The 1990s

A Decade of Contemporary British Fiction

Titles in *The Decades Series*

The 1970s: A Decade of Contemporary British Fiction
edited by Nick Hubble, John McLeod and Philip Tew

The 1980s: A Decade of Contemporary British Fiction
edited by Emily Horton, Philip Tew and Leigh Wilson

The 1990s: A Decade of Contemporary British Fiction
edited by Nick Hubble, Philip Tew and Leigh Wilson

The 2000s: A Decade of Contemporary British Fiction
edited by Nick Bentley, Nick Hubble and Leigh Wilson

The 1990s

A Decade of Contemporary British Fiction

Edited by

Nick Hubble, Philip Tew and Leigh Wilson

Bloomsbury Academic
An imprint of Bloomsbury Publishing Plc

B L O O M S B U R Y
LONDON • OXFORD • NEW YORK • NEW DELHI • SYDNEY

Bloomsbury Academic
An imprint of Bloomsbury Publishing Plc

50 Bedford Square
London
WC1B 3DP
UK

1385 Broadway
New York
NY 10018
USA

www.bloomsbury.com

BLOOMSBURY and the Diana logo are trademarks of Bloomsbury Publishing Plc

First published 2015
Reprinted by Bloomsbury Academic 2016
First published in paperback 2017

© Nick Hubble, Philip Tew, Leigh Wilson and contributors, 2015, 2017

All rights reserved. No part of this publication may be reproduced or transmitted in any form or by any means, electronic or mechanical, including photocopying, recording, or any information storage or retrieval system, without prior permission in writing from the publishers.

No responsibility for loss caused to any individual or organization acting on or refraining from action as a result of the material in this publication can be accepted by Bloomsbury or the author.

British Library Cataloguing-in-Publication Data
A catalogue record for this book is available from the British Library.

ISBN: HB: 978-1-4411-7258-7
PB: 978-1-3500-0541-9
ePDF: 978-1-4742-4242-4
ePub: 978-1-4742-4241-7

Library of Congress Cataloging-in-Publication Data
A catalog record for this book is available from the Library of Congress.

Series: The Decades Series

Cover design: Eleanor Rose

Typeset by Integra Software Services Pvt. Ltd.

In memoriam

Graham Joyce

22 October 1954 to 9 September 2014

Contents

Contributors		ix
Series Editors' Preface		xii
Acknowledgements		xv
Critical Introduction: Recovering the 1990s *Philip Tew, Leigh Wilson and Nick Hubble*		1
1	Literary History of the Decade: The Emergence of Post-Industrial British Fiction *Martyn Colebrook*	37
2	Special Topic 1: Rewriting National Identities in 1990s British Fiction *Nick Bentley*	67
3	Special Topic 2: Satirical Apocalypse: Endism and the 1990s Fictions of Will Self *Katy Shaw and Philip Tew*	95
4	Postcolonial and Diasporic Voices – Bringing Black to the Union Jack: Ethnic Fictions and the Politics of Possibility *Sara Upstone*	123
5	Historical Representations: Between the Short and Long Twentieth Centuries: Temporal Displacement in the Historical Fiction of the 1990s *Nick Hubble*	149
6	Generic Discontinuities and Variations: Experimental Enunciations in 1990s British Fiction *Mark P. Williams*	181
7	International Contexts 1: Whatever do the Germans Want? 1990s British Fiction and the Condition of Germany *Anja Müller-Wood*	213

8	International Contexts 2: National Identity and the Immigrant *Paoi Hwang*	239

Timeline of Works	263
Timeline of National Events	266
Timeline of International Events	272
Biographies of Writers	278
Index	290

Contributors

Nick Bentley is Senior Lecturer in English literature at Keele University in the United Kingdom. His main research interests are in post-1945 British literature and literary and cultural theory, and especially in intersections of postmodernism, postcolonialism and contemporary fiction and culture. He is the author of *Martin Amis: Writers and Their Work* (Northcote House, 2014), *Contemporary British Fiction* (Edinburgh University Press, 2008) and *Radical Fictions: The English Novel in the 1950s* (Peter Lang, 2007), and he is the editor of *British Fiction of the 1990s* (Routledge, 2005). He is currently working on two books: *Contemporary British Fiction: The Essential Criticism* (Palgrave, 2015) and the representation of youth subcultures in fiction and film 1950–2010. He is also the co-editor of *The 2000s: A Decade of Contemporary British Fiction* in The Decades Series (Continuum, 2015).

Martyn Colebrook is an independent researcher. He completed a PhD focusing on the novels of Iain (M.) Banks at the University of Hull (2012). He co-edited the first collection of scholarly essays on Banks, *The Transgressive Iain Banks* with Katharine Cox (McFarland 2013) and has published individually and collaboratively within the field of twentieth-century fiction with chapters including 'Contemporary Scottish Crime Fiction and Terrorism', '*The Wasp Factory*, the Gothic and Mental Disorder', 'Paul Auster and Alienation' and 'Gordon Burn, *Somebody's Husband, Somebody's Son* and the Yorkshire Ripper'. Additionally, he has organized conferences focusing on, among other topics, 'Representations of 9/11', 'Millennial and Apocalypse Fiction', 'Michael Moorcock' (with Mark Williams, University of Mainz) and 'Angela Carter'.

Nick Hubble is Reader in English at Brunel University London, United Kingdom. He is the author of *Mass-Observation and Everyday Life: Culture, History, Theory* (2006; second edition 2010) and the co-author of *Ageing, Narrative and Identity* (2013). He is the co-editor of *The Science Fiction Handbook* (2013), *The 1970s: A Decade of Contemporary British Fiction* (2014) and special issues of the journals *EnterText, Literary London* and *New Formations*. He has published journal articles or book chapters on writers including Pat Barker, Ford Madox

Ford, B.S. Johnson, Naomi Mitchison, George Orwell, Christopher Priest, John Sommerfield and Edward Upward.

Paoi Hwang holds a PhD from Royal Holloway, University of London. She was a lecturer in the Department of Foreign Languages and Literatures at National Taiwan University from 2003 to 2010. Currently, she resides in Britain and teaches part-time at Durham University. Her academic papers, reviews and creative stories have appeared in *Partial Answers, EurAmerica, Wenshan Review, Asiatic* and other journals and magazines. She is also the Deputy Editor of National Taiwan University Press's *East-West Cultural Encounters* series and she continues to serve on the advisory board of the journal *Encounters* (http://encounters.zu.ac.ae/).

Anja Müller-Wood is Professor of English Literature at Johannes Gutenberg-Universität in Mainz. Her main areas of interest are the literature and culture of early modern England and twentieth-century and contemporary Anglophone literatures. She is the author of *Angela Carter: Identity Constructed/Deconstructed* (1997) and *The Theatre of Civilized Excess: New Perspectives on Jacobean Tragedy* (2007), as well as of many articles and chapters in journals and books.

Katy Shaw is Principal Lecturer in Contemporary Literature and Director of Centre 21 at the University of Brighton. Her research interests include twenty-first century writings, contemporary literature, especially working-class literature, cultural representations of Gothic post-industrial regeneration and the languages of comedy. Shaw's publications include *David Peace: Texts and Contexts* (Sussex Academic Press, 2010), *Analysing David Peace* (Cambridge Scholars, 2011), and *Mining the Meaning: Cultural Representations of the 1984-5 UK Miners' Strike* (Cambridge Scholars, 2012), and she edited with Deborah Phillips *Literary Politics: The Politics of Literature and the Literature of Politics* (Palgrave Macmillan, 2013). She is also the editor of *C21 Literature: Journal of 21st-Century Writings* and on the editorial board of *Comedy Studies*.

Philip Tew is Professor in English (Post-1900 Literature) at Brunel University London, United Kingdom, and a fellow of the Royal Society of Arts. Among his main publications are *B. S. Johnson: A Critical Reading* (Manchester UP, 2001), *The Contemporary British Novel* (Continuum, 2004; rev. second ed. 2007) and *Jim Crace* (Manchester UP, 2006), and he co-edited with Glyn White *Re-reading B. S. Johnson* (Palgrave Macmillan, 2007). Tew is the founding Director of both the Modern & Contemporary Fiction Studies Network and the B.S. Johnson Society. More recent books have included a multi-authored policy report on ageing, *Coming of Age* (Demos, 2011) and *Ageing Narrative and Identity* (Palgrave Macmillan, 2013) co-written with Nick Hubble; a solely edited collection, *Reading Zadie Smith* (Bloomsbury, 2013); and edited with Jonathan Coe and Julia Jordan, *Well Done God! Selected Prose and Drama of B.S. Johnson* (Picador, 2013).

Sara Upstone is Principal Lecturer in English Literature at Kingston University, London. She specializes in contemporary postcolonial, British and American literature. She is the author of *Spatial Politics in the Postcolonial Novel* (Ashgate, 2009) and *British Asian Fiction: Twenty-First-Century Voices* (Manchester University Press, 2010), as well as the editor (with Andrew Teverson) of *Postcolonial Spaces: the Politics of Place in Contemporary Culture* (Palgrave, 2011). She is currently researching the relationship between literary genre and representations of race in contemporary fiction.

Mark P. Williams has taught literature at Victoria University of Wellington, New Zealand and University of East Anglia. He is international editor for the Scoop Review of Books (http://books.scoop.co.nz). His primary research interests lie in contemporary literature and politics, specializing in the relationship between Science Fiction and Fantasy and the avant-garde. In 2008, he co-organized 'The New World Entropy: A Conference on Michael Moorcock' and he has been a contributor to various journals, including *The Literary London Journal*, *The Irish Journal of Gothic and Horror Studies* and *Critical Engagements: Journal of the UK Network for Modern Fiction Studies* (UKNMFS) and *Alluvium Journal of 21st Century Writing*. He published 'Selective Traditions: Refreshing the Literary History of the Seventies' in *The 1970s: A Decade of Contemporary British Fiction* (2014).

Series Editors' Preface

Nick Hubble, Philip Tew and Leigh Wilson

Contemporary British fiction published from 1970 to the present has expanded into a major area of academic study in the last twenty years and attracts a seemingly ever-increasing global scholarship. However, the very speed of the growth of research in this field has perhaps precluded any really nuanced analysis of its key defining terms and has restricted consideration of its chronological development. This series addresses such issues in an informative and structured manner through a set of extended contributions that combine wide-reaching survey work with in-depth research-led analysis. Naturally, many older British academics assume at least some personal knowledge in charting the field of the contemporary, but increasingly, many of these coordinates represent the distant past of pre-birth or childhood not only for students, both undergraduate and postgraduate, but also for younger academics. Given that most people's memories of their first five to ten years are vague and localized, an academic born in the early to mid-1980s will only have real first-hand knowledge of less than half these forty years, while a member of the current generation of undergraduates, born in the mid-1990s, will have no adult experience of the period at all. The rather self-evident nature of this chronological, experiential reality disguises the rather complex challenges it poses to any assessment of the contemporary. Therefore, the aim of these volumes, which include timelines and biographical information on the writers covered, is to provide the contextual framework that is now necessary for the study of the British fiction of these four decades.

Each of the volumes in this Decades Series emerged from a series of workshops hosted by the Brunel Centre for Contemporary Writing (BCCW) located in the School of Arts at Brunel University London, United Kingdom. These events assembled specially invited teams of leading internationally recognized scholars in the field, together with emergent younger figures, in order that they might together examine critically the periodization of contemporary British fiction by dividing it into its four constituent decades: the 1970s symposium was held on 12 March 2010; the 1980s on 7 July 2010; the 1990s on 3 December 2010; and the 2000s on 1 April 2011. During these workshops, draft papers were offered and discussions ensued, with the aim of exchanging ideas and ensuring both continuity and also fruitful interaction (including productive dissonances) between what would become chapters of volumes that would hopefully exceed the sum of their parts.

The division of the series by decade could be charged with being too obvious and therefore rather too contentious. In the latter camp, no doubt, would be Ferdinand Mount, who in a 2006 article for the *London Review of Books* concerned primarily with the 1950s, 'The Doctrine of Unripe Time', complained 'When did decaditis first strike? When did people begin to think that slicing the past up into periods of ten years was a useful thing to do?' However, he does admit still that such characterization has long been associated with aesthetic production and its relationship to a larger sense of the times. As Frank Kermode so influentially argued in *The Sense of an Ending: Studies in the Theory of Fiction*, published in 1967, just before the period covered by this series began, divisions of time, like novels, are ways of making meaning. And, clearly, both can also shape our comprehension of an ideological and aesthetic period that seems to coexist but are perhaps not necessarily coterminous in their dominant inflections. The scholars involved in our symposia discussed the potential arbitrariness of all periodizations, but nevertheless acknowledged the importance of such divisions, their experiential resonances and symbolic possibilities. They analysed the decades in question in terms of not only leading figures, the cultural zeitgeist and socio-historical perspectives, but also in the context of the changing configuration of Britishness within larger, shifting global processes. The volume participants also reconsidered the effects and meaning of headline events and cultural shifts such as the miners' strike of 1984–85, the collapse of communism, Blairism and cool Britannia, 9/11 and 7/7, to name only a very few. Perhaps ironically to prove the point about the possibilities inherent in such an approach, in his *LRB* article Mount concedes that 'For the historian ... if the 1950s are famous for anything, it is for being dull', adding a comment on the 'shiny barbarism of the new affluence'. Hence, even for Mount, a decade may still possess certain unifying qualities, those shaping and shaped by its overriding cultural mood.

After the symposia had taken place at Brunel, the individuals dispersed and wrote up their papers into full-length chapters (generally 10,000–12,000 words), revised in the light of other papers, the workshop discussions and subsequent further research. These chapters form the core of the book series, which, therefore, may be seen as the result of a collaborative research project bringing together twenty-four academics from Britain, Europe and North America.

Each volume shares a common structure. Following the introduction, the first chapter of each volume addresses the 'Literary History of the Decade' by offering an overview of the key writers, themes, issues and debates, including such factors as emergent literary practices, deaths, prizes, controversies, key developments, movements and bestsellers. The next two chapters are themed around topics that have been specially chosen for each decade, and which also relate to themes of the preceding and succeeding decades, enabling detailed readings of key texts to emerge in full historical and theoretical context. The tone and context having been set in this way, the remaining chapters fill out a complex but comprehensible picture of each decade. A 'Postcolonial Voices' chapter addresses the ongoing legacy of Britain's Empire and the rise of globalization, which is arguably the most significant long-term influence on contemporary British writing. 'Historical Representations' is concerned not just with historical novels but the construction of the past in general, and thus the later volumes will be considering constructions of the earlier decades, so that a complex multilayered account of the historicity of the contemporary will emerge over the series. The chapter on 'Generic Discontinuities' highlights the interaction between the sociocultural contexts, established in earlier chapters, and aesthetic concerns. The 'International Contexts' chapters allow the selected academics from non-British cultures to write about the key international aspects of the British fiction of the particular decade on which they are focusing from a different perspective. This might variously concern how such fiction relates to international ideological, aesthetic and other relevant movements and/or how the fiction influenced international fiction and/or international reader reception. Each decade is different, but common threads may emerge.

In the future, it is hoped to expand the Decades Series by adding to the first four planned volumes others that extend the period of 'Contemporary British Fiction': both by covering subsequent decades as they complete their course and also by featuring precursory decades, extending the focus of study backwards in time to cover the British fiction of the modern and post-war periods.

Works Cited

Kermode, Frank. *The Sense of an Ending: Studies in the Theory of Fiction*. Oxford: Oxford University Press, 1967.

Mount, Ferdinand. 'The Doctrine of Unripe Time'. *London Review of Books* 28 (22) (16 November 2006): 28–30; http://www.lrb.co.uk/v28/n22/ferdinand-mount/the-doctrine-of-unripe-time. n.p.

Acknowledgements

We would like to thank all our contributors for their expertise, patience and generosity when responding to our queries and guidance as this book has gradually taken shape. We have enjoyed excellent support throughout from the editorial team at Bloomsbury, especially David Avital and Mark Richardson, who have been instrumental in bringing this book to fruition.

We gratefully acknowledge the support of the Brunel University London's Research and Knowledge Transfer Committee for providing the funding which enabled the Brunel Centre for Contemporary Writing to host the 'Contemporary British Fiction Decades Seminar Series' during 2010 and 2011, which has led to the publication of the volumes in this book series. Without the support of administrative and catering staff at Brunel, these events could not have taken place. We would also like to thank all the academics and postgraduate students who attended and contributed to the discussions at these events.

We would also like to mention the staff at Brunel University London Library, the British Library, the National Library of Wales and other research libraries who have provided support to the contributors to this volume.

Critical Introduction
Recovering the 1990s

Philip Tew, Leigh Wilson and Nick Hubble

This introduction attempts to contextualize the 1990s through key aspects of that decade perceived from a distinctly British perspective, but will do so with regard to a range of far wider issues including an emergent globalism and certain dynamic geopolitical events that dominated both the political and news agendas of the period – and thereby impacted upon the public consciousness – such as the death of and apparent collective public mourning for Diana, Princess of Wales, the genocidal massacres of Tutsis and moderate Hutus in Rwanda and the political turmoil in the Balkans followed by the NATO bombing of Serbia. In doing so, the introduction attempts to challenge a number of the cultural and ideological myths propounded by the political class and reported widely in mainstream media during the decade and often repeated in subsequent historical accounts. Importantly, this introduction will interrogate the grounds of such errors and also address the issue of a local-global culture in rapid flux in very many ways – ideologically, technologically, culturally and in terms of lived experience. In outlining such features, it is our hope that the following critical introduction will offer a backdrop against which the reader might contextualize the following chapters, allowing a more detailed reading that incorporates the complexities of the decade and certain of its various legacies. Many of these chapters touch upon the hyper-individuality that typified the processes of identity that characterized this period, a Thatcherite legacy of the primordial sense of the self, which, as Michael Brennan makes clear, was inherent in the public mourning for Princess Diana after her death, the significance of which is explored in this introduction below. Brennan argues that

> the work of mourning a lost love-object is intimately bound up with the work of (personal) identity; only by exploring the latter can we understand the former. Mourning is in this sense not simply the outward or public display (as a set of

social practices) that intimates the experience of private loss but is instead a process which is integral to development of the self. (209)

The 1990s: Political, economic and social overview

The 1990s is often (mis)remembered as a time of relative peacefulness and optimism, especially as it preceded 9/11 and the ongoing wars and regional instabilities in Afghanistan and Iraq. Nick Bentley, for example, reduces the period's major conflicts and its turbulence to anxieties about everything 'from global warming to wayward asteroids to millennium bugs' (6). Fred Botting concludes that 'The shift in political perspectives from society to individualism was accompanied by various forms of identity politics [...]' (27). Certainly, much of the new British television output of the period mirrored such an individualistic zeitgeist, with the explosion of youth-oriented, populist and seemingly more spontaneous programming, working from apparently unscripted events. Such shows included *The Big Breakfast, TFI Friday, The Word* and even *Noel's House Party*, and they drew members of the public actively into the frame of the screen, seemingly democratizing this visual culture. Importantly, such cultural optimism appeared to draw upon other larger headline events, for the decade did appear imbued from the beginning with the influence of promising and positive geopolitical occurrences, including the fall of the Berlin Wall, beginning on 9 November 1989 and continuing apace in early 1990, bringing about the end of the Cold War, with much talk of a 'peace dividend' that would lead to non-conflict-oriented economic growth. This idea became so widespread that it attracted warnings from policy advisors of the military such as William T. Johnsen of the Strategic Studies Institute in 1995, who cautioned that the 'peace dividend' was impacting negatively on the European NATO countries' military spending, capabilities and strategies (27). In terms of other developments that contributed to an overarching sense of promise, there was also the widely publicized end of Nelson Mandela's long incarceration, after which he was elected as South Africa's first post-Apartheid president in 1994. Former trade union leader and activist Lech Walesa became the First President of post-communist Poland in 1991, the year that also saw the collapse of the Soviet Union, the US expedition to 'free' Kuwait after Saddam Hussein's invasion in Operation Desert Storm, in which conflict Britain participated, and South Africa repealing its Apartheid Laws. In 1992 came the official end of the Cold War. For escapists, the first Harry Potter novel by J.K. Rowling was published in 1997, a series that inspired millions to read fiction.

Such optimistic notions of progress were bolstered by radical technological changes including advances in computers and digital technology which began affecting Western economies with far-reaching consequences in many political and social areas including the constant and at times seemingly unregulated circulation of news and information, a process which the political classes began to manipulate. Some of the technical coordinates of innovation seem modest and mundane in retrospect, but they contributed to a literal technological *and* social revolution. Hand-held mobile phones become smaller and more affordable throughout the decade facilitated by advances in batteries and energy-efficient electronics, the 'second generation' systems emerged using digital transmission, and satellite technology was revolutionized. In 1990, the World Wide Web/Internet protocol (HTTP) and WWW language (HTML) were created by Tim Berners-Lee, and in 1991, the Internet became available to the public – on 6 August, the first website dedicated to information about the Web went live. The first SMS text message was sent in 1992. By 1993, the then groundbreaking fast Pentium processor had been invented, followed by technological developments that would lead to the 56K bit/sec modem, revolutionary hardware using standard analogue dial-up phone line connections allowing high-speed data transfer between computers. Internet usage grew throughout the decade from 16 million users in 1995 to 204 million in March 2000, as did the widespread use of mobile phones. Mobile phone ownership in Britain was around a million subscribers in 1993; it increased noticeably only after the end of the recession, to 27 per cent in 1998 when pay-as-you-go contracts were introduced with around 9 million subscribers, rising to 54 per cent in 2000, and reaching 73 per cent by 2001 (Crabtree, Nathan and Roberts 10). Despite enthusiasm for this new technology, various conflicting but widely reported research projects resulted in reports that appeared in the late 1990s concerning the potential health risks of mobile phone radiation, largely ignored by eager consumers. High-definition (HD) TV was first broadcast in field tests in the early 1990s, the first broadcast followed on 23 July 1996 in Raleigh, North Carolina. In 1988, Sony and Ampex had co-developed and marketed the D2 digital videocassette format, allowing single-cable composite video connections, followed by video compression systems revolutionizing editing processes. DVDs became available in 1997, virtually rendering video tape cassettes obsolete. Plasma flat panel televisions were commercially available in the late 1990s, and full colour flat panel computer monitors were released commercially in the decade, competing against CRT televisions. In 1995, the first book was purchased on Amazon, a new mode of online retailing. In 1999, a two-way email pager, the first BlackBerry device, was introduced. A so-called 'dotcom' bubble of the 1990s reflected the decade's overall optimism, later proved to actually be based on often unrealistic trading and investing in stock of any company focused on the new electronic media, and it was to be followed by the dotcom crash in March 2000, finally ending a certain naïve positivity, if only in terms of the financial sphere.

In 1989, Sky Television's satellite service was launched, and in the same year, the government introduced a Broadcasting Bill to deregulate commercial television (passed in 2000). On 25 March 1990, British Satellite Broadcasting (BSB) began, only to merge in November with Sky, launching a digital satellite provision in 1998. Cable television companies had earlier been granted the right to offer telephony and the 1990s saw a series of mergers, with NTL and Telewest by far the largest at the end of the decade (eventually to merge in 2006, rebranded as Virgin Media in 2007). Many of the technological parameters of a cultural and economic world that were to be taken for granted in the 2010s emerged during the 1990s, a plethora of apparent modest innovations forming what would later seem almost a cultural tsunami. In terms of economic and transport infrastructure, Canary Wharf in the east of London was developed, and London's Docklands expanded despite the property slump of the early 1990s, following an unsustainable boom based on optimism unsustainable by either average incomes or rent levels and ended by economic factors such as a credit squeeze. The Docklands Light Railway was expanded in two phases, and by 1993, London City Airport which served the City was used by 245,000 passengers after its extended runway had been approved and opened on 5 March 1992. Its flights carried over a million people by 1997 according to 'Celebrating 25 Years of London City Airport' (9).

Technology was slower in its effects upon traditional print media. As a report by Justin Lewis et al. indicates, the beginning of online news coverage was cautious, restricted to 'the launch of the online "Electronic Telegraph"... in 1994, and the launch of the "Guardian Unlimited" in 1999' (9). In the 1990s, newspapers still generated high levels of pre-tax profits and profit margins throughout the 1990s, apart from during the 1991 collapse for the *Mirror* group following the death of Robert Maxwell, and even there profitability soon recovered (9). And, yet, the above report also demonstrates the numbers of staff employed by the British press, and broadcast news was cut progressively in most of the twenty years from 1985, with an associated increase in workloads (6) and dependence upon 'public relations and other media (especially wire services)' (3) grew. The report 'found that 19% of newspaper stories and 17% of broadcast stories were verifiably derived *mainly or wholly* from PR material, while less than half the stories we looked at appeared to be entirely independent of traceable PR' (3). Hence spin prevailed, particularly in public affairs in the 1990s, although less obviously since 'political stories in the press contain less identifiable PR material than any other kind' (20), making some news little more than establishment propaganda. Combined with the increasing use of electronic media to gather information and report news, the 1990s saw the beginning of a decline in independent journalism.

Although initially the decade seemed to extend the ongoing Anglo-Irish troubles and saw a continued Irish Republican bombing campaign, including on 20 July 1990 a Provisional IRA attack on the London Stock Exchange and on 15 June 1996 the Manchester City Centre bomb, injuring over 200, nevertheless a gradual path to peace emerged in Northern Ireland after the Downing Street declaration on Northern Ireland was agreed in 1993, a peace proposal issued jointly with the British and Irish governments designed to end the Troubles. From 1995, under the chairmanship of American Senator George Mitchell, the agreement led to talks between all major parties to end the conflict in the province, culminating in the Belfast Peace Agreement signed on Good Friday 1998 and subsequently known as the 'Good Friday Agreement'. However, on 15 August 1998, the Omagh bombing by dissident republicans in the Real IRA killed twenty-nine civilians. Despite this, from May 2000 the decommissioning of weapons held by most paramilitary groups went ahead, alongside the normalization of security arrangements in Northern Ireland and democratic local regional elections, a move forward in reinstituting a more generally stable and accepted democratic process.

However, despite the general sense of apparent progress technologically and in terms of conflict resolution, the 1990s cultural scene was not simply defined by such progressive change and optimism; in contrast to this move towards peace in Ireland, both nationally and internationally various new kinds of struggles came to characterize the 1990s, and conflict was as much part of this decade as any apparent optimism. From 1 April 1990, the Thatcher government introduced the 'Community Charge' – widely known as the 'poll tax' – on all citizens in England and Wales which provoked protest rallies and widespread disorder and disobedience; a largely peaceful central London march ended with serious rioting in Trafalgar Square. Just over a year later, on 22 November 1990, Thatcher, who had become an increasingly unpopular Prime Minister both inside and outside her government, resigned, just days after the Iron Lady had somewhat manically declared her intention 'I fight on; I fight to win'. She had secured the first round of a leadership contest, but without the required majority to stop a second round of voting. This represented the culmination of resistance to her leadership in the Conservative Party, leading to John Major becoming Prime Minister. Following Thatcher's 'Big Bang' or deregulation of the Stock Exchange in 1986, which essentially introduced the free-market doctrines of unrestrained competition and meritocracy, the City of London and speculation in the markets and in property played an increasing role in the nation's economy, especially as much of the nation's industry had ceased to function. Initially, the Conservatives were successful and, in 1992, won the April general election, returning Major as prime minister. However, by 16 September, or 'Black Wednesday', speculators on money markets forced Britain to withdraw from the European Union's Exchange Rate Mechanism, costing the Treasury at least £3.3 billion, with £27 billion reserves having been spent in propping up the pound, and losing a potential £2.4 billion profit had sterling been devalued in a more timely fashion. After the ERM crisis, Britain remained cautious, and although a member of the European Union throughout the decade, Britain maintained a large degree of financial independence when the nation did not join the Euro, the new European currency launched on 1 January 1999.

Other domestic events also offered a sense of a turbulent period in the face of natural and cultural challenges. While waiting for a bus on the evening of 22 April 1993 in Eltham, London, Stephen Lawrence was stabbed and killed by a gang of youths undertaking a racist attack. The Crown Prosecution Service (CPS) dropped charges against five suspects on 29 July 1993, citing insufficient evidence. After an internal Metropolitan Police Service review begun in August 1993, on 16 April 1994, the CPS reaffirmed there was insufficient evidence for murder charges against anyone else. In April 1994, the Lawrence family initiated a private prosecution against the five suspects; concerning two there was again found to be insufficient evidence while three others were acquitted. The flawed police investigation became a cause célèbre, particularly after a public enquiry in 1998, headed by Sir William Macpherson examining the original Metropolitan Police Service investigation, concluded that the force was 'institutionally racist'. However, later research of the police's own opinions by Foster, Newburn and Souhami indicated that 'officers perceived the MPS's failings to be rooted in incompetence rather than racist practices' (10), and their report suggests that negativity prevails among the police concerning the Macpherson enquiry:

> During the in-depth fieldwork many police officers suggested the Lawrence Inquiry had been unfair and that the police had been singled out for attack. Large numbers of front-line officers felt unsupported by their managers, and suggested they had been made scapegoats. (21)

However, Mapherson's view prevailed among official circles, and a more critical view incorporating the concept of 'institutional racism' led to changes in many institutions including police forces. Much later, in response to the furore over the case and subsequent to a campaign by Stephen's mother, Doreen Lawrence, in 2003 in the Criminal Justice Act, parliament revoked the 800-year legal principle of 'double jeopardy' and the change was applied retrospectively, much to the dismay of some legal experts and civil liberties groups. After a cold case review in June 2006, a new trial convicted Gary Dobson and David Norris, two of the original suspects, of Lawrence's murder, after the former's previous acquittal had been quashed.

In 1996, bovine spongiform encephalopathy (BSE) – known popularly as Mad Cow Disease – was first diagnosed in Britain, and in 1997, Dolly the sheep was cloned by scientists at the Roslin Institute in Scotland, raising the spectre of the dangers of biogenetic manipulation. Certain other controversies were high profile in terms of press reporting in newspapers and television in the 1990s, reflecting a growing distrust among the general public concerning both experts and the state itself. This was exemplified by a UK media storm around the use of the combined vaccine to inoculate children against measles, mumps and rubella (MMR). Taking up claims by Andrew Wakefield and others in research published in *The Lancet* in 1998 that the vaccine had led in a number of cases to a bowel disorder and autism, the media reporting led to much panic among parents and a significant dip in the take up of the vaccine. Lewis et al. identify 'the failure of the media to interrogate claims made by Andrew Wakefield linking the MMR vaccine with autism' (39) as a determining factor in the controversy. Such controversies seemed to provide growing evidence of an increasing distrust among the majority of the population concerning both the establishment and supposed experts. This was also evidenced in responses to the South Ronaldsay child-abuse scandal when in 1991 overzealous police and social workers removed some children from their homes in Orkney, Scotland, because of allegations of child abuse involving satanic rituals, despite denials by the children and no corroborating evidence from medical examinations. The child interviews were led by a social worker involved in the 1990 Rochdale 'Satanic Abuse' case. Lord Clyde's later official enquiry criticized official conduct in both cases.

As well as such controversies being played out on television news, there was also increasing coverage and associated debate concerning matters of an international nature, often with a certain voyeuristic character concerning the horrors of events involving conflict, violence, death and suffering. Such reporting became a major staple of twenty-four hour news coverage in the 1990s, and stories were often conveyed simplistically and with a degree of Western bias. One story that dominated the news came with the dissolution of the Soviet Union on 26 December 1991, which was followed by the establishment of the Russian Federation with policies of liberalization, stabilization and privatization. A struggle for central authority ensued which led Boris Yeltsin, the Federation's first president, to dissolve parliament in September 1993, ordering new elections and a referendum on a new constitution. When parliament resisted, Yeltsin's tanks surrounded their 'White House' building and parliament capitulated. Russia faced conflict in various republics as in Chechnya, where two wars occurred in 1994 and 1999. In the Russian Federation, a strong Presidential system was instituted, but the economy suffered a severe depression by the mid-1990s, a further financial crash in 1998, only commencing its recovery in 1999–2000.

These crises meant that the United States as leader of the West was emboldened to increase military intervention as a tool for shaping foreign affairs, based largely on the myth of American exceptionalism (a grandiose version of the notion of manifest destiny), which came to shape the political rhetoric of Anglo-American leaders in supporting foreign interventionism when it was in their own strategic interests. As Godfrey Hodgson notes in *The Myth of American Exceptionalism*, 'American history has been forced into a distorted and selective narrative of exceptional virtue' (xxi). This propensity and Russian weakness also heightened a hubristic sense of invincibility which took hold in triumphalist neoconservative circles, with their 'New World order', and which through the 'special relationship' between the United States and the United Kingdom came to permeate some key members of the British political class thrilling in the apparent power of a vicarious neocolonialism. As Donald E. Pease says in *The New American Exceptionalism*, as the quintessential modern state, the United States indulges in a 'state fantasy' (1) upon which is based 'its monopoly of legitimate violence' (2) using 'traumatic events [to] precipitate states of emergency' (5) in quasi-Orwellian fashion. Britain under a new prime minster would be drawn into these conflicts, staring in the Balkans. Although initially popular after New Labour's landslide election in 1997, Tony Blair was not only accused of populism, but other problematic affinities with Thatcher became apparent. Not only did the limits of Britain's democracy become all too apparent with later protests against the imminent Iraq War, but its failure to apply any such principles elsewhere had already emerged in 1990s foreign policy. Some, like Chomsky and Žižek, have argued that a neocolonialism emerged in terms of foreign adventurism supported by either bombing or the threat of force, which would have far-reaching and unexpected consequences with the retaliatory 9/11 attacks. In the 1990s, international events indicated not only a world in flux, but increasingly a zeitgeist centred upon local belligerence and conflict.

Media manipulation in the West became a political imperative for some in public office, attempting to shape the forthcoming millennium ideologically, as detailed in Howard Kurtz's *Spin Cycle: How the White House and the Media Manipulate the News* (1998), which specifies how spin doctors representing Clinton's administration went about 'alternately seducing, misleading and sometimes intimidating the press' (xiv) in 'a daily struggle to control the agenda, to seize the public's attention' (xv) often with the growing complicity of the media, practices that had already been copied extensively by the Blair government. Two such cases were the civil war and genocide in Rwanda and the crisis and ethnic cleansing in the Balkans. Each of these, and their aftermath, dominated television broadcasts for a protracted period without offering a full picture of the initial wilful lack of action in Rwanda by the West and its complicity in an accelerated collapse of Yugoslavia. Ethnic cleansing was an old practice, but the term coined in the Balkans was used in the 1990s widely for such events, and these two occurrences shocked the world and led to a sense of moral outrage as if people had been confronted with something unheard of. Political leaders in Britain and America agitated for military action. In contrast, significantly in Rwanda, the possibility of intervention was eschewed, despite perhaps some of the most extreme and shocking of circumstances imaginable. In 1994, civil war brought what was a genocide to the country on 6 April after a plane carrying President Habyarimana, a moderate Hutu, was shot down by two missiles as it approached the capital, Tigali (Hutu President Cyprien Ntaryamira of Burundi was also aboard). This reignited the civil war and destabilized the Great Lakes region. An unpublished 225-page report by French anti-terrorist judge Jean-Louis Bruguière, leaked to *Le Monde*, blamed current President Paul Kagame, who was and is still supported and highly praised by former President Clinton and former British Prime Minister, Tony Blair. Kagame sought Rwandan membership of the British Commonwealth of Nations, which was granted in 2009.

According to the International Criminal Tribunal for Rwanda, early on 7 April 1994 Prime Minister Agathe Uwilingiyimana was arrested by the presidential guard, sexually assaulted and shot, after taking refuge in the UN compound. Subsequently, the ten Belgian UN troops who had previously protected her at her home were tortured, castrated, gagged with their severed genitalia, further mutilated and murdered by rebel Hutu forces intent on overthrowing the government and initiating a genocide. Other political and cultural leaders were hunted and murdered despite the UN peacekeeping presence. As the United Human Rights Council's 'Genocide in Rwanda' says at that point 'Rwanda's population of seven million was composed of three ethnic groups: Hutu (approximately 85%), Tutsi (14%) and Twa (1%)'. Very little of this was reported at the time in mainstream media in the West. Over 8,00,000 people were to be killed in around 100 days by the Rwandan Patriotic Front, most of the victims were Tutsis, but the dead also included Hutus who opposed the organized slaughter. Furthermore, many women were to be systematically raped, as Chiseche Salome Mibenge suggests in *Sex and International Tribunals: The Erasure of Gender from the War Narrative*, by both 'opportunistic predators' and others conducting 'widespread and systematic sexual exploitation and abuse' (84). This was so widespread that in the aftermath 'the woman who was not raped is the exception' (61). Despite a general view that a new government, of which Kagame was Vice President and Minister of Defence, ended the violence, as Filip Reyntjens makes evident in *The Great African War: Congo and Regional Geopolitics, 1996–2006*, the post-genocidal regime headed by the RPF continued 'government-sponsored violence' and killing (26). Reyntjens argues that at the time many international leaders denied these events and refused to challenge the legitimacy of Rwanda's genocidal government. In terms of its mission, the UN's own report identified an 'overriding failure' (30). Although contemporaneously under-reported in terms of the scale of horror, the mediatization, sanitizing and commercialization of even such horrific events have become rapid processes in the contemporary world, as seen by subsequent general news coverage of the crisis as if it had almost been a natural disaster (no blame attributed) and even the appearance of the sympathetically scripted film *Hotel Rwanda* (2004), co-written by its British director, Terry George.

Another example of a series of events that were featured on the news channels with a great degree of bias occurred around the scale of local inter-ethnic violence (see Herman and Peterson 345) when the Balkan conflicts dominated news schedules from 1991 to 1995 and beyond, in part to justify Western intervention, particularly with regard to targeting Serb forces and depicting Bosnian and Kosovar Muslims as victims of 'genocide'. During the 1980s, Yugoslavia had suffered political instability, especially with various ethnic tensions and conflicts between religious-ethic groups. By 1991, all but one of its six republics had proclaimed independence, with only Serbia and Montenegro still federated, creating the four new states of Slovenia, Croatia, Bosnia and Herzegovina and Macedonia. Subsequently, this part of the Balkans descended into a series of conflicts and bouts of ethnic cleansing – including the infamous 'genocide' undertaken by Republika Srpska forces in Srebrenica. These conflicts were often responses to the legacies of previous inter-ethnic and ideological wars and genocide during the Second World War, during which almost a million people, many Serbs and Roma from Bosnia and Herzegovina, had been killed. However, in *The Politics of Genocide*, Edward Herman and David Peterson conclude that

> not only 'ethnic cleansing' but also the words 'massacre' and 'genocide' were quickly applied to Serb operations. The remarkable inflation of claims of Serb evil and violence (and playing down of NATO clients' violence), with fabricated 'concentration camps,' 'rape camps,' and similar Nazi- and Auschwitz-like analogies, caused the onetime head of the U.S. intelligence section in Sarajevo, Lieutenant Colonel John Sray, to go public even before the end of the wars in Bosnia with his claim that 'America has not been so pathetically deceived since Robert McNamara helped to micromanage and escalate the Vietnam War'. (46)

The mainstream media in the West mainly ignored such deceptions, in which in fact they were complicit. Ironically, given the later 9/11 attacks on America, interestingly, there are credible reports from journalists on the ground including Renate Flottau and Eve-Ann Prentice which did not feature in the mainstream press – that Osama bin Laden, who had been issued a Bosnian passport, met Bosnian Muslim President Alija Izetbegovic in order to involve other Muslim fighters, a tactic which had been used in Afghanistan.

The Bosnian War concluded on 14 December 1995 after a NATO bombing campaign against Bosnian Serb positions. Reports suggest that, as part of this campaign, the British and Americans were involved in supporting the Croatian ethnic cleansing of Serbs from Krajina. And, as John R. Schindler explains in *Unholy Terror: Bosnia Al-Qa'ida and the Rise of Global Jihad*, this conflict was a forging ground for extreme Islamism, whom some argue were given tacit approval by US officials, ironic since several 9/11 hijackers were either trained or fought in Bosnia, and such training would continue with the Kosovo Liberation Army (KLA) to further destabilize Yugoslavia.

Later from 24 March 1999 to 10 June 1999, Britain not only participated in a full-scale NATO bombing of Yugoslavia after its government refused peace proposals that demanded a full-scale NATO occupation, but Blair and American leaders cited Serbian attacks on and killings of hundreds of thousands of Kosovar civilians as being akin to the holocaust. Bill Clinton's Statement on Kosovo on 24 March 1999 referred specifically to the Holocaust, explicitly likening events in Nazi Germany to those in Kosovo. Subsequently, he stressed the need 'to deter an even bloodier offensive against innocent civilians in Kosovo and, if necessary, to seriously damage the Serbian military's capacity to harm the people of Kosovo'.[1] As John Pilger reflected retrospectively, 'Tony Blair invoked the Holocaust and "the spirit of the Second World War"'. Blair agitated for the NATO attacks on Yugoslavia (undertaken without approval of the UN Security Council), a series of supposed 'humanitarian' bombings that were to facilitate the independence of Kosovo, preventing a so-called genocide of Kosovar Albanians being the purported motivating force. John Pilger has claimed that the NATO attacks 'killed hundreds of people in hospitals, schools, churches, parks and television studios, and destroyed economic infrastructure'. On Tuesday 4 May 1999 of the bombing of Serbia, Alistair Campbell records in his diaries that '*The Independent* led on Serb claims of twenty dead in the bus attack. I sent them a letter pointing out that even where mistakes were admitted that does not mean they should take at face value Serb accounts of the consequences' (8). In a highly controversial fashion, many attacks by Western bombers deployed either cluster bombs or munitions containing depleted uranium. As Herman and Peterson make clear, 'British Defence Secretary George Robertson acknowledged to his Parliament on the very day that NATO launched its war that, through January 1999, more people had been killed in Kosovo by the KLA than by the Serbs' (49). As Pilger concludes from later inspections, 'There was no genocide in Kosovo. The "holocaust" was a lie. The Nato attack had been fraudulent'. Noam Chomsky concurs in an interview noting that the KLA were CIA-backed. Various commentators including Chomsky have since assessed the underlying cause of the NATO bombing to have been Yugoslavian resistance to political and economic reforms the West desired. Chomsky argues that 'Serbia was not carrying out the required social and economic reforms, meaning it was the last corner of Europe which had not subordinated itself to the US-run neoliberal programs, so therefore it had to be eliminated'. Certainly, Alexandros Yannis comments that 'one might wonder whether "greed not grievance" is at the root of the Kosovo conflict' (175), and he cites various sources as evidence that the KLA, whom the West supported, was linked financially to 'Albanian organized criminal groups' (176) and was itself involved in the drug trade and prostitution (176). According to Yannis, the lawless aftermath following Serbian withdrawal was characterized by 'warlordism and economic opportunism' (197) of a savage kind which almost caused a civil war in neighbouring Macedonia (186), and significant ethnic cleansing of Serbs from most of Kosovo. Certainly, Serb forces had undertaken a number of local massacres and widespread intimidation of civilians and attacked Kosovar Albanian settlements, but according to Pilger and others, including Carla Del Ponte in *Madame Prosecutor: Confrontations with Humanity's Worst Criminals and the Culture of Impunity*, widespread evidence has emerged subsequently that Kosovar militants were involved in massacres of groups of Serbs, Roma and collaborating ethnic Kosovar Albanians, and in some cases, organs were harvested from those killed in criminal enterprises.

On 23 April 1999, NATO bombed the Radio Television of Serbia headquarters, killing sixteen employees and injuring others. Three days later, television presenter Jill Dando was assassinated outside her home in West London, a murder which occurred after she had hosted a BBC Kosovo Crisis appeal for refugees on Tuesday 6 April and which had raised millions of pounds, followed by Serbian protests. Given that the highly dubious conviction of a local man, Barry George, was overturned, the crime still remains unsolved, although numerous press reports have speculated over the link to the Kosovan situation and Serbia's response (Myall and Myers; Myer).

Clearly, in the face of such overwhelming superpower hardware as seen in Yugoslavia, conflict against the major Western powers was to become increasingly asymmetrical, as seen in October 2000 when al-Qaida organized the bombing of the *USS Cole*. This oppositional dynamic had been percolating for all of the 1990s. Significantly, a later world-changing cataclysm was presaged by an earlier attack in 1993 when terrorists planted a truck-bomb in the basement of the North Tower of the World Trade Center (intended to topple it into the South Tower), killing six and injuring 1,042 people, an attack led by Ramzi Yousef (whose uncle Khalid Sheikh Mohammed would later mastermind the 9/11 attacks) who attended an Afghanistan-based al-Qaida training camp in early 1991. Violent response was not just the purview of foreign terrorists, however. In Britain, David Copeland, an English Neo-Nazi militant, known as the 'London Nail Bomber', undertook a 13-day bombing campaign in April 1999 aimed at London's black, Bangladeshi and gay communities, killing three people and injuring over a hundred, some severely.

As New Labour prime minister following the so-called Third Way, Tony Blair seemed, as Roger Luckhurst has argued, 'to transcend old ideological divisions of Left and right and to marry the best practice of European social-democratic parties with neo-liberal economics' (81). In *The End of Politics: New Labour and the Folly of Managerialism* (2007), Chris Dillow says that in an unrealistic fashion, New Labour offered a social commitment to 'a belief that equality and efficiency are mutually compatible' (9). Much of Blair's grand illusion would be later thoroughly shattered following Britain's involvement in the invasion of Iraq, despite the largest protest in British history, on evidence that it would later emerge was clearly managed. This was unsurprising since Blair heralded more a new brand of managerialism that appeared both in politics and culture more generally in the decade, where the primary aim in politics and institutional management appeared to be to attain control of situations by all or any means and the methods included the use of spin or even repeated untruthfulness. As Dillow explains, Blair's New Labour was characterized by 'an ideology which tries to eliminate political debate about the rival merit of competing ideals. In its stead, managerialism relies on a central elite which believes that it, and it alone, has the skill and know-how to devise policies to cope with the inexorable forces of economic change', thereby reconciling 'conflicting objectives' (11). A prime example of this in foreign policy had been Blair's 'humanitarian bombing' of the Balkans. Another was to be the capacity for the apparently left-liberal leaning Blair to offer unquestioning support to a new, bellicose, far-right American President George W. Bush, despite the latter being elected in 2000 in extremely controversial circumstances with widespread electoral irregularities (including an entirely prejudicial refusal of many black voters) that favoured the Republican and did not receive sufficient scrutiny across the mass media. In Florida, Republican Governor of Texas Bush appeared to beat the previous Democratic Vice President Al Gore in suspicious circumstances, by 537 votes out of around 6 million in a state where Bush's brother Jeb was governor, after a recount of 'hanging chad' votes was suspended (machine voting and counting proved imperfect as many of the holes punched into ballots were partial, hence many such ballots required physical inspection which the Republicans opposed and were determined to disallow). Organized Republican mobs prevented a local Dade County recount through physical intimidation of the election board, and the Palm Beach canvassing board was refused a short recount extension by Florida's Secretary of State, Katherine Harris, part of a wider extra-electoral campaign to secure for Bush Florida's crucial twenty-five Electoral College votes. Despite the subsequent Supreme Court's decision awarding victory to Bush, most independent analyses judge that in reality Gore had achieved sufficient support for victory (because of various suspect practices, he lost an estimated 15,000–25,000 votes) and would have done so if a visual recount had been undertaken, thereby winning both the college and popular Presidential votes nationwide. Such a corrupt, right-wing theft of a popular election through fraud and intimidation was the appalling legacy of 1990s managerialism, with its spurious capacity to supposedly reconcile matters or issues which are diametrically opposed, to muddle fact and opinion and to blur lines of actual responsibility.

'Don't Look Back in Anger': Culture in the 1990s

'Don't look Back in Anger', the second single to go to number 1 in the charts for the British rock band Oasis, taken from their second album, *(What's the Story) Morning Glory* (1996), can tell us much about British culture in the 1990s. Written in 1995 by Noel Gallagher, the song became one of the band's central anthems, was their best-selling single and was voted the fourth most popular song on the occasion of the UK chart's 60th anniversary in 2012 ('Queen's "Bohemian Rhapsody" Voted Nation's No. 1 Single'). The song was part of the soundtrack of the late 1990s, and the track's chopped up, dislocated lyrics coupled with a yearning, soaring chorus twice made it the choice to indicate something crucial about politics, change and the future during the decade, although on each of these occasions its selection was for a very different purpose. In September 1996, the song was used at a 'Youth Experience Rally' put on during the Labour Party conference and part funded by Alan McGee, the head of Oasis's record label, Creation. It played as Tony Blair, the Labour leader, walked on to the stage at the rally, to be presented with a platinum disc which the band had been awarded (Brooker 118). Even before its landslide victory at the General Election of May 1997, then, the Labour Party was using youth culture to signify its up-to-date qualities, its investment in the future and as a strategy by which it might claim hope as one of its central values. In the *Vanity Fair* article from March 1997 which coined the term 'Cool Britannia', Blair was quoted as saying that 'The hope that change will bring ... is outweighing the fear of change' (Kamp n.p.). In this article, a perceived revival in contemporary British culture – in its novels, its fashion, its art, its music, its food – is linked to the possibility for political, social and economic transformation which the main opposition party under Blair seemed to offer. In this article, which was to become incredibly influential in creating the atmosphere of the second half of the decade – its cover featured Oasis's lead singer Liam Gallagher and his then girlfriend Patsy Kensit in a bed made up with Union Jack bed linen – the dynamism of the present is linked clearly to future change. Indeed, some months earlier, *Newsweek* had named London 'the coolest city on the planet' (McGuire 35). Such a designation also suggested that contemporary London, and by implication British culture generally, was important because of a successful temporal combination. The article claimed that London's coolness was the result of 'a hip compromise between the non-stop newness of Los Angeles and the aspic-preserved beauty of Paris sharpened to New York's edge' (34). London was considered cool in the article because it managed well the relative claims of the past and the present, and this seemed to bode well for the future. Rather than 'looking back in anger', the mid-1990s combination of a potential political change and a renewed flourishing of popular and youth culture suggested to many the possibility of a brave new Labour world in the future where Britain's past – its loss of great power status, the ramifications of post-colonialism, the destruction of its manufacturing base – no longer cast a stultifying shadow.

In the same year, as Blair's use of the Oasis anthem for his triumphal entry to the youth rally, however, 'Don't Look Back in Anger' had been put to very different use, one that suggested that any such temporal harmony, such a resolved reckoning of the present with the past, was an illusion. In early 1996, BBC2 broadcast a drama in nine episodes, *Our Friends from the North*, written by Peter Flannery and directed by Simon Cellan Jones, Pedr James and Stuart Urban. Set between 1964 and 1995, the series intertwined the lives of four fictional friends with real events from those years, including political corruption in local government and the polarizing miners' strike of 1984–5. Each episode was named after the year in which it was set and followed the four friends from youth through to middle age. The final episode, *1995*, was broadcast in March 1996 and showed the friends, though reunited, wounded, compromised and chastened by their experience of three conflictual decades of British history. The final credits rolled to 'Don't Look Back in Anger', both connecting the drama's vision of Britain to the present moment – the song was number one the week that the final episode was aired – and giving the lie to the 'shiny newness' of contemporary Britain that was to be so evocatively described in the *Vanity Fair* article the very next year. The use of the Oasis song was ironic at the same time as its yearning, soaring chorus expressed the ache of loss and missed opportunity in recent British experience; the drama suggested that one really should look back in anger, for the last thirty years of British history had been made up of circumstances and decisions shaped by a lack of vision, by corruption, by elitism and by certain destructive political impulses – a nasty concoction that had been neither eradicated nor properly admitted or mediated. *Our Friends from The North* suggested that the underlying issues had not been faced squarely, and that Britain's sense of its immediate past was an illusory one.

The use of the song in these two very different ways – to signal a break with the past and the apparent shininess of all things new, on the one hand, and an aching acknowledgement of the still powerful and destructive effects of the past on the other – points to a tension at the heart of British culture in the 1990s. The decade saw itself, and has continued to be seen since, as marking a sea change in terms of new technologies and an attendant obsession with the moment of the present, as a time somehow impossibly existing outside of the conflict and struggle of history, which, as has been suggested in the section above on the political, economic and social turbulence and conflicts of the 1990s, is an absurd notion. However, the decade has also been seen as the moment where any sense of a faith in the future had finally disappeared, and when a particular kind of regressive obsession with the past took its place. Gallagher's song tells us not to look back, but the song itself looks back in a number of ways. Oasis's title incorporates multiple allusions, most specifically to David Bowie's 'Look Back in Anger' from his 1979 album *Lodger*, and to John Osborne's play, *Look Back in Anger*, first performed at the Royal Court in London in 1956, cultural coordinates indicative of a pre-Thatcherite world still imbued with a sense of expansion, confidence and cultural agitation against the dead hand of privilege and the establishment. In addition, the Oasis song's lyrics make use of lines apparently spoken by John Lennon in tapes he was making of his memoirs at the time of his death in 1980, where he talks of 'trying to start a revolution from me bed, because they said the brains I had went to my head' ('The Making of Don't Look Back in Anger by Oasis' *Uncut* 34), referring to the 'Bed Peace' protests against the Vietnam War put on by Lennon and Yoko Ono in Amsterdam in 1969. In addition to Gallagher using Lennon's words, the opening chords of the Oasis single use those from Lennon's *Imagine*, from 1971. The lyrics and the production of the Oasis track then look back to and reference various moments of post-war popular countercultural resistance and utopianism, but they do so in a way that suggests that the very energy of such radical ideological commitments was exhausted and that such a sense of cultural possibilities had already been lost. It was as if the 1990s were indeed, as has been suggested by Lynn Segal, 'the most politically tedious decade in living memory' (142), stripped of the future vision which was only superficially gestured towards in New Labour rhetoric, and it is therefore no surprise that in this song, as indeed in Oasis' work in general, pastiche replaced a sense that the new could make a positive intervention in the world which could make the future different from both the past and the present. Fredric Jameson, in his *Postmodernism, Or the Cultural Logic of Late Capitalism*, famously defined pastiche as, like parody, 'speech in a dead language', but unlike parody, he argued, it is without 'ulterior motives, amputated of the satiric impulse, devoid of laughter' (17). For Jameson, the dominance of pastiche in 'postmodernsim' signals, rather than a connection to the past, a sundering from it (18), and such a sundering negates any idea of historical change, any idea that the future could be transformed, be in any fashion significantly different. The shifting in conceptions of temporality suggested by repetition, Joe Brooker has argued, marked many aspects of culture in the 1990s, including those previously thought countercultural, such as Indie music, such that Britpop, the genre to which Oasis belonged, is named by him as a 'karaoke pop movement' (112). As Mark Mazower has glossed it, 'The only new Worlds still to be discovered in the 1990s lay in the past' (357). It would seem that revivalism replaced radicalism, and an ersatz nostalgia displaced both anticipation and expectation.

As this reading of 'Don't Look Back in Anger' suggests, work in the arts and culture in the 1990s can be seen as reproducing and reinforcing the freezing of temporal relations perceived in the world of politics and economics, what the conservative US writer Charles Krauthammer, looking back at the 1990s from the early twenty-first century, called a 'holiday from history' (quoted in Bentley 3). A sense of the loss of overarching mechanisms of historical change – centrally those theorized by Marxism – lost through the philosophical undermining of 'grand narratives' and the collapse of actually existing Communist states after 1989 changed the way the past, the present and the future were perceived and represented. At the same time, as marking this as a curiously intermediary and undifferentiated phase – where past, present and future merged as if coalescent – though, the decade was also marked by a freezing of affect, by both a loss and a lack. Throughout the decade, not the least of the paradoxical effects of this was that, as a sense of a productive connection to the past waned, in its place came a relation to the past that was traumatic, pathological and tortured. Lynn Segal has argued that '[i]n place of political ideals and collective action, mourning and melancholia have never been more popular than they became in the 1990s' (143). This is perhaps why the death of Princess Diana in August 1997 had such a huge impact. Jon Simons concluded in the year of her death: 'Diana may not prove to be enduring, but endearing she certainly was because she embodied key aspects of contemporary British culture, defined ... as a therapeutic, confessional society, or a culture of intimacy'. Certainly, over 1 million people lined the route of her funeral procession, and 2.5 billion people worldwide watched the funeral on television. The widespread public mourning which followed the death was accounted for by a number of writers as a response to more than the death of one woman, as indicative of a widespread experience of loss and alienation. In comparing Diana's death to that of Princess Charlotte in 1817, as Stephen C. Berhendt indicates such a socio-individual process involves a staged theatricality (89) eliciting a complex, highly ritualized (78) and significant response:

> The activities of mourning, while they of course memorialized the object of grief, performed a larger social function in enabling the mourners to participate in the actual and symbolic worth (or import) of the object of their activities.

Mourning becomes in these circumstances a public performance in which the distinctions normally separating the elite object of mourning from both the common individual and 'the people' collectively are reduced or even nullified and the mourned individual is fused symbolically with the 'common' public. (75)

There is also an inherent refusal to fully and realistically contemplate the death. As Freud so influentially argued in his essay of 1917, 'Mourning and Melancholia', both of these conditions are formed around an inability to accept that something which existed in the past has not continued into the present. For Freud, while mourning is a necessary point on the road to recovery and acceptance of this loss, in contrast, melancholia marks a frozen moment, where the subject, unable to accept the loss, takes the lost object into themselves and so treats the self as in some way itself dead. The ensuing struggle within the melancholic self Freud describes at the end of his essay as a 'painful wound' (258), and indeed the decade which Segal has described as melancholic had at the centre of its sense of connection to the past, both personal and collective, the concept of trauma, from the Greek for 'wound'. As Roger Luckhurst has argued in his *The Trauma Question* (2008), while the idea of trauma is centrally linked to modernity per se, the beginning of the 1990s saw a new and powerful conception of it which shaped all modes of representation through the decade. The 'Memory Wars' of the early 1990s, beginning in the United States and then spreading, were fought over the nature of the relation between memory, eventfulness and trauma, specifically with regard to memories of abuse in childhood. The consequences of such a dispute were entangled with very real effects in the world. As Luckhurst recounts, in 1990 in the United States, George Franklin was imprisoned 'on the sole evidence of his daughter who had, with her therapist, recovered repressed memories of the murder of a childhood friend from 1969' (11). In 1994 in the United States, the False Memory Syndrome Foundation was founded to challenge the claim that memories of traumatic childhood experiences could be recovered in pristine and mimetic fashion, that they could tell a straightforward truth about the past. In the United Kingdom in 1990 and 1991, there were two high-profile court cases, in Rochdale and in Orkney respectively, based on claims that children had been systematically abused in satanic rituals in those areas. Both trials collapsed, but such models of recovered memory lay at the basis of a sizeable amount of academic and clinical work too, such as the controversial collection of essays edited by Valerie Sinason in 1994, *Treating Survivors of Satanic Abuse*. Through the decade, the struggle over the nature of memory became the assumed shape of all human relations to the past. The assertion of 'recovered memory' claimed that we could be fully reconnected to our past, but that such reconnection would always be to a site of trauma; the challenge to such claims asserted that our connection to the past was always fallible, always contingent, always in some way a fiction, but that such a loss of any 'real' connection was itself traumatic. So, while the nature of the trauma differed – on one side was the 'truth' of the trauma of abuse in childhood, on the other there was the trauma of our never fully possible connection to the past – what the 'memory wars' and their repercussions constructed was the relation between the past and the present as per se traumatic.

The reconstruction of this relation had important consequences for the broad shape of the British novel during the decade. As many critics have noted, in the 1990s, the novel took a 'historical turn' (see De Groot, Keen). However, as Jerome De Groot has argued, the historical novel of the 1990s differed significantly from the 'historigraphic metaficiton' named by Linda Hutcheon in her *The Politics of Postmodernism* (1989, 14). While Hutcheon's postmodernist novel was playful, using a multiplicity of voices and metanarrative to undermine the truth value of grand narratives and assert a more nuanced and inclusive version of history, in the 1990s, '[t]his self-consciousness, relatively shorn from its radical roots' became 'a commonplace in fiction' (de Groot 120). For De Groot, beginning with Rose Tremain's *Restoration* (1989), the decade saw a 're-bourgeoising' (98) of the novel which engaged with history, the beginning of what Nick Bentley has called 'popular postmodernism' (4). The most critically and commercially successful novels of the decade were all historical: A.S. Byatt's *Possession* (1990), Pat Barker's *Regeneration trilogy* (1991–5), Michael Ondaatje's *The English Patient* (1992), Sebastian Faulk's *Birdsong* (1994), and into the beginning of the next decade, Zadie Smith's *White Teeth* (2000), and Ian McEwan's *Atonement* (2001). De Groot argues that, despite these novels losing some of the political bite of 1980s experiment with historical modes, they retained a certain resistance:

> These bourgeois novels clearly demonstrate the influence of postmodern style and form. They take the tools of postmodern historiographic metafiction and make them mainstream and popular. In so doing these novelists drew some of the political sting from such techniques, but each is still self-conscious enough in style and form to suggest an interest in questioning authority and legitimacy. These novels demonstrate the assertion...that the techniques of historical fiction *necessarily* imply a form that is self-conscious, complex and questioning. (100, emphasis in original)

However, seen through the lens of trauma, the 'historical turn' of the 1990s sits uneasily between the two opposing sides of the 'memory wars'. As de Groot suggests, such novels are on the whole broadly realist in their strategies and effects. They allow the reader the illusion that the past, like the supposedly 'recovered memories' from childhood, can be reached without the incursion of loss, or the effects of distortion or fantasy. At the same time, it is possible to argue that the narrative focus of so many of these novels in the most disturbing and shattering moments of the relatively recent past – the two world wars, the Holocaust, colonialism and its legacies – produce historical relation as per se traumatic. The immersive effects of realism then seduce the reader not into consolation but into the horror of history. What this might mean for a final assessment of the 'historical turn' is a difficult question. De Groot argues that the historical novel cannot be anything but a reminder of the difficult relation between past and present, and that

> the techniques of postmodernism... have become the techniques of the modern historical novel. Questioning the legitimacy of narrative and undermining authority are fundamental to the ways that contemporary novelists approach the past. Once again, this indeterminacy and dissident complexity are fundamental to the historical novel as a phenomenon or format. (108)

This assumes, of course, the radical nature of 'postmodernism', but it also stops short of including the nature of the novels' consumption in a final assessment of their effects. Roger Luckhurst has argued that the sites of recommendation and consumption of novels in what he calls in his *New Formations* article 'traumaculture' have profoundly determined the nature of the contemporary novel. The Oprah Book Club, began in 1995 by US talk show host Oprah Winfrey, and the Richard and Judy Book Club began by the British talk-show hosts Richard Madeley and Judy Finnigan in 2001, both grew out of their hosts' parts in the genre of daytime TV confession and their own openness about their lives past and present. During the runs of their TV book clubs each could make the fortunes of the titles chosen, so that the nature of their choices profoundly affected novel selling, reading and even writing. As Luckhurst argues, in the TV book clubs:

> [b]ooks favoured are narratives of pain, suffering and/or injustice eventually overcome... Novels do feature in these Book Clubs, but have to conform to this narrative model of tribulation and ultimate moral uplift. The reading mode encouraged is one of complete identification, affective connection rather than aesthetic analysis. (134)

While the TV book clubs could be dismissed as the obvious purveyors of such easy pleasures, there is evidence that reading groups more generally are formed around and promote a reading culture that has these 'values' at its heart. Jenny

Hartley, in her *Reading Groups* (2001), acknowledges that reading groups and book clubs have existed at least since the eighteenth century but chart their meteoric rise through the 1990s. By the end of the 1990s, there were an estimated 50,000 reading groups in the United Kingdom and most national newspapers, BBC Radio 4 and a number of TV channels had their own book clubs (Hartley vii). From the end of the decade on, the Internet was increasingly the site of such 'shared reading', and reading groups could be found also in libraries, bookshops, workplaces, hospitals and so on. In 2000, the *Guardian* newspaper used reading groups for the first time to pick its First Book Award ('Judging Panel Announced for Guardian First Book Award 2000'), a tacit acknowledgement of their centrality in literary culture by this time. Slightly later, in 2002/3, a television comedy series aired on Channel 4 entitled *The Book Club*, written and directed by Annie Griffin, featuring a newly arrived American in Glasgow who starts up such a group to make new friends. While Hartley does not set out to ask what might account for this explosion of reading groups in the 1990s, the results of her survey of 350 reading groups suggest much about what, why and how they read. Hartley acknowledges that for reading groups 'the premium is on empathy, the core reading-group value' (132). The results of her survey show that empathy is valued as the primary mode of engagement between members of the group, between author and character, and between reader and character. This accounts, she argues, for the preference shown among her groups for realism (135), with its onus on the construction of 'life-like' characters with whom the reader can identify. The importance of this 'core value' is particularly interesting when considering the novels most often chosen and read by the groups. Of the top thirty books read by the groups surveyed between June and December 1999, all are broadly contemporary titles, seventeen are historical novels, and three more are historical memoirs or biographies (165–6), all are broadly realist. The novels read include stories of recovered memories of sexual abuse in childhood, such as Jane Smiley's *A Thousand Acres* (1991)), stories set in the First and Second World War (for example, Sebastian Faulks' *Birdsong* (1993), Pat Barker's *Regeneration* (1991), Louis de Bernière's *Captain Corelli's Mandolin* (1994)) and those focusing on the Holocaust (Anne Michaels' *Fugitive Pieces* (1996) and Bernard Schlink's *The Reader* (1995). The question is, then, if traumatic subjects constitute the bulk of these works, but they are articulated through the consolations of a fairly conventional realism, what is the residue left by such reading experiences? If a disturbing residue can be seen, does the experience of reading within the setting of the reading group mitigate it, or is in fact the contagious nature of trauma noted by Luckhurst – he describes it as 'worryingly transmissible' (3) – responsible for the rise of such groups?

The complex nature of these questions in any reading of the decade is made even more difficult by the fact that the concept of trauma came to dominate not just popular cultural discourse, the novel and wider literary culture, but also much literary critical and cultural analysis itself. Importantly, initiated and shaped by the work of Cathy Caruth, 'trauma studies' had come by the end of the decade to dominate significant parts of the humanities. While the field had at its heart profound debates over the nature of human experience, the constitution of memory, the relation between memory and narrative and the potential of various kinds of therapeutics, what its existence nevertheless implicitly affirmed was the existence of 'trauma' and its centrality to human experience and indeed subjectivity per se. That the writers of novels should be so concerned with trauma, then, may not so much attest to its actual existence as much as to the increasing dominance among British writers of those with degrees in the humanities, in particular in English literature, and so schooled in the theoretical and conceptual discourses of the time.

The decade did produce, however, a number of writers who, while using the concept of trauma, attempted to go beyond the either/or of 'recovered memory' and scepticism about any possible connection with history. As Andrzej Gąsiorek has noted, a number of writers in Britain were forceful in asserting through the 1990s the still powerful connection to history. Writers such as Andrew O'Hagan, Rachel Lichtenstein, Iain Sinclair and W.G. Sebald, Gąsiorek argues, resist the 'temporal stasis' that results if the present sees itself as cut off from the past, and their interest in the past is a claim for a historical sense which continues to be invested in the possibility of the future. What is clear about most of these writers, though, is that they are less wedded to realism than the 'rebourgoised' historical novel discussed above, while at the same time, they eschew postmodernism's scepticism about any possible connection with history. In W.G. Sebald's *Austerlitz* (2001), the legacy of perhaps the most rending event of recent history, at least for the European imaginary, the Holocaust or Shoah, is marked by a layered, complex narrative, its suffocating, unavoidable horror enacted by the chapterless, paragraphless writing and the Russian doll-like set of narrative voices. While the work insists on the visibility of modes of telling – the voices of the anonymous narrator, of his friend Jacques Austerliz and of the various people whose words Austerliz repeats insistently *speak*, they are characters and bodies in contrast to the disembodied omniscient narrator of classic realism – it does not substitute stories for history. The narrative construction of *Austerliz* is both the result of the repression of Austerliz's memories of his childhood in Prague, his journey to England on the *kindertransport* and his loss of his parents in the Holocaust *and* an indication that the past is not lost, that its legacies remain and that the act of writing can be seen as itself a resistance to 'temporal stasis' through its necessary entwining of past, present and future.

As Gąsiorek also notes, the commodified world of the present where 'temporal stasis' is, far from being challenged, taken for granted is powerfully represented in the work of J.G. Ballard, particularly in his work of the late 1990s and early twenty-first century:

> Human beings are, in novels such as *Cocaine Nights*, *Super-Cannes* and *Millennium People*, systematically subordinated to the urban and technological environments that dwarf them. In this version of postmodernity as a terminal zone, time ceases to have meaning and the future is construed solely in terms of a further domination of space: more road networks, business parks, retirement pueblos, shopping malls. (48)

Time in Ballard's work is a dead zone, filled with repetition rather than change, the sating of short-term desire rather than the construction of long-term hope. It pictures not history, but its disappearance as nightmare. Elsewhere in the decade, though, the disappearance of the past and of faith in any mechanisms of historical change was not represented as nightmare but embraced as the rule of the new. The supposed 'triumph' of capitalism marked by the fall of the Berlin Wall and the dissolution of the Soviet Union, as we have seen, led some to argue for the 'end of history', and at the same time, the lack of an existing alternative meant that all was folded into capitalism's insatiable reification of the new and the now. In British culture, the effects of this triumph on the forms of artistic production were perhaps most obviously and notoriously seen in the visual arts. The inclusion of those artists who came to be known as yBas (young British artists) in the rise of 'Cool Britannia' was an indication of how these artists and their work, while lauded by some for bringing verve to the British art scene, increasing gallery visits and public engagement generally with the visual arts, were enmeshed in the intertwined networks of celebrity, scandal, consumption and political spin. As forcefully argued by Marxist curator and art historian Julian Stallabrass in his *High Art Lite* (1999), the origins and construction of the new British art scene in the 1990s were utterly imbricated with an aggressive capitalism in the form of Charles Saatchi, whose collecting of the work of very young artists – sometimes buying their degree show work – at the end of the 1980s and the beginning of the 1990s created the phenomenon of the yBas. Saatchi and his brother Maurice had founded the advertising agency Saatchi & Saatchi in 1970, and by the 1980s, the firm had become synonymous with the decade's voracious business culture, not least through their association with the Conservative Party for whom the agency produced the 'Britain Isn't Working' campaign in the run up to the general election in 1979. Saatchi and his brother left the agency they had founded in 1995, by which time Saatchi had already become the most influential collector of art in the United Kingdom. His position as the most powerful collector of new art in the United Kingdom was consolidated when he in the early 1990s sold his collection of the work of older, established painters and of the leading artists of the 1980s – including the work of, for example, Lucian Freud, Howard Hodgkin, Anselm Kiefer and Julian Schnabel – and concentrated his buying on very young and unheard of artists of a particular kind. Saatchi favoured works that were accessible, often punning and witty, and had a direct and immediate effect; the description, one could claim, of a successful advert. Michael Bracewell has seen the aesthetic properties of this new art as utterly reflecting, rather than challenging, the economic and political orthodoxies of the decade:

> The art itself, for the most part, was a cleverly crafted, ironic spin on Pop minimalism – part joke, part camp, part affectation of grunge nihilism, but with a heavy veneer (a kind of department store sheen) of sheer aesthetic gorgeousness. And as such the phenomenon of YBA was an astute articulation of the surface values of its times: a luxurious surfer ride across the in-shore shallows of the zeitgeist, as slick and as satisfying as any ride could be. (Bracewell 23)

What is significant here is the way that, via Saatchi, the priorities and language of advertising and the market became visible in the aesthetic realm in a quite different way from previously because of his buying choices and the promotion of his subsequent collection. In addition, the activities of those artists who came to be bought by Saatchi, even before they became Saatchi artists, were very much complicit with, rather than a direct challenge to, the hegemony of the market. The nucleus of the yBas studied at Goldsmiths' in London and took part in the Damien Hirst organized show, *Freeze*, held in an empty London Port Authority building in Docklands in 1988, the first show of young artists attended by Saatchi, and showing work by, among others, Sarah Lucas, Gary Hume, Matt Collishaw and Michael Landy. The early, self-organized shows, while appearing to be literally and figuratively sited outside the mainstream London art scene, were often sponsored (*Freeze* had been sponsored by the London Docklands Development Corporation and by the property developers

Olympia and York), so from the beginning such art was imbricated in capital's priorities and needs.

More broadly, the new artistic culture begun by these younger artists, in resisting the elitist orthodox art world, moved instead to the commodified realm of popular culture. The art magazine *frieze*, set up in 1991 and linked through the 1990s to the new British artists, as well as covering this scene, had articles on film, photography, design and fashion. In a retrospective look at the yBas, Dan Fox, one of the current editors of *frieze*, has acknowledged that at the time the magazine and young artists were as interested in *The Face* – a fashion, music and culture magazine – as they were in the academic journal of contemporary art and theory, *October* (Fox 101).

The particular inflection and effects of this were most visibly seen towards the end of the decade in the *Sensation* exhibition at the Royal Academy in the autumn of 1997, a show comprised entirely of Saatchi's collection of young British artists, and for much of the general public their first introduction to the yBas. Controversy and scandal attended the exhibition for much of its run in London (and on its transfer elsewhere), as Stallabrass argues; indeed, such controversy was clearly part of the RA's aim in staging the exhibition (Stallabrass 202; see also Cashell, Chapter 2). The exhibition was one of the most successful in terms of visitor numbers the Royal Academy had ever staged and was particularly successful in attracting younger people into the somewhat staid institution (see Jury n.p.). These two things are not unrelated, and the show enacted the tendency of yBas art itself to concentrate on potentially shocking material in a way that reproduced the culture of the now without obvious reflection or commentary that might historicize it. The work in *Sensation* that produced the most controversy and debate was Marcus Harvey's *Myra* (1995), a large portrait of Myra Hindley, the so-called Moors Murderer, who had been convicted in 1966, alongside her then lover Ian Brady, of abducting, torturing and murdering three children. The pair much later confessed to the murders of two more children. The portrait reproduced a black and white photograph of Hindley taken at the time of her arrest and used over and over again in the press in the intervening thirty years. The pixelated nature of so many newsprint reproductions was simulated in Harvey's portrait by applying the paint with the cast of a small, child-sized handprint. Families of the children murdered by Hindley and Brady protested. Winnie Johnson, the mother of Keith Bennett, who was 12 when murdered by Hindley and Brady, and whose body has never been found, picketed the gallery, and Ann West, the mother of Lesley Ann Downey, who was 10 when murdered by them, called for a boycott of the exhibition.

Rather than such a boycott, however, what followed was an explosion of media comment and debate concerning the painting and the ethics of its production, split between those who justified it as a comment on society's obsession with and glamorization of such criminals and crimes, and those who saw its creation as an offence against the real events, the real children who lost their lives in such horrific fashion, and their families who were still living with the after effects of those events. At stake in this, as many acknowledged, was the nature of the relation between representation and the real events of history, the nature of art's responsibility to the truth of what really happens or happened in the world. What outraged critics of the work was what they saw as the painting's non-engagement with the truth of the crimes committed by Hindley, its reproduction of the frozen moment of a photograph without a powerful enough intervention that would engage the image with the real of history. For many critics, in common with much of the work of the yBas, rather than effecting such an intervention, *Myra* is 'extraordinarily mute' (Stallabrass 206) and indifferent in its relation to its subject (Julius 167).

The relationship between shock and capitalism's undoing of meaningful historical sequence has been recognized at least since Walter Benjamin's work from the 1930s, but in the 1990s, in one area at least, and against Benjamin's hope, the publicity generating and commercial possibilities of shock won out over any hope that it might dislocate or undo capitalism's push to amnesia. The domination of British art in the 1990s by the Saatchi-created yBas was strongly linked to another art institution that constructed itself around publicity and controversy, the Turner Prize, and the prize is an indication of the way that such resistance to history can be seen as part of, rather than incompatible with, the British novel's historical turn in the decade. The Turner Prize was inaugurated in 1984 by the Tate Gallery, in order to promote new British art, although it really found its identity only in 1991, after a year of suspension, when it remade its criteria and processes, and when Channel 4 became its sponsor and televised the award ceremony for the first time. In her account of the history of the prize, Victoria Button acknowledges that the prize has 'always actively sought publicity' but locates the scandals associated with it not in any intention on the part of the Tate, but in the resistance of the British media and general public to the new in art per se (15). However, what might be more powerful in the relation between the prize and its interlocutors is not so much the new in art as the question of the 'newsworthy'. Button's history of the prize is to a significant extent a history of those aspects of it that made the news. She reproduces tabloid cartoons lampooning new art and charts the relation between the prize and the media in some detail. The privileging of the newsworthy over the aesthetically new with regard to the prize is clear, for example, from the continued assumption that Tracey Emin, shortlisted in 1999 for her *Bed*, won the prize. She didn't; the prize that year was in fact won by *Deadpan* (1997), a video work by Steven McQueen based on Buster Keaton's film, *Steamboat Bill, Jr* (1928), with its famous shot of a house front falling on Keaton's character, only for him to be improbably saved as he is standing at the precise spot where the house's open upper doorway comes to rest. McQueen's film was, like Keaton's, both black-and-white and silent, lacking most of the elements which came to be seen as newsworthy in a work of art in the 1990s – the autobiographical, sexual content, or the flagrant rejection of the more traditional practices and materials of art.

Newsworthiness as the most privileged value was not limited to the Turner, but inherent in prize culture more generally. James English has argued that scandal and controversy attend the judging of every prize because such scandals 'go to the very heart of the prize's initially fragile claim to legitimacy' (7) – that is, any prize's attempt to unite aesthetic and commercial values. It is also the case, though, that through the 1990s, such scandals and controversy increasingly became the reason for such prizes. As English argues, by the early twenty-first century, prize culture had reached 'the point of a kind of cultural frenzy' (18).

If prizes are constructed around the generation of 'news' – the scandal and controversy that suggests something new and attention-worthy in culture – it may appear something of a paradox that so many of the novels that won prizes, critical acclaims and high sales figures in the 1990s were historical novels. It would seem that the novel's repeated return to past was being validated by system which was complicit with capitalism's privileging of the isolated, amnesiac present. Through the decade, for example, of the eleven winners (it was shared by two novels in 1992) of the Booker Prize, the United Kingdom's most remunerative literary prize, half were historical novels, a ratio which rises in the next decade, when seven of the ten winners were either historical novels or novels centrally concerned with memories of the past.

As we have seen illustrated and discussed in the first section above concerned with the political, economic and social dynamics of this period, by the end of the decade the new technologies of communication had begun to reshape and redetermine the everyday lives of the majority of people in the United Kingdom, while the media diverted their attention from the underlying dynamics of the geopolitical flux. The consequences of this have been (and will continue to be) deeply significant for the novel and for cultures of reading into the twenty-first century, not least in the continued reshaping of temporal relation. As John Tomlinson has noted:

> The technologies of communication with and through which we routinely interact create the *impression* of a general effortlessness and ubiquity of contact which seems to be distinct from the purposiveness of mechanically accomplished speed. It is as if the gap between departure and arrival, here and elsewhere, now and later, a certain order of desire and its fulfilment, has been closed by a technological *legerdemain*. (21)

1990s: A decade in contemporary British fiction

Martyn Colebrook's 'The Emergence of Post-industrial British Fiction: A Literary History of the Nineties' begins by discussing the reconfiguration of the term 'literary' into a marketing category that occurred during the 1990s as a consequence of linked processes such as the ending of the Net Book Agreement (NBA), the so-called 'Waterstonisation' of bookselling – the process of discounting books and offering '3 for the price of 2' deals – and the rise of the celebrity 'bestseller' which could be bought in local supermarkets. Colebrook relates these developments to the changed social context of Britain following the sharp decline in manufacturing industries which had occurred during the Thatcherite 1980s. Arguing that oppositional literary discourses were often restricted to independent presses, micro-publishing initiatives and those writing from marginalized positions, he focuses in particular on how writers such as Irvine Welsh, James Kelman and John King addressed the problems associated with representing white, working-class masculinity in this post-industrial period. In conclusion, he argues that the literary history of the decade demonstrates how innovative combinations of independent publishing activities and imaginative representational strategies were able to create identities in fiction that met the social needs of a readership who otherwise felt bereft of any sense of agency or authenticity.

In 'Re-Writing National Identities in 1990s British Fiction', Nick Bentley considers how selected novels and authors explored Englishness, Northern Irishness, Scottishness and Welshness as both thematic literary themes and as Britain's dominant internal national identities, doing so, as Bentley stresses, in a period that focused on both the conception of and renewed interest in the sustainability of a national identity whose project is 'permanently incomplete because the missing part always remains beyond concrete definition' (67). Clearly, the context was of a nation, the United Kingdom or Great Britain, undergoing radical processes of devolution in a decade where, as Michael Rosie and Ross Bond observe, north of the border there was 'a substantial subsequent drop ... in the proportions choosing British as their best identity and a symmetrical rise in the proportion choosing Scottish' (56). As Rosie and Bond add, even England saw 'a gradual strengthening of Englishness ... and a similar decrease in Britishness' (57). Through a broad reading of Scottish, Welsh and Northern Irish novels, as well as novels by authors whose identities have their roots beyond the British Isles, Bentley explores the shifting dynamics of national identity in the decade.

In 'Satirical Apocalypse: Endism and the 1990s Fictions of Will Self', Katy Shaw and Philip Tew detail ways in which the satiric tradition has been both inflected and reconfigured in a number of Self's fictions, exploring how these prose narratives also engage specifically with and yet multiply the concepts of the apocalyptic and the transformational. In doing so, this chapter explores a range of Self's fictions; it draws illustratively upon *My Idea of Fun* (1993), *Grey Area* (1994), *The Sweet Smell of Psychosis* (1996) and *How the Dead Live* (2000); and it critically examines in close detail *The Quantity Theory of Insanity* (1991), *Cock and Bull* (1992) and *Great Apes* (1997). Shaw and Tew argue for Self's capacity to fictionalize both 'the undifferentiated incongruities of the life-world and satire's revelatory and corrective possibilities concerning the contradictions in human understanding' (98), while considering in these readings the potential influence of and Self's rejection of contemporaneous thinkers such as Francis Fukuyama. Through the chapter, Shaw and Tew demonstrate how Self uses 'satire to illuminate the fragile and fluid boundaries between reality and fiction, the word and the world' (110).

Sara Upstone, in her chapter 'Bringing Black to the Union Jack: Ethnic Fictions and the Politics of Possibility', brings to the reading of fiction by black British writers a much-needed attention to form. Upstone argues that, while broadly committed to realist forms, a consideration of the generic choices of black British writing is 'essential to appreciating its definitive contribution to British literature' during the decade. In particular, her reading of the formal choices of a range of black British writers highlights a commitment to the possibility of an ethnically diverse future for the country. The existence of this 'utopian realism' she charts through the work of, among others, Caryl Phillips, Hanif Kureishi, Courttia Newland and Diran Adebayo.

In 'Between the Short and Long Twentieth Centuries: Temporal Displacement in the Historical Fiction of the 1990s', Nick Hubble considers in a bold and complex fashion the significance of various novels, including A.S. Byatt's *Possession* (1990), Lawrence Norfolk's *Lemprière's Dictionary* (1991), Pat

Barker's *Regeneration trilogy* (1991–5), Kim Newman's *Anno Dracula* (1992), Christopher Priest's *The Prestige* (1996), Sarah Waters's *Tipping the Velvet* (1998), and Mary Gentle's *Ash: A Secret History* (1999). Hubble situates his analysis within the cultural, ideological and aesthetic fallout of the fall of the 'Iron Curtain', the subsequent dissolution of the Soviet Union in 1991, and the apparent legitimization of Francis Fukuyama's assertion of 'The End of History' and the consequent claims for various postmodern conceptions of history and historical fiction as advanced by theorists such as Fredric Jameson and Linda Hutcheon. Drawing on a range of theories, such as Max Saunders's concept of 'autobiografiction' and the ideas of quantum mechanics which influenced fiction in the 1990s, and sources including Giovanni Arrighi's *The Long Twentieth Century* (1994) and Walter Benjamin's 'Theses on the Philosophy of History', Hubble discusses how the 1870–1914 period – which marked both the final phase of a long nineteenth century and the opening of a long twentieth century – came into its own as a background for historical writers seeking to explore contemporary *fin-de-siècle* concerns.

In 'Experimental Enunciations in 1990s British Fiction', Mark P. Williams surveys the range of experimental fiction written in the 1990s in the light of theoretical sources including Christine Brooke-Rose's *Rhetoric of the Unreal* (1983) and Pierre Macherey's *A Theory of Literary Production* (1966). Focusing on the idea that experimental texts highlight and expose the intersubjective character of fiction, he examines work by authors including Brooke-Rose, Will Self, Martin Amis, Irvine Welsh, Indra Sinha, David Britton, Alan Moore, Grant Morrison, Iain Sinclair and Kim Newman amongst others. By analysing how these texts draw readers into entering active positions, Williams argues that the experimental fiction of the decade called into question our relationship with all forms of social enunciation.

In her chapter, Anja Müller-Wood presents a view of British fiction in the 1990s from the outside. Meticulously charting the reception of the British novel, and British culture more generally, in Germany through the decade, the chapter argues that a number of sometimes conflicting versions of both were used to cover over Germany's tensions and to provide a model for its hopes following unification. In doing so, Müller-Wood presents a refreshing and sometimes provocative reading of the work of, among others, Salman Rushdie, Hanif Kureishi and Nick Hornby.

In 'National Identity and the Immigrant', Paoi Hwang discusses the parallels between Britain and Taiwan in the 1990s within the context of the more general Western influence on Taiwan during this period. Having established key themes and issues, she proceeds to make a detailed comparative reading of Hanif Kureishi's *The Buddha of Suburbia* (1990) and Tachun Chang's *My Kid Sister* (1993). By reflecting on the relationship between narrative, identity and sexuality in these two texts, Hwang assesses how both writers use 'immigrant' voices to comment on and distance themselves from the society about which they write.

Note

1   Clinton's comparative ploy, its widespread circulation and its manipulative intention are discussed by Benjamin R. Bates in 'Circulation of the World War II/Holocaust analogy in the 1999 Kosovo intervention: Articulating a vocabulary for international conflict'.

Works Cited

Anon. 'Genocide in Rwanda'. United Human Rights Council. Undated, http://www.unitedhumanrights.org/genocide/genocide_in_rwanda.htm

Anon. *Report of the Independent Inquiry into the Actions of the United Nations during the 1994 Genocide in Rwanda.* 15 December 1999, http://daccess-dds-ny.un.org/doc/UNDOC/GEN/N99/395/47/IMG/N9939547.pdf?OpenElement

Bates, Benjamin R. 'Circulation of the World War II/Holocaust Analogy in the 1999 Kosovo Intervention: Articulating a Vocabulary for International Conflict'. *Journal of Language and Politics* 8.1 (2009): 28–51.

Behrendt, Stephen C. 'Mourning, Myth and Merchandising: The Public Death of Princess Charlotte'. In *Responses to Death: The Literary Work of Mourning*. Ed. Christian Riegel. Edmonton: University of Alberta Press, 2005, 75–96.

Bentley, Nick. 'Introduction: Mapping the Millenium. Themes and Trends in Contemporary British Fiction'. In *British Fiction of the 1990s*. Ed. Nick Bentley. London and New York: Routledge, 2005, 1–18.

Botting, Fred. 'From Excess to the New World Order'. In *British Fiction of the 1990s*. Ed. Nick Bentley. London and New York: Routledge, 2005, 21–41.

Bracewell, Michael. 'New Image Glasgow to Young British Art: Introducing the 1990s'. In *New Formations: Remembering the 1990s*. Eds Joe Brooker and Roger Luckhurst. Number 50, Autumn 2003: 22–7.

Brennan, Michael. 'Towards a Sociology of (Public) Mourning?' *Sociology* 35.1 (2001): 205–12, also: http://wrap.warwick.ac.uk/798/1/WRAP_Brennan_Sociology_public_mourning.pdf

Brooker, Joe. 'Commercial Alternative'. In *New Formations: Remembering the 1990s*. Eds Joe Brooker and Roger Luckhurst. Number 50, Autumn 2003: 106–22.
Button, Virginia. *The Turner Prize: Twenty Years*. London: Tate, 2003.
Campbell, Alistair. *Diaries: Volume Three: Power and Responsibility*. London: Arrow Books, 2012.
Caruth, Cathy. 'Introduction to Psychoanalysis, Trauma and Culture I'. *American Imago* 48.1 (1991): 1–12.
———. (ed.) *Trauma: Explorations in Memory*. Baltimore: Johns Hopkins University Press, 1995.
———. *Unclaimed Experience: Trauma, Narrative, and History*. Baltimore: Johns Hopkins University Press, 1996.
'Celebrating 25 Years of London City Airport'. *London City Airport Runway News* 23, Autumn/Winter (2012): 9, https://www.londoncityairport.com/content/pdf/Runway_News_Edition_Twenty_Three_Autumn_2012.pdf
Chomsky, Noam. 'On the NATO Bombing of Yugoslavia: Interviewed by Danilo Mandic'. *RTS Online* (25 April 2006): n.p., http://www.chomsky.info/interviews/20060425.htm
Crabtree, James, Max Nathan and Simon Roberts. *MobileUK: Mobile Phones and Everyday Life*. London: The Work Foundation, 2003, http://www.theworkfoundation.com/assets/docs/publications/103_mobileuk.pdf
De Groot, Jerome. *The Historical Novel*. London: Routledge, 2010.
Del Ponte, Carla and Chuck Sudetic. *Madame Prosecutor: Confrontations with Humanity's Worst Criminals and the Culture of Impunity*. New York: Other Press, 2009.
Dillow, Chris. *The End of Politics: New Labour and the Folly of Managerialism*. Petersfield: Harriman House, 2007.
English, James F. *The Economy of Prestige: Prizes, Awards and the Circulation of Cultural Value*. Cambridge: Harvard University Press, 2005.
Foster, Janet, Tim Newburn and Anna Souhami. *Assessing the Impact of the Stephen Lawrence Inquiry*. Home Office Research Study 294. Home Office Research, Development and Statistics Directorate: London, 2005, http://webarchive.nationalarchives.gov.uk/20110218135832/rds.homeoffice.gov.uk/rds/pdfs05/hors294.pdf
Fox, Dan. 'Then and Now: British Art and the 1990s'. *Frieze* 159 (November–December 2013): 100–7.
Freud, Sigmund. *Mourning and Melancholia (1917)*. Standard Edition. Volume 14. London: Hogarth Press, 1953: 237–58.
Gąsiorek, Andrzej. '"Refugees from Time": History, Death and the Flight from Reality in Contemporary Writing'. In *British Fiction of the 1990s*. Ed. Nick Bentley. London: Routledge, 2005.
Griffin, Annie. *The Book Club*. Channel 4. 2002–3.
Hartley, Jenny. *Reading Groups*. Oxford: Oxford University Press, 2001.

Herman, Edward and David Peterson. *The Politics of Genocide*. New York: Monthly Review Press, 2010.

Hodgson, Godfrey. *The Myth of American Exceptionalism*. New Haven and London: Yale University Press, 2009.

Hutcheon, Linda. *The Politics of Postmodernism*. London and New York: Routledge, 1989.

Jameson, Fredric. *Postmodernism, or the Cultural Logic of Late Capitalism*. London: Verso, 1991.

Johnsen, William T. *NATO Strategy in the 1990s: Reaping the Peace Dividend or the Whirlwind?* Carlisle: Strategic Studies Institute, United States Army War College, 25 May 1995, http://www.strategicstudiesinstitute.army.mil/pubs/display.cfm?pubID=165

'Judging panel announced for Guardian First Book Award 2000'. *Guardian* (1 July 2000), http://www.theguardian.com/books/2000/jul/01/guardianfirstbookaward1999.guardianfirstbookaward

Julius, Anthony. *Transgression: The Offences of Art*. London: Thames & Hudson, 2002.

Jury, Louise. 'Royal Academy's "Sensation" Proves to Be a Shockingly Good Crowd-Puller'. *The Independent* (30 December 1997), http://www.independent.co.uk/news/royal-academys-sensation-proves-to-be-a-shockingly-good-crowd-puller-1291068.html (accessed 13 June 2014)

Kamp, David. 'London Swings! Again!' *Vanity Fair* (March 1997), http://www.vanityfair.com/magazine/archive/1997/03/london199703 (accessed 6 June 2014).

Keen, Suzanne. *Romances of the Archive in Contemporary British Fiction*. Toronto: University of Toronto Press, 2003.

———. 'The Historical Turn in British Fiction'. In *A Concise Companion to Contemporary British Fiction*. Ed. James English. Oxford: Blackwell, 2006, 167–87.

Kurtz, Howard. *Spin Cycle: How the White House and the Media Manipulate the News*. New York: Simon & Schuster, 1998.

Lewis, Justin, et al. *The Quality and Independence of British Journalism: Tracking the Changes over 20 Years*. Cardiff: Cardiff University School of Journalism, Medias and Cultural Studies/Public Trust Project, 2005, http://www.cardiff.ac.uk/jomec/resources/QualityIndependenceofBritishJournalism.pdf

Luckhurst, Roger. 'British Science Fiction in the 1990s: Politics and Genre'. In *British Fiction of the 1990s*. Ed. Nick Bentley. London and New York: Routledge, 2005, 78–91.

———. *The Trauma Question*. London: Routledge, 2008.

Mazower, Mark. *Dark Continent: Europe's Twentieth Century*. London: Penguin, 1998.

McGuire, Stryker, et al. 'London Reigns'. *Newsweek* (4 November 1996): 34–6.

Mibenge, Chiseche Salome. *Sex and International Tribunals: The Erasure of Gender from the War Narrative*. Philadelphia: University of Pennsylvania Press, 2013.

Myall, Steve and Russell Myers. 'New Jill Dando Murder Probe: Serbian "Assassins" Questioned'. *The Daily Mirror* (24 February 2014). n.p., http://www.mirror.co.uk/news/new-jill-dando-murder-probe-3178020#ixzz2waCDvhXt

Myer, Patrick. 'Jill Dando "Murdered by Serbian Hitman"'. *The Telegraph* (3 March 2012); http://www.telegraph.co.uk/news/uknews/crime/9120523/Jill-Dando-murdered-by-Serbian-hitman.html

Pease, Donald E. *The New American Exceptionalism*. Minneapolis: University of Minnesota Press, 2009.

Pilger, John. 'Don't Forget What Happened in Yugoslavia'. *The New Statesman* (14 August 2008): n.p., http://www.newstatesman.com/europe/2008/08/pilger-kosovo-war-nato-serbs Online.

'Queen's "Bohemian Rhapsody" Voted Nation's Favourite No. 1 'Single', 16 July 2012, http://www.smoothradio.com/music-news/bohemian-rhapsody-nations-no1/

Reyntjens, Filip. *The Great African War: Congo and Regional Geopolitics, 1996–2006*. Cambridge: Cambridge University Press, 2009.

Rosie, Michael and Ross Bond. 'National Identities and Politics after Devolution'. *Radical Statistics* 97 (2008): 47–65, http://www.radstats.org.uk/no097/RosieBond97/.pdf

Sebald, W.G. *Austerlitz*. London: Hamish Hamilton, 2001.

———. 'Theoretical Perspectives: Poor Rich White Folks Play the Blues'. In *New Formations: Remembering the 1990s*. Eds Joe Brooker and Roger Luckhurst, 50 (Autumn 2003): 142–56.

Simons, Jon. 'The Dialectics of Diana as Empty Signifier'. *Theory & Event* 1 (4) (1997): n.p., https://muse.jhu.edu/login?auth=0&type=summary&url=/journals/theory_and_event/v001/1.4simons.html

Sinason, Valerie Sinason (ed.) *Treating Survivors of Satanic Abuse*. London: Routledge, 1994.

Stallanbrass, Julian. *High Art in the 1990s*. London: Verso, 1999

———. 'The Making of Don't Look Back in Anger', *Uncut* (August 2007): 34–6.

Tomlinson, John. 'The Agenda of Globalisation'. In *New Formations: Remembering the 1990s*. Eds Joe Brooker and Roger Luckhurst. 50 (Autumn 2003): 10–21.

Yannis, Alexandros. 'Kosovo: The Political Economy of Conflict and Peacebuilding'. In *The Political Economy of Armed Conflict: Beyond Greed and Grievance*. Eds Karen Ballentine and Jake Sherman. Bolder: Lynne Rienner Publishers, 2003, 167–96.

1

Literary History of the Decade
The Emergence of Post-Industrial British Fiction

Martyn Colebrook

In terms of book publishing, the 1990s were a significant period, being the decade which included variously: the last banning of a book for obscenity – David Britton's *Lord Horror* (1990), the ending of the Net Book Agreement (NBA), the rise of the celebrity 'bestseller' and the reconfiguration of the term 'literary' into a marketing category associated with a proliferating field of high-profile prizes. Alongside these changes to the publishing industry, one of the other most noteworthy developments of the decade was the emergence of fiction which engaged with the onset of the post-industrial society, as instigated by the deleterious and destructive excesses of the Thatcher Government in the 1980s. 'Post-industrial' is an adjective which has come to be associated with culture, gender, socio-economics, space and nation, themes with which the literary texts featured in this chapter address and engage in a dialogue throughout. In particular, there will be an analysis of how Irvine Welsh, James Kelman and John King set about, in their own particular ways, to debate with or negotiate the methods of representation and problems associated with representations of the 'post-industrial male' and 'white, working-class masculinity' and, in doing so, adopted particular techniques which allowed them to construct an 'authenticity' within their fiction. Throughout the twentieth century, British publishing was controlled by the NBA, which had been introduced in 1900 as an agreement between publishers and booksellers that all books would be sold at an agreed price. If any bookseller was found selling a book below the agreed price, then the publisher in question would immediately cease to supply them. However, the decision of the large bookstore chains, Dillons and Waterstones, to start discounting books at the beginning of the 1990s eventually led to the Office of Fair Trading referring the NBA to the Restrictive Practices Court. Over the course of the review process, debate around the issue grew and several leading publishers, including Reed Books and Hodder Headline, withdrew from the agreement before the Court finally in March 1997 ruled the NBA contrary to public interest and therefore illegal. As predicted by supporters of the NBA, the market for bookselling immediately expanded to include retail outlets which had not traditionally sold books, such as the supermarkets Asda and Tesco, which took full advantage of the removal of restrictions on prices to sell best-selling books at a significant discount as loss leaders. Those in favour of keeping the NBA had argued that abandoning it would lead to a reduction in booksellers' profits and, therefore, also a reduction in the number of books being printed. In contrast, those in favour of scrapping the agreement had claimed that this would force the publishers to be more discerning in their selection of titles and, therefore, stimulate a greater interest in literary fiction amongst the reading public, who would now be able to buy these books more cheaply than hitherto. Either outcome would have impacted upon the means by which cultural production appropriated and disseminated the main tenets of literary and popular fiction and thereby influenced taste and trends. In reality, despite the doom-saying from the publishers and booksellers, there was no visible disaster, and the number of novels published increased in spite of the changes to the material conditions under which publishing operated.

However, while the quantity and variety of books increased, the environment in which they were retailed changed radically. Perhaps in an effort to distinguish themselves from the non-traditional retail outlets, the bookstore chains Waterstones (which had incorporated Dillons by the end of the decade) and Borders began offering 'a complete leisure experience' where 'you can relax over coffee in the "spacious, comfortable seating area" and "enjoy one of the regular live music performances"' (Barker 1999: n.p.) – the jargon phrase was 'lifestyle bookselling' but the phenomenon became more popularly known as 'Waterstonisation'. By blending the consumption of 'literature' with other cultural components, the era of corporate-sponsored culture emerged with a host of prizes: onto the victors, the status of 'literature' was conferred. This culture of prize-winning, which has come to represent one of the defining aspects of creating 'literature', also evolved in relation to the marketing strategies adopted by publishers. As evidence of the different strata in which fiction could be positioned, the British public were showered with offerings from the Orange Prize for Fiction (which has since become the Baileys Woman's Prize for Fiction), the Costa Book Awards, the Costa Short Story Awards and the Man Booker Prize. The status of these prizes and their shortlists reminds the reader that they are engaging with

'Literature-with-a-capital-L' and that 'This market is a global one [...]' (Zimring n.p.). For the public, participating in these prizes – by reading the books and paying attention to who wins – functioned as a 'cultural event' equivalent to a trip to a heritage site or a weekend break. Furthermore, given that the Booker Prize is a method by which the judges can be seen to 'legitimise the multicultural, the exotic, and the foreign' (Müller 2002: 50), another cultural exchange takes place by which 'Booker Plc gains status as a postcolonial literary patron, as a recogniser, judge, and consumer of refined culture [and so] gains prestige in a realm typically beyond its field of influence and action' (Müller 2002: 49).

This new, commercialized, branded prize-giving literary culture had wide-reaching consequences. As the analysis of *Trainspotting* in the following pages will demonstrate, complicities developed between the gatekeepers, the arbiters of taste and culture and the publishing industry, which applied even to the work of apparent literary outsiders. However, in response to the new conditions of the publishing and bookselling industry, pockets of regional resistance – such as the Scottish publishing scene – and alternative outlets – small and independent presses – took on a new importance as the main sources of alternatives to an increasingly homogeniszd literary culture. In particular, independent publishing projects which came to prominence in the 1990s, such as Savoy Books and Attack! Books, subverted and contested the notions of 'literature' and 'culture' at the height of their marketization. In particular, the publication by Savoy of *Lord Horror*, written by the firm's co-founder, David Britton, in 1989 (although it is dated 1990) and its subsequent banning and pulping in accordance with the Obscene Publications Act acted as a prologue that highlighted the issues surrounding culture that would be at stake – albeit often less sensationally – during the 1990s. While, at the other end of the decade, the emergence of Steven Wells's Millennial leftist project, Attack! Books, with its intent to 'self consciously problematise the notion of canon' (Williams 18) – a project which can be aligned with various anthologies of that period such as Stewart Home's *Suspect Device: A Reader in Hard Edged Fiction* (1998) and Tony White's *Britpulp!* (1999) – formed a suitable epilogue: Wells's venture. More generally, the significance of the small presses for the decade can be seen in the emergence of writers such as Irvine Welsh and John King, who would go on to major critical and commercial success, with early short stories. Despite the enshrinement of prizes celebrating literature, the 1990s was marked by a continual breaching of the false distinctions between 'high' and 'low' culture.

This chapter, therefore, is about the transgressive impulse in contemporary fiction published in the 1990s, with a general focus on the emergence of fictions from marginal presses and their subsequent relationship with the canon. More specifically, the texts discussed in this chapter provide a method by which one can plot and then navigate a cartography of novels and novelists who are concerned with the problematizing of white, working-class masculinity *and* an attempt to describe transnational post-industrial identities.

Cult status by appointment of the State: 'The last banned book in Britain'

In 1976, David Britton and Michael Butterworth co-founded Savoy Publishers, an alternative outlet based in Manchester. Savoy describe drawing their inspirations from a number of significant publishers:

> We were inspired by the US houses Lancer Books and Ace Books (the fantasy range under Donald Wollheim's control), for the way they updated the American pulp tradition in their jacket design, and Arkham House, publishers of HP Lovecraft's first work. In the UK we looked to Picador, who were using the large-size 'trade' format to present paperback literary fiction in a distinctive way, and Allison & Busby, out-of-category champions of alternative fiction and black writers. (Savoy)

Savoy set out to position themselves in a number of traditions which are relevant to the other fiction under discussion in this chapter. The presence of pulp is an underpinning influence, as is Picador, which are using a specific format in order to make distinctive the paperback literary fiction they publish. That Allison and Busby promote fiction which is 'out of category' is telling when considering how genre becomes such a powerful tool for the formation of canons and sub-canons in contemporary publishing. One of Savoy's earliest creations, Lord Horror, came to prominence as the eponymous central character of *Lord Horror*, which was eventually published in 1989, although it had been written some years earlier. Subsequent to this debut, Lord Horror has appeared in comic books and also become known for his appearances on a number of record releases. Occasionally working with fellow Savoyards, Britton and Butterworth have created and published every item in the Lord Horror franchise: now several decades' worth of novels, comics, anthologies, records, CDs.

In the same year as Savoy was formed, James Anderton was appointed Chief Inspector in the Greater Manchester. Anderton, who was notorious (or famous, depending on one's point of view) for his 'muscular Christianity' and 'outspoken illiberalism') created a local Obscene Publications Squad (the only one in Britain apart from a London-based organization) to undertake an orchestrated assault on the sale of pornography in his region; as a consequence of this mission, Britton's Manchester shop was regularly raided during the 1980s and various materials were seized, among which some of Savoy Books' own titles including, of course, *Lord Horror*. There is a distinct irony to this sequence of events because outspoken anti-gay pronouncements by Anderton had been transposed into the narrative of *Lord Horror*: Britton and Butterworth pointedly replacing each instance of the word '*gay*' with '*Jew*'. The effect of this transformation was that real hate speech became the subject of satire, subverting both the intended output and the interlocutor.

Lord Horror, which, as discussed, was eventually banned under the Obscene Publications Act in 1991, uses tropes of monstrosity in its discussion of fascism and the Holocaust. Working in the tradition of Swift, Hogarth and Dickens, the text represents a confrontational, genuinely provocative and offensive scatological satire which, according to Michael Moorcock, succeeds because it:

> confronts hypocrisy, violence, racialism, sexism, prejudice in all its hideous modern forms – ill-formed fears of homosexuals, people of colour and the jobless classes. Everything *Lord Horror* attacks is representative of that evil which the English pride themselves on defeating... by forcing us to confront the obscenities in our own society we are made to consider our own attitudes, perhaps even our own complicity. (Morgan 2004: n.p.)

The complexity of Britton's vision informs a text whose characters epitomize and come to embody the monstrous in a multitude of forms and representations. As D.M. Mitchell suggests, *Lord Horror* contains 'encapsulations of every major train of thought and belief that has made the 20th century the horror we see today' (Mitchell). In its aggressive and direct confrontation of the transgressive impulse, this text deploys strategies which can be traced directly from speculative and fantasy genres, but simply to focus on the lineage from which *Lord Horror* emerges is to offer a disservice to its creators; such a richness of imagination, brilliance of execution and unrivalled levels of provocation need not be buried under an unhelpful weight of academic detective work. In much the same vein as many of the texts under discussion in this chapter, the tone of the controversy and debates sparked by such works of fiction can prove to be as telling and valuable as cultural and political indices as the fictions themselves. For example, Elizabeth Young took up the baton for the moral guardians of the reviewing press in condemning the work, complaining in *The New Statesmen* that '*Lord Horror* is a book that outrages current taboos on racism: taboos so strangulating that no one may transgress them... *American Psycho* outrages no contemporary taboos' (Young). Her comments led to an exchange in the letters page of *Private Eye*[1] with Robert Meadley and David Butterworth, in which she clarifies her contention that *American Psycho* (1991) was an 'acceptable' work of literature and breaks no taboo because the violence is entirely in Patrick Bateman's mind. With Young's 'expert' analysis in mind, it is worth examining the view from the other side of the spectrum as represented, for example, by Tony Williams's argument that '*Lord Horror* is one of the most carefully constructed works emanating from contemporary alternative British literature' (Williams). The point, as emphasized by Williams's use of the term 'construction', is surely that whatever else might be said about *Lord Horror*, it is ludicrous to suggest that it is anything but a work of imagination. Furthermore, as Frances D'Souza notes, 'It is particularly ironic that a book dealing with the totalitarian notions of a fictional character could be destroyed by police, without benefit of a jury trial' (D'Souza).

Attempts to summarize or indicate the plot of *Lord Horror* are futile, given that it contains no discernible plotline, instead being composed of a sequence of sketches or vignettes in which Horror travels through time with his assistants, Meng and Ecker, committing horrendous acts of violence against Jewish citizens. The passage which is often cited as being potentially the most anti-semitic is also underpinned with a sense of both hyperbole and utter brilliance in its depiction of the protagonist literally ingesting a Jew. After swallowing half the Jew, Lord Horror

> heaved himself onto his feet. He propped himself unsteadily against the wall, wreathed in steam, with the two bent legs of the Jew brazenly dangling from his mouth. He raised his hands to the pain in his head, clasped it, stared up at the big moon. When the white orb tossed down light, the loose legs swung and crossed one over the other as though the old Jew inside had seated himself casually in a roomy armchair. (Britton 160)

Even so, with a scenario which owes as much to Dali or Bosch as it does to the self-conscious send-up of its complicity with the horrific acts committed by Lord Horror, the text is not content to stop there. Earlier in the narrative, it is observed that 'Lord Horror's avowed anti-semitism was a cartoon, a burlesque, a technicolour replica of Hitler's own Jewish stance... Horror was just a brushstroke in a tapestry without substance, his actions far too Grand Guignol theatrical to be truly convincing' (Britton 37). Such a self-conscious commentary on the status of the text as *not* endorsing the acts within the narrative makes it clear that Britton and Butterworth's strategies are to critique the subject of their narrative from within.

Subsequently to *Lord Horror*, Butterworth and Britton worked on a second and third text in the sequence: *Motherfuckers: The Auschwitz of Oz* (1996) and *Baptised in the Blood of Millions* (2000). At the time of writing, *Motherfuckers* and *Baptised in the Blood of Millions* are both stocked by Amazon, yet *Lord Horror* remains pulped, and as the Savoy website proclaims, Britton and Butterworth have no plans for a reprint. Keith Seward commented on the follow-up to *Lord Horror*: 'its domain: the same avant-garde, cultish, transgressive form of literature produced by the author of *Naked Lunch*. Its delirium is not demented but deliberate. *Motherfuckers* is a literary work of the most serious intention and the highest art' (Seward). Similarly resisting its appropriation by the academic canon, James Marriott correctly suggests that 'Calls to add Lord Horror to the academic canon seem similarly misplaced: academic appraisal is sure to draw the sting from even the most brutal work, while Savoyards have long celebrated the obscure, unsung and hopelessly irredeemable' (Marriott 2008: n.p.).

New voices and new writing: Revolution from the fringes

Scottish fiction re-emerged as a force in the 1970s, which saw the debuts of William McIlvanney and James Kelman, the former, initially, through a small US publishing house. The impact of McIlvanney's socialist realist fiction and how it was being taken as a contribution to 'literature' was emphasized when his first crime novel, *Laidlaw*, was reviewed as genre fiction from a *serious* novelist. This was the start of a process, which would see Scottish fiction become the dominant force within contemporary British fiction by the 1990s; a state of affairs that was acknowledged by mainstream literary culture, when Kelman's shortlisting for the 1989 Booker Prize, for *A Disaffection*, was followed by his winning it with *How Late it Was, How Late* in 1994.

The rise of Scottish fiction in the 1980s – the subject of Monica Germanà's chapter in the *1980s: A Decade of Contemporary British Fiction* (2014) – was marked by milestones such as the publication of Alasdair Gray's *Lanark: A Life in Four Books* (1981), another major breakthrough for Scottish literature in terms of critical reception as opposed to a commercial success – marketed in the United States as science fiction, it sank without a trace. However, 1984 saw the publication of Iain Banks' *The Wasp Factory* which, following an aggressive marketing campaign in which all the negative reviews were published with the novel, became a 'cult classic' and bestseller overnight. In many respects, the markers set down by Gray and Banks, two 'Highlanders' of contemporary

Scottish fiction, highlight two competing facets of contemporary fiction, commercial and canonical success, as well as the manner in which such successes are achieved or recognized.

In terms of the practical aspects of publishing, Duncan McLean's Clocktower Press began publishing short stories from writers such as Ron Butlin (already established as a poet), Janice Galloway, A.L. Kennedy, Irvine Welsh and Gordon Legge – authors who were hitherto unrecognized outside Scotland's artistic circles. From these origins, the force that is contemporary Scottish fiction emerged, and using their own specific techniques, other novelists began writing back against specific constructions of regional and national identity, as well as the particular genres in which their fiction was positioned. In this context, the appearance of *Lanark* in 1981 represented a watershed because it provided a model for how Scotland could be narrated as a post-industrial space, and it inspired and motivated other novelists to explore the new narrative contours and opportunities provided by this space (see Colebrook 2013). With fresh territory to explore came the exposition of a darker side of the contemporary psyche, writing which has come to be labelled the 'Contemporary Scottish Gothic'. In 2001, Alan Bissett produced an anthology of writing entitled *Damage Land: Contemporary Scottish Gothic*, written in the wake of David Punter's essay 'Heart Lands: Contemporary Scottish Gothic' (1999) which was one of the first treatments of the subject matter. Revisiting his motives for writing *Damage Land*, Bissett claims that:

> I was excited by the way in which he had positioned the likes of Galloway, James Kelman, A.L. Kennedy and Irvine Welsh as investigators of psychological disturbances and breakdown. A collection of fiction seemed like the next step in making a case for these Gothic textures in contemporary Scottish literature. (Bissett 2009)

The excitement that Bissett experienced would become a hallmark of the fiction which this coterie of novelists and their colleagues produced in the 1990s. Tellingly, despite Kelman's open resistance to genre fiction, Bissett observes that 'Kelman scholars may be interested to know that he pointed me towards two of his stories, "O jesus, here come the dwarfs" and "A Nightboilerman's notes" from *Lean Tales* (1985), as ones which he himself felt displayed Gothic effects' (Bissett 2009). The function of the Scottish Gothic as a theme of literature in the 1990s is its responsiveness to the expected shift from an outgoing Conservative Government and the accompanying Thatcherite project and prevailing economic conditions which would accompany the newly elected Labour Government under Tony Blair. The absence of a markedly different political agenda, the emphasis on the acquisition of personal wealth and consumerism – the 'society of choice' – meant that contemporary Scottish Gothic could be seen as a spectre or shadow of the 'auspices of Thatcher's and Blair's free-market utopia, [it] is a dark doppelganger of it, if you will' (Bissett 2009).

Focusing on Irvine Welsh's *Trainspotting* (1993) and James Kelman's *How Late it Was, How Late* (1994) as the central texts from Scottish writing in the 1990s, and with brief reference to their contemporaries, the section discusses both the transgressive and the post-industrial in a two-pronged incursion into the heartlands of Scottish fiction in the 1990s. Each text 'posit[s] the Scottish consciousness as haunted by itself, by its own internal demons, as it were' (Bissett 2009: 1), and these demons take the form of drug and alcohol abuse, and subversions of gender constructions.

In these instances, Scottish Gothic is identified as proposing a sequence of concepts which undermine the myths inscribed upon Scotland by the political, economic and cultural powerhouses which constitute England and Literary London. Wallace claims that

> [t]here is a new cultural identity celebrated in recent Scottish fiction, but an identity whose instability and claustrophobic intimacy with psychological maiming writers inevitably deplore, yet appear incapable of forsaking. (218)

The cultural identity seems to be riddled with ambiguous or contrary values. That it is celebrated does not mean that the writings are positive, but that they are revelling in their own fascination with the carnivalesque or the transgressive. This is suggested by the juxtaposition of the 'deplorable' identity with the 'incapability of forsaking' it – asserting that the persistent presentation of this identity type in Scottish writing has become an intrinsic part of the nation's culture, despite the writers' and critics' dislike of its presence. There is a sense of frustration and despair here, that to write about such individuals and their 'instability' and 'psychological maiming' has become an expectation rather than an opportunity for exploration. The despair is particularly evident given that for Wallace the argument remains that

> such motifs have become entrenched as readily identifiable and assimilable literary tropes which, despite their continued creative appeal, may have not only outlived their function, but also become the internalised submission to a condition in which the Scottish imagination will eventually colonise itself. (220)

Arguably, the trope has become too familiar and is in danger of being exhausted – there is a cause for concern that its repeated use will cause the genre to impose limitations of creativity on the authors using it. In each of the novelists under discussion in this chapter, the invigoration of the trope is demonstrated and its creative potential and appeal remains apparent, and it is simply the method by which the trope manifests itself which is left open to question.

News just in from the fringe: Irvine Welsh and James Kelman

Ezra Pound said that literature is news that stays news. Commentators tend to focus on the notion of permanence in that statement, but it seems to me that the 'news' part is at least as important. (Mclean xiv)

There are distinct differences between the media personae and methods of James Kelman and Irvine Welsh. As Drew Milne argues, Kelman should be considered in the context of European modernism as well as a part of contemporary Scottish writing (see Milne 2001, 2003). Nonetheless, the two writers shared a number of commonalities, including the same publisher: Secker and Warburg. In a process similar to Kelman's own emergence into the public domain, Welsh's success was supported by a writing group that was 'modelled on Glasgow's a decade earlier and the creation of outlets such as Duncan McLean's Clocktower Press and Kevin Williamson's Rebel Inc which not only supplemented established showcases such as *New Writing Scotland* but were able to make the newest writing available in the shortest possible time' (Morace 2007: 22). The significance of the impact of small presses and litzines was evident in the earlier discussion of *Lord Horror* and it is this continued resistance to the corrosive 'Waterstonisation' of contemporary literature, as well as the rapacious appetites of expansionist conglomerates and publishing giants such as Random House, which highlights the importance of ventures such as Williamson's and McLean's or, indeed, of regional publishers such as Canongate. The speed at which small presses can print and distribute material also heightens their value, ensuring more exposure and a wider audience for fiction which would otherwise be neglected or rejected by the perceived mainstream publishers. The name, 'litzines', is a clear indicator of the manner in which their output, processes and origins destabilize distinctions between the 'popular' and the 'literary' and challenge the reader's preconceived notions about the cultural expectations of the medium.

Originally brought to life under the title 'Past Tense: Four Stories from a Novel' and drawing on journals which Welsh had kept in the early 1980s, *Trainspotting* was, at its inception, a sequence of short stories published by Clocktower Press in 1992. As McLean recalls: 'Our slowest seller was undoubtedly *Past Tense: Four Stories from a Novel* by Irvine Welsh ... In those days to write about heroin addicts on a run-down Edinburgh estate was far from the easy commercialism critics often accuse Irvine of having adopted' (McLean xiv). In response to the accusations of such easy commercialism, Welsh contends that he was more concerned with getting the book published than the amount of money he would receive. In a television interview, Welsh claimed that 'The motivation for writing *Trainspotting* was because there were so many people that I'd known that were just dropping dead, were getting infected. For me it was like trying to work out through fiction how that was happening' (Welsh 1995: n.p.). There remains, however, the legacy of suspicion which was provoked by the promotion-savvy Welsh's self-styled persona as the 'illiterate savage from the Scottish backwaters' who turned out to be an MBA-educated, middle-management white male professional. Whilst his detractors bring their own particular agenda to their reviews and criticism, it is arguable that Welsh's fiction should be viewed with a cautious sense of cynicism and an appreciation for the cultural complicity between marketing profile, aggressive publication briefs and an author who is more than happy to play up his 'wild-child' reputation.

In advance of the publication of *Trainspotting* by Secker and Warburg in 1993, Alan Chadwick, writing in *Herald Scotland*, announced: 'Critics, prize-giving juries, and readers alike are hereby served notice: *Trainspotting* marks the arrival of a major new talent' (Chadwick 1993: x). Along with Rebel Inc's provocative endorsement that 'This book deserves to sell more copies than the Bible' (Welsh 1993: x), each press release and circulation set about the process of promoting Welsh and his novel to 'the more or less closed ranks of the literary establishment of gatekeepers (reviewers and prize juries) and in the literary marketplace as part of the category that has come to be known as "literary fiction"' (Morace 2007: 35). That Morace identifies these ranks as 'closed' clearly highlights further the weight of value which the small presses bring to ensuring exposure for novelists who are operating in zones which are rejected or otherwise ignored by the culture-makers. This space was reinforced by the efforts of Secker and Warburg who organized a pre-release excerpt and feature in the *Literary Review* as well as arranging a reading by Welsh at the Edinburgh Festival in 1993 (also featuring Duncan McLean); both of which were subject to significant publicity in advance. It is arguable that the amount of pre-release exposure and the extent of the efforts which Secker and Warburg undertook to herald this novel indicated a degree of anxiety and lack of confidence over the financial reward *Trainspotting* would return on their investment.

In contrast with the avenues in which his work was promoted, Welsh's own view on the success of *Trainspotting* is that it is a consequence of the 'colonial guilt-trip, a sense that the mainstream of writers has run out of ideas, that they're just the same middle-class Oxbridge voices writing about the same stuff [...]. Literary culture exists for its own references and just goes up its own arse' (Walsh in Kelly 2005: 73). Similarly, he expressed unease at the manner in which *Trainspotting*'s film adaptation differed from the book and reworked the economic and social values he was writing about in line with 'institutional and distributional realities' (Kelly: 73). There is often confusion as to the relationship between the instant box-office success of Danny Boyle's *Trainspotting* (1996) and the impact of the novel before the film came out. By the time the film had been released, *Trainspotting* had sold around 1,00,000 copies; an extraordinary number for a debut but even so the novel had not been the media and reviewing sensation it was to become.

A crucial distinction between *Trainspotting* and the lineage in which critics seemed keen to insert it was that, as opposed to continuing the presentation of the junkie as 'decadent, bohemian addict' (Kelly 2005: 36) – the hallmark of the earlier Scottish cult writer Alexander Trocchi – Welsh relocated the surroundings to the disenfranchised working-class housing schemes of Edinburgh and the run-down port of Leith. The different context necessitated a new sociocultural focus: the working class in the 1980s, whose inhabitation of the wastelands and shanty towns on the outskirts of major urban locations was a direct consequence of the unemployment and economic hardship which stemmed from the decline of the industrial base within Britain. As the title suggests, *Trainspotting* explores these tensions by implicitly acknowledging the railway as a powerful symbol of the industrial revolution while focusing on the bystanders engaged in a pastime which allows one to 'fill in time but is otherwise completely futile' (Grant 1993: 14). Attempts to relieve boredom by achieving a high or imposing a regulated order on an otherwise random sequence of chaotic markers are all characteristics of the crises which have beset the modern post-industrial male and his simultaneous resistance to and experience of 'anonymity and despair' (Tew: 116). Drug users and their suppliers remain the subjects of media 'moral panics', and elaborate media-inspired fictional constructs, through their threat to the solidity of the social fabric. Welsh states:

> I've always found the treatment of someone who's got drug problems a bit offensive in Scottish literature. In classic Scottish fiction you see the junkie coming into their books as a shadowy cardboard cut-out figure who's there to undermine or subvert decent Scottish working-class values. (Young 33)

Welsh justifies the prominence of drug addicts in his work on the grounds that their relationship both to the drugs and the networks of fellow drug users and dealers highlights how individuals are connected to social and cultural networks even when they apparently epitomize marginality and anti-social behaviour. Suggesting that he felt it appropriate to demonstrate the junkie as one who is not 'isolated and cut off', Welsh highlights a sense of the community which combines with and informs the bodily metaphor at the heart of *Trainspotting*. As Johnny Swan, Renton's dealer, comments with a darkly ironic tone when Sick Boy refuses to share needles: 'Now that's nae very social, nae sharin, nae shooting'. For Swann, there are 'no friends in this game, just associates'. As Renton opines:

> We are all acquaintances now. It seems tae go beyond our personal circumstances; a brilliant metaphor for our times. (Welsh 1993: 11)

This represents a complicit agreement with the prominent (almost infamous) proclamation from Margaret Thatcher in 1987 that 'there is no such thing as society' (Keay: n.p.). The idea of 'acquaintances' suggests that the jump from Edinburgh schemie to Edinburgh's nouveau-riche may not be as massive a jump as one may think, and that the presence of such individuals in close proximity to each other persistently offers an uncomfortable lack of distance between two different forms of social structure connected by the practices of consumption and consumerism. For example, a dimension which is present in other fiction from the 1990s is the status of drug use as a fashion accessory for the discerning consumer with a suitable disposable income, what Aaron Kelly refers to as 'Heroin Chic' (Kelly: 73). Drug use and consumerism connects *Trainspotting* with Iain Banks' *Complicity* (1993) which similarly addresses the role of transgression and fantasy in the identity crisis faced by the post-industrial male. Escapism through a different form of addictive hallucinatory fantasy frames a novel that is equally as contemporary in its concerns, and set in Edinburgh.

Lynne Stark notes that addictions 'have a particular resonance in baroque modernity because they attempt to resolve the wider social struggle between physical release and cogitative control at the lead of the individual body' (Stark 2002: 59) and represent 'distinctly (post)modern patholog[ies], relating as they do to the issues of consumption and control' (Stark 2002: 52). Consumption is a dominant theme at the heart of *Complicity*, particularly through the character Cameron Colley, journalist, drug user, champagne (or rather malt whisky) socialist and fantasist. Cameron represents an interesting figure through his drug use because, whilst he is not an addict, he represents the post-industrial male, for whom drug use represents a form of fashion choice and a further stimulus for his fantasy lifestyle. Despite this, his casual drug use has connections with the significance of addictions in contemporary culture. In his personal life, Colley is fluent in the vocabulary of the contemporary consumer rhetoric, referring to his 'bleeper, mobile, Tosh, Nicads' whilst overdosing on the computer game *Despot*, 'a world-builder game from the HeadCrash Brothers' which is able to continue 'building your world for you if you leave it alone', 'it actually *watches* you', 'it *knows* you', 'it will try its little damnedest to *become* you' (Banks 1993: 53). There are echoes of this speech in Mark Renton's patter:

> Society invents a spurious convoluted logic tae absorb and change people whae's behaviour is outside its mainstream. Suppose that ah ken aw the pros and cons, know that ah'm gaunnae huv a short life, am ay sound mind etcetera, etcetera, but still want ta use smack? They won't let you dae it. They won't let ye dae it, because it's seen as ah sign ay thir ain failure. The fact that ye jist simply choose to reject whit they have tae offer. Choose us. Choose life. Choose mortgage payments; choose washing machines; choose cars; choose sitting oan a couch watching mind-numbing and spirit-crushing game shows, stuffing fuckin junk food intae yir mooth. Choose rotting away, pishing and shiteing yersel in a home, a total fuckin embarrassment tae the selfish, fucked-up brats ye've produced. Choose life. Well, ah choose no tae life. If the cunts cannot handle it, it's their fuckin problem. (Welsh 1993: 187–8)

Renton and Cameron share a hatred of what they perceive as a mainstream culture predicated on false concepts of 'life' and both like to feel they exist outside of this mainstream, yet both are complicit with capitalist culture through their consumption of drugs and use of them to provoke fantasies. Cairns Craig argues that rather than viewing them as being symptomatic of isolation and rebellion:

> Welsh's addicts and pushers and users are the mirror image of the free market capitalism which they believe themselves to have refused: rather than its antithesis, they simply perform at its most extreme both the inability to become a Person [...] – and the lack of responsibility for others that means the one with the drugs is the one with the power. (Craig 97)

By refuting the 'alternative' presentation of drugs as a consumer choice, Welsh highlights the complicity and convergences between differing structures of capitalism and their relationships to the socio-economic status of their consumers. Welsh thus identifies and highlights the increasing incompatibility of capitalist systems with individual agency and questions of class and identity. As Kelly observes, 'The contradiction between the content of the novel's critique of consumer capitalism and the implication of *Trainspotting* as product in precisely those economic imperatives is an issue that impinges upon all of Welsh's subsequent work' (Kelly 74). Acting as an analogy for these differing paradigms of capitalist structures, Welsh demonstrates the dark consequences of the demarcation between customers and suppliers, the addictive status of consumerism and the bitter consequences of a neoliberal Thatcherite agenda which eroded the traditional male working-class identity and abandoned them in the wastelands of a disrupted post-industrial landscape.

In the era of social media and corporate client complicity, emergent in the 1980s and rampant through the 1990s, networking bears a number of different connotations: the relationship between supplier and customer, the possibility of moving or improving one's social hierarchy through interaction with peers, the transport service which ferries passengers throughout the Scottish highlands and lowlands into the cities' conurbations. Networks are, however, susceptible to breakdown and viral infection which impose upon and destroy from the inside. Similarly, the characters' bodies in *Trainspotting* are persistently in danger from threats such as pneumonia and AIDS, which haunt the former residents of Leith who have shared the notorious 'shooting galleries' in Edinburgh's less salubrious areas. The presentation of these bodies and the disruption of contemporary gender paradigms is another theme which literature about post-industrial culture has sought to embrace. In keeping with the tone and formal narrative structures at work within the novel, *Trainspotting* begins with this image:

> The sweat wis lashing ofay Sick Boy; he wis trembling. Ah wis jist sitting thair, focusing oan the telly, trying no tae notice the cunt. He wis bringing me doon. Ah tried tae keep my attention oan the Jean Claude van Damme video. (Welsh 1993: 3)

Comparing the 'fantasy body' in the video with the decaying body of Sick Boy means Welsh 'severs *Trainspotting* from a Scottish West Coast tradition of working-class writing' (Kelly 40) and emphasizes the assault on the perception of how the male body *should* be seen. In the absence of industrial employment, the unemployed body has little option but to descend into decline. Stark suggests that 'the baroque modern body is a phenomenon that occurs within the context of postmodernity' (Stark 2002: 36), and the decomposition and breakdown of the male body is in marked opposition to postmodern muscle-bound body which exists as the escape for Renton. The emphasis on the film highlights his need for fantasy in order to avoid having to acknowledge the onset of decay in Sick Boy's body, a differentiation which ensures Renton can maintain a notional psychosocial superiority to his ailing companion despite their mutual drug consumption.

One of the transgressive aspects of *Trainspotting* remains Welsh's use of vernacular which destabilizes traditional linguistic expectations and narrative form: 'The interplay of a multiplicity of voices in Welsh's work fully embodies Bakhtin's concept of *heteroglossia*. Welsh's writing revels in what Bakhtin calls *grammatical jocose*, the transgression of conventional grammatical order' (Kelly 25). The significance of the vernacular as a method for disrupting the conventional structures of Standard English can be seen in the reception of novelists and their works that have been bracketed within Welsh's legacy – for instance, Niall Griffiths's *Grits* (2000), which is set in West Wales and Kevin Barry's *City of Bohane* (2011) set in West Ireland. Griffiths' debut novel was endorsed with approving jacket quotes from Welsh and this continuum was extended when Barry's fiction received rave reviews in the quality press, particularly from Griffiths. The case in point is that in order to capitalize upon the growing success and popularity of these regional variants, Griffiths's and Barry's works must be marketed with public support from a novelist who was published in the margins but has now been embraced by the mainstream and the canon. The process by which canons and anti-canons inform each other can be seen as an analogy for the processes of transnational exchange which underpin the fiction under consideration in this chapter. In this respect, as will be discussed further below, 'to read John King is to read an English "Highlander"' (Williams 3).

And the critics said … the case of James Kelman

Kelman grabbed the attention of the critics through the brouhaha in which he became embroiled in 1994 following the decision by the judges to award *How Late it Was, How Late* the Booker Prize. Kelman's career is similar to Welsh in its relationship to the literary establishment and, conversely, the literary establishment's relationship to his work. Drew Milne observes that Kelman himself was a marginal writer, first publishing with a small press in the United States and his first two novels with Polygon, Edinburgh University's publishing house, when it was still student run (Tew 2007, Milne 2003: 158). He is thus another notable figure in contemporary literature to have emerged from the small presses.

Just as Welsh demonstrated his objection to the appropriation of *Trainspotting* by New Labour and his artistic differences with Danny Boyle, the director of

Trainspotting, Kelman has a similarly fractious relationship with the academic and reviewing community. In his acceptance speech for the Booker Prize, Kelman highlighted a commentator's assessment of his work:

> A couple of weeks ago a feature writer for a Quality Newspaper suggested that the term 'culture' was inappropriate to my work, that the characters peopling my pages were 'pre-culture' – or was it 'primeval'? I can't quite recall. (Kelman n.p.)

The origin of the reviewer's comment seems to be founded on Kelman's use of a particular tradition, a highly stylized and carefully constructed form of the vernacular. Kelman infuses the narrative with idiom, colloquialisms and obscenities in order to remove what he perceives as the hegemonic implications of using Standard English. The deployment of such transgressive language means that Kelman is able to expose a gap or space between 'official' literary representations and what he perceives as the reality around him:

> A theory of transgression... draws attention to popular culture's role in struggles over meaning. It argues that the popular text is successful because it operates at the borders of what is socially acceptable; and, in order to provoke a widespread interest, the text must, at some level, breach the bounds of that acceptability. It must, in other words, challenge social standards and norms. (McCracken 1998: 158)

Language as a means of identity formation and representation is crucial to Kelman's oeuvre, marking out a resistance to what he perceives as 'imperialism and the language of the coloniser' (Bantick 1997: 8), and he further problematizes attempts to theorize his work by rejecting terms such as 'idiom' or 'vernacular' on the grounds that they seem to be 'euphemism[s] or synonym[s] for language' (Bantick 1997: 8). Preferring to see his writing as the Scottish working-class way of speaking, Kelman argues that couching the style in a vocabulary which is both exclusive and specific to academic or intellectual spheres enables the agencies who apply cultural prestige to his work to sanitize or hide its impact. This resistance is a means of opposing the critical perception that he is writing in a debased form of English. By opposing the imposed value-system of Literary London, Kelman aims to achieve what he terms 'value-free prose' (McLean 1989: 72). Through a process of translation, he is able to intersperse demotic language with Standard English and the outcome is a language which he feels 'could be mine'.

When Kelman received the Booker Prize, he became the first Scottish novelist to win this award and it is here that the processes of appropriation and resistance began to emerge. Just as the marketing of Welsh attempted to create a space for his novel, the literary industry and the Booker Prize demonstrated the processes for ensuring a synthesis between a novel's reception and its incorporation into the canon. The adjudication and evaluations which take place demonstrate collusion between publishers, reviewers, retailers of books and agents in order to construct and impose a concord of accreditation and acceptability around a particular text. This allows the respective stakeholders to obtain their own 'return on investment' and 'allow the "legitimisers" the "right to judge" and "stake a claim" in the writer's work' (Bourdieu, 1993). In addition to providing financial and cultural capital to the recipient, the Booker Prize also gives what Muller sees as access 'into the "right" social circles and closed social groups [...]. When Kelman was shortlisted in 1989 for the Booker Prize, he declined to attend the award ceremony because he did not want to "swan around" with the literati' (Wynne-Jones, 1997: 8–11). The concept of policing a text written by an author who is ultimately 'Resisting Arrest' (Craig) and the idea of a capitalist entity offering its endorsement for a product which is ultimately trying to subvert its practices provides a method by which Kelman's text can be interrogated. Notably, against a pattern already established, Kelman's novel is one of the few winners of the Booker Prize not to become a bestseller.

Set in Glasgow, the novel narrates the story of Sammy Samuels, who wakes from a two-day drinking session and is arrested by the police, only to find he has been left virtually blind after being assaulted by them. As he attempts to find his bearings, Sammy dimly sees a group of people he presumes are tourists:

> Maybe they were tourists, they might have been tourists; strangers to the city for some big fucking business event. And here they were courtesy of the town council promotions office, being guided by some beautiful female publicity officer with the smart tailored suit and scarlet lips with the quiet smile, seeing him here, obliged no to hide things; to take them everywhere in the line of duty, these gentlemen foreigners, so they could see it all, the lot, it was probably part of the deal otherwise they werenay gony invest their hardwon fortunes. (Kelman 2)

The perception of tourists as consumers of cultural capital and the 'strangers' who seek to invest actual capital into the city informs Kelman's perception of Glasgow's Capital of Culture status in 1990. The relationship is reinforced by the complicity between the officialdom of the City Council officers who court the attentions of big business and the capitalists' desire to 'see it all, the lot', even the aspects of Glasgow which are not perceived as desirable for strangers to the city. The publicity officer's 'quiet smile' connotes both a knowing acknowledgement that Sammy should not be presented to the tourists and the silence which is imposed upon him as an aspect of his socio-economic position. The 'quiet' also operates as a link to denying Sammy the chance to articulate his views on *his* version of culture and *his* city. In this respect, Kelman's work provides a voice for the voiceless of Glasgow, those who he feels will not and who those in power deem cannot be allowed to be heard or seen. As Sammy gets closer, he realizes just who the 'tourists' are: 'He caught sight of the tourists again. Only they were nay tourists, no this time anyway they were sodjers, fucking bastards, ye could smell it; even without the uniforms' (Kelman 3). The shift from business tourists to police is significant, as is the use of the term 'sodjers' because both possess status as enforcers of specific power, through legal and cultural legitimation. The term also has connotations of groups which punish people who transgress by making them disappear out of sight, whether it is through jail or by the process of gentrification. At this point, it is possible to connect Kelman with Welsh here through their depictions of the ways by which such people are ghettoized in housing schemes. Both sets of people facilitate the actions and desires of the establishment in such a way as to suppress dissent or disorder, receiving their own capital as reward for enacting these processes.

The motif of blindness that Kelman uses is understood by Punter to represent 'a projection of the wilful blindness of the society around him. Essentially, Kelman's book is a book about culture itself; it probes the boundary beyond which it is not possible to go without entering the wilderness' (Punter 2000). The lack of vision is a disempowerment – Sammy cannot see, as well as in official terms needing to be hidden or remain unseen.

The boundaries which Punter identifies are not confined to the cultural sphere. As Sammy attempts to make his way home or to a place of safety, he realizes that in negotiating the city, his recollection of events does not fit with official accounts. In his interrogation with the police, Sammy is told firmly 'Don't use the word "cunts" again, it doesnay fit in with the computer' (Kelman 160) and is accused of being 'illiterate'. In his subsequent interview with the Job Centre, the following exchange takes place:

> What's entered here is the phrase 'they gave me a doing', and it's entered expressly as a quotation. But it's a colloquialism and not everyone who deals with yer claim will understand what it means. I felt that it was fair to use physical beating by way of an exposition but if you would prefer something else... is there anything else ye can think of? (Kelman 103)

Samuels's language means he is excluded from official structures and he cannot be understood, the meaning of his phrases cannot be translated. Even the process of transcription means his phrases are designated by quotation marks, isolated from the official accounts of his treatment by the police. When asked to find an 'alternative' expression, Samuels finds that his own words have been translated but cannot be certain that the meaning and nuance of his version have been captured. What each of these events represents are 'issues of repetition and dominance, of the repetition *of* dominance, of the compulsion of power' (Punter 2000: 114) by which the post-industrial male finds himself persecuted by representations of official power structures and unable to access the necessary assistance to be able to survive.

Two Scotsmen walk into a bar: Welsh and Kelman

In their respective fictions and their respective receptions, the writing that Welsh and Kelman produce demonstrates characteristics which demonstrate a 'radical and progressive dimension' (Maley 2000: 68). Furthermore, the legacy which Welsh takes from Kelman is conspicuous in his use of the vernacular and his portrayal of working-class life and socio-economic disenfranchisement. However, where they diverge is the 'political: the "commitment" and "integrity" of the one, the anarchy and disintegration of the other' (Maley 2000: 194).

Paradoxically, Welsh and Kelman have all too often been accused of reinforcing or even endorsing stereotypes of Scotland and the Scottish through their portrayal of the 'Scottish experience' – a paradoxical term in itself, given the highly self-conscious and artificially constructed techniques which inform the writing produced by these novelists. Noting Giles Gordon's assessment, Robert Morace suggests that *Trainspotting* is the type of novel which will either prove once more the power of contemporary Scottish writing or it will provide 'further evidence of the Scottish cringe in its presentation of "Scots as the English like to see them: drunken or drugged, aggressive, illiterate, socially inept, boorish"' (Gordon cited Morace 2007: 35). It is the engagement with and subversion of such presentations and stereotypes – a writing back if you will – which has informed the dynamics of contemporary Scottish literature within the 1990s and thrust it firmly into the public consciousness.

When discussing the idea of writing back against specific presentations of identity, John King might be regarded as a writer of contemporary Englishness. King writes largely about the white working class and frequently about immigration. He is connected through personal friendship to Stewart Home and, as this chapter indicates, by a shared technique which performs a specific form of identity which has its roots in pulp novels, amongst others.

Punk-as-fuck and no-holds barred: John King and *The Football Factory*

The significance of emergent small presses such as Canongate and Clocktower Press in the 1990s was not just restricted to Scotland. Litzines, or literary magazines, were the locations where novelists such as John King and Irvine Welsh cut their teeth. As the name 'Litzine' suggests, there is an emphasis on blurring the distinctions between the 'popular' and the 'literary', publishing 'literature' but in a format which is more associated with 'popular' models of writing. With King's debut, *The Football Factory*, the title suggests, at one level the nights and day-jobs, the lives and losses (there are never loves, only one-night stands) of a group of English 'football hooligans' who are following Chelsea in the London of the near-past-present. Published with approving quotes from the 'Gritty Scotsman', Irvine Welsh, this endorsement proved to be more of a marketing ruse than a genuine reflection of the content within. Simon Sellars offers the most scathing commentary on this publisher's trick, warning 'But don't be fooled by the Irvine Welsh endorsement on the cover. King writes about working class mores, football and drugs, less the sloppiness and incomprehensible self-indulgence peddled by the Scottish writer' (Sellars 1999: n.p.). The titles of King's later work make it apparent his concerns political and polemical: *Human Punk* (2000), *White Trash* (2002), *The Prison House* (2004) and *Skinheads* (2008) demonstrate a recurrent engagement with the dynamics of class, the post-industrial landscape and, as King described *White Trash*, 'a defence of the NHS' (Thwaite 2008: n.p.).

In his review of King's debut novel, Sellars's main question concerns the rationale behind King's debut novel being written about in glowing terms in a publication concerned predominantly with science fiction and the 'fantastic'. Andres Vaccari suggested that the major challenge facing science fiction is its 'failure to engage with some dominant (and curiously "science fictional") languages of our era: the languages of advertising [and] propaganda ...' (Vaccari in Sellars 1999: 62), and when considering *Trainspotting* with this in mind, it becomes apparent that works of 'social realism' from the 1990s appear to have ventured boldly into this territory. As Sellars claims, 'this is precisely the focus of *The Football Factory*, with King fictionalising the bewildering experience of living within a literalised media landscape and the resultant pre-millennium tension. The book does not speak science fiction – it lives it, in everyday life' (Sellars 1999: n.p.). The 'literalised media landscape' about which King writes is part of the post-industrial landscape which is under discussion in the introduction to this chapter and which can be seen to emerge as a dominant theme within the novels discussed here. This landscape is one where 'authenticity' is constructed, mediated and performed, as techniques are deployed to simulate the real. King demonstrates this mediation with a noticeable change of tone, away from the language of the terrace and into the corporate speak of the Premier League with its promises of 'live and exclusive' coverage: 'Powerful winds battered the multi-million pound structure, yet for the assorted players, officials, sponsors and media personnel cocooned inside the East Stand it could just as easily have been a warm summer's evening' (King 1997: 52). The 'multi-million pound structure' immediately connotes a new cash injection from another owner; no longer just a football stadium, it has become a multifunctional entertainment venue. The 'assorted' individuals who are protected from the elements by sealed glass windows and a distorted sense of distance from the arena now comprise the capitalist stakeholders whose investment is in the club and, more likely, the players. Whether that investment is through sponsorship or image rights enhancement with a preferable write-up in the national newspapers, or negotiation of a new contract, they require a demonstration of their corporate partnership and the protection of their brand.

As the football journalist, Will Dobson, explains to his reporter-in-training, the upper-class Jennifer Simpson, about the current 'realities' of British football, King's tone becomes more acerbic:

> The game was a bit boring as well, don't you think? Where were the hooligans we read so much about?
> In here, Will laughed, tapping his temple. A figment of the imagination. An editor's wet dream. Sadly our hooligan friends are a thing of the past. [...]
> Lowering his voice because the subject was a taboo which turned off the sponsors. Before they were a bloody nuisance, but they shifted papers and journalism's all about circulation figures. (53)

The 'figment of the imagination' that Dobson refers to is the media construction of the proverbial footballing cultural bogeyman, a rampaging hooligan with a bulldog tattoo, bellicose aggression and shaven head, beered-up and brawling with the opposing fans. That Dobson must ensure the sponsors do not overhear his conversation makes it apparent how King positions the dominance of the capitalists in their control over the way the media portray football clubs and their fan base. That hooligans 'shifted papers and journalism's all about circulation figures' emphasizes the complicity between the practitioners of the media landscape and media's desire to demonize and drive away the elements who they see as disruptive to the 'beautiful game' and its pre-packaged, sanitized entertainment awaiting delivery to the global consumers through the mediation of BSkyB. As King has argued elsewhere when discussing the formation of culture, 'If something comes from the top down it is usually via a power-propelled committee or a money-motivated business interest' (Thwaite 2008: n.p.). The manner in which this mediation takes place is demonstrated further in the novel:

> First come the titillation and the gory details, then the condemnation which masks the pleasure the reader's had from the story. Call for the return of the cat o'nine tails and demand some good old fashioned square-bashing and everyone's happy. It makes the public feel secure. (58)

The reduction of journalism to rhetorical devices and constructed depictions which sell newspapers on the grounds of sensationalism presents once more the complicity between capital and the media to enact a form of Orwellian Hate Week whereby the populist masses are provided with propaganda by which they can identify and enact a lynch-mob mentality against the latest enemy of the state. In this is instance King conveys both the demonization of the white working-class male by the media and the manner in which cultural and social values are expressed and communicated through a 'mediated' yet 'lived' experience for the consumer. As Steve Redmond suggests, 'the question of the "real" in *The Football Factory*, is a much more complicated issue and relates directly to previous attempts at promoting social realism in British cinema and literature in the late 1950s and early 1960s and the reworking of such representations in the era of postmodernism in the 1980s and 1990s' (Redmond 92). The constructions underpinning King's work are a process of complex exchange between different authorial strategies which emerge from strands of punk writing and music. Like Kelman and Welsh, King represents what he understands as the language of the street but the creative process he undertakes is as responsive to the media as *Trainspotting* is, if not more.

For King, the consumers within the football ground and the fans about whom he writes are identified within a specific social bracket: 'It's one o'clock and we're having a pre-match pint. It's been a hard week at the warehouse and the lager gives me a kick-start. Stacking boxes five days solid takes it out of you' (King 1996: 2). The designation of Tom Johnson's employment, manual labour, positions him in a working-class socio-economic group. His weeks are dominated by the routine of a stultifying manufacturing job, whilst his weekends are reserved for football, fighting, drinking to the usual excess and engaging in non-too-discerning casual sex. For Tom, 'the fighting is a release from the drudgery of his factory job and from the mind-numbing monotony of consumer society' (Sellars 1999: n.p.). Similarly, his views represent an unreconstructed view of gender roles and the ways in which men are conditioned to behave in the society he perceives around him, 'Men are always going to kick fuck out of each other then go off and shag some bird' (King 2). However, this attitude is tempered when it comes to men who transgress the unspoken codes: those whom the media construct as dangers to society, the moral panics over the 'nonces' and 'rapists', the paedophiles and the monsters. When Tom and his friends visit a member of their Firm, Marshall, he shows them a film involving a young woman being raped by a gang of squaddies:

> When it was over Marshall said it was the real item. Paid a hundred quid for the video. It was made in Aldershot. Authentic rape. Authentic squaddies. The lads just laughed, but you knew they didn't like that kind of scene. You have to be a fucking nonce to get off watching rape. [...] After I left John Nicholson threatened him with a knife from the kitchen. Kicked him in the head and said he was a cunt. Then he put a chair through the screen. Only honest bloke there. (King 10)

Initially believing that what they are viewing is hardcore pornography, Marshall then reveals it was unsimulated, that the rape actually took place. The group's reaction is one of disgust – both with Marshall and themselves for consuming the act willingly. Such deployment of mediated images is another aspect of the contemporary landscape, where fantasy and revulsion, constructed fictions and reality make the authentic even harder to discern.

This mediated experience is imitated in the structure of the novel. Similarly to *Trainspotting*, which alternates between 'Junk Dreams' and 'Come Downs', King's novel is organized around a series of self-contained chapters. Within most of the sequences, the reader is informed by Tom's

> internal monologues ruminating at length upon the nature of the modern British police state. In King's London, surveillance cameras record, edit and wipe over lives with clinical efficiency; the economical, tight prose (aided by the book's disjointed narrative structure) zooms in on each character, filing their personal details for later reference and further developments. (Sellars 1999: n.p.)

The onset of the Surveillance State and CCTV is reflected in King's prose and narrative, where Tom's fights are conducted away from the football ground, the spotters and potential infiltration by the police, and where individual characters swiftly become the focus of writing which summarizes the basic facts about their status, interests and habits, documenting and moving onto the next person. To Tom, the police who control the CCTV and imprison those who are fighting represent 'Fucking scum the lot of them hiding behind uniforms, licking the paymaster's arse' (62). Demonstrating a considerable overlap with the manipulation of the police by the state and echoing the experiences of Sammy Samuels, the difference here is that in King's society, the individual cannot fail to be seen or recorded, this is the point where they are exposed through the media and their danger to the social fabric becomes exaggerated to the point of ridicule. The global media saturation of the 1990s (which is ongoing into the Noughties) is perhaps summed up emphatically by this reflection from Tom: 'Nothing's changed. We're just more global and the village idiot gets a documentary made about him by all those people who want to be John Pilger' (103). Through the figure of Tom, King identifies the urban spacemen of London, 'the digital ghost', wandering through the wastelands in search of his disembodied self.

The end of the decade: Towards a new literature: Attack! Books

This generation needs a NEW literature – writing that apes, matches, parodies and supersedes the flickeringly fast 900 MPH ATTACK! ATTACK! ATTACK! velocity of early 21st century popular culture at its most mEnTaL! We will publish writers who think they're rock stars, rock stars who think they're writers and we will make supernovas of the stuttering, wild-eyed, slack-jawed drooling idiot-geek geniuses who lurk in the fanzine/internet shadows... (Gallix, 2001)

The end of the 1990s saw readers return full-circle to the beginning with the small presses coming to prominence again. Formed in 1999, Attack! Books was an avant-pulp imprint operating under the aegis of Creation Books. Encompassing writing which was operating partly as a homage to Richard Allen and British action comics, partly working within a Surrealist tradition and partly revelling in the excesses of ultraviolence, the titles were under the editorial jurisdiction of Steven Wells. The epigraph to this section provides evidence of the imprint's mission statement whilst a more outspoken and exuberant view from Wells claims that, in order to succeed, *'The self-perpetuating ponce-mafia oligarchy of effete bourgeois wankers who run the "literary scene" must be swept aside by a tidal wave of screaming urchin tits-out teenage terror totty and DESTROYED! ATTACK! ATTACK! ATTACK!* (ref). With contributors such as Stewart Home and tabloid-baiting titles such as *Tits Out Teenage Terror Totty*, Wells's imprint represents a press dedicated to embracing the strategies deployed by both punk musicians and punk writers, texts which, like the outputs from Clocktower Press or LitZines, engage in the process of different cultural exchanges in order to flourish in the zones and interstitial spaces reserved for popular fictions. It is also somewhat appropriate to conclude this 'moment' with the view of one Elizabeth Young, detractor and condemner of *Lord Horror* for its 'outrage', she silently seethes at Attack! Books whilst issuing the following damning praise:

> Only the most mean-spirited could deny the sheer energy and animation of the ATTACK! books. Its authors were forged in the DIY crucible of Punk where destruction and creation became indistinguishable. And certainly the ATTACK! books evoke all the sick humour and terminal cynicism of the country we really live in. (Young 1999 n.p.)

The image of the 'terminal' cynicism brings to mind the iconography of *Trainspotting*, but the excessive 'assault' which Wells claims he wishes to enact on 'literature' suggests the novels will engage in the same processes of cultural production which came to produce and endorse the work of Kelman, Welsh and King. By the same method which Punk came to be appropriated by capital and commercialism, the desire for a more authenticated experience through our reading means that the flurries of activity which emerge around the small presses will continue to prove vital and important 'moments' in rupturing, albeit temporarily, the dominant forces of cultural acquisition and legitimization.

Note

1 This exchange cited by Young is quoted in full on the Savoy Books *Lord of Horror* website; see: http://www.savoy.abel.co.uk/HTML/lhorror.html

Works Cited

Banks, Iain. *Complicity*. London: Little and Brown, 1993.
Bantick, Christopher. 'Street Talk'. *The Courier Mail: Weekend* (Brisbane, Australia) (25 January 1997), 8.

Barker, Paul. 'The War of Words.' *New Statesman* 23 August 1999: n.p. http://www.newstatesman.com/node/135472. Online.
Barry, Kevin. *City of Bohane*. London: Vintage, 2011.
Bissett, Alan. *Damage Land: Contemporary Scottish Gothic*. Edinburgh: Polygon, 2001.
———. 'Damage Land Revisited: Scottish Gothic in the Noughties'. *The Bottle Imp* 6, 2009, 1–2. http://www.arts.gla.ac.uk/ScotLit/ASLS/SWE/TBI/TBIIssue6/Damage_Land.pdf
Bourdieu, Pierre. *The Field of Cultural Production*. New York: Columbia University Press, 1993.
Boyle, Danny (dir.) *Trainspotting*. (dir. Danny Boyle) Channel Four Films, 1996.
Britton, David. *Lord Horror*. Manchester: Savoy, 1990.
———. *Motherfuckers: The Auschwitz of Oz: A Novel*. Manchester: Savoy, 1996.
Britton, David and Michael Butterworth. *Baptised in the Blood of Millions*. Manchester: Savoy 2000.
Chadwick, Alan. 'Fear and Lothian'. *The Herald* Saturday 31 July 1993, n.p. http://www.heraldscotland.com/sport/spl/aberdeen/fear-and-lothian-1.748591
Colebrook, Martyn. 'Lanark and The Bridge: Narrating Scotland as Post-Industrial Space'. In *The Transgressive Iain Banks*. Eds. Martyn Colebrook and Katharine Cox. Jefferson, NC and London: McFarland, 2013, 28–44.
Craig, Cairns. *The Modern Scottish Novel: Narrative and the National Imagination*. Edinburgh: Edinburgh University Press, 1999.
———. 'Resisting Arrest'. In *The Scottish Novel since the Seventies: New Visions, Old Dreams*. Eds. Gavin Wallace and Randall Sevenson. Edinburgh: Edinburgh University Press, 1993, 99–114.
D'Souza, Frances. 'Article 19 (International Centre against Censorship after *Lord Horror* Was Found Obscene'. http://www.savoy.abel.co.uk/HTML/lhorror.html#anchor230500
Easton Ellis, Brett. *American Psycho*. London: Picador, 2006.
Gallix, Andrew. 'Attack! Books: Meet the New Barbarians. Andrew Gallix Interviews Steve Wells.' *3AM Magazine* Issue 5, 2001: n.p. http://www.3ammagazine.com/magazine/issue_5/articles/attack_books.html. Online.
Germanà, Monica. 'The Awakening of Caledonias? Scottish Literature in the 1980s'. In *The 1980s: A Decade of Contemporary British Fiction*. Eds. Emily Horton, Philip Tew and Leigh Wilson. London: Bloomsbury, 2014, 51–74.
Grant, Iain. 'Dealing Out the Capital Punishment'. *Sunday Times* (5 September 1993): 14.
Gray, Alasdair. *Lanark: A Life in Four Books*. Edinburgh: Canongate, 1981.
Griffiths, Niall. *Grits*. London: Jonathan Cape, 2000.
Home, Stewart. 'Proletarian Postmodernism, or from the Romantic Sublime to the Comic Picturesque'. In *Suspect Device: A Reader in Hard-Edged Fiction*. Ed. Stewart Home. London: Serpent's Tail, 1998, 53–60.

———. *Suspect Device: A Reader in Hard-Edged Fiction*. London: Serpents Tail, 1998.
Keay, Douglas. 'Aids, Education and the Year 2000!'. *Woman's Own*. 23 September 1987. 8–10; Rpt. Margaret Thatcher Foundation. http://www.margaretthatcher.org/document/106689: n.p.
Kelly, Aaron. *Irvine Welsh*. Manchester: Manchester University Press, 2005.
Kelman, James. 'A Nightboilerman's Notes.' In *Lean Tales*. Eds Alasdair Gray, James Kelman and Agnes Owens. London: Abacus, 1985, 91–100.
———. 'O Jesus, Here Come the Dwarfs'. In *Lean Tales*. Eds Alasdair Gray, James Kelman and Agnes Owens. London: Abacus, 1985, 65–86.
———. 'Elitist Slurs Are Racism by Another Name' [Booker Prize acceptance speech]. *Scotland on Sunday*, 16 October 1994.
———. *How Late It Was How Late*. London: Secker and Warburg, 1994.
King, John. *The Football Factory*. London: Jonathan Cape, 1996.
———. *The Headhunters*. London: Jonathan Cape, 1997.
———. *England Away*. London: Jonathan Cape, 1998.
———. *Human Punk*. London: Jonathan Cape, 2000.
———. *White Trash*. London: Jonathan Cape, 2002.
——— *The Prison House*. London: Cape, 2004.
——— *Skinheads*. London: Cape, 2008.
Maley, Willy. 'Subversion and Squirrility in Irvine Welsh's Shorter Fiction'. In *Subversion and Scurrility: Popular Discourse in European from 1500 to the Present*. Eds. Dermot Cavanagh and Tim Kirk. Aldershot: Ashgate, 2000, 190–204.
Marriott, James. 'Untitled Review: Horror Panegryric'. *London Book Review.com* 2008: n.p. http://www.londonbookreview.com/lbr0047.html. Online.
McCracken, Scott. *Transgression and Popular Culture*. Manchester: Manchester University Press, 1998.
McLean, Duncan. 'James Kelman Interviewed'. *Edinburgh: Edinburgh Review* 71(1989): 64–80.
———. 'Introduction'. In *Ahead of Its Time: A Clocktower Press Anthology*. Ed. Duncan MacLean. London: Jonathan Cape, 1997, 1–8.
Milne, Drew. 'Broken English: James Kelman's Translated Accounts'. *Edinburgh Review* 108 (2001): 106–15.
———. 'The Fiction of James Kelman and Irvine Welsh: Accents, Speech and Writing'. In *Contemporary British Fiction*. Eds. Richard Lane, Rod Mengham and Philip Tew. London and New York: Polity, 2003, 158–73.
Mitchell, David. 'The Horror of It All: Savoy, David Britton and Lord Horror'. *SAVOYWEB* 1995. http://www.savoy.abel.co.uk/HTML/horofitb.html
Morace, Robert. *Irvine Welsh*. Basingstoke: Palgrave Macmillan, 2007.
Morgan, Cheryl. 'Interview: Savoy Books'. *Emerald City* 108 (2004). n.p. http://www.emcit.com/emcit108.shtml#Savoy
Müller, C. Amanda 'How James Kelman Survived the Booker Prize'. *Counterpoints: The Flinders University Online Journal of Interdisciplinary Conference Papers* 2 (1)

July 2002: n.p. http://ehlt.flinders.edu.au/projects/counterpoints/Proc_2002/A6.htm. Online.

Punter, David. 'Heartlands: Contemporary Scottish Gothic'. *Gothic Studies* 1.1 (August 1999): 101–18.

———. *Postcolonial Imaginings: Fictions of a New World Order*. Maryland: Rowman and Littlefield, 2000.

Savoy, 'The History of Savoy I, II and III'. *SAVOYWEB* Undated. http://www.savoy.abel.co.uk/1book.html

Sellars, Simon. 'John King: *The Football Factory*'. In *Abaddon Review* 2.2. Carlingford: New South Wales, 13 April 1999, 65–7. http://www.andresvaccari.net/abaddon_archivos/ab02_reviews.pdf

Seward, Keith. *Horror Panegyric*. Manchester: Savoy, 2008.

Smith, Zadie. *White Teeth*. London: Hamish Hamilton, 2000.

Stark, Lynne. 'Beyond Skin: The Exposed Body and Modern Scottish Fiction.' Unpublished Ph.D. Thesis. University of Edinburgh. 2002.

Tew, Philip. *The Contemporary British Novel*. 2nd Edition. London: Continuum, 2007.

Thwaite, Mark. 'Interview with John King'. *BookDepository.com* 9 December 2008, n.p.: http://www.bookdepository.com/blog/post/tag/John-King

Wallace, Gavin. 'Voices in Empty Houses: The Novel of Damaged Identity'. In *The Scottish Novel since the Seventies: New Visions, Old Dreams*. Eds. Gavin Wallace and Randall Sevenson Edinburgh: Edinburgh University Press, 1993, 217–31.

Wells, Steven. *Tits-Out Teenage Terror Totty*. London: Attack! Books, Creation, 1999.

Welsh, Irvine. *Trainspotting*. London: Secker and Warburg, 1993.

———. *'In Your Face. Irvine Welsh: Condemn More, Understand Less*. Broadcast 27th November 1995.

White, Tony. *Britpulp! New Fast and Furious Stories from the Literary Underground*. London: Sceptre, 1999.

Williams, Mark P. 'In Defence of Literature: The Counter-Cultural Critique of Steven Wells' Attack! Books (Because the Best Defence Is a Strong Offence)'. *Critical Engagements* 2.2 (2008): 15–45.

Williams, Tony. 'Commentary on Lord Horror'. *SAVOYWEB* n.d.: http://www.savoy.abel.co.uk/HTML/lhorror.html

Wynne-Jones, Ros. (1997) 'Time to Publish'. *Independent on Sunday*, 14 September 1997. 8–11.

Young, Elizabeth. 'We're Brutal But Brilliant.' The Guardian. 20 November 1999: n.p. http://www.theguardian.com/books/1999/nov/20/fiction.reviews. Online.

———. 'Blood on the Tracks'. *Guardian* (14 August 1993), 33.

Young, Elizabeth J. 'Psycho Killers. Last Lines: How to Shock the English.' *New Statesman & Society* (5 April 1991), 24.

Zimring, Rishona. 'Exotic Souvenirs: Reflections on Britain's Booker Prize.' *Open Spaces: Views from the Northwest* 2014, n.p.: http://www.open-spaces.com/article-v1n3-zimring.php.

2

Special Topic 1
Rewriting National Identities in 1990s British Fiction[1]

Nick Bentley

Writing in 1993, Slavoj Žižek introduces his book *Tarrying with the Negative: Kant, Hegel and the Critique of Ideology* with a powerful image of nationalism in crisis through his description of the flag used by Romanian rebels involved in overthrowing Nicolae Ceausescu's regime in which the red star had been cut from the centre of the national flag, representing for Žižek, 'that intermediate phase when the former Master-Signifier, although it had already lost its hegemonical power, has not yet been replaced by the new one' (1). Although Žižek is referring to the image as a moment in which power is in flux and is historically specific, the idea of the national flag with a hole at its centre, for me, embodies a way of thinking about how national identity is conceived more generally. This can be considered in two ways: first, when national belonging is invoked at certain specific moments such as Royal weddings, war memorials or international football matches, the individual is asked to plug the hole, fill the gap and complete the collective social bond that constitutes the unified nation. Second, this image can also be evoked when thinking about the ways in which one might define the salient characteristics of, say, Scottishness or Frenchness in that it is a vain attempt to complete a concept that is permanently incomplete because the missing part always remains beyond concrete definition; there is a supplement that is endlessly deferred, either to a nostalgic past or to a future reconstruction of the originating moment; an ideal other to the insufficient present. Such a process is particularly pertinent to situating *and* understanding the 1990s. In an international context, the fall of the Berlin Wall and the dismantling of the Soviet Union's direct political influence in Eastern bloc nations and the peripheries of its boundaries (Latvia, Lithuania, Estonia, Ukraine, Kazakhstan, Turkmenistan, Uzbekistan, etc.), as well as the nationalistic inflection driving the Balkan Wars and break-up of Yugoslavia, marked a renewed interest in nationalism on a scale that, arguably, had not been seen since the nineteenth century.

The 1990s also saw renewed interest in national identity in domestic British politics due to the devolution of governmental power for several constituent areas in the United Kingdom, an issue debated and argued about for most of the 1990s and achieved to a significant degree after 1997 when Scotland and Wales established their own national parliament or assembly respectively, each with a significant range of regional legislative powers. This in turn generated a renewed focus on the concept of Englishness, both politically and in the popular cultural imagination. In addition, the Peace Process in Northern Ireland and the establishment of the Northern Ireland Assembly at Stormont also generated continued analysis of Irish national identities.

Inevitably, such extensive interest in nations and national identity found a significant source of expression in literature. The definitions and discourses of discrete national identities within Britain (Englishness, Northern Irishness, Scottishness, Welshness) were a thematic concern in much British fiction in the 1990s. This chapter will explore some of the ways in which this focus on Britain's range of internal national identities was articulated in selected fiction of the period. In terms of Scotland, it can be argued that there was something of a renaissance in fiction during this time. Alasdair Gray and James Kelman, publishing throughout the eighties, continued to produce influential texts in the 1990s that were concerned with articulating a sense of Scottish identity, whilst a newer generation of Scottish writers emerged that offered more ambivalent engagements with the discourses of the nation, writers such as A.L. Kennedy, Alan Warner and Irvine Welsh. These later writers tended to approach national identity through association with youth cultures and subcultures, and the same connection can be made with Welsh writing of the period. The 1990s renaissance of Welshness was most visibly articulated through popular cultural forms and, in particular, the celebration of Welsh national identity by bands such as the Manic Street Preachers and Catatonia, as well as the re-imagining of Cardiff as a cosmopolitan European capital represented symbolically by the new Millennium Stadium. The focus on youth culture and Welshness was also articulated in the writing of Niall Griffiths (an Englishman with Welsh family ties who has spent periods living in Wales) and John Williams in the late 1990s and early 2000s. In Northern Ireland, the continuing 'Troubles' and the politics of the 'Peace Process' with its attempts at reconciling divisions in the community were most often articulated in poetry and drama rather than fiction, although Brian Moore's *Lies of Silence* (1990), Glenn Patterson's *Fat Lad* (1992), Seamus Deane's *Reading in the Dark* (1996), Deirdre Madden's *One by One in the Darkness* (1996), Robert McLiam Wilson's *Eureka Street* (1996) and Bernard MacClaverty's *Grace Notes* (1997) are notable exceptions. English identity also attracted increasing attention over the decade fuelled by nostalgic reconstructions of the myths of Englishness in the political rhetoric of Conservative Prime Minister John Major, as well as the continuing influence on the English psyche of devolution, postcolonialism, the end of empire and the emergence of multiculturalism and difference as influencing alternative models of the nation. Novels such as Hanif Kureishi's *The Buddha of Suburbia* (1990), Adam Thorpe's *Ulverton* (1992), Julian Barnes's *England, England* (1998), John King's *England Away* (1999), and Zadie Smith's *White Teeth* (2000) place some of these issues at their centre.

Before discussing individual novels, it is worth reflecting on some theoretical approaches to the way in which the nation has been imagined in literary and cultural contexts. Perhaps the most often cited recent model of national identity is Benedict Anderson's conception of the nation as an 'imagined community' which develops a sense of the nation as both imaginary and as a shared 'comradeship' (6 7). This model identifies the nation as a construct, but one with practical power to affect people's lived ideologies and material practices. To accept that national identities are artificial constructs also implies that they can be manipulated by interested parties (cultural, aesthetic and political) to support particular versions, each with their own implied and modelled ideologies. The search for the 'real' Britain, or some defining quality of Britishness, is thus primarily rhetorical rather than being epistemological or ontological. For example, when the Blair Labour government introduced the Life in the United Kingdom test in 2002, which is often seen as a test of Britishness, it presented the attainability of authentic national identity as a scientifically calibrated concept that could be read off against a number of fixed criteria. This concern with categorizing Britishness is, of course, fraught with contention but in a way reveals the culmination of a decade of cultural and societal concerns with what national identity means.

As an extension to Anderson's model of national identity, the British context (as most national contexts would be) is complicated by the presence of other discrete national and cultural identities under the umbrella of the political entity called the United Kingdom of Great Britain and Northern Ireland. Britishness is always already engaged in a fraught attempt to centrifugally define itself against a series of overlapping but distinctly different national identities: Englishness,

Irishness, Scottishness and Welshness, each of which is contested and historically contingent. Anderson's concept, in the case of Britain, is inevitably pluralized beyond any clear sense of a 'community', suggesting that contemporary Britain is more accurately described as a series of competing social, cultural and ethnic communities, each of which negotiates the larger concept of Britishness. This plurality is extended even further with respect to discourses of multiculturalism that begin to gain influence in the 1990s overlaying the four national identities incorporated in the United Kingdom. It could be argued, therefore, that the very complexity of national identity increased in the last quarter or so of the twentieth century, and that a similar complexity can be seen in the attempt to render the nation in literary fiction. As Philip Tew has noted: 'To deal with contemporary fiction... requires understanding that writers from the mid-1970s onward have been responding not only to traditions of representation, but more fundamentally to a shift in Britain's intellectual and geographic culture' (31). To put it bluntly, representing a sense of national identity in fiction in the 1990s became much more vexed. Nevertheless, many writers were concerned during the decade with the attempt to imagine the nation whilst acknowledging these very profound changes in sociocultural conditions. It is likely, in fact, that the desire to identify a convincing model of national identity increases at a time when the older conceptions of the nation are felt to be loosening.

The 1990s saw a dismantling and fracturing of discourses of national identity, both in terms of older nationalistic discourses and in terms of externalized stereotypical constructions. This can be evidenced in several of the novels I discuss in this chapter. Literary expression of national identity is, of course, one of the most powerful ways in which the nation has been constructed, reinforced and challenged. The nation can be seen as a grand narrative that locates originating myths alongside projections into the future, as well as the desire to reclaim, maintain or progress perceived national characteristics. To think of the nation as a narrative, therefore, establishes a sequential quality, and Timothy Brennan, for one, has identified a 'national longing for form' in this context (44–70). Homi Bhabha, in 'DissemiNation: Time, Narrative, and the Margins of the Modern Nation', has gone on to consider the genre in which a national narrative might construct itself by combining a series of forms: fictional, historical and mythical. Furthermore, the literary mode deployed can determine the type of nation that is evoked. For example, a sense of traditional national identity has been equated with the realist mode of fiction. Bhabha writes, 'Such a form of temporality produces a symbolic structure of the nation as "imagined community" which, in keeping with the scale and diversity of the modern nation, works like the plot of a realist novel' (308). To extrapolate from Bhabha's point, if the realist novel represents the dominant literary mode for expressing the nation, then formal experimentation, for example postmodernism, can be said to represent a formal disruption of that national grand narrative. In this context, the 1990s can be seen as the decade of high postmodernism, or, as I've argued elsewhere, the period of popular postmodernism, when the mode lost any potentially radical outlook it had and it was embraced by those devising more popular forms of culture from the Simpsons to the retro-pop of Blur, Oasis and Pulp (2005). The adoption of literary modes in novels that address national identity and move away from realism can, therefore, be seen to be challenging the established and prevailing ideologies of the nation. This is an important factor to bear in mind when analysing the way in which the writers discussed in this chapter negotiate constructions and reconfigurations of respective national identities. The chapter is organized with respect to novels that offer engagement with the four main national identities contained with the United Kingdom in the order: Northern Ireland, Wales, Scotland and England. The final part looks at fiction that addresses national identity with respect to multicultural discourses and the development of new ethnicities within Britain.

Northern Ireland

Towards the end of August1997, the British and Republic of Ireland governments signed an agreement to decommission weapons stockpiled by the IRA and the Ulster Unionists. This effectively announced (publically at least) the end of the Troubles that had dogged Northern Ireland since the late 1960s. This followed on from a series of negotiations, talks and projected ceasefires, alongside continued terrorist action in the early to mid-1990s both in Northern Ireland and on the British mainland. This most visible success of the new Blair government seemed to promise a new peace in the territory. The process became the touchstone for a number of writers during the 1990s including novelists, dramatists and poets, some newly emerging alongside many who continued to build their literary careers. It is probably fair to say that the literary scene in Northern Ireland in the last quarter of the twentieth century was dominated by poetry, with such major figures as Seamus Heaney, Michael Longley, Ciaran Carson, Paul Muldoon and Tom Paulin all writing some of their best work during the period. The novelists are less well known, yet a significant number of their 1990s novels engaged in different ways with the Troubles, including Brian Moore's *Lies of Silence* (1990), *Resurrection Man* (1994) by Eoin McNamee, *Reading In The Dark* (1996) by Seamus Deane and Bernard McLaverty's *Grace*

Notes. And, in this chapter, I will discuss Deirdre Madden's *One by One in the Darkness* (1996) before going on to discuss, briefly, novels by writers who came to prominence during the decade: Glenn Patterson's *Fat Lad* (1992) and Robert McLiam Wilson's *Eureka Street* (1996).

Deirdre Madden's *One By One in the Darkness* follows the experiences of two sisters, Cate and Helen Quinn, from a Northern Irish Catholic family. Helen, the elder, is a solicitor who specializes in cases of terrorist activities and who has continued to work in Northern Ireland, while her younger sister has moved to London. As the novel opens, Cate returns to Northern Ireland to attend the funeral of her father, Charlie, who has been murdered in a sectarian killing. The novel's chapters alternate between the contemporary 1990s setting and sections set during the sisters' childhood in rural Northern Ireland; we learn that 'Cate' has in fact changed her name from 'Kate' in an attempt to create an adult identity that distances her from her childhood. Consequently, she is referred to as Cate in the 1990s and Kate in the 1970s. The 1970s narratives refer to significant events for Kate and Helen that shaped their later lives and career choices and their relationships with variously family, nation, the Catholic religion and the Troubles. The family includes a third sister, Sally, who is a primary school teacher and who it is assumed at the outset is contented to stay in Ireland, although it is discovered later that she is doing so only to support her mother, especially following Charlie's death.

The novel addresses the construction of Northern Irish identity in a number of ways, one of which focuses on press coverage of the Troubles. The way her father's death was reported in the British media angers Helen in particular, 'where the death was reported coldly and without sympathy, much being made of Brian's [Charlie's brother] Sinn Fein membership ... The inference was that he had only got what was coming to him' (47). Helen's distaste for the press is emphasized at several points in the novel, for example, she criticizes the 'making up of stories out of a few facts, and presenting them as though that interpretation was the absolute truth' (50). The implicit bias she notes in the media stresses the way in which assumptions are made based on ideological concerns that mask the pain and hurt felt by individual families. The book is primarily concerned with the way in which the British press is seen to misrepresent the fraught political tensions in Ireland; however, the novel is far from an apology for IRA terrorism. At one point, Helen describes the disconcerting moral position in which she is placed in defending a man who has been accused of a sectarian killing, and who is clearly guilty. The text focuses on the terrorist's mother, who is also portrayed as a victim, one that cannot come to terms with the violence in which her son has been involved. The novel attempts to understand, or at least contextualize, the situation from which the violence emerges – the everyday and mundane sectarian prejudice, the stop checks by police as well as the apparently random and casual beatings that Catholics are forced to endure, and which had included Helen and Cate's uncles Brian and Peter in the 1970s sections. The arbitrary nature of this violence is stressed in this section; although Peter is an IRA sympathizer, he has never been actively political. Overall, the narrative suggests that guilt by association has ultimately led to her father's death; Charlie has been murdered while visiting Brian's house and as the latter suggests, 'It was me they wanted' (28). Ironically, certain sections from the past confirm the divisions within the family over Irish politics; at what turns out to be an IRA funeral, 'Their Uncle Brian was one of the men who clapped hardest of all, but their father didn't join in' (105). The injustice of Charlie's murder, therefore, is emphasized and demonstrates how consideration of particularities is abandoned in the generalities of the taking of sides *and* in media reporting of the sectarian conflict, as well as the response by both the authorities and the paramilitary organizations.

Returning to Northern Ireland from the career she has established in London provides Cate with a different perspective on events. Cate sees herself as having escaped the Troubles, but a sense of guilt attends this liberation. Cate's crisis of identity is paralleled by the difficulties in identifying a simple sense of Northern Irish national identity. This is, of course, complicated in the case of Northern Ireland by religious, class and gender identities. As one story from the 1970s section shows, when filling out UCCA forms to attend university, Sister Philomena, Helen's form teacher, has instructed pupils to put Irish instead of British in the space for nationality. When this causes a parent to complain, 'Sister Philomena told the girls to ask their parents what they should put there' (154). The situation emphasizes, first, that national identity is dependent upon family background and, second, that there is no straightforward response to the question of national identity in Northern Ireland, most especially for Catholics. That Cate has left for London and now returned resurrects this implicit sense of identity crisis in both individual and national terms. On her visits back to her family, Cate often drives around the countryside alone 'trying to fathom Northern Ireland in a way which wasn't, if you still lived there, necessary. Or advisable she thought. Or possible even' (82). There is a long passage in the novel that describes what she finds on these trips, including 'pinched villages where the edges of footpaths were painted red, white, and blue, where there were Orange lodges and locked churches ... [and] villages where unemployed men stood on street corners and dragged on cigarettes, or ambled up and down between the chip shop and the bookie's, past walls which bore Republican graffiti' (82). She concludes with the thought that 'if she had been asked to pick a single word to sum up her feelings towards Northern Ireland she would have been at a complete loss' (83). Cate's feelings are exacerbated by her father's murder and this is also registered in Helen's disillusion about her ambitions to change things by becoming a Catholic lawyer. As a child in the 1970s, she explains to a careers advice teacher that her wish to study law was fuelled by the fact that 'we need our Catholic teachers and doctors and nurses and lawyers' (158). Although in the 1990s Helen is beginning to have doubts about her vocation, her original ambition is seen to have been justified as, when she asks her friend David to describe the difference between then and now, he replies: 'We are. The educated Catholic middle class' (60). The novel, on the whole, bears out this positive change. The emphasis on education is clearly something that is represented as a way out of the present difficulties, both in the 1970s sections and as a future ideal for both sides in the sectarian divide in Northern Ireland.

Nevertheless, the individual disillusion for Helen is exacerbated by her father's murder. This is poignantly stressed in the final chapter where a description of her habit of trying to get to sleep by imagining a space between waking and sleeping provides two images divided across the two main time frames of the novel. First, there is a description of Helen's childhood vision of Ireland in her imagination between waking and sleeping as she remembers a teacher shining a torch on a globe, and in her waking dream, she imagines focusing in first onto Europe, then Ireland and then Northern Ireland and further down to her family's house with her father smoking on the kitchen sofa and her and her sisters safe in bed (180). This image parallels the move from the general to the particular, and specifically from the generalization of external, mediated assumptions about people and events in Northern Ireland during the Troubles to the particularity of individual lives and emotions. The ending of the novel suggests a similar move and begins by evoking James Joyce's closing image in 'The Dead', the last story in *Dubliners* (1914) in which 'snow was general all over Ireland' (225). However, in Helen's half-dream, this is not a stultifying, paralysing snow, but an ideal image of welcome respite from the Troubles in the easy security of family life. This childhood image is then disturbed by Helen imagining the details of her father's murder and the 'searing grief came from the tension between that smallness and the enormity of infinite time and space' (181). The novel carves out the space between these two visions of Northern Ireland: between an image of peaceful domesticity and the sectarian violence that shatters it.

If *One by One in the Darkness* offers a poignant and serious examination of the Troubles in terms of looking back to the 1970s, then Glenn Patterson's *Fat Lad* attempts to move away from that past and record the vibrant youth culture in Belfast that appears to be emerging from the two decades of conflict preceding the 1990s. Patterson's comic novel registers the sectarian divide but is more interested in deconstructing traditional images of Belfast and reconfiguring Northern Irish identity. As the main character, Drew notes on returning to Belfast from England:

> The Belfast he left, the Belfast the Expats forswore, was a city dying on its feet: cratered sites and hunger strikes; atrophied, self-abased. But the Belfast he had reports of this past while, the Belfast he had seen with his own eyes last month, was a city in the process of recasting itself entirely... Restaurants, bars and takeaways proliferated along the lately coined Golden Mile, running south from the refurbished Opera House, and new names had appeared in the shopping streets: Next, Body Shop, Tie Rack, Principles. (5)

This recasting of Belfast is driven by market forces, and Drew's job as a sales manager for 'Bookstore', an up-and-coming retailer, sits well with Belfast's potential to join the other areas of inner city renewal in the United Kingdom in the 1990s, such as Manchester, Birmingham, Glasgow and Cardiff. Drew himself is indicative of this new culture where national and regional identities are shown to be less important in the face of the cosmopolitanism of 1990s consumer society. As we learn early on, 'One place was as good as any other to him' (9). As the novel moves forward, however, the legacies of the Troubles begin to show through the surface rendering of the new Belfast, ultimately resulting in Drew leaving Northern Ireland, as the restrictions placed on him by the political situation prove to be too difficult to overcome.

This sense of a new youth-inflected Irishness butting up against old prejudices is also evident in Robert McLiam Wilson's 1996 novel *Eureka Street*. One of the novel's main characters, Jake Jackson, is a working-class Catholic, but he tries to keep his religious identity out of the way in his day-to-day dealings as a bailiff. The second is Chuckie Logan, a Protestant who is involved in various nefarious practices, and who as a child recollects that, 'I liked the Troubles. They were like television' (48). As with *Fat Lad*, however, the initial attempts of both characters to play down the effects of the Troubles on their personal lives are frustrated. Wilson's novel registers the way in which twenty years of the Troubles have resulted in a waning of affect and a sense that violence now permeates the everyday lives of the Belfast population. Whereas in the 1970s, in the aftermath of terrorist bombs, 'the colour of the streets always seemed drained and muted as if the colours, too, had been blown away', in the 1990s, 'it was all just an inconvenience, all just a traffic jam' (82). The banality of violence becomes part of the lives of the two characters, but this is not driven by sectarian ideologies or passionate adherence to collective identities, merely a response to the environment and the novel makes it clear that the divisions in Northern Irish society are more determined by economic and class differences than religious affiliations. Wilson's style has a greater poetry than Patterson's, and *Eureka Street* has sparkling linguistic dexterity, however, in terms of outlook, as Richard Bradford has noted, both novels ultimately seem to present the idea that 'Northern Ireland is possessed of a self-perpetuating malignancy' (Bradford, 230).

Wales

While Northern Irish fiction had a significant number of writers addressing issues during the 1990s, Welsh fiction is marked by its relative paucity. As Bradford has noted, 'recent Welsh fiction is as sparsely populated as the more attractive parts of the national landscape' (219). Perhaps expressions of national identity find their mode of expression in different forms at different times, and in Wales, rock, pop and indie bands seemed to carry the flag for a new configuration of Welsh identity. The Manic Street Preachers, Catatonia, Super Furry Animals and the Stereophonics produced a Welsh-inflected counterpoint to Britpop in the 1990s that chimed with a sense of a renaissance of Welsh culture bound up with the establishment of the National Assembly for Wales in 1998 and the regeneration of Cardiff into a vibrant European capital. This optimism, however, overlaid continued economic strife in certain areas of Wales, including parts of the rural north, and the continuing legacy of the closure of the pits in the Welsh valleys in the 1980s.

In fiction, Emyr Humphreys continued to produce works that reflected, usually with a backwards looking focus, on life in Wales. His novel *Bonds of Attraction* (1991), the last part of his Land of the Living novel sequence, is set in the 1960s and details, through a dual narrative, an attempt to disrupt the investiture of Prince Charles at Caernarfon Castle in 1969. John Williams's *Five Pubs, Two Bars, and a Nightclub* (1999) tried to do for Wales what Glenn Patterson and Robert McLiam Wilson were doing for Belfast and Irvine Welsh for Edinburgh. The title of Williams's novel appears to be a parody of *Four Weddings and a Funeral*, the highest grossing British film of the 1990s, with its representation of a particular kind of upper-class Englishness tailored for an American market. Williams's novel clearly aims to show an oppositional aspect of contemporary Britishness both in terms of class and region. It fits into the genre of the hard-boiled crime novel but reveals a Cardiff made up of several ethnicities and reveals an alternative vision to the attempts by the Welsh Tourist Board to re-imagine Cardiff in the 1990s. Perhaps ironically, given its subject matter, Welsh's *Trainspotting* probably contributed to attracting younger tourists to the Scottish capital, but the same could not be said for Williams's novel.

Niall Griffiths's *Grits* (2000) is a darker and better-crafted novel than *Five Pubs* and involves the coming together in and around Aberystwyth of a number of characters who have dropped out of mainstream society. The novel does not address Welsh's national identity specifically but reveals a subculture of dropouts trying to locate meaning in their individual lives, as a kind of coming down from the hedonistic lifestyles pursued by several of the characters in the rave culture of the late 1980s and 1990s. The novel is divided into several first-person narratives, and it is difficult to disentangle individual viewpoints from the author's, but a general sense emerges in which what are seen as older narratives of community and national identity have been replaced by either new social groupings along alternative cultural practices, such as the use of (specific) illegal drugs, or a sense of opting out of mainstream culture. For example, Paul, who has moved from London and is living in the communal house in Aberystwyth that forms the main location for the novel, contemplates: 'What is it that binds yuh together? Thuh nationalists talk about nationhood, cultural unity, stuff like that ... But a think that the stuff that binds yuh together as probly got more tuh do with, erm, a dunno, recognizing something in others that either yuh want to see in yuhself or are too scared tuh see in yuhself' (31). Here, group association is not defined in terms of broader, external discourses such as class or the nation, but as a connection between individuals from disparate backgrounds. As Paul explains, the main characters that have come together in the house are 'all from diffrunt parts uv the country' (31), and in this sense, it becomes a metaphor for the variety of identities in the contemporary nation. As with Paul, each voice in the novel is transcribed with a particular attention to demotic characteristics forming a whole that corresponds to Mikhail Bakhtin's understanding of a heteroglossic linguistic framework within the nation (1981). In Griffiths's novel, the centrifugal forces of language are in the ascendant, and yet, despite this diversity, connections are made on personal levels.

One of the Welsh characters in the novel specifically challenges traditional constructions of Welsh identity in a scene that involves him hallucinating when placed in an isolated part of the countryside. Roger's narrative relates his experience of being involved in a murder when serving for the British Army in Northern Ireland, and his subsequent time in prison and dismissal from the army. In one particular LSD trip, Roger sees a dragon, although he knows 'it's not *rirly* a dragon like' on the mountains, which turns out to be a stag. His army training kicks in and he eventually stalks and kills the stag (68). Such symbolism suggests not only that Roger is coping with his personal demons, but also that he is killing off a sense of traditionally constructed Welsh identity in the form of the dragon/stag. As he explains 'iss is wild fuckin Wales boy ... a keep imadginin a fuckin stag prowlin round ee ouse, starin in at-a window with glowing red eyes ... snortin ... tossin its ead' (69). This combination of hallucinatory experience and mythopoeia serves to show Roger as an emblem of a contemporary rejection of Welshness as a viable hook on which to hang a sense of personal identity.

Scotland

In comparison with the relative lack of Welsh novelists engaging with national identity in the 1990s, Scottish literature flourished during the decade with the emergence of several key Scottish novelists including Irvine Welsh, A.L. Kennedy and Alan Warner, alongside the consolidation of a slightly older generation of novelists such as Janice Galloway, Alasdair Gray and James Kelman. As Matt McGuire notes, 'The latter decades of the twentieth century witnessed a dramatic transformation in the public profile and critical esteem afforded to Scottish literature' (1). As in Northern Ireland and Wales, the process of devolution during the decade added to the renewed interest in what constituted Scottish national identity as distinct from Britishness. As Cristie L. March has noted, contemporary Scottish writers have offered 'new visions of Scotland that play between the traditional rural and urban models of Scottishness' (2) perhaps to the extent that Scotland itself, as Kaye Mitchell speculates, is just a 'collection of disparate and contradictory narratives' (16). The sheer diversity of Scottish fiction during the period testifies to this claim of diversity, from Gray's and Kennedy's playful postmodernisms, to Welsh and Warner's focus on youth subcultures, to Kelman's social realism and Galloway's examination of mental health. What links all these novelists, however, is their political commentary on contemporary society from a broadly left-wing position, whether through a critical examination of a decade of Thatcherism, or as a mission to represent marginalized, working-class Scottish voices.

Perhaps the other inevitable context that links these novelists is their engagement with a distinctly Scottish literary and philosophic tradition, whether that be to reject or reposition themselves, whilst at the same time looking askance at English, European and wider literary traditions. Alasdair Gray's *Poor Things* (1992) is particularly interesting in this context as it uses national identity as a way of mapping out ideologies in Victorian society in its historiographic metafictional parody of Mary Shelley's *Frankenstein*. Gray is a staunch socialist writer, and his setting of the novel in the late nineteenth century aims, in part, to counter contemporary right-wing rhetoric of the desire for a return to Victorian values. The novel sets out, through a technique borrowed from the *tabula rasa* approach of the Martian poets, to interrogate the material effects of late Victorian culture in terms of its ideologies of class, gender and national identity. The fantastic conceit of the novelist is that the Frankenstein-like scientist Godwin Bysshe Baxter (his name reflecting several connections with Mary Shelley) has succeeded in transplanting the brain of a baby into the dead body of its mother, thus creating the figure of Bella Baxter. Subsequently Bella is able to encounter the world afresh, gradually becoming aware of the absurdities of late-Victorian patriarchal capitalism.

Gray's playful metafictional technique forces the reader to question the reliability of all narratives, and yet, in the tradition of the early-eighteenth-century novel, Gray's book presents Bella's narrative as a true story, with Gray claiming to be the editor of a found manuscript rather than the author of the text. In fact, the editor persuades us to believe the fantastical tale over counterclaims that the manuscript is merely the crazed ravings of its author, Archie MacCandless, who becomes Bella's husband. The main manuscript is bookended by the editor's introduction and a letter by a Victoria MacCandless, around whom Archie has constructed his non-realistic narrative. Victoria's letter provides a rational explanation of Archie's story, suggesting that it is his inability to come to terms with her successful career as a doctor, undermining his masculinity within the gender-coded patriarchy of the late nineteenth century, that has resulted in his attempt to present Victoria (Bella) as a monstrous aberration. The novel then is partly about female empowerment (hence the shift in names from Bella to Victoria). The text also includes part fact/part fictional 'Historical notes' which further complicates the truth claims of the narratives.

In terms of national identity, the novel is interested in connecting certain ideologies with certain national characteristics associated especially with the male characters who attempt to control, contain and exert power over Bella. This can be seen in a number of ways. Scottishness is divided between, first,

Godwin, heir to the Scottish scientific and philosophy Enlightenment tradition of David Hume, Adam Smith, Joseph Black and James Hutton, and, second, Archie, a (mock-)romantic hero who is a parody of the heroes of Walter Scott and Robert Louis Stevenson. Englishness is also divided between two characters: Astley, the intellectual cynic who provides Bella with an education in a variety of nineteenth-century political ideologies, all of which he rejects, and General Sir Aubrey de la Pole Blessington Bart V.C., who represents the imperialist tradition in English culture. Englishness is thus identified as either coldly cynical or aggressively militaristic as distinct from the tension between romanticism and scientific rationalism in the Scottish tradition. Formally, the novel can best be described as socialist postmodernism, adhering to a certain set of political positions whilst playfully rejecting textual representations of truth claims, and blurring the relationship between fact and fiction, between historical truth and partial representation of the past.

Of all the Scottish novels produced during the decade, perhaps the one that made most impact on the British literary and cultural scene is Irvine Welsh's *Trainspotting* (1993), due in no small part to Danny Boyle's 1996 film adaptation. Welsh's novel offers an antidote to the traditional image of Scotland as litany of 'kilts, bagpipes, green hills and thick Scottish brogues' as Cristie L. March puts it (1). Rather than the rural idyll, the novel presents, through its disparate narratives, a descent into the hellish world of the Edinburgh skagboy subculture of the 1980s. Within this culture, all traditional markers of identity are lost to the imperative of the next hit – the drug subculture taking precedence over any allegiance to nation, class, gender or indeed fellow human feeling. National identity is either mocked or rejected by the main character Renton and his drug buddies, Sick Boy, Spud and, later, Tommy. As Renton argues of the Scots at one point in the novel:

> Fuckin failures in a country ay failures. It's nae good blamin it oan the English fir colonising us. Ah don't hate the English. They're just wankers. We are colonised by wankers. We can't even pick a decent, vibrant, healthy culture to be colonised by. No. We're ruled by effete arseholes. What does that make us? The lowest of the fuckin low, tha's what, the scum of the earth. The most wretched, servile, miserable, pathetic trash that was ever shat intae creation. Ah don't hate the English. They just git oan wi the shite thuv goat. Ah hate the Scots. (78)

Unlike Gray's novel, in which the national identity of the English is critiqued, in Welsh's novel, Renton's bile is reserved for the Scots themselves. This critique from inside challenges English national identity and Scottish nationalism simultaneously and enhances the novel's rejection of national identity as a relevant form of cohesion for contemporary youth culture. In Boyle's film adaptation, Renton moves to London to become involved in property development, representing the aggressive individualism that exemplifies the Thatcherite ideology of 'there's no such thing as society'. And, specifically in the film (although not the novel), Renton thus rejects family and friends in his pursuit of self-gratification.[2] In this sense, this emphasizes the selfishness of the heroin subculture, and it is presented as the other side of the coin to the 1980s imperative of individualism; heroin is the emblematic drug of this culture, in the same way that marijuana represented the communalism advocated in 1960s countercultures. As Robert Morace has argued, Welsh's fiction emerges out of a range of sociopolitical contexts that includes the processes of devolution alongside 'high unemployment, punk's aggressively anti-art DIY aesthetic and anti-bourgeois ethic' as well as AIDS, heroin and, later, rave culture and Ecstasy (15–16).

A sense of a distinct national consciousness emerges most directly through the use of the vernacular, although as Gavin Miller has shown in 'Welsh and Identity Politics' this is not simply the use of a generic Scottish demotic in opposition to Standard English. As with Griffiths's *Grits*, the novel uses a heteroglossic range of speech styles in its several first-person narratives; however, a form of collective voice can be said to emerge that is reminiscent of Deleuze and Guattari's definition of one of the functions of a 'minor literature' in their discussion of Franz Kafka's work. For Deleuze and Guattari, a minor literature inevitably voices a 'collective enunciation' of the marginalized position of a literary expression from one who feels part of that minority. As they write:

> The third characteristic of a minor literature is that everything takes on a collective value ... what each other says individually already constitutes a common action, and what he or she says or does is necessarily political ... literature finds itself positively charged with the role and function of collective, and even revolutionary, enunciation. It is literature that produces an active solidarity in spite of skepticism; and if the writer is in the margins or completely outside of his fragile community, this situation allows the writer all the more the possibility to express another possible community and to forge the means for another consciousness and another sensibility. (17)

In Welsh's case, the minority voice is registered in three contexts: nation, class and age. Welsh's use of a particular form of speaking for Renton, Sick Boy and Spud is distanced from Standard English, in the sense of its amalgam of Scottish (Edinburgh) vernacular, working-class demotic and subcultural argot. The particularity of this voice might extend to other identity categories, as Gavin Miller has argued, to specific sectarian contexts in Edinburgh as registered in the minority Catholic culture of the main characters.

Concentration on the use of language and voice as inherently political is also taken up by James Kelman in his Booker Prize winning novel of 1994, *How Late it Was, How Late*. Kelman's narrative drifts between first person, free indirect discourse and interior monologue, with sections also in the second person that serve to draw the reader into a collective grouping with the main characters: 'Ye wake in a corner and stay there hoping yer body will disappear' (1). Kelman's concentration is on urban working-class experience, and like Gray, he places a particular emphasis on Glasgow. For Kelman, Scottish national identity is not something that needs to be discussed directly, rather it lies in the warp and weft of the language itself. The use of non-Standard English, as with Irvine Welsh, works in terms of an implicit commentary on the tradition of the novel in English, distancing it from the dominant middle-class interpretive community upon which it has traditionally rested. Kelman and Welsh's work can be seen as experimental in this regard, but the former is closer to the modernism of James Joyce and Virginia Woolf, whereas Welsh's fracturing of narrative into smaller chunks of contemporary experience relates well to a postmodern reflection of fragmentation in contemporary society.

England

Postmodern techniques are also deployed in several novels of the decade that address Englishness. Richard Bradford has argued that contemporary novels that 'address some element of Englishness are significant because of their rarity, and even within this eclectic subgenre there are no tangible similarities between texts or implicit notions of comradeship between authors' (177). As we have seen, Bradford's second point could also be made about fiction from Scotland and Northern Ireland and to a lesser extent Wales, but the point about rarity becomes arguable in the 1990s. In fact, Englishness gained much attention during the decade and into the early part of the twenty-first century, both in academic work and in the mainstream. Several books of fiction, history, literary criticism and cultural commentary were engaged in trying to define, locate or examine Englishness, such as Robert Colls's *The Identity of England* (2002), Roger Scruton's *England: An Elegy* (2000), Paul Langford's *Englishness Identified* (2000), Peter Ackroyd's *Albion: The Origins of the English Imagination* (2002),

Jeremy Paxman's *The English: A Portrait of a People* (1998), John McLeod and David Rogers's *The Revision of Englishness* (2004) and Kristan Kumar's *The Making of English National Identity* (2003). What links these books is a feeling that English national identity was undergoing a period of crisis and transformation in the fourth quarter of the twentieth century. As suggested earlier, this is fuelled by a sense of the break-up of the constituent nations within the United Kingdom, as Tom Nairn has discussed at great length in *The Break-Up of Britain*, and with a sense in which England as an old imperial centre needs to come to terms with the gradual and yet profound loss of international power. In the 1990s, in particular, an assessment of where that leaves Englishness seemed to be an inevitable consequence amid millennial fears of what the new century might bring.

There is something of this engagement with the idea of Englishness in crisis in Julian Barnes's 1998 novel, *England, England*, in which the nation is reduced to a series of commodified symbols. The conceit of the novel is that a theme park, based on Englishness as a concept, is to be constructed on the Isle of Wight catering for the public nostalgia for the past alongside a willingness to be able to buy a product that promises to fulfil their desire. The park is the project of Sir Jack Pitman, a businessman who clearly embraces Thatcherite economics and entrepreneurship, and whose name is surely an ironic reference to the pit closures of the 1980s. The theme park acts as an emblem for the commercialization of history as witnessed in the development of the heritage industry in the 1980s and 1990s. In the same way that working mines, steel works and pottery factories were replaced by mining and pottery museums and centres for the celebration of Britain's industrial past, the theme park built on the Isle of Wight stands for an England that has itself been consigned to history. If, for Jean Baudrillard in *America* (1988), Disneyland encapsulates the whole of America, then in Barnes's novel, the eponymous theme park stands in for the nation as a whole. The difference, however, is that in Barnes's theme park it is not the present but English history and mythology that is trawled for iconic images. As the marketing consultant hired by Sir Jack argues:

> You – we – England – my client – is – are – a nation of great age, great history, great accumulated wisdom. Social and cultural history – stacks of it, reams of it – eminently marketable, never more so than in the current climate. Shakespeare, Queen Victoria, Industrial Revolution, gardening, that sort of thing. If I may coin, no copyright a phrase, *We are already what others may hope to become*. This isn't self-pity, this is the strength of our position, our glory, our product

placement. We are the new pioneers. We must sell our past to other nations as their future! (39–40)

The park itself becomes a paradigm of capitalist enterprise, an image of the nation without interference from democratically elected governmental restrictions. As a financial analyst explains: 'It's [the theme park] a pure market state. There's no interference from government because there *is* no government. So there's no foreign or domestic policy, only economic policy. It's a pure interface between buyers and sellers without the market being skewed by central government' (183). Such an image of an ideal Englishness exemplifies the discourse prominent in the 1990s of the 'End of History', fuelled primarily by Francis Fukuyama's work. According to a simplified, yet widely accepted account of Fukuyama's theory, the collapse of the Soviet Union in the early 1990s resulted in an end to a dialectic sense of history as a series of competing economic forces, with capitalism as finally triumphant. History, in this sense, ends. In *England, England*, this is represented by the effective end of English history in that it is confined solely to the past: 'There was no history except Pitco history' (202). The gathering of iconic images of English popular history in the theme park – kings and queens, the Battle of Britain pilots, Dr Johnson, Nell Gwynn, and so on – effectively confines England to the recycling of past images called up unthinkingly in the present and effectively removes the sense of the future in the ever-present now of postmodern consumerism. As Fredric Jameson, in *Postmodernism, or the Cultural Logic of Late Capitalism* (1991), identifies in what he calls the 'nostalgia mode', it is easy to see the novel as a critique of postmodernism's love affair with ahistoricity and surfaces at the detriment of real historical contexts. Postmodern theory is personified in the novel by a French intellectual who Sir Jack invites to speak to the team developing the project and who asserts: 'It is well established – and indeed it has been incontrovertibly proved by many of those I have earlier cited – that nowadays we prefer the replica to the original' (53). This is a clear parody of Baudrillard's theories, the irony being that Baudrillard's critique of postmodern culture is recycled for the benefit of Sir Jack's project as a celebration of the market economy.

The novel is divided into three sections: the first of which describes the early life of Martha Cochrane, who later becomes part of Sir Jack's team, while the second recounts the development and opening of the theme park. Once the theme park is opened, a strange thing begins to happen, as revealed in the third section, in that some of the people employed to act out roles from English myth and history begin to merge into their adopted characters. For example, the character acting as Dr Johnson begins to garner complaints from customers because he smells, eats voraciously and becomes 'either bullyingly dominant, or else sunk in silence' (208), while the team playing the Battle of Britain Squadron begin to sleep in the Nissen huts waiting for the scramble call, and the Cornish smugglers start to circulate contraband until the park authorities have to stage a raid on the village benefitting from their illicit activities (with tickets snapped up by the Premier Visitors to watch). As the novel suggests, 'They were happy to be who they had become' (198). The park, then, dramatizes a deeper psychological need for the constructed securities of past identities that suture themselves easily to recognized narratives of Englishness. It becomes a kind of escape from the disrupted communities and identities of a postmodern society in which consumption has replaced production. The crafted authenticity of the roles becomes more than just a ruse to sell the idea. Also in the third section, we find Martha, now as an old woman, returned to mainland England, which itself has become a rural backwater.

Despite its engagement with postmodern ideas of simulations and simulacra and the constructedness of all grand narratives, including those attached to the nation, ultimately the novel casts a wistful eye on the pre-postmodern securities of an Enlightenment model of fixed identities and cohesive national communities, whilst at the same time recognizing that authentic places of origin never really exist other than in the minds of those who choose to accept them. In this way, it describes the preference for the simplified simulacra enmeshed with the psychological need for a sense of authenticity, which are, in fact, identified as coterminous. What Martha begins to understand in the final section of the book is that to fulfil the desire to recover a lost past – a garden show, our image of rural England, Cornish smugglers, Robin Hood – it is necessary to suspend knowledge of the very inauthenticity and artificiality of such constructions. This does not, however, make them any the less real to the conscious mind. The first section of the novel already supplies an indication of this kind of thinking, in Martha's description of memory: 'There's always a memory just behind your first memory, and you can't quite get at it' (3). Englishness in this context is seen in the novel to be a series of facing mirrors, offering a *mise en abyme* into the unreachable distance. Barnes is a reluctant postmodernist. *England, England* laments the fact that a true or accurate or ultimately fixed idea of the nation can never be recovered, because it never existed. This, however, is not a cause for celebration as a liberation from some kind of a national grand narrative, but a wistful regret that our sense of the nation has moved from a song of innocence to one of experience. The novel then reveals a cultural crisis in the meaning of Englishness that is particularly pertinent to the 1990s, both in its reflection of postmodernism and the crisis under which the nation is placed due to competing discourses of devolution and multiculturalism which threaten to undermine older constructions based on location, race and ethnicity.

New ethnicities

One gap, then, in Barnes's novel is its lack of concern with contemporary issues of multiculturalism or ethnic diversity. In its focus on a lost Englishness, it decides not to include a reference to alternative models of the nation that incorporate alternative ethnicities. In addition to the moves towards devolution in the United Kingdom, the impact of immigration and the development of multicultural communities in Britain during the same period contributed to a reconfiguration of national identity as it came to terms with (often exaggerated) anxieties about a sense of a weakening of traditional notions of Englishness. As John McLeod has argued in his 'Introduction: Measuring Englishness', post-war immigration to Britain has resulted in 'a new multicultural English population as well as triggering myths of an embattled national identity which turned increasingly to race and heterosexuality as the prime marker of legitimacy and belonging' (3). Paul Langford emphasizes the 'mongrel nature' of the English historically, whilst acknowledging that 'the creation of a self-consciously multiracial society... might have startled many who sought to summarize the English character between the mid-seventeenth and mid-nineteenth century' (318). Discourses of the nation are, of course, bound up with definitions of class, gender, sexuality, race and ethnicity, all of which can be seen to have been put under pressure in the last quarter or so of the twentieth century. Stuart Hall, for example, offers a detailed analysis of the variety of areas in which the subject has been decentred in post-war societies. Hall summarized this approach in his chapter in *Modernity and Its Futures* from 1992:

> a distinctive type of structural change is transforming modern societies in the late twentieth century. This is fragmenting the cultural landscapes of class, gender, sexuality, ethnicity, race and nationality which gave us firm locations as social individuals. These transformations are also shifting our personal identities, undermining ourselves as integrated subjects. This loss of a stable 'sense of self' is sometimes called the dislocation or de-centring of the subject. This set of double displacements – de-centring individuals both from their place

in the social and cultural world, and from themselves – constitutes a 'crisis of identity' for the individual. (274–5)

The crisis of national identity is thus overlaid in terms of a more general crisis of personal identity. Out of this crisis, however, new paradigms of identity develop, especially with respect to the increased mixing of peoples and cultures as a legacy of the postcolonial process in Britain after the Second World War including immigration to Britain and the development of distinct marginalized communities; what Hall, in an earlier work, describes as 'new ethnicities' in his essay of the same name. Two novels of the period that were particularly interested in this decentring of the national subject and the creation of new ethnicities are Hanif Kureishi's *The Buddha of Suburbia* (1990) and Zadie Smith's *White Teeth* (2000).

The question of national identity is introduced in the opening sentence of Kureishi's novel: 'My name is Karim Amir, and I am an Englishman born and bred, almost'. The tensions established here between the traditional and the new mark out a central interest in the novel. The hesitancy of that 'almost' represents the difference felt by Karim despite his very English background. It is significant that the 'born and bred' phrase itself sounds old-fashioned in this context, slightly out of phase generationally with Karim's age at the opening of the novel – nineteen. He continues: 'I am often considered to be a funny kind of Englishman, a new breed as it were, having emerged from two old histories. But I don't care – Englishman I am (though not proud of it), from the suburbs and going somewhere' (3). This opening passage raises issues about whether national identity is specifically cultural or biological, undercutting older notions of race being stitched directly to nation. This tension is embodied in Karim's parentage – his mother is White English, his father British Asian – and as he explains his restlessness is difficult to define, though he speculates a reason to be his 'mixing of continents and blood, of here and there, of belonging and not' (3), the combining of the biological, the geographical and the cultural creating a complex mix. It is this complex interaction that extends in the novel to describe a nation itself in flux and struggling to come to terms with differing notions of identity.

The sense of crisis in identity is initially seen as empowering for Karim as he experiments with drugs, sexuality and (sub)cultural possibilities drawn from a number of ethnic and national contexts. As Karim explains at one point in the novel with respect to his cousin Jamila, 'sometimes we were French, Jammie and I, and other times we went black American' (53). Karim and Jamila here look beyond England in their sampling of alternative cultural identities, and as this passage shows, cultural identity is seen as detachable from specific ethnic or racial identity. The sense both that identity can be constructed and performed can be seen in the bricolage attitude adopted by Karim in the earlier parts of the text. When getting ready for an evening out, attention is paid to his donning of clothes drawn form a range of cultures:

> It took me several months to get ready: I changed my entire outfit three times. At seven o'clock I came downstairs in what I knew were the right clothes for Eva's evening. I wore turquoise flared trousers, a blue and white flower-patterned see-through shirt, blue suede boots with Cuban heels, and a scarlet Indian waistcoat with gold stitching round the edges. I'd pulled on a headband to control my shoulder-length frizzy hair. I'd washed my face in Old Spice. (6)

Here, the flared trousers, flowered shirt and headband relate to 1960s hippy culture, while the blue suede shoes suggest earlier rock'n'roll and the Cuban heels Black American street culture, the Indian waistcoat is far from authentic in Karim's context as it is very probably filtered through George Harrison and the Beatles' orientalizing of Indian mysticism. The bathos of the traditional, suburban male aftershave indicates the jumble of cultural signifiers that mark out Karim's attempt to carve out his own adolescent identity.

However, despite this innocent embracing of different cultures, the society Karim encounters as he moves from his parental security is not as open to change. The novel also describes aspects of racism in 1970s Britain experienced by characters from non-white ethnic backgrounds. Such racism takes different forms dependent on context, but it is presented as a tenacious aspect of British society. It is encountered in physically violent ways; for example, the shop owned by Jamila's parents is in an area 'full of neo-fascist groups' (56) and is targeted by right-wing thugs. When he arrives from Bangladesh, Jamila's husband, Changez, is attacked by a gang of National Front supporters who attempt to carve the initials 'NF' on his chest with razor blades (224). Karim suffers racist abuse from the father of a white, suburban girl he dates while still at school, who sets his Great Dane on Karim when he calls round to their house to pick her up.

These incidents of racist violence occur in the working- and lower-middle-class environments where Karim grows up, but he also encounters more subtle forms of racism in the apparently liberal middle and upper-middle-class circles in which he begins to move when he becomes an actor. The first acting role he gets is playing Mowgli in an adaptation of *The Jungle Book*, for which he has to 'black up' because his skin is not quite dark enough for the defined role. He also has to adopt the speech of a cod Indian character to emphasize his oriental status. The director of the play, Shadwell, thus subjects Karim to a re-orientalizing that undermines his English suburban background in order to effectively re-colonize

Karim's identity. Karim tries to resist this process by 'suddenly relapsing into cockney at odd times' (158), but the inauthentic position in which he is placed is recognized by both his father and Jamila when they come to see the play; as the latter comments, 'It was disgusting, the accent and the shit you had smeared over you. You were just pandering to prejudices' (157). This is an example of what Paul Gilroy, in *There Ain't No Black in the Union Jack* (1987), has identified as 'cultural racism' where prejudice based on the perceived cultural practices of a particular ethnic group is employed in order to re-establish colonial power relationships.

Thus, the novel shows the complexities of racist behaviour as a set of lived ideologies and practices and suggests that one of the causes is the legacy of colonialism. For some in the novel, the postcolonial dismantling of the empire produces a residual desire for a world in which the traditional racial hierarchies still hold. As Karim's father argues: 'The whites will never promote us ... they still think they have an Empire when they don't have two pennies to rub together' (27). In one scene, Shadwell articulates this sense of resentment by emphasizing what he sees as the ironies of Karim's place within a postcolonial England for which the legacies of empire are lingering:

> What a breed of people two hundred years of imperialism has given birth to. If the pioneers from the East India Company could see you. What puzzlement there'd be. Everyone looks at you, I'm sure, and thinks: an Indian boy, how exotic, how interesting, what stories of aunties and elephants we'll hear now from him. And you're from Orpington. (141)

Although Shadwell's tone is mocking, he highlights a possible explanation for the kind of racism Karim suffers in that the dominant ideologies are not yet able to fathom the contradictions of this 'new breed' of Englishman (3). In Kureishi's novel, the new ethnicities of which Stuart Hall speaks may represent the potential for a new understanding of race and nation, but they are clearly not (yet) embraced by the majority.

It could be argued that these forms of racial prejudice are specific to the 1970s context, but the impact the novel (and perhaps the BBC TV adaptation, first shown in 1993, even more so) had suggests that these concerns were still prevalent in the early 1990s. In his next novel, *The Black Album* (1995), Kureishi explores racial tensions in contemporary Britain by focusing on the ways in which young British Asians in particular are drawn to differing cultural and transnational affiliations, complicating any allegiances to discrete national identities. Like *The Buddha of Suburbia*, the novel is a Bildungsroman which tracks a range of influences on its central character, Shahid, who at the opening of the novel has just moved to north-west London to study at a local college. These influences include an affair with Deedee Osgood, a lecturer at the college in her early thirties who introduces him to the emerging rave scene, whilst also filling him in on the left-leaning cultural politics of the 1980s to which she is still attached but concerning which she is, to a certain extent, becoming disillusioned. The second major influence is from a British-grown radical Islamic group headed by Riaz Al-Hussain with whom Shahid becomes friend when he moves, at the opening of the novel, into a six-storey house that has been divided into small bedsits. It is tempting to see this house, filled as it is with a variety of ethnicities, as a metaphor for the contemporary nation, and indeed, the narrative is driven by Shahid's oscillation between competing ethnic and ideological influences, resulting in a complicated series of divided identities: 'He would wake up with this feeling: who would he turn out to be on this day? How many warring selves were there within him? Which was his real, natural self? Was there such a thing?' (122). This postmodern fragmentation of individual identity could be seen as an aspect of the essential adolescent journey into adulthood, but it is given specific historical context in the description of discrete factions in the society in which Shahid finds himself:

> He had noticed, during the days that he'd walked around the area, that the races were divided. The black kids stuck with each other, the Pakistanis went to one another's houses, the Bengalis knew each other from way back, and the whites too... wasn't the world breaking up into political and religious tribes? The divisions were taken for granted, each to his own. (111)

Shahid continues to explore his sexual relationship with Deedee, alongside fighting with Riaz's group against racist attacks on local Asian communities. However, balancing his oppositional allegiances becomes increasingly difficult, as each is suspicious of the other's influence on Shahid. The novel culminates in him being drawn, reluctantly, into a public book-burning of Salman Rushdie's *The Satanic Verses* at the college, as Riaz's group's local response to the fatwa against Rushdie issued by the Ayatollah Khomeini. This event brings to a head the stand-off in Shahid's confused identity-formation between the attractions of the libertarian left represented by Deedee and the rise of a religiously informed youth resistance movement to Western capitalism crystallized at this juncture around the issue of Rushdie's novel. This moment forces Shahid's decision to reject what are initially seen as the attractive ideologies of Riaz's group and the novel ends with him planning to continue his affair with Deedee, at least 'until it stops being fun' (230).

Despite Shahid finding a tentatively stable life beyond his vacillating influences, the novel as a whole presents the image of a nation of fragmented and tribal cultural allegiances which does not sit well with the emerging discourse of a positive multiculturalism in the 1990s. It is perhaps not until the end of the decade that a novel appears, on the surface at least, to offer a vision of Englishness that embraces multicultural diversity. Zadie Smith's novel *White Teeth* was published in January 2000 and thus represents a retrospective view from the very edge of the twentieth century, as well as of the 1990s (and presumably the novel must have been completed and in production during the last months of the decade). In fact, in the last scene, the novel projects towards events that take place on New Year's Eve 1999, although the main events in the novel take place in the 1970s, 1980s and early 1990s. Smith's novel develops Kureishi's sense of individuals with new ethnicities to describe the multiracial interactions of a range of ethnicities. The legacies and problems of colonialism are still apparent, but the novel ends on a note of hopeful projection to a world in which roots and historical legacies can be, if not rejected, at least evaded. The novel has a number of story lines, one of which is the creation of a genetically engineered 'Future Mouse', who despite the fact that its life is determined by genetic engineering manages to escape its pre-programmed destiny when it is inadvertently freed at the end of the novel by Archie Jones, one of the novel's central characters. Archie emerges as one of the unlikely heroes of the novel, perhaps the other being Irie Jones, Archie's daughter. The father of Irie's baby will remain unknown, even to DNA testing, as she has slept with both Magid and Millat (the twin sons of the novel's other main character Samad Iqbal) who in their own ways are locked in a perpetual struggle due primarily to their own particular responses to the legacies of colonialism. Perhaps the final events of the novel (chronologically speaking) offer a neat emblem to this sense of potential freedom from past restrictions dependent on colonial power and ethnicity and the possibility of a more liberating world. The last chapter, although set mainly in 1992, projects momentarily forward to New Year's Eve 1999, when Archie and Samad's favourite drinking haunt, O'Connells, the 'Irish pool house run by Arabs with no pool tables' (183), opens its doors for the first time to women, suggesting the removal of cultural restrictions with respect to gender to match its open policy on ethnicity and sees a tentative projection to a new conception of the nation fit for the new millennium. At least, that is, until the events of 11 September 2001, in which new configurations of national identity are required to meet a whole new set of tensions and demands.

Notes

1 This chapter develops some ideas first presented in a previous article. See Bentley (2007).
2 Aaron Kelly notes that this aspect of the film is not included in the novel and, following Alan Sinfield, argues this undermines Renton's implicit resistance to Thatcherite ideologies in the novel (70).

Works Cited

Ackroyd, Peter. *Albion: The Origins of the English Imagination*. London: Chatto and Windus, 2002.

Anderson, Benedict. *Imagined Communities: Reflections on the Origin and Spread of Nationalism*. London: Verso and New Left Books, 1983.

Bakhtin, Mikhail M. 'Discourse in the Novel'. In *The Dialogic Imagination: Four Essays by M.M. Bakhtin*. Ed. Michael Holquist. Trans. Carl Emerson and Michael Holquist. Austin: University of Texas Press, 1981, 259–422.

Barnes, Julian. *England, England*. London: Jonathan Cape, 1998.

Baudrillard, Jean. *Simulations*. Trans. Paul Foss, Paul Patton and Philip Beitchman. New York, Semiotext[e], 1983.

———. *America*. Trans. Chris Turner. London: Verso, 1988.

Bentley, Nick. 'Introduction: Mapping the Millennium: Themes and Trends in Contemporary British Fiction'. In *British Fiction of the 1990s*. Ed. Nick Bentley. London and New York: Routledge, 2005.

———. 'Re-Writing Englishness: Imagining the Nation in Julian Barnes's *England, England* and Zadie Smith's *White Teeth*'. *Textual Practice* 21.3 (2007): 483–504.

Bhabha, Homi. 'DissemiNation: Time, Narrative, and the Margins of the Modern Nation'. In *Nation and Nation*. Ed. Homi Bhabha. London: Routledge, 1990, 291–322.

Boyle, Danny (dir.) *Trainspotting*. Channel Four Films, Figment Films, Noel Gay Motion Picture Company, 1996.

Bradford, Richard. *The Novel Now: Contemporary British Fiction*. Oxford and Malden: Blackwell, 2007.

Brennan, Timothy. 'The National Longing for Form'. In *Nation and Narration*. Ed. Homi Bhabha. London: Routledge, 1990, 44–70.

Colls, Robert. *Identity of England*. Oxford: Oxford University Press, 2002.

Deane, Seamus. *Reading in the Dark*. London: Jonathan Cape, 1996.

Deleuze, Gilles and Felix Guattari. *Kafka: Toward a Minor Literature*. Trans. by Dana Polan. Minneapolis: University of Minnesota Press, 1986.

Fukuyama, Francis. *The End of History and the Last Man*. London: Hamish Hamilton, 1992.

Gilroy, Paul. *There Ain't No Black in the Union Jack: The Cultural Politics of Race and Nation*. London: Hutchinson, 1987.

Gray, Alasdair. *Poor Things*. London: Bloomsbury, 1992

Griffiths, Niall. *Grits*. London: Jonathan Cape, 2000.

Hall, Stuart. 'The Question of Cultural Identity'. In *Modernity and Its Futures*. Eds. Stuart Hall, David Held, and Tony McGrew. Cambridge: Polity, 1992.

———. 'New Ethnicities' [1989]. In *Stuart Hall: Critical Dialogues in Cultural Studies*. Eds David Morley and Kuan-Hsing Chen. London and New York: Routledge, 1996, 441–9.

Humphreys, Emyr. *Bonds of Attraction*. Cardiff: University of Wales Press, [1991] 2001.

Jameson, Fredric. *Postmodernism, or The Cultural Logic of Late Capitalism*. London: Verso, 1991.

Joyce, James. *Dubliners*. Harmondsworth: Penguin, [1914] 2000.

Kelly, Aaron. *Irvine Welsh*. Manchester: Manchester University Press, 2005.

Kelman, James. *How Late It Was, How Late*. London: Secker and Warburg, 1994.

King, John. *England Away*. London: Jonathan Cape, 1999.

Kumar, Krishan. *The Making of English National Identity*. Cambridge: Cambridge University Press, 2003.

Kureishi, Hanif. *The Buddha of Suburbia*. London: Faber and Faber, 1990.

———. *The Black Album*. London: Faber and Faber, 1995.

Langford, Paul. *Englishness Identified: Manners and Character 1650 1850*. Oxford and New York: Oxford University Press, 2000.

MacClaverty, Bernard. *Grace Notes*. London: Jonathan Cape, 1997.

Madden, Deirdre. *One by One in the Darkness*. London: Faber and Faber, 1996.

March, Cristie L. *Rewriting Scotland: Welsh, Mclean, Warner, Banks, Galloway and Kennedy*. Manchester: Manchester University Press, 2002.

McGuire, Matt. *Contemporary Scottish Literature*. Basingstoke: Palgrave, 2009.

McLeod, John. 'Introduction: Measuring Englishness'. In *The Revision of Englishness*. Eds. John McLeod and David Rogers. Manchester: Manchester University Press, 2004, 1–14.

——— and David Rogers (eds) *The Revision of Englishness*. Manchester: Manchester University Press, 2004.

McNamee, Eoin. *Resurrection Man*. London: Picador,1994.

Mike Newell (dir.) *Four Weddings and a Funeral*. PolyGram, Channel Four Films, Working Title Films, 1994.

Miller, Gavin. 'Welsh and Identity Politics'. In *The Edinburgh Companion to Irvine Welsh*. Ed. Berthold Schoene. Edinburgh: Edinburgh University Press, 2010, 89–99.

Mitchell, Kaye. *A.L. Kennedy*. Basingstoke: Palgrave, 2008.

Moore, Brian. *Lies of Silence*. London: Bloomsbury, 1990.

Morace, Robert. *Irvine Welsh*. Basingstoke: Palgrave, 2007.

Nairn, Tom. *The Break-Up of Britain: Crisis and Neonationalism*. 2nd Edition. London: New Left Books, [1977] 1982.

Patterson, Glenn. *Fat Lad*. Belfast: Blackstaff Press, [1992] 2008.

Paxman, Jeremy. *The English People: A Portrait of a People*. London: Michael Joseph, 1998.
Roger Michell (dir.) *The Buddha of Suburbia*. BBC, 1993.
Scruton, Roger. *England: An Elegy*. London: Chatto and Windus, 2000.
Smith, Zadie. *White Teeth*. Harmondsworth: Penguin, [2000] 2001.
Tew, Philip. *The Contemporary British Novel*, 2nd Edition. London: Continuum, 2007.
Thorpe, Adam. *Ulverton*. London: Secker and Warburg, 1992.
Welsh, Irvine. *Trainspotting*. London: Secker and Warburg, 1993.
Williams, John. *Five Pubs, Two Bars and a Nightclub*. London: Bloomsbury, 1999.
Wilson, Robert McLiam. *Eureka Street*. London: Secker and Warburg, 1996.
Žižek, Slavoj. *Tarrying with the Negative: Kant, Hegel and the Critique of Ideology*. Durham: Duke University Press, 1993.

Special Topic 2
Satirical Apocalypse: Endism and the 1990s Fictions of Will Self

Katy Shaw and Philip Tew

[T]he 1990s will come to be seen as the Gotterdammerung of periodicity itself. […] [N]ever again will the brute fact of what year it is matter so much in cultural terms.

(Will Self, 'Ingenious Bubble Wrap', 26)

In 'The Valley of the Corn Dollies' in the *Guardian* in 1994, Will Self said of his homeland: 'It is a culture of profound and productive oppositions. And I believe, personally, the best possible country for someone with a satirical bent to live in. I'd go further: England has the world's top satirical culture' (*Junk Mail*, 204). Elsewhere in 'Conversations: Martin Amis', Self 'unquestionably' situates himself as part of that heritage (408), working in literary satire, aware of his antecedents. Satire itself has a long tradition, traced back variously to Ancient Egypt and to Greece, to the Romans and to Medieval Europe, although arguably the role of satire as a mode of social commentary came into even sharper focus during the Enlightenment, with seminal literary satires published in Britain such as Alexander Pope's *The Rape of the Lock* (1714) and the writings of Jonathan Swift and Daniel Defoe. And certainly, the latter two figures are direct influences on Will Self, whose satirical narratives of the 1990s are the focus of this chapter. Satire is generally public-spirited, using ridicule and denigration in order to either restore truth and justice or at the very least identify evil and venality in the world. There are a range of possibilities in satire, some approaches seemingly in contradiction to others, but at an intentional level unified by an implicit sense of moral critique and social corrective. In his dictionary, Dr Johnson defined satire as a text 'in which wickedness or folly is censured', while in *The Battle of the*

Books, Swift argued that 'satire is a sort of glass, wherein beholders do generally discover everybody's face but their own, which is the chief reason for that kind of reception it meets in the world, and that so very few are offended with it' (137). People in essence project their social failures and deficiencies onto others by this account, accepting certain realities, but simply not applied to the self on first reading. Deploying what Pope in the *Epilogue of the Satires* calls 'Truth's defence' (l.212), satire presents, according to Melville Clark, 'a chameleon-like surface' by using all the tones of its spectrum, 'wit, ridicule, irony, sarcasm, cynicism, the sardonic and invective' (32). Below, this essay will set out a sense of Self's adaptations of this tradition.

Self has been the focus of much critical attention since his first collection of short stories *The Quantity Theory of Insanity* (1991) was published. He has enjoyed a love/hate relationship with both his peers and with literary critics and Self claims to have 'always relished the idea of my work being not simply misunderstood by ordinary readers, but also comprehensively misinterpreted by the professionals' ('You Ask The Questions' 7). Despite being a recognized 'enfant terrible' of the 1990s, Self was also praised by Sam Leith as one of the most gifted young writers of the period. As an author whose fictions document 'an entire version of reality: a sort of extensio ad absurdum' (n.p.), Self was lauded by Brian Finney as 'the most original new fiction writer to appear in Britain during the 1990s' (n.p.). Self featured on *Granta*'s 1993 list of best young British novelists before his first novel had even been published, and he quickly became 'a cult figure' (Rushdie 24), concerning whom many heavyweights of the literary world joined in a chorus of approval. Salman Rushdie claimed that Self was 'someone who stands as a one-off' (quoted in Shone 39), Doris Lessing deemed him 'a genuine comic writer', while Beryl Bainbridge applauded his black, macabre and relentless vision of the world (quoted in Shone 39). Self's dark, distorted visions garnered widespread critical praise, perhaps culminating in Zoe Heller's assessment of Self as 'a very cruel writer – thrillingly heartless, terrifyingly brainy… Self has probably won more praise – and praise of a more uninhibited kind – than any writer to emerge in the last decade' (126).

Over the course of the 1990s, Self generated an impressive oeuvre including short stories, novels, journalism and even a comic strip that was anthologized. As suggested above, *The Quantity Theory of Insanity* was praised by the UK literary establishment. It was shortlisted for the 1992 John Llewellyn Rhys Prize and won the Geoffrey Faber Memorial Prize. Subsequently, Self published two novellas, *Cock* and *Bull* (1992), a novel, *My Idea of Fun* (1993), another short story collection, *Grey Area* (1994), *Junk Mail* (1995), a collection of journalism, interviews and essays and *Great Apes* (1997), a second novel. As well as his prolific output during the decade, Self also attracted attention as a media personality and celebrity. Almost immediately Self became aware that alongside the critical acclaim and literary prizes 'there's the fame shit too, and swaggering around in a silk suit and having your catamite buff your toenails – I went for all that' (quoted in Kinson). And, in 2000, Stephen Moss quoted Julie Burchill, a devotee, along with Self, of the Groucho Club in the 1990s, as having 'announced to the world that she no longer fancied him':

> 'To get the full clout of this', she explained, 'you've got to understand what Will Self represented, sexually, in the 90s. Despite his drug and alcohol intake, to us London media babes he was a sexual icon packing the oomph of Jimi Hendrix, Robbie Williams and Gordon Brown all rolled into one. Every man wanted to be him and every woman wanted to have him. They usually did, too'.

As Lesley White wrote in *The Times*, 'Most of us have never met Will Self… but we are all aware of his pose, his junkie past, the naughtiness that once declared it was as easy to get crack as a rail ticket at Kings Cross station' (quoted in Pattern). Over the course of the decade, Self quickly achieved, as Pattern suggests, 'a certain literary reputation' and a pronounced degree of 'personal notoriety' along with the critical acclaim. Arguably, the climax of such opprobrium came in the run-up to the general election of 1997 when Self was accused of snorting heroin in the toilet of the campaign jet of John Major, the then UK Prime Minister. Subsequently, Self was sacked by *The Observer* for whom he was reporting on the election and found himself subject to a veritable storm of media coverage. His experiences and his own mediatized image as a symbol of transgression might be argued to have enhanced Self's sense of the possibilities of what Malcolm Bull in *Seeing Things Hidden: Apocalypse, Vision and Totality* (1999) identifies in visions of the final days: 'What is seen in apocalyptic vision is more often than not a series of symbols embodying what is otherwise prohibited' (71). Bull argues that satire embraces the curious ruptures of the apocalyptic imagination, and certainly, Self's tabooed behaviour might be argued to mirror the prohibitions that appear to be threatened by apocalypse. The controversy also catapulted Self onto a national stage, where increasingly (if erroneously at times) he came to typify the 1990s. During this period, the public perception of the author changed. As Hunter Hayes indicates, 'In the wake of unbidden media coverage, he published his second novel, a more significant event in his career' (124). Possibly, but ironically one consequence of this affair, as Nick Rennison explains, was that 'Will Self has a significantly higher public profile than the majority of "literary" novelists' (149) about which Self remained 'deeply ambivalent' (150).

Even before these momentous few weeks in 1997, Self's shifting narrative surfaces had incorporated various of the satiric coordinates alluded to above, as can be seen in the naïve and gentle irony of 'The North London Book of the Dead' in his first collection in 1991, where a son encounters his dead mother unexpectedly in a London street, baffled by her new choice of home. Equally the extended ridicule, comic grotesqueries and sarcasm underpinning *How the Dead Live* (2000), a novel very largely composed at the very end of the 1990s, incorporates many of that decade's social realities by depicting whole additional London suburbs populated by the dead, many commuting to work among the living but unnoticed by them.

Marked by a highly self-conscious style, such fictions manipulate generic conventions to disrupt readerly expectations, using extended conceits, parody, pastiche, intertextuality and conceptual innovation to offer a sense of the tensions inherent in the turn of the century but subsumed within an overarching satirical framework. Self's 1990s fictions drew upon exaggeration, the absurd and unexpectedly surreal elements in order to rewrite rather than reject satirical tradition, and clearly, he still drew upon examples from the past as an energizing force. Self operates as a linguistic agent provocateur, mobilizing an eighteenth-century Swiftian tradition with more fantastical elements of the contemporary, such as with his human-ape transformations within the setting of a recognizable London in *The Great Apes*, and the grotesque sexualized transformation at the end of *The Sweet Smell of Psychosis* discussed below. Moreover, Self deployed a satirical perspective to expose disconcerting truths about the pre-millennial human condition, reflecting upon a present where some were obsessed with the decade's 'endism'. Malcolm Bull draws parallels between apocalyptic thinking's capacity to unpick the undifferentiated incongruities of the lifeworld and satire's revelatory and corrective possibilities concerning the contradictions in human understanding (and therefore behaviour) relating to the world (59). Having been nominated by the media as the quintessential 'bad boy' of the 1990s literary scene, Self evoked and interrogated this undercurrent of the apocalyptic that fascinated this anxious society, worried about limits and behaviour, capturing a period that foregrounded the very concept of a whole variety of potential endings. As Bull indicates, it is possible to 'define [the] apocalyptic as the revelation of contradiction and indeterminacy' (113), and Self's fictions do this *par excellence*. So, can the 1990s be truly considered to be an apocalyptic period? In 1989, Francis Fukuyama indicated some sort of finality in an essay entitled 'The End of History?' announcing a triumphant liberal democracy in a post-ideological world, which in his subsequent book, *The End of History and the Last Man* (1992), he couched in apocalyptic terms: 'I argued that liberal democracy may constitute the "end point of mankind's ideological evolution" and the "final form of human government," and as such constituted the "end of history"' (xi). As Self reflected in 'In praise of pessimism', had his dying and pessimistic mother survived:

> My mother would have had to hang on only a few months in order to prop herself up in bed, or possibly lie supine, while I read aloud to her Francis Fukuyama's essay in the *National Interest* 'The End of History?'. How she would have snorted derisively at Fukuyama's assertion that the end of the cold war would be followed by the worldwide dissemination of benign western liberal democracy.

Self's mother was pessimistic in all things, perhaps an impulse akin to that of satire. Yet, however absurd Fukuyama's view might appear retrospectively, after the numerous disruptions to the social and world order, that view was influential throughout the 1990s. Certainly, in a more mundane way, the press reflected widely upon public fears that the approaching millennium might be marked by a new set of challenges and threats to society, and the fragmentation, discontinuities and generic instabilities of Self's texts considered below mirror the anomie and doubt of those years.

Self's cartography of what may be variously considered from adjacent perspectives as a sense of apocalypse (anticipation of either prophetic revelation and/or the end of time) or endism (the belief in the radical rupture of historical power as it has been previously known, a fissure of cultures, as critiqued by Samuel P. Huntington) is very particular in its emphasis, and its coordinates feature two of the five possibilities concerning the apocalyptic posed by Malcolm Bull. He asks whether it might represent: 'A teleological framework for the understanding of evil? ... A tone of disclosure, perhaps distinct from the content of the discourse, revelatory if only in that it reveals itself?' (47). Hence, arguably, Self's prose in its very insistence on an exuberant and unusual vocabulary that declares the primacy of its own presence irrespective of whatever is being described mirrors a deep apocalyptic impulse, as does his search for the causes of what the narrator dismisses in *My Idea of Fun* as 'The horror of it all, the ghastly anti-human horror? ... the Holocaust writ small' (4) when describing the gory act of ripping off a tramp's head from his body.

Elsewhere Self focuses on both individuals and systems that fall short of his exacting (if implied) standards of required human behaviour, thereby offering a series of scathing judgements of contemporary society, its mores and erroneous belief systems. *The Sweet Smell of Psychosis* (1996), with its darkly grotesque illustrations by Martin Rowson, concerns members of the media and creative professions who are the habitual denizens of the Sealink Club (for which read the Groucho Club, of which Self was himself a member), and Self's narrator observes: 'They all seemed to smoke, they all seemed to drink, they all held themselves in exaggerated postures, heads jerking around, on the lookout for better social prospects lying behind the heads – or the bodies – of their interlocutors' (7). Self conveys variously the insincerity, unoriginality and lack of creativity of a particular cultural set which is assumed by the wider culture to be bright and creative. In the club, around half are journalists or 'hacks' who 'were transmitters of trivia, broadcasters of banality, and disseminators of drek' (10). They form a clique around Bell, a newspaper columnist and TV personality. Self's critique is directed broadly, exposing everything to derision, holding up as hideous elements found in the real world. The story's narrative later reflects upon an editorial meeting of *Rendezvous*, a journal where various Sealink members work, including protagonist Richard, its deputy head of previews:

> But after all, Richard thought, what did work consist of? Reducing some forthcoming event still further than it reduced itself? Producing a kind of stock of the culture? He would write a hundred and fifty words on a novel, a play, an album, append it to a photograph the size of a postage stamp, and often – in his unhumble opinion – he would have dealt with the subject matter, the themes, better than the original.
>
> This morning's meeting was more than averagely awful. The Editor, whose patter was compounded in equal parts of managementspeak and manipulation, was making it his business to humiliate the editor of the performance section, an unstable man with a burgeoning heroin habit. (33–4)

The narrator's sense of dismissal is self-evident, the motivations of the editor are petty and vindictive; the interrelations of this group are subtended by indifference and hostility, but such negative responses are normalized by them. In his fiction, Self subjects a gamut of other issues – including those of gender, power, time and the very notion of any possibility of a common humanity – to his satirical gaze in order to identify tangible gaps between the ideal (or at least the humanly desirable) and the actual appalling state of things, and in so doing, Self's satires represent a pre-millennial attempt to indicate both the petty and gross errors of humanity, a deviation from a balanced set of relations, although the representation of so much darkness seems to indicate that the restoration of any such equanimity is unlikely. A final rupture emanates as a climax from the set of seemingly mundane, habitual and indifferent social interactions animated by various degraded impulses: erotic desire, career ambition, drug-related hedonism, the craving for minor celebrity, all part of 'the howling vacuity, at the epicentre of Bell's clique' (66). At the end of *The Sweet Smell of Psychosis*, Richard appears to have seduced Ursula, a woman he has desired because he thought she might have been wealthy, and 'to Richard, silly fool, she redeemed him, her, all of the sordidity and torpor, the tragic bathos that he felt sloshing about the Sealink'. However, during sex there comes a moment when Richard attempts to defer his climax and to prolong his pleasure by thinking of Bell, whom Richard finds so disgusting. Shockingly, and in an instant Ursula is literally transformed into Bell, who proceeds to rape Richard, a disturbingly Juvenalian encounter: 'It wasn't Ursula's voice that was urging Richard on any more, it was a deeper, throatier voice, a voice not of abandonment – but of damnation' (89). Self's use of grotesque degradation in this mutative coupling brings to mind Northrop Frye's conjunction of elements allied to satire in *Anatomy of Criticism* (1967):

> Satire demands at least a token fantasy, a content which the reader recognizes as grotesque, and at least an implicit moral standard, the latter being essential in a militant attitude to experience. (7)

Richard's sexual encounter is variously an undermining fantasy, an obliteration of desire and a demonstration of the high degree of ambivalence permeating Self's satirical world, with its instability expressed in terms of an incapacity to sustain identity or sociality, indicating an innate incoherence.

In a general sense, Self's satires are also intensely interested in the breakdown of both societies and individuals and in their depiction of such fractured experiences his fictions foreground the absurd and grotesque, testing what Hayes terms 'the limits of narrative propriety' (4). Self has described his two earlier novellas published together as *Cock & Bull* (1992) as 'an elaborate joke about the failure of narrative' and has openly confessed, in 'Martin Amis', to not being 'interested in character at all. Indeed, I don't even really believe in the whole idea of psychological realism. I see it as dying with the nineteenth-century novel' (*Junk Mail* 381). He has found instead an aesthetic freedom through a series of transgressions and excesses, mobilizing a challenging and often highly intellectual vocabulary to suggest alternative and perhaps unfamiliar modes of representation. According to Self, in 1997, there are 'two ways of getting someone to suspend disbelief. One is to present a fantastic conceit – like Kafka – and the other is to very gradually try and convince somebody of something wildly preposterous' ('News' 52). As a writer who regularly opts for the latter approach (whilst also at times incorporating aspects of the former), he claims that 'my heart lies in a particular kind of fiction, fiction of the alternative world. The great liberty of the fictional writer is to let the imagination out of the traces and see it gallop off over the horizon' ('Penguin Book Authors').

In satire, there are a number of inherent tensions, including that between a position of assumed moral authority and one of hypocrisy if the author falls short of the ideals propounded by their work. Self's literary representations might evidence a sharp consciousness of the vices and flaws inherent to his fellow humans, yet as a literary satirist, he assumes a position of 'Janus-like ambivalence', at once both anti-establishment and prone to drug-fuelled rages while at the same time exhibiting undeniable establishment credentials as an upper-middle-class graduate from a respectable, well-to-do family. These postures or impostures may well be revealing, for as Malcolm Bull says, 'Pretending not-to-be may be equivalent to hiding, but pretending itself seems to involve hiding without actually causing something to be hidden' (9). Hence the co-existence of the two selves, and any concealment or attempt at disguise becomes curiously revelatory, highlighting certain innate contradictions. As Self admitted later in life, 'I am very anti-establishment [...]. But I am also very obviously a middle-aged bourgeois man, so it is difficult to quite maintain the edge' (quoted in Guignery 137). In fact in contrast to his notorious 1990s reputation, and as Rennison concludes, Will Self had been raised 'as much at the heart of the establishment as you can get' (150), at least in intellectual and literary terms. The product of Jewish-American and Anglican parents – a union that produced a sense of a split identity that Self draws on throughout his work – his upbringing was remarkably stable, progressing from Christ's College Grammar School to Oxford to read PPE at Exeter College. However, he quickly became more interested in the drug culture of Oxford than its teaching. He left university with a third-class degree and discovered a personal capacity for self-destruction. Subsequently, during the 1990s, Self plundered what he called in 2011 the 'toxic landscape of carcinogena – the yards of liquor, the sooty furlongs left behind by chased heroin, the miles driven and limped for over a decade to score crack which then scoured its way into my lungs. The prosaically giant haystacks of Virginia tobacco hardly bear mentioning – being, in contrast, merely bucolic' ('There Will Be Blood' 2). He describes his addiction to drugs as a horror that 'cast a long shadow over my life and the lives of my family, and infiltrated my fictive inscape, poisoning its field margins, salting its earth' (3). Interestingly, such breaching of norms also has echoes in Bull's observation that one can position '[t]he identification of the apocalyptic time of mixture with the transgression of taboo' (70–1). Self's rebellion incorporates a desire perhaps to break away from and/or terminate the influences of his youth. However, there is a paradoxical impasse in such impulses for as Maurice Blanchot suggests in *The Writing of the Disaster* (1980) 'We are on the edge of disaster without being able to situate it in the future: it is rather always already in the past, and yet we are on the edge or under the threat, all formulations which would imply the future – that which is yet to come' (1). A sense of the apocalypse and of endism both anticipate aspects of the world that cannot be fully imagined or realized without recourse to past horrors, fusing past and present, incorporating a retrospective impulse, a common strategy in much satirical writing. Throughout the 1990s, away from the page, Self remained a Soho regular, with a propensity for long nights and controversial situations, most especially at the Groucho Club which, as discussed above, he satirized savagely despite being one of its stalwarts. As also indicated earlier, his excesses continued well into the 1990s. After championing, in *Junk Mail*, 'the social and spiritual value of intoxication' (19), later Self spent time in rehab for his addiction to drink and drugs, an experience which formed the basis of his short story 'Ward 9' and his recurring character Dr Zack Busner, which can both be seen as explicit evidence of his later change of approach to narcotics and to creativity. Despite a liberal approach to drug culture in his private life, Self's fictions in the 1990s focus on the trauma, rather than the glamour, of addiction, featuring mostly middle-class characters whose lives are damaged or ruined by experiences with mind or mood altering substances. In 'New Crack City', he reflects on the realities of drugs, of the life of a dealer he knows, of the minutiae of such consumption: 'And you could while away the evening doing pipe after pipe, with an odd chase of smack in between to stop yourself having a heart attack, or a stroke, or the screaming ad dabs' (*Junk Mail* 15). Tembe in 'The Rock of Crack as Big as the Ritz' is upbraided by his brother for his disordered life, his addiction and finally he cannot resist the product, taking a pipe of crack until 'The edges of his vision were fuzzing black with deathly, velvet pleasure' (*Tough, Tough Toys for Tough, Tough Boys* 22). Self uses such fiction to examine the relationship between illness and psychology, repeatedly returning to issues of addiction, illness and morality as paradigms for considering the relation of the individual to contemporary society. Successful satire demands detachment from the world under examination and, in Self's case, involves using reflexive or formally aware aesthetic tactics. He delights in inventing worlds with which to negotiate the relationship between fantasy and reality, and while such satires achieve a distancing from the spirit of his age, his fictions still reflect upon, and engage with, the moral, social and cultural zeitgeist of the times. Self's narratives define themselves against the various social, political and historical values in which his characters are implicated, systems of belief which Self seeks to subvert or undermine, using fantastic conceits and scenarios to communicate alternative perspectives concerning humanity. As will be considered below, across *The Quantity Theory of Insanity, Cock* and *Bull* and *Great Apes*, Self reveals the true horror underlying the apparently (at least initially) ordinary everyday lives of his characters, the disintegrations and transformations represented as a logical manifestation of humanity's own sense of loss and fragmentation at the end of the twentieth century. As Malcolm Bull indicates, the 'Apocalyptic does not merely invert the processes embodied in taboo and sacrifice, it also differs from these practices in that it positively welcomes the intrusion of chaos into the existing cosmos' (78). In his satirical fiction, Self's sense of such potential chaos is insistent and strong throughout, and as Philip Tew observes, 'His satirical vision largely reworks the complexity of his life' (116).

Self's views on the 1990s are well documented. He has described the decade as having 'the merest trace of *maquillage*, daubed across the awful, ravaged face of decadence' ('Ingenious Bubble Wrap' 26). His 1990s writing focuses on themes of regression and degeneration depicted through a hybrid of dreams, nightmares and alternative realities which serve to both highlight and explore the heightened anxiety of his age and offer a mediation on the darkness of civilization at the dawn of the new millennium. All such projections respond to and critique underlying and headline political realities in the public domain. Beginning with Thatcher, high unemployment and riots, and ending in Blair, promises of economic prosperity and 'Cool Britannia', various social, political and economic contexts shape Self's fictions. For instance, while the 1990s are widely regarded as the beginning of a new information age characterized rise of the Internet, Self's work interrogates any concomitant sense of this as representing progress, suggesting rather that humanity stood on the brink of degeneration at the turn of the century. Self's fictions of the 1990s mobilize satire to point towards residing discourses of doubt and discomfort and to reveal spectacles of difference and tension within a wider pre-millennial anxiety. For Self, 'a culture lost in a hopeless fugue' is the 'defining characteristic of the 1990s'. As 'a 24.7 celebration of sexuality and death', he has argued that the 1990s 'existed in dyadic relationships with two other decades, the 1980s – for which they were a rerun with knobs on, sort of: 1980s * – and the 1890s' ('Ingenious Bubble Wrap' 26). Highlighting a fin de siècle sentiment which sees in the decadence of the age a pronounced awareness of an unavoidably approaching end, his work offers the imaginative worlds of fictive creation as a renewed means of comprehending the looming unknown, potentially offering a social role for fiction in the face of 'endism'.

If the 1990s fictions of Will Self are grounded in this sense of 'endism', of a conclusion marked out by uncertainty and apprehension, the year 2000 appeared to mark a crucial turning point for society and for contemporary literature, amid doubts concerning what, if anything, the new millennium might bring. A host of disturbing social indicators culminated in a broader cultural millennial anxiety, whose symptoms in Britain included declining voter turnout, decaying levels of trust in government, in cultural institutions and even in other people, a widening gap between rich and poor and a rise in the number of the clinically depressed. There was a much-hyped swelling of millennial anxiety concerning myriad doom-laden projections related to 'Y2K' also referred to as the 'millennium bug', a problem for both digital and non-digital documentation and data storage situations resulting from the practice of abbreviating a four-digit year to simply two digits. As Jessica Tinklenberg deVega notes:

> Millions of dollars were spent in the U.S. alone to correct this programming problem by reprogramming software to use a four-digit year code. The programmers who made the coding adjustment expressed more concern about the growing public hysteria than any of the potential glitches...
>
> The Y2K bug itself, then was not an insurmountable technical obstacle but the portrayal of the issue in the press was often over-hyped. (149–50)

As deVega adds 'Soon, at least in popular imagination, Y2K became synonymous with apocalyptic devastation' (150). There were apocalyptic biblical prophecies, proliferating cults and militia groups and metastasizing religious and ethnic conflicts. Generally, the anticipation of the year 2000 became a source of fear as well as a time for hope and optimism about the future. As Malcolm Bradbury argued earlier in the decade:

> Industrial pollution surges, environmental terrors reign, and plagues and earthquakes spread. Our pleasures have become our pains: our food and drink, our sex and smoking, all threaten to injure us. We have new visions of choking, collapsed, crime and drug ridden cities, wasted landscapes, fundamentalist conflicts and genocidal wars, shrinking ice-caps, the widening of the ozone hole... seen from this turning point, our century is most likely to seem uniquely terrible, less the age of visionary hopes and fantastic utopian prospects... more a time of terrors, crimes, political disasters and technological horrors. (87)

Fukuyama also reflected on the underlying fear of an atavistic cultural failure: 'The possibility of the cataclysmic destruction of our modern, technological civilization and its sudden return to barbarism has been a constant subject of science fiction' (82). And of course this very genre had been of great influence on Self in his teens, and especially J.G. Ballard, whose work helped shape his writing, both influences confirmed when interviewed by Philip Tew in December 2006 (108). Self's fiction during the 1990s focused on the experiences and thoughts of individuals in such a seemingly chaotic and apocalyptic world facing imminent threat. Reshaping recognizable reality, Self's narratives distort matters of scale, offering uncanny images of the formerly recognizable, using literature as a diffracting lens through which to project new satirical perspectives on science, art and the nature of narrative itself. Much maligned by Hayes for his 'lumpy' (4) and by Leith 'abstruse vocabulary', Self's prose style has been likened by Finney to '[Martin] Amis going cold turkey with a thesaurus'. Valentine Cunningham too has suggested that, as Amis's 'satirical heir', Self goes beyond even the thematic and linguistic grotesqueries of his predecessor (412). In the *Guardian*, Julian Evans reflected in a feature on the author: 'Self leaves no adjective unsaid, no metaphor unturned' (12). The author's famously verbose style even won his first novel, *My Idea of Fun*, the 1993 '*Sunday Times* Purple Prose Award' for outstandingly pompous or pretentious verbosity. Such verbal extremes extend his narratives beyond the evident autobiographical elements, despite being grounded in his own experiences. Both his satirical prose and vast 'lexical palette' ('Martin Amis' 401) have been heavily criticized, but Self defends this style as key to his literary approach. In interview with Lynn Barber, Self has argued that his reliance on a thesaurus is not unusual, since 'a writer saying he doesn't use one is like a mechanic saying he doesn't use a socket set' (17). As Walsh indicates, arguably Self's hybrid of journalese, high metaphors and metatextual references seems designed to 'obscure rather than to illuminate' (28). However, such an extremity or exaggeration serves not only as an innate quality of his style, but effectively captures the heightened emotional and physical states of flux that characterize his satirical writings. And, as Jeremy Scott notes, this 'is Self's trademark: a prodigious, eclectic and often obscure vocabulary' (175). Additionally, Scott suggests that the transatlantic nature of both Self's style and his influences mean that 'in Self's work, the epithet "English" seems to take on the tenor of a term of abuse' (152). For satirical purposes, Self situates himself as an outsider looking in on our absurdities with which, nevertheless, he is still complicit.

Raised in East Finchley, Self is repeatedly drawn back to London as a backdrop to his alternative fictional worlds. If part of the capital can be classified as 'Amiscountry', there is almost certainly a case for Soho and the suburbs of North London being classified as 'Selfcountry' ('Martin Amis: The Misinformation' 321). Certainly, such suburbs are of particular significance to Self's vision of London and are often related to a particular satire on city life that partakes of the potentially repetitive lives of those dwelling in suburbia. Interrogating this relationship between humans and space, Self uses London as his muse, mediating physical and imaginative topographies of the city. In a conversation with J.G. Ballard reproduced in *Junk Mail*, Self confesses to being 'a writer who is very attached to the idea of place', one who views the idea of writing about locations away from the capital as akin to 'pulling a tablecloth from under your imagination' ('J.G. Ballard' 353–4). Loosely aligning himself with a field of 'psychogeographers', Self's fictive topographies 'are wholly mutated out of the ones that we really occupy' (quoted in McCarthy). Offering a tight focus on events specifically produced by, and situated in London, his work begins at this psychological and geographical 'centre' to decentralize and explore alternative perceptions of the city. Across Self's work, characters traverse the city to explore its topography as a metaphor of their own inner traumas. Defamiliarizing the most familiar space in order to satirize our relationship with it and our practices and routines within it, his fictions explore the relationship between landscape and the people that occupy it to focus on contemporary disconnections from urban living and alienation in the modern city.

Self's first collection, *The Quantity Theory of Insanity*, uses the capital city as a site for six short stories interconnected by repeated characters, events and locations. Exploring anxieties about revulsion, attraction, psychiatry, civilization, death and mortality, the dominance of the first person establishes a sense of personal confession and reflection which augments the topics under discussion. Self's fictions are fuelled by the conviction that, as Self expresses it, 'writing is about expressing something new and exploring the form in new ways' (quoted in Murray). Self's short stories function to establish ideas later reproduced, and in some cases developed, by his longer works. Such a technique enables Self to author sustained satires employing recognized characters who react and respond to changing contexts which mirror the contemporary world. The interrelated themes and the recurrence of character-types are part of an arrangement of his short stories' collections in a particular fashion where each story is not only a narrative in its own right, when considered as a whole the various stories also constitute fractured, disjointed novel-like structures. The role of form in Self's repetition, revisiting and construction of a fictional parallel reality was recognized by fellow 1990s novelist Nick Hornby who described *The Quantity Theory of Insanity* 'as not so much stories as a series of feature articles on an alternative world' (quoted in 'Penguin Book Authors'). Self's oeuvre to date can be considered a kind of *roman-fleuve*, a set of independent yet interrelated fictional works with reappearing characters that work around a set of distinct themes and concerns. As Self reflects, 'writing can be kind of an addiction' (quoted in Heller 149), and throughout his fiction, he returns to the same locations, protagonists and concerns to enhance and enrich his satirical representations.

The first collection opens with a story that has come to define Self's approach to fiction. 'The North London Book of the Dead' is narrated by a middle-aged man whose mother's death involves her relocation to an afterlife in the London suburbs as part of an extended community of the suburban un-dead. The story proposes immortality as a concept perhaps more frightening than death, one which, in the fictional world of Will Self, simply involves relocation to the leafier parts of London. Across Self's oeuvre, death overshadows everything and its imminence can be felt across each story in this collection. Exploring bereavement and a fascination with the darker side of stasis, 'The North London Book of the Dead' creates an alarming juxtaposition from which Self satirizes the concept of an afterlife by allowing it to intrude upon and likening it to present-day reality. Proposing the afterlife as a form of 'deathocracy... a kind of self-help group run by the dead themselves' (Self in McCarthy, 2001), the tedium of the ultimate establishes an initial interest in endism which is developed in his subsequent work.

Read in the context of Self's wider oeuvre, *The Quantity Theory of Insanity* plays a vital role in establishing locations (including London's suburbs, hospital wards and riverside spaces), characters and concepts (such as Dr Busner and the Urbororo) and approaches to narrative that underpin his later work. Like the patients in the collection's Chekhovian 'Ward 9', readers quickly become aware that Self's characters are not active agents but merely respond to events around or beyond them. They do not evidence free will and even though the presence of choice is regularly highlighted – his characters can be dead or alive, sober or high, patient or doctor – they often choose to remain in limbo, trapped by an inability to commit to a single role or state. As the collection immediately establishes, even the boundaries between the living and the dead are not immune from transgression or satirical derision in the hands of Will Self.

Identifying in death an 'inconsistent iconisation of violence and sensuality' (Self in Gloer 15), Self adopts a heterogeneous approach to death in his writings. He has said that 'What excites me... is to disturb the reader's fundamental assumptions. I want to make them feel that certain categories within which they are used to perceiving the world are unstable' (Self in Gloer 15). One example is where death as an immutable ending or beginning of a spiritual journey is challenged in *How the Dead Live*, with its contradictory title and its parodic premise of additional suburbs of London (that most of the living fail to notice) populated by the departed with a literal presence, from which areas some of the dead even commute to their paying jobs elsewhere. As Magdalena Maczynska says, the novel relies on its 'uncanny urban topography' (68) amidst which protagonist Lily Bloom lives in Dulston (only marginally reworking the real Dalston), an 'eerie district' (70) to where she has moved after death. As Maczynska adds:

> Throughout *How the Dead Live*, Self develops a sustained critique of the spatial and ideological structures of twentieth-century suburban life, denouncing its failed communality, class isolationism, oppressive patriarchal regime, and infantilizing consumerism through a playful exploration of fantasized London topographies. (70)

Satire depends on the solidity of certain underlying cultural assumptions, against which actual things and events from the reworked (often exaggerated) narrative reality are contrasted negatively. Thus, with readers at least implicitly depending upon shared notions of humanity, assumed approaches to life and death and a normative commonality of experience, Self challenges them, disrupting such comfortable visions of reality in his fictions, his reworked cityscapes offering a critique, based on alternative, often seemingly counter-factual perspectives and judgements. Why, for instance, in a huge city like London could not an afterlife be led among the living, simply unnoticed in the enormity and dullness of suburban life? And, in a curious sense nothing could evoke the anti-apocalyptic – which validates that which it negates – more than death. Drawing upon Hegel, as Malcolm Bull says, 'if the finite excludes the infinite, then the infinite too has a limit, with the consequence that it is, by definition, not infinite, but finite' (103). Self's novel dramatizes such a paradox in terms of life and death *and* also evokes the inherent fearfulness necessary to alterity and loss, for as Blanchot notes 'The death of the Other: a double death, for the Other is death already, and weighs upon me like an obsession with death' (19).

At the heart of Self's satirical working of the relation between fictional and real worlds is the idea of transformation. Concerned with the breakdown of the human form, Self's fiction explores mutations – of people, psyches, sensibilities, attitudes, gender, ideas and landscapes – to energize narrative with a new, satirical power. Self claims that 'metamorphosis is the key condition; we are always in a state of change and flux, and it's really only received constraints in our language that try to block that from us and straight-jacket us into definable states' (Self in McCarthy). Confessing that 'transmogrification, particularly horrible metamorphosis, tends to lie at the core of most of what I write' (Self in McCarthy), Self explores distortions of scale and elements of the fantastic to present a seemingly irreconcilable, intelligent and visceral re-visioning of society. Representing change and alternatives via the grotesque, parody and metamorphosis, Self's invention lies in his use of satire to illuminate the fragile and fluid boundaries between reality and fiction, the word and the world. As Richard Bradford notes, 'Self's trademark is to constantly invite us into an act of recognition while almost simultaneously dispersing it' (51).

Mobilizing the underused form of the novella as a convenient mid-ground between the formal discipline of the short story and the lengthier novel and exercising its satirical potential to comment on the novel form, Self followed the success of *The Quantity Theory of Insanity* in 1992 with his paired novellas, *Cock* and *Bull*. In *The Quantity Theory of Insanity* Self progresses from the boundaries between life and death, re-examining that final, yet most basic and familiar form of mutation, to gender and sexuality in *Cock* and *Bull*, where he uses the form of the novella to offer paired satires on gender and power relations at the turn of the century. As Bradford notes of both protagonists, 'Before their anatomical transformations occur Dan and Carol are presented very effectively as normal individuals, average to the point of cliché' (51). *Cock*'s protagonist Carol is initially established as a passive female in an unfulfilling relationship. She is submissive, seemingly without agency and at the mercy of events around her in her job, family and relationship. Indeed, it is Carol's propensity 'always to take the line of least resistance in all that she ever said, or did, or even thought, that gives this story its peculiar combination of cock and bull' (*Cock and Bull* 4). The growth of a small pubic mound begins to change this behaviour and leads to her engaging in more masculine behaviour. Significantly, Carol becomes aware of this change in the domestic setting of her dining room when 'she sawed too vigorously at her M&S chicken kiev' and 'a spurt of butter marinade shot from the ruptured fowl and fell, appropriately enough, like jism on Dan's crotch' (10). This comical and symbolic ejaculation foreshadows Carol's ultimate transformation from domestic cook into sexualized killer.

Satirizing the restricted gender role and repetitive, limited existence Carol occupies as a woman in the beginning of the novella, Self exposes his protagonist to a total metamorphosis. Rejecting her 'cramped and pedestrian sex life' (10–11), Carol begins to collect caged birds, has sex with a woman, buys a dildo and 'masturbated for the first time' (24). Embracing a liberated and performative sexuality, Carol's cock mutates from 'a tree growing in a gulley' (28) to a 'miniature volcanic column' (29), culminating in Chapter Five's titular descriptor 'It' (51). Carol does DIY, takes up driving lessons (55) and notices that she is 'getting more aggressive' (57) but also 'empowered... she felt her status as a potentially effective agent' (69). This power reaches a pinnacle when she crumbles cantharides into the drinks of her partner Dan and his friend 'Dave 2' and anally rapes them. By this point, a man is simply 'an empty thing, a vessel, a field upon which the majestic battle may rage' (112). The reader is asked to accept that the growth of a cock 'somehow *made* Carol aggressive, made her a rapist' (113). The transformation of Carol into a rapist was, claims Self, 'a very facile or simple-minded enjoinder or endorsement of the early seventies feminist argument that anybody with a penis is a potential rapist; I was just taking that to its logical conclusion' (Self in McCarthy). Self claims to have the 'ability to actually feel disgusted with sex' (*Junk Mail* 418) and recalls that he originally 'wrote *Cock* out of rage at the involuntary character of my own sexual arousal' (*Junk Mail* 422). Where it does occur in his work, sex is a form of exploitation, an act of theft or manipulation inextricably bound up with power. As bodies mutate both physically and metaphorically, so too does Self's fiction, using literary form and genre to satirize gender roles and role performance in contemporary society.

In an interview in 1995, Self has stated that he 'wrote most of the first draft [of *Cock* and *Bull*] in about ten days' (*Junk Mail* 410). Bearing a clear debt to the *Metamorphosis* of both Kafka and Ovid (the first chapter of *Bull* even borrows from Ovid's title), the novellas offer transformation as a problematic experience. Opening with quotations from Byron's *Don Juan*, the first novella establishes an early expectation of the labyrinthine narrative to come. In *Cock*, Self's narrative takes the form of two competing voices which vie for dominance. Only at the end of the novella is it revealed that the 'don' who relates Carol's tale is actually an elderly version of Carol, who goes on to viciously rape his fellow male passenger while holding a knife to his throat. The interplay of this female (in possession of a cock) and male voice forms a dialogue that centres on conflict and makes the reader radically question the reliability of the narration provided. In reading both narratives, Emma Parker has argued that: 'Will Self appropriates the Lawrentian conceit of cocksure women and hensure men to explore what he describes as "this strange situation we find ourselves in at the moment in Western societies", a situation of "utter confusion, with gender roles flung around on the ground of the id like pick-up sticks"' (229–30).

In *Cock*, the voice of the don and the passenger break the narrative into fragmented sections. The don furthers this fragmentation, '*addressing*' the passenger '*personally, directly and not simply as a unitary audience*' (76), in order to detach from the voyeurism of his/her mutation. Staging the tale as a '*performance*' (44), the uncomfortable intimacy of the don and passenger encourages reflection upon the role of the author and the nature of narrative itself. The don is used to wryly reflect on 'the value of good narrative [...]. [T]he positive values of storytelling' (102). Effectively combined with such self-reflection, the narrative offers its own potential interpretation through strategies such as aggressive warnings: 'I hope you aren't deriving any signifiers or symbols from Carol's penis. I hope you aren't undertaking some convoluted analysis of this story in your sick sheeny mind. [...] Only a faggot would do such a thing' (105). Self also includes a self-conscious satire on fiction as a genre: 'If you don't watch it some purely local story, some commuting tale, will mow you down, cleave you in two, finally separate your dialogue from your characterisation' (101). Effectively, the don offers a jaded warning to the literary critic. Under strict instruction that one ought not 'go looking for the hidden meaning' or 'try to pick away at the surface of things, pretending to find some "psychological" sub-structure' (90–1), the role of the reader is undermined to offer a scathing perspective on the relationship between writers and literary critics. Refusing his reduction to an 'amusing character, an oddity, a type!' (55), the standard font and direct speech of the don are fragmented by the italicized reflections of the passenger. As their literal and metaphorical journeys progress, the passenger reports that the don was *'metamorphosising into someone else altogether'* (71). Noting that the *'don was playing with himself'* (128), the passenger predicts the climax of the story and the don's frantic excitement as Carol is revealed to be his *'fictional alter-ego'* (140). After the don attacks the passenger he flees leaving his victim in fear of contacting the police in case they 'conclude that you were asking for it. [...] [Y]ou wanted to be an audience. [...] That is what you get if you sit there like a prat, listening to a load of cock ... and bull' (145). Echoing concerns usually reserved for female rape victims, Self reverses gender roles and expectations as well as mocking the desire for narrative closure, surprising his captive readership before allowing the narrator to disappear into the night without explanation.

While *Cock* claims that a woman's body is 'Totally unlike a man's body, which never changes, which is static and lifeless' (35), its sister novella *Bull* counters this claim. *Bull* opens with a reference to Tennyson's poem 'Maud' (1855) which, with its connotations of sexual maturity, secrets and death, functions as a chilling warning of events to come. At the beginning of the novella, male protagonist Bull is athletic, well-built and defensive of his gender identity. In contrast to the narrative complexities of *Cock, Bull*'s story is told in the third person through a broadly linear plot, broken occasionally through rhetorical questions. Beginning without preamble, the novella's opening line immediately informs us that 'Bull, a large and heavyset young man, awoke one morning to find that while he had slept he had acquired another primary sexual characteristic: to wit, a vagina' (149). This opening line clearly alludes to the opening of Franz Kafka's novella *Metamorphosis* (1915), and its description of Gregor Samsa's transformation into 'Ungeziefer' (often translated as vermin). Whereas, however, Kafka's story of an impossible transformation makes radically uncertain the relation between the fictional world and the real world and so leaves the reader estranged and disorientated, Self's satirical intent points always back to the world that we know, familiar if disgusting and wrong. Jonathan Swift's 'glass, wherein beholders do generally discover everybody's face but their own' provokes wry laughter, not estrangement.

Bull is pursued by Alan, a doctor whose medical care of Bull extends beyond the treatment room. Lust makes Alan view 'Bull-as-a-woman; Bull as inside, rather than outside' (230) and together they have 'contorted sex' (302). Although his own physical state remains intact, Alan is not immune to mutation and transformation. His awareness of the London landscape evolves across the novella until he experiences a Ballardian vision when:

> Alan saw for the first time that the line of the flyover formed the stick shape of an enormous woman. [...]
> Alan's car was charging like a runaway vibrator, towards the very crotch of the flyover. Alan appreciated that he was about to penetrate the woman-figure with 170 brake horsepower. He felt just fine. [...]
> He revelled in it!' (242–43).

Faced with the ultimate revelation that London is entirely comprised of 'cunts' (249), Bull is left to reflect that 'It was patently absurd to describe the city's architecture, as Bull had heard the art critic at *Get Out!* do, as "phallic". The church spires, the war memorials, the clock towers, the skyscrapers [...] they were all terminally irrelevant, ultimately spare pricks. The real lifeblood of the city, Bull now saw, was transported in and out of quintillions of vaginas' (249–50).

Trapped in such an 'ugly knot of revelation' (223), Bull struggles 'to make sense of his own identity' (228) and 'a new loss of self, a new *petit mort*' (229). In this horrific orgasm, Bull adopts the role of a passive, emotional dependent. Dismissed from his job as a reviewer of cabaret for a barely fictionalized version of London listings magazine *Time Out* and replaced by his aggressive female friend Juniper, Bull is repeatedly left asking 'Who am I?' (282). Rejecting his male friends – feeling 'oppressed by their self-assurance, their seemingly unquestioning masculinity',

250) – instead, he has earlier found solace in Ramona, a transsexual prostitute. This 'He/She' (262), an ex-welder from Wearside, possesses an intense Northern masculinity that constitutes the ultimate reversal of gender roles. The novella concludes with a claim to unoriginality. Declaring the tale an 'everyday story […]. There's nothing new under this red dwarf emotional sun of ours' (298), it ends in conventional narrative closure – Bull establishing a home in the quiet domestic setting of San Francisco with a son Kenneth, the result of his affair with Alan, and who is, ironically, 'popular with the local kids, very much one of the boys' (310).

The twin novellas *Cock* and *Bull* represent gender and sexuality as forms of power which Carol and Bull master as a result of their respective mutations. While Carol finds herself empowered and inclined to consume without morality, Bull finds himself crippled by a new emotional awareness and responsibility. Where the *petit mort* of orgasm signals an escape from frustration for Carol, it marks a loss of identity for Bull. Indeed, for all these narratives appear to promote liberation from strict gender roles via metamorphosis, they are actually rather inhibited, excessively absurd and, like the pained stand-up comic who berates Bull, they try a little bit too hard. Self claims that he has not re-read this 'dicktych' (Self in McCarthy) since he wrote it, and at times, the novellas do feel dated, especially in respect to their polemic representations of gender and power. Marked by tales of impotent individuals, forced to stand by and watch or be subjected to aggressive acts, the two novellas, like much of Self's work, concern themselves with the grotesque, exaggerated to the point of the absurd, to reveal profound tensions in contemporary culture. As Rennison observes, 'All the strange, metamorphosed couplings Self imagines – and describes in unsqueamish detail – might be considered pornographic but are played as black farce' (151). Significantly, the novellas do not offer solutions to the debates with which they engage. Instead, these extended cock and bull stories, tales of nonsense – or in an alternative expression of the phrase, plain 'bullshit" – actualize transformation and mutation to enact change. As satires, they point to the contemporary social norms behind such inversions to suggest the need for change.

Self's use of a wildly preposterous world fuelled by the physical alteration of states perhaps reached a climax in Self's *Great Apes*. Valentine Cunningham has noted the 'extensive simianizing' (407) of twentieth-century satirical fiction:

> Monkey business is the modern satirists' usual trade, their regular trope. Modern satire takes up residence on a planet of the apes. Humans have turned everywhere into monkeys – a degree zero of the human animal, devoid of spiritual life and intellectual worth, a parody of civility and culture, repellent, charmless, disgusting. (405)

Adding to the power of this 'regular trope', during the 1990s, several major news stories concerning animals captured the British imagination. In 1992, Damian Hirst – a key member of the yBas (Young British Artists) – exhibited his now infamous work *The Physical Impossibility of Death in the Mind of Someone Living*, a tiger shark suspended in a formaldehyde filled vitrine, at the Saatchi Gallery, London. In 1996, attention turned again to matters of humanity and evolution in the ground-breaking genetic cloning of 'Dolly the Sheep'. Echoes of these events can be detected in Self's approach to the relationship between humans and animals in *Great Apes* (1997) which explores an ethological crisis centred around the intrinsic connection between humans and animals. Ethology, an offshoot of zoology, became popular in the 1990s as a means of understanding human behaviour. Claiming that humans are remarkably like animals in respect of reproduction, workplace behaviour and recreational habits, ethnologists propose that through appreciating this revelation, humans can understand their ancestors and the mechanisms of evolution that led to the final, superior position of humanity. Ethology therefore not only seeks to illuminate political and social interactions but re-frame them, to throw new light on the human condition.

The central conceit of *Great Apes* is that the evolutionary teleology of existence has been reversed in some way, and in Self's universe, apes have been triumphant in the evolutionary game. As Paul Maliszewski suggests, 'this novel is about boundaries and the perception that creates them' (238). Self integrates transgressions and mutations of boundaries both in thematic and formal terms, with a surprising intertextual dimension. Self reanimates and develops previously human characters and settings drawn from earlier fiction into his absurd new parallel simian universe to great comic effect. With humans decentred in favour of the evolutionary dominance of apes, Self takes a satirical swipe at anthropocentricism. Opening with an epigraph from Kafka's 'Report on the Academy', Self situates his own narrative within a long-established tradition of literary interventions on the subject. Elsewhere, references to the *Planet of the Apes* – a 1974 television series, which drew on a 1968 Hollywood film adaptation of an original French novel published in 1963 – and to Swift's bestial Yahoos from *Gulliver's Travels* (1726) foreground a cultural heritage of questioning the assumed superiority of the human race. Setting humanism against animal rights, Self takes this conceit as far as it will go to draw attention to the assumptive nature of anthropocentrism. In his novel of hierarchy, the most shocking and satirical revelation is how far down the dominant order humanity has fallen.

Self's ape-run vision of contemporary London presents a world in which humans have swapped roles with apes and become 'domesticated' beasts 'employed for scientific purposes'. 'Held in large compounds, isolated, diseased, in pain, malnourished' (*Great Apes* x), humans are cast as wild creatures whose primeval cry 'Fuuuuuuckoooooffff- Fuuuuuuckoooooffff' (484) is indicative of their declining evolutionary potential. Mocked for their 'primitive forms of ideology' including mating for life (xi) – a practice derided on the grounds that it offers 'no genetic advantage' (xii) – humans are presented as 'worthy of some small measure of our sympathy' (x). Kept in zoos, circuses or PG Tips adverts (227), perhaps the ultimate cultural inversion of the novel, humans are relegated to the role of beasts while apes drive cars, staff hospitals and run a country unsettlingly similar to the United Kingdom during the 1990s. Self's regular cast of fictional characters, including Simon Dykes and Dr Zack Busner, are not immune from this satirical transformation, translated here into their simian-counter-selves. Although perhaps this trope of inversion begins to become vexing when extended across several hundred pages, it is generally successful in attempting to create an imaginative space that, despite its absurd and frightening scenario, retains enough elements of reality to anchor Self's criticisms in the real world.

The opening chapters of *Great Apes* offer a subtle and suggestively satirical focus on animalistic aspects of the human world, perhaps even human nature. As Maliszewski notes, 'what the world of chimps grants Self is a new perspective on the human behaviour' (238). For artist Simon Dykes, even in his pre-ape state, 'intimacy was defined by sexual interaction' (13), by 'Bodies dragged by thin shanks through thick mud, bodies smashed and pulverised, throats slashed red, given free tracheotomies so that the afflicted could breathe their last' (16) before intercourse. Vanessa, an art critic Simon encounters at a gallery, is a classic Selfian female, an idiot whose ignorance of ethnologist Levi-Strauss is flaunted for the benefit of knowing male nods. Simon regards Vanessa as an alien, sending 'one psychic probe into her anus, the other into her left nostril. He turned her anatomy inside out, sockwise, and in the process quite forgot who the fuck she was, what the fuck she has said up until now, and so told her' (6).

As Parker indicates, Self has been criticized for his blatant sexism and for reproducing older, sexist views of men and women, a view subject to critical distain (236–37), a perspective she challenges. Across his fiction, Self could be seen as traversing the divide between naughty schoolboy and blatant misogynist, tempering his limited and problematic characterizations with 'groaningly cheap jokes' (Leith 28) about the differences between men and women. Taking *Cock and Bull* as a starting point, however, for Parker 'Self offers a satirical deconstruction of gender and sexual difference' (230). Despite this, in *Great Apes*, Selfian gender relations reach a new low as female apes are immediately subordinated to their males counterparts, who do not even 'discard the morning paper before effecting penetration' (40). Drugs fuel a similar primal promiscuity for Simon in human-form, making him 'feel like penetrating everybody in sight... a conga-line of copulation, where a cock-thrust here would produce a cunt-throb way over there' (11). Simon calls his girlfriend Sarah 'my little monkey' (51), noting 'her imperfections... the too thin lips... pointed canine teeth' (83) and her 'covering of coarse blonde fur' (89), descriptions actualized in the subsequent transformation to her ape-self. Propositioned by suitors at a bar in the human-world, Sarah reflects that the 'men were like apes... attempting to impress her by waving and kicking about in a display of mock potency' (18). Culminating in Simon's vision of King Kong attacking a busy Oxford Circus (31), this early focus on 'the darkness at the edge of the sun, and these bulletins of disembodiment, discorporation updates' (16) sows the seeds of transitions to come. Simon's 'series of modern apocalyptic paintings' (29), inspired by the apocalyptic visions of nineteenth-century painter John Martin, foreshadow his own descent into chaos, the end of the human world and the birth of the planet of the (great) apes.

After the interjection of a chapter introducing an alternative ape society, Self's narrative returns to the human, culminating in a drug-induced dream in which Sarah transforms into an ape who swings through the trees surrounded by phallic imagery. Simon awakes to a world in which reverse Darwinism has taken effect to produce a mirror image of evolutionary progress. After this point, the novel is situated solely in an alternative reality where Simon's 'human delusion' (231) is blamed on his drug induced psychosis and he is sectioned in an ape-run hospital. Ape society liberates the boundaries of the human, presenting Simon with a culture in which racism and misogyny underpin social interactions and where incest, paedophilia and (literal) arse licking are accepted models of behaviour. Thrown into this 'ghastly planet of the apes world' (473), Simon reflects that he 'had gone to sleep with his human lover and when he awoke the following morning she was a chimpanzee and so was everyone else in the world' (94). Identified by the media-savy Selfian regular Dr Busner as a 'great ape' (131), Simon proves an ideal 'case to manipulate' (99). Long forgotten for the 'doctoral excesses of *The Quantity Theory of Insantiy*, with which he had been associated' (34), Self's recurring character Dr Busner might look like an ape but is otherwise unchanged. He is interested in Dyke's case solely because other 'case histories' of patients like Simon have 'made great copy and highly entertaining television' (36).

The novel finally reveals that Simon's psychosis of humanity is not caused by his apocalyptic paintings, feelings towards women or his children, but simply by 'a satirical trope' (493) imposed by its author. Focussing on the 'numinous dividing line between man and chimp' (xiii), *Great Apes* suggests that humanity itself is a form of psychosis, that all anthropocentrism is madness, and that it is only when Simon accepts his true nature that he is cured. This satire is based on a normative position that implies that humans should be more than apes, yet the similarities across the novel are too frequent to be dismissed. Simon is left to reflect, 'What, after all, were the apes, if not distorted versions of the body?' (223). An omniscient narrator guides a narrative that attempts to underpin this unhinged reality with misanthropic humour and parody to offer a satire on mankind's distorted relationship with the human body and evolutionary superiority. The function of this satire is to convince the reader to identify the behaviour highlighted and align themselves with the satirist in condemning it and considering alternatives to those perceived by humanity at the turn of the century.

Self's 1990s fiction delights in dismantling fundamental binary oppositions, exploring a divided self through the transformation of variously the living to the dead, female to male, male to female and man to ape. Literally working out the internal beast, his texts reverse humanity's place in the evolutionary cycle and, in doing so, invert the dominant narratives of the age. Complicating the concept of accurate representation, these devolutionary scenarios suggest that the true horror of his 1990s fictions lies in their revelation of the terrifying familiarity at the heart of 'otherness'. In *Great Apes*, Dr Busner describes Simon Dykes's condition as 'the *Zeitgeist*...fused with psychosis' (325). In many ways, this diagnosis might be applied as an effective description of Self's early oeuvre. His 1990s fictions combine irony and satire to engage with a perceived decadence of 1990s Britain as it edged towards the new millennium. Trialling new forms of imaginative narration to reflect the 'endism' inherent to this era, his fiction evinces a millennial anxiety in which a sense of a serio-comic entertainment is interwoven with stark truths to create alternative perspectives. Describing this approach as a 'kind of miscegenation, a kind of rubbing up against the traditional categories of English literary concern' ('Penguin Book Authors'), Self reveals the capacity of his fictions to draw upon satirical traditions of the past to fuel new critiques of *fin de millennial* society. Filled with polemical statements and archetypal profiles rather than subtle characterization and plot development, his writings from this period can be viewed as a kind of '"movement" fiction...a book where you work consciously to unite your individual voice – in some way – with the *Zeitgeist*' ('Martin Amis' 405).

Self's writings not only look beneath the surface of reality but also expose familiar aspects of our world, rendering them uncomfortable, shining a newly illuminating light to – as Coleridge commented of Wordsworth – 'awaken the mind's attention from the lethargy of custom' (Coleridge in Jackson, 122). By exposing the shibboleths of the familiar world, Self's prose suggests at least obliquely a more logical and fairer worldview, although not an easy one, as he admits in 'In Praise of Pessimism': 'We do not arrive at any idea of what is best for the collective unless we are prepared to seize the day and practise it on our own behalf. Most mature individuals understand what this means in respect of themselves – it's just all those feckless others that they don't trust to act appropriately.' By making people laugh, in a dark fashion, whilst making them interrogate their beliefs, Self's texts reveal structures of power and the inherent flaws in the social order. Turning a critical focus both within and outwardly, Self explores that 'Gotterdammerung of periodicity' – or disastrous conclusion to events – that was the 1990s, to suggest certain potential trajectories for humanity at the end of the millennium: transformation, regression or death. As Self's character Bull reminds us, in 'this world where all are mad and none are bad, we all know that the finger points backwards' (266), while the paired novella, *Cock*, reflects that 'as the cock of progress thrusts through social form and change, it is at once and the same time taking itself from behind' (74). Self imagines alternative worlds in which change occurs through mutation rather than by deploying any sense of progress or teleology. These are mutative transformations but may be regressive, atavistic. The reader is left uncertain as to overriding value of such changes. His characters are altered both physically and psychologically, moving from life to death, madness to sanity, from an active demeanour to a passive one, male to female and even human to animal. As Valentine Cunningham reflects, 'Satire does not do happy endings. Its wastings and trashings go on irreversibly [...]. Badness is unalleviated' (419). In Self's fiction with such fundamental transformations, identity and notions of the self are altered, various boundaries are reached while others are constructed. These transformations in an age obsessed with difference and a diversity of identities also alert the reader to what Malcolm Ball labels the 'primary factors of experience' (51), a set of universal ways of being. Self's work during this final decade of the millennium deploys satire to interrogate contexts central to and familiar in terms of the overall trajectory of post-war British literature that includes issues of identity, morality, gender, class, social change, addiction, the media and threats to the nuclear family within the universal framework of the experiential. Marked by the particular social, economic and political conditions of the 1990s, these fictions respond to a series of problems – of lives, ideas, relationships, of sanity and identity – that are the coordinates of new satirical psychogeographies of mutation and transgression, suggesting potential pathways leading away from the perceived 'endism' of the twentieth century, readying his readers for the uncertainties of the twenty-first.

Works Cited

Barber, Lynn. 'Self Control'. *The Observer* (11 June 2000): 17.
Blanchot, Maurice. *The Writing of the Disaster*. Trans. Ann Smock. Lincoln and London: University of Nebraska Press, 1995 [1980].
Bradbury, Malcolm. *The Modern British Novel*. London: Penguin, 1993.
Bradford, Richard. *The Novel Now: Contemporary British Fiction*. Malden and Oxford: Blackwell, 2007.
Bull, Malcolm. *Seeing Things Hidden: Apocalypse, Vision and Totality*. London and New York: Verso, 1999.
Cunningham, Valentine. 'Twentieth-Century Fictional Satire'. In *A Companion to Satire*. Ed. Ruben Quintero. Oxford: Blackwell, 2007, 400–33.
deVega, Jessica Tinklenberg. *Guesses, Goofs & Prophetic Failures: What to Think When the World Doesn't End*. Nashville: Thomas Nelson, 2012.
Evans, Julian. 'A Severed Neck'. *The Guardian*, Features (14 September 1992): 12.
Evans, Lloyd. 'Self Abuse'. *The Spectator* (31 January 2004), http://www.spectator.co.uk/essays/11875/self-abuse.thtml
Finney, Brian. 'The Sweet Smell of Excess: Will Self's Fiction, Bataille and Transgression', 2006, http://www.csulb.edu/~bhfinney/selfsweetsmell.html (accessed 1 May 2013).
Frye, Northrop. *Anatomy of Criticism: Four Essays*. Princeton: Princeton University Press, 1967.
Fukuyama, Francis. 'The End of History'. *The National Interest* 16 (Summer 1989): 3–18.
———. *The End of History and the Last Man*. New York: The Free Press, 1992.
Gloer, Will. 'His Heroin Habit and a Bad Case of Self Abuse: Profile'. *The Scotsman* (1 May 1997): 15.
Guignery, Vanessa (ed.) *Novelists in the New Millennium: Conversations with Writers*. London: Palgrave, 2013.
Hayes, M. Hunter. *Understanding Will Self*. Columbia: University of South Carolina Press, 1997.
Heller, Zoe. 'Self-Examination'. *Vanity Fair* (June 1993): 126–7.
Huntington, Samuel P. 'No Exit: The Errors of Endism'. *National Interest* 17 (Fall 1989): 3–11.
Jackson, H.J. (ed.) *Samuel Taylor Coleridge's Biographia Literaria*. Oxford: Oxford University Press, 1985.
Kinson, Sarah. 'Why I Write'. *The Guardian* (9 May 2007), http://www.guardian.co.uk/books/2007/may/09/willself (accessed 1 May 2013).
Leith, Sam. 'He's A Wimp She's A Chimp'. *The Observer* (11 May 1997), http://www.guardian.co.uk/books/1997/may/11/fiction.willself (accessed 1 May 2013).

Maczynska, Magdalena. 'This Monstrous City: Urban Visionary Satire in the Fiction of Martin Amis, Will Self, China Miéville, and Maggie Gee'. *Contemporary Literature* 51.1 (Spring 2010): 58–86.
Maliszewski, Paul. 'Great Apes'. *Review of Contemporary Fiction* 18.1 (Spring 1998): 238.
McCarthy, Tom. 'The Necronautical Society Interviews Will Self'. *The Necronautical Society* (3 April 2001), http://www.necronauts.org/interviews_will.htm (accessed 1 May 2013).
Melville Clark, Arthur. *Studies in Literary Modes*. London: Folcroft Library Editions, 1946.
Moss, Stephen. '*How the Dead Live* by Will Self'. *The Guardian* (22 June 2000), http://www.theguardian.com/books/2000/jun/22/willself (accessed 23 July 2014).
Murray, Janet. 'Can You Teach Creative Writing?' *The Guardian* (10 May 2011), http://www.guardian.co.uk/books/2004/jan/11/fiction.willself (accessed 1 May 2013).
Parker, Emma. 'Kicks against the Pricks: Gender, Sex and Satire in Will Self's *Cock & Bull*'. *English* 60.230 (2011): 229–50.
Pattern, Dominic. 'Self Promotion'. *Salon Media Circus* 1997, http://www1.salon.com/july97/media/media970716.html (accessed 1 May 2013).
Pope, Alexander. *Epilogue of the Satires*. London: J Nutt, 1738.
Rennison, Nick. *Contemporary British Novelists*. London: Routledge, 2005.
Rushdie, Salman. '20-20 Vision'. *The Independent on Sunday* (17 January 1993): 4.
Scott, Jeremy. *The Demotic Voice in Contemporary British Fiction*. Basingstoke and New York: Palgrave Macmillan, 2009.
Self, Will. *The Quantity Theory of Insanity*. London: Bloomsbury, 1991.
——. *Cock and Bull*. London: Bloomsbury, 1992.
——. *My Idea of Fun*. London: Bloosmbury, 1993.
——. *Grey Area*. London: Bloomsbury, 1994.
——. 'Martin Amis'. *Junk Mail*. London: Bloomsbury, 1995, 372-402.
——. 'Martin Amis: The Misinformation'. *Junk Mail*. London: Bloomsbury, 1995, 299–313.
——. 'The Valley of the Corn Dollies'. *Junk Mail*. London: Bloomsbury, 1995, 202–218.
——. 'J.G. Ballard'. *Junk Mail*. London: Bloomsbury, 1995, 329–371.
——. *Junk Mail*. London: Bloomsbury, 1995.
——. *The Sweet Smell of Psychosis*. London: Bloomsbury, 1996. Illustrations Martin Rowson.
——. *Great Apes*. London: Bloomsbury, 1997.
—— 'News'. *Publishers Weekly*. 8 September 1997: 53.
——. *Tough, Tough Toys for Tough, Tough Boys*. London: Bloomsbury, 1998.
——. *How the Dead Live*. London: Bloomsbury, 2000.
——. 'You Ask The Questions: Will Self'. *The Independent* (6 June 2001): 7.
——. 'Ingenious Bubble Wrap'. *New Statesman* (15 July 2002): 26.
——. 'Introduction.' In Alisdair Grey, *1982, Janine*. Edinburgh: Canongate, 2003. i-xviii.
——. *Will Self in Un veritable naturalisme litteraire est-il possible ou memem souhaitable?* Naimes: Editions Plains Feux, 2003: 44–6.

———. Untitled Essay. In *Confidential*. Ed. Alison Jackson. London: Taschen, 2007: 246-249; see also: 'The Rotting Fruit of Fame, Alison Jackson's Celebrity Lookalike Pictures.' *The Telegraph*. 13 October 2007: n.p.; http://www.telegraph.co.uk/culture/theatre/3668498/The-rotting-fruit-of-fame.html.

———. 'The Rotting Fruit of Fame, Alison Jackson's Celebrity Lookalike Pictures'. In *Confidential*. Ed. Alison Jackson. London: Taschen, 2007.

——— 'Penguin Book Authors, Interview with Will Self", *Penguin Online*, 2008, http://www.penguin.co.uk/nf/Author/AuthorPage/0100004872600.html (accessed 1 May 2013).

———. 'There Will Be Blood'. *The Guardian*, Review Section (22 October 2011): 2–4.

———. 'In Praise of Pessimism'. *New Statesman* (29 July 2013), http://www.newstatesman.com/culture/2013/07/praise-pessimism (accessed 23 July 2014).

Shone, Tom. 'The Complete, Unexpurgated Self'. *Sunday Times Magazine* (5 September 1993): 39–42.

Swift, Jonathan. *The Battle of the Books*. London: J Nutt, 1704.

Tew, Philip. 'Will Self'. In *Writers Talk*. Eds Philip Tew, Fiona Tolan and Leigh Wilson. London and New York: Continuum, 2008, 105–124.

Walsh, John. 'Bully Puts His Soul Up for Sale'. *The Independent* (18 September 1993): 28.

4

Postcolonial and Diasporic Voices – Bringing Black to the Union Jack

Ethnic Fictions and the Politics of Possibility

Sara Upstone

In 1998, Caryl Phillips wrote an essay 'The Pioneers: Fifty Years of Caribbean Migration to Britain' in which he spoke for what he called 'my generation' of black Britons. This generation, Phillips declared, would be committed to changing the face of British society:

> [O]ur response was different from that of our parents, who often held their tongues in order that they might protect their children. We were invested in British society in a way in which they were not and it was clear to us that a British future involved not only kicking back when kicked, but continuing to kick until a few doors opened and things changed. We, the second generation, had to change British society with our intransigence, or what the police force called our 'attitude', because British society was certainly not going to change of its own volition. (276)

This generation would not hold their tongues. They would speak. And by the 1990s, when Phillips wrote his essay, they would be shouting loudly. If the 1980s was the decade in which the concept of 'black British Literature' established itself, then the 1990s was the decade in which this writing found its confidence and declared itself as a permanent fixture on the literary map.

To speak of 'black British literature' is to generalize about a diverse range of writings, recognized already in the 1990s by a movement away from this broad identification – so useful for political alliance in the previous decades – towards more fragmented and particular identities such as 'African British' and 'British Asian'. Indeed, as a significant part of 1990s criticism was devoted to deconstructing essentialist ethnic identities, to speak even of a 'Caribbean British literature' or an 'African British literature' would be equally problematic.

The discussion that follows is framed explicitly with an awareness of these limitations and the questions they raise.

Nevertheless, 'black British literature' maintains its usefulness for exploring a range of home-grown ethnic literatures that were established in contrast to traditions of both postcolonial and migrant writing in Britain, to the extent that it is no longer appropriate to speak about these terms as synonymous (Dawes 258). This critical distinction would gather pace by the 1990s, as Timothy Brennan asked 'In a land as literary as Britain, why are its black writers invisible – at least as *British* writers?' (5). By the end of the decade, an established body of literary anthologies and academic texts pointed to the critical importance of black British writing (Antoine; McCarthy; Sissay; Dennis and Khan; Baker Jr, Diawara and Lindeborg; Owusu; Procter; Wambu; Newland and Sesay; Mercer; Lee). Events such as the British Council's 1997 gathering of those working in 'minority communities', 'Re-Inventing Britain', the London Museum's 1997 conference on black British Literature, the founding by Marsha Hunt of the Saga Prize for new black British writing in 1994, the establishment in 1993 of the X-Press by Steve Pope and Dotun Adebayo to publish popular black British fiction and the events to commemorate the fiftieth anniversary of Empire Windrush in 1998 spoke to the confident place of black British literature.

A significant body of criticism now exists emphasizing the difference in outlook between the migrant and/or postcolonial novel and black British writing; the best of this draws attention to such distinctions being not simply a matter of time of writing, but of specifics of outlook, so that it is recognized that a young migrant writer, writing today, would perhaps be more likely to produce fiction resonant with the concerns of Sam Selvon than with his or her contemporary British counterparts (see Sesay, 'Transformations'). These discussions emphasize the shift from the focus of the former on themes of alienation, dislocation and transformation, to the latter's assertion of confidence, settlement and citizenship rights. Yet, there are also formal and generic differences. Windrush migrant writing in Britain has been defined almost exclusively by Selvon's *The Lonely Londoners* (1956) (the only text routinely taught and consistently in print), with its modernist flourishes. The contemporary postcolonial form, at least how it was consumed and popularly read in the West in the 1990s, was frequently highly experimental, often categorized as either postmodern or magical-realist, and associated with Booker Prize winners Ben Okri, Keri Hulme, J.M. Coetzee and, most notably, Salman Rushdie, whose *Midnight's Children* (1981) and *The Satanic Verses* (1988) for very different reasons dominated the beginning and the end, respectively, of the 1980s. Other Windrush generation writers still in print, such as Wilson Harris, can be defined by a fusion of these modernist and magical-realist stylings. In contrast to this, black British writers of the 1990s offered a scaled back, sparse, realist style, often urban in setting and frequently gritty and hard hitting. Particular attention is taken of the specifics of place in terms of street names and postcodes, heavy use of is made of street dialect and slang, urban dress, music and popular culture are highlighted, all of which root texts explicitly in both time and place. Socially and historically grounded and refusing both extravagant experimental flourishes and literary playfulness, they bore little comparison with the most well-known of either postcolonial or migrant writings. Discussion of how publishing demands obscure the diversity of migrant and postcolonial writing is well established by texts such as Huggan's *The Postcolonial Exotic* (2001). I draw attention here, therefore, to the specifics of a popular and dominant form of writing with which black British texts are in dialogue, and this should not be taken to deny the rich diversity of genres and styles offered by migrant and postcolonial texts more generally.

The significance of these generic choices is often overlooked in criticism of black British writing, which understandably hones in on the discursive differences between this literature and migrant and postcolonial texts, yet they are essential to appreciating its definitive contribution to British literature of the decade. When Phillips, writing in 1995, discussed the rise of ethnic writing, he insightfully declared that 'form, how to tell one's story, is the ultimate challenge' ('Extravagant' 293). In the same essay, when he listed his selection of the most radical formal innovators in English literature, he located their innovation in their connection to 'alternative cultures and traditions' (291); this shared experience could, for Phillips, unite authors as different as Thackeray and Rushdie. It would not be a unity of plot that would connect them, but rather a commitment to formal innovation: 'to constant questioning and reinvention of the most vigorous type' because 'they cannot accept the comfort zone of "continuity"' (293) and thus 'discover new formal strategies which will expand our understanding of what is possible in literary form' (296).

Where, then, to place black British writers in Phillips's own classificatory system? Not with the writers born elsewhere with the 'most vigorous' formal innovations. Yet, at the same time, not with those born into Englishness and several generations of history and racial privilege, with their easy acceptance of the realist form. Phillips argues they should be classified with writers such as Virginia Woolf, for whom marginalization of another kind could lead to the same formal radicalism. Yet, the character of black British writing itself speaks to something somewhat different: to a form both realist and speculative;

fantastic not in the elaborate flourishes of magical-realist texts, but with a quietly transformative character; experimental not with the dramatic interruptive power of the postmodern or modernist text, but rather with a tendency towards subtle innovations and restrained but nevertheless affecting stylistic departures. It is perhaps because such texts are defined by their realism that the relationship between genre and content in these texts is so often overlooked; realism, in comparison to more experimental choices, appears as almost an empty signifier, a 'non-form' rather than a specific intervention. The exception to this is Magdalena Maczynska, whose essay 'The Aesthetics of Realism in Contemporary Black London Fiction' (2007) offers not only a detailed investigation into the realist form in black British fiction, but also useful clarification of the problems of such generic classifications. Maczynska's conclusions, however, ultimately uphold the status of realism as a 'non-form' as she juxtaposes 'mimetic' black British realism with 'an increased interest in alterative [sic] modes of representation' (147) that are seen as more 'radical'.

That such literature also lacks the more explicit experimentation of the first generation of British migrant writers such as Selvon and Harris, writing from the 1950s and 1960s, can be said to bear witness to a genuine improvement in circumstance; as Phillips contends that he would 'rather have a less vigorous literature and a healthier nation' ('Extravagant' 297), so it follows that the more positive climate of the 1990s would produce a less obviously experimental literature than earlier decades, as the stylistic vibrancy born of anti-racist resistance discourse in earlier decades might give way to less explicit 'subversions'. More importantly, however, the realism of black British fiction, in particular, can be read not as striving for 'authenticity' or 'representation' as much as for an illusion of *verisimilitude* designed to direct the reader towards desired conclusions about British society. Most importantly, these conclusions speak not to the status quo, or to present circumstance, but more powerfully to the possible future for an ethnically diverse Britain.

It is difficult to label such choices, and any terminology will by its very nature be reductive. Yet, in the 1990s, the convergence of this formal character with certain choices in terms of plot, particularly in terms of narrative conclusions, does suggest possible labelling. It is useful to think of these fictions as what might be termed 'utopian realisms'. Such texts show preference for the realist form, to produce socially and historically rooted texts. Yet, at the same time, they often include scenarios and denouements in particular which transcend realist definition and move the texts into speculative fiction. These speculations are reinforced by other formal choices regarding narrative style such as multi-voiced, non-linear and linguistically neologic narratives that renew and refresh the realist form. Following Phillips's own definition, such realism is not specifically ethnic ('Extravagant' 294); rather, ethnic fictions can be seen as the most pronounced locale of this stylistic trend. What John McLeod in his 'Diaspora and Utopia' defines in terms of Phillips's work as 'progressive utopianism' (3) can profitably be seen as indicative of a more general movement in black British fiction in this decade that is rooted not only in the novel's message but also in its aesthetics, reflective of what Arana draws attention to as the need to recognize that black British artists 'embody not merely *a politics of identity*, but *an aesthetics of identity* as well' ('Introduction' 2). In this utopian realist moment, realism becomes an intentional choice; its counterpoint to the non-linear, magical and extra-worldly speaks intentionally to the declaration of a distinct genre and an alternative perspective, aesthetically defined.

The utopian nature of this realism can be specifically situated in sociopolitical terms. In the 1970s and 1980s, a starkly realist form of black British writing already existed, driving forward and imagining the existence of a black British political identity as a strident opposition to racist, and particularly Thatcherite, politics. In the 1990s, the utopian turn in black British realism reflects an optimism drawn from political change and yet also the continued role of literature as a shaping and defining force in positing a future vision. As McLeod so insightfully argued in his essay in the 1970s volume for this series, the literature of this earlier decade needs to be read not as simplistically representational, but rather as self-consciously creating a black British identity for its readers that might resist the violence of white racism at both local and institutional scales. This intention is captured by Phillips in an essay he wrote three years before 'The Pioneers', arguing that 'for the past fifteen years it would be fair to say that the only truly functional multicultural and multiracial area of British life – aside from the national athletics team – has been the literature' ('Extravagant' 295). The fiction of the 1990s can be seen as extending this project in its self-conscious projection not simply of a black British identity, but of the creating of a social space of inclusion for the black British community.

In this regard, black British realism in the 1990s can be seen as an intentional and definite authorial choice with particular applicability to the discursive impact of the fictions in question. By the end of the 1990s, Phillips felt confident enough to declare that 'British concern with a continuous past, with fixity, with a racially conscious rigidity, is these days playing an increasingly small part in how the nation thinks of itself' ('Pioneers' 281). In this sense, literature of the decade may have got progressively more hopeful, but conversely less utopian as this hopefulness became more rooted in actual circumstance and less distant from social and political realities. In acknowledging this, it is important not to idealize a decade which was also the decade of the Stephen Lawrence murder (1993) and the subsequent police mishandling of the investigation. The Lawrence murder inquiry spans the decade: the initial prosecution case collapsed in 1996; in 1997, the Police Complaints Authority opened an investigation into the handling of the case; the MacPherson Report which highlighted police failings was published in 1999. Convictions against two men for the murder were only achieved in 2012.

If, however, in terms of criticism, the 1980s was the decade of Gilroy's *There Ain't No Black in the Union Jack* (1987), then the 1990s would be the decade of his *Between Camps* (2000), with its calls for a post-racial society in which the 'liberation from "race"' might lead to 'planetary humanism' (15): a nonracial humanism focused on shared humanity rather than cultural difference. With the inauguration of the 'New Labour' government under Tony Blair in 1997 and the defeat of the Conservative Party after eighteen years in power, there was an emerging sense of the possibility of a new state of race relations in twenty-first-century Britain. Blair, in his speech to the Labour Party conference in September of that year, would call for more black people in office and public life, 'reminding ourselves just how much negative discrimination there is'. This was reflected in the emergence of multiculturalism as a conceptual framework for British society: the Commission for the Future of Multi-Ethnic Britain, set up by the Runnymede Trust think-tank, was established in 1998 and its 2000 report called for a new definition of the United Kingdom that would reflect an established multicultural nation. Even before this, the weight of expectation after the resignation of Margaret Thatcher in 1990, the more moderate government of John Major – marked most notably by the abolition of the poll tax and a softer stance on European integration – and a Labour Party campaigning as the party for whom 'racism has no place' (Smith), can be felt in a literature that dared to speak more boldly of the possibility for social change. The Conservative government of this decade, influenced strongly by more liberal party members such as pro-Europeans Kenneth Clarke and Michael Heseltine, spoke of a more inclusive Britain which, although still haunted by the Thatcherite era and the unrest of the 1980s, seemed to offer a route towards a less divided Britain both racially and economically, a partial resurrection of 'One Nation' Conservatism which has subsequently been taken up more prominently by David Cameron and the Tory–Liberal coalition government which defeated Labour in the 2010 general election.

Utopian realism, then, is centred upon projecting the possible future of British society. Instead of an imagined past – the province of xenophobes and nationalists – it fixates upon presenting an imagined present as route to an imagined future. This resonates with the focus of those working in black British studies on this strategy – appropriating Edward Said's call for the postcolonial intellectual to offer revised versions of the past 'tending towards a future' (quoted in Baker Jnr, Diawara and Lindeborg 6). An imagined present, paradoxically, can itself take the form of a re-visioned past: such pasts are directed through both veiled and explicit reference towards a future, as they speak to contemporary circumstance. They are not imagined, in that they frequently serve as a corrective to the partial discourse of colonial histories. For example, the new generation of writers of the 1990s is often read as replacing the migrant generation's focus on the pain of dislocation and a racist reception in Britain with new narratives of settlement. Yet, equally, such writers also return to this narrative in utopian realist form. Knowledge of Britain speaks to the dual positioning of the double-voiced author as simultaneously insider and outsider in a society in which he or she is now fully immersed. Novels such as S.I. Martin's *Incomparable World* (1996) offer detailed and accurate mapping of London's streets and landmarks, and the characters' movement between them represents the discourse of the knowing insider. Such novels stake a claim to Britain through the ability to realistically map its contours and therefore have the narrative itself identified as a discourse originating from a position of 'belonging'. This confidence opens the way for a strategic rewriting of historical events to reflect a burgeoning hopefulness.

R. Victoria Arana emphasizes this strategy in her reading of the representation of the 1980s in black British writing. Discussing contemporary writers such as Jackie Kay, Diran Adebayo and Bernadine Evaristo, she notes:

> Each has responded in one way or another to the cultural legacy of the 1980s and participated in the radical retheorising of British identity that has overtaken the British Isles ever since the countrywide race riots of 1981. Nevertheless, their writings do not reflect the same sort of bitterness and anger evident in the works of the 1980s' generation. (Arana, 'The 1980s' 230)

Compare, for example, the exclusively black world of Selvon's immigrants with the lives of the young men in Rocky Carr's *Brixton Bwoy* (1998). In the latter, the central character of Pupatee is part of an ethnically diverse gang, led by the blond haired, blue eyed Jimmy, in which 'colour counted for nothing' (34). In this re-imagining of Brixton history, the local gangs of the Herbies and the Rebels are colour-blind: 'What made you a Rebel or a Herbie wasn't the colour of your skin, but growing up in Brixton and the friends you had' (89). A similar utopianism is evident in Martin's *Incomparable World*, a novel set in eighteenth-century London but explicitly speaking to contemporary circumstances, a disjunction which led Kwame Dawes to describe the novel's characters as 'disturbingly British' ('Negotiating' 256). The novel asks whether 'another two centuries' (175) will bring any change to the poverty and racism the central character, Buckram, sees on London's streets, and frames his experience in terms of discourses of repatriation resonant with a 1980s BNP agenda. Despite this reality, the opening of the novel, in the Charioteer pub with its diverse clientele, speaks to a multiethnic allegiance. Equally, the final lines of the novel speak to the possibility of black individuals claiming nationality:

> He's charging through the white of winter, a black man on a black horse. He throws back his head and laughs in the cold, wild air. He is heading north now and speeding into Christmas Day, ready to claim whatever present the heart of England holds for him. (178)

Rich with metaphorical significance, these final lines see Buckram pushing through whiteness, confident in a blackness that claims a right to be accepted into Englishness. On Christmas Day, a day of miraculous births and new beginnings stands the promise of a rebirth of English society. That Martin posits this possibility in the wake of the hardship of eighteenth-century society, and identifies Buckram's experience with the cyclical nature of the black experience (98), suggests a similar hope on the eve of Labour's ascendance to power. Eighteenth-century London is already multicultural, not just in the sense of a definite black presence, but also in the sense of the mixed race relationships, and social groupings, that populate the novel.

That such utopianism can encompass the experiences of British-born individuals is evidenced in the work of Andrea Levy, who published her first novels in this decade. Levy's first novel, *Every Light in the House Burnin'* (1994), reworks the migrant narrative through the perspective of a daughter, recounting familiar experiences of failed dreams with particular poignancy and emotion. The experience of Angela, the daughter, who intersperses her father's story with that of her own childhood, is told without revision, as Levy highlights the racial prejudice faced growing up in England in the 1960s. In Levy's two subsequent novels, however, the shift to a more concentrated focus on the younger generation brings with it more optimistic scenarios. Telling the story of two sisters born in Britain to Jamaican parents, *Never Far From Nowhere* (1996) charts how light-skinned Vivien and dark-skinned Olive fare differently growing up in racist 1970s Britain. The novel is filled with examples of institutional racism, skinhead violence and widespread societal prejudice. In the novel's penultimate chapter, Olive, who is being prosecuted for cannabis possession, planted on her by the police, declares her intention to return to Jamaica, lambasting her sister for failing to understand that, in England, 'people like her are never far from Nowhere' (273). Yet, rather than end the novel in these terms, the final page instead sees Vivien able to assert her national belonging and stake a claim for her right to British nationality:

> On the train back to Herne Bay a white-haired old woman wanted to talk... 'Where do you come from, dear?' I looked at my reflection in the train window – I've come a long way, I thought. Then I wondered what country she would want me to come from as I looked in her eyes. 'My family are from Jamaica', I told her. 'But I am English.' (282)

Claiming not just Britishness, but the more exclusive Englishness, Vivien stands not so much for 1970s optimism, but for the 1990s commitment to black British confidence and belonging; the novel must be read coterminously through both time of setting and time of writing to unravel the jarring positivity of its final page. Levy's fiction embodies a strategic use of denouement here that privileges future-focused optimism over present-day realism; decisions at the level of discourse order ambivalent plots in favour of more hopeful emphases. At the end of the decade, Levy would be equally positive in *Fruit of the Lemon* (1999). The central protagonist, Faith, grows up in an England riddled with racism. Yet, Faith announces at the novel's conclusion that she is 'coming home' to England, fully confident in her right to national belonging. Having made a journey to her parents' birthplace of Jamaica which connects her to her diasporic identity, she repeats the assertion of Vivien: she is 'coming home' (339).

That such choices should stake a claim for black Britishness is integral to Levy's own strong commitment to Englishness as a multiracial identity (Lima 73). Moreover, they also reflect her commitment to literature as socially transformative. In the latter context, Levy's utopian decisions make even more sense. If her novels are not always as hard on racism as they might be (Lima 70), allowing at least her 'less black' characters to begin to stake a claim for their birthright, then this can be seen as an intentional choice to further the impetus to social transformation provided by her novels. Moreover, this choice is for Levy explicitly connected to realism: a 'belief that if you can represent reality, you can attempt to change it' (Lima 80).

Tracing the decade: Caryl Phillips and Hanif Kureishi

In a decade of such political change, the nuances of such a strategy shift and modify. To trace the different moments in the utopian realist project, it is useful to consider in more detail the work of perhaps the two most prominent ethnic writers of the 1990s: Hanif Kureishi and Caryl Phillips. Both authors published three novels, their work spanning the decade; in very different ways, in each case, the novels trace a trajectory that embodies the movement from tentative possibility in the immediate post-Thatcher period, to mid-decade speculative utopianism, to end-of-decade optimism – more hopeful but less utopian – in the wake of increased self-assurance.

Kureishi's first novel of the decade, *The Buddha of Suburbia* (1990) is a stark example of the discursive privileging of positive conclusions as a means of emphasizing a hopeful future beyond present circumstances. In 1990, the novel's denouement is most utopian, coming before Thatcher's resignation in November of that year. Kureishi's novel feeds into a sense of imminent change – the end of an era he had so powerfully documented in *My Beautiful Launderette* (1986). Brilliantly comic, it employs the utopian reshaping of history as 1970s Britain, for his mixed race protagonist offers the possibility of hybrid identities, both racial and gendered, despite racial prejudice. Karim captures the experience of a generation with the right to be British, but the experience too of exclusion, declaring 'we were supposed to be English, but to the English we were always wogs and nigs and Pakis and the rest of it' (53). Yet, in the wake of this, Karim stakes his claim. Much is made in criticism of Karim's opening line: 'I am an Englishman born and bred, almost.' Much less is made of the words that follow it: 'Englishman I am' (3), a confident reversal not to be found in the migrant's narrative. Although this ambivalence dominates the novel to its conclusion, Kureishi's final words are a utopian moment: 'I thought of what a mess everything had been, but that it *wouldn't always* be that way' (my emphasis, 284). Such words do not betray Karim's confusion, or the tension between his hyperbolic spirit and the oppressive weight of racism. Yet, at the same time, they speak explicitly to a future.

That *Buddha* is a historical novel suggests that – at the time of reading – such a moment of change must be upon us, or at least imminent. It pushes the reader towards action and enacts, like Levy's work, a social function as stimulus for change. Kureishi's work is the fictional counterpart to Stuart Hall's writing in the decade on the end of the essential black subject. By the end of the decade, in 1998, Hall would be declaring a black Britishness 'confident beyond its own measure in its own identity', with the possibility of being both 'Black and British ... simply taken for granted as an aspect of life' (128). Kureishi's characters assume this confidence even in the 1970s: they can play with racial identities, assuming them ironically, for comic or performative effect. This is not 1990s political multiculturalism in the sense that it is not a discourse of toleration of cultural communities as much as it is a manifesto for endless transformation and strategic allegiances. Those who embody such features are not alienated but advantaged; those who lack them are limited and lost: Margaret, for example, laments the fact that she is 'only English' (5).

Phillips's first novel of the decade, *Cambridge* (1991), is in essence the bleakest, and it may initially seem strange to suggest that the same strategy as Kureishi's might be employed in this very different fiction. What exists, however, is more of a difference of emphasis than a difference in kind. Phillips is in reality the most subtle proponent of this new form, which glimmers only tentatively from beneath his often very grim realities; whereas writers such as Kureishi more obviously embody its strategies explicitly. Phillips recounts stories too bleak to be revisioned for the benefit of contemporary resonance. This difference has led McLeod, when discussing Phillips's later writing, to distinguish between Gilroy's optimism – for McLeod inflated and unrealistic – and Phillips's more tempered vision ('Diaspora and Utopia'). In *Cambridge*, this difference is starkly evident. Ending in the death of both the eponymous slave and also his mistress, the Englishwoman Emily, *Cambridge*, finds little space for cross-cultural communication. The reality of nineteenth-century humanism, embodied in Emily's desire for her father to accept the iniquity of slavery, is rendered in stark contrast to Gilroy's planetary humanist ideal, as neither Emily nor Cambridge manage to escape the racial and gendered inequalities of slave-holding society. It is left to Cambridge alone to uphold this in his own nineteenth-century Christian form, declaring God to have 'made of one blood all nations of men' (167). As in Martin's *Incomparable World*, representation of the free blacks of London reinforces the history of black settlement in England (142); yet, the genuine alliances of Martin's characters are replaced here with the sense of free blacks as a 'fashionable appendage' (142) for privileged whites. In this respect, the novel is entirely realistic and rooted in its historical circumstance, with little sense that this circumstance is being rewritten to offer a metaphor for contemporary Britain, or being rendered more hopeful to project into an imaginary future. Indeed, in different contexts, Phillips has been vocal about his dislike of such rewritings, highly critical of the Hollywood film industry that would offer a 'happy' ending to the slave experience ('Amistad' 77).

The contemporary resonances of *Cambridge*, in this context, are about acknowledging the trauma of diaspora. So Emily declares:

> Perhaps the commonest of all the negro airs that I have given ear to, and one of the very few that I have been able to distinguish as *English*, reflects the rootlessness of these people who have been torn from their native soil and thrust into the busy commerce of our civilized world. It is much to be doubted that they will ever again reclaim a true sense of self. The evidence before my eyes suggests that such a process will unfold only after the passage of many decades, perhaps many centuries. It will not be swift. (71)

What Phillips does not do, in 1991, is speculate upon the alleviation of these traumas: realist novels, as Emily herself knows, are not about fortune smiling, but about clouds of doom descending (118). For Phillips hope is harder to find, and his ability to do this makes the utopianism of his narratives even stronger. So, even here, one can detect the hints of hopefulness – in Cambridge's marriage to an Englishwoman, Anna, and his positive relationships with Christian reformers in London; in his relationship with the clerk, John Williams, who teaches Cambridge English 'without concern for my complexion' (140). Most notably, hope is evidenced in the defining and mutually affectionate relationship between Emily and her housemaid, Stella: Phillips's movement to third person narration in the final part of the book emphasizes that just as Emily will end her life thinking of Stella, not as her black housemaid but 'her friend' (184), so Stella comes to her with a touch that is 'tender' (180).

Mid-decade, Phillips was writing in his non-fiction of the 'personal ambivalence' black Britons 'not born in Britain' (including himself) would feel towards the country ('Extravagant' 296), and his second novel of the decade, *Crossing the River* (1993), reflects this. Telling the story of three 'siblings' situated in three very different locations and times, it makes the greatest departure of Phillips's fiction from realism, presenting a non-linear progression of different voices, the same movement between third and first person narrative used in *Cambridge*, and an almost magical-realist timeline with its time-travelling protagonists, shifting in its final pages to fragmented prose to represent the unimaginable trauma of the concentration camp. Yet, the weight of the novel's subject matter, and attention to the detail of this, speaks still to a realist form, so that utopianism comes to be a formal quality of the text; glimmers of experimentation speak to a world beyond the heaviness of the subject matter. The bulk of the novel finds little space to echo this formal utopianism in events, however. There are moments of hope – in the love felt for Nash Williams by his master; in the mixed race love affair between the GI and the English woman. Yet, these are rendered tragic, stories haunted by death and abandonment and, more than anything, by the loss of children, be they adopted or birth-given. They point to a love that fails, defeated by prejudice, intolerance and outright savage racism.

However, as with *Cambridge*, Phillips's resistance to transforming the historical is in tension with a subtly utopian conclusion. The two short narratives of the 'father' who sells his children into slavery that frame the text as opening and closing say something quite different to that of the rest of novel-proper. In the wake of his terrible loss, the father finds hope:

> You are beyond. Broken-off, like limbs from a tree. But not lost, for you carry within your bodies the seeds of new trees. Sinking your hopeful roots into difficult soil. (2)

In his concluding monologue, the father speaks again as he does in the opening of there being 'no return' from his 'foolishness'. Yet, the novel's final line – 'But they arrived on the far bank of the river, loved' (237) – speaks for the hope that the black community can survive. That the conclusion reworks the opening, and chooses to privilege the hope rather than the loss, dramatically alters the novel's final tone. These stories will be told; these voices will be heard. Phillips's trend for revisiting and rewriting his own words would continue as the decade went on: in 1996, he adapted his 1985 novel *The Final Passage* for Channel 4 television; yet, whereas his original novel ends bleakly, the adaptation allows the viewer to see a happier conclusion. Phillips in an interview locates this shift in the demands of the medium – television, for which 'you have to offer some slightly positive – not glossy or romantic – sense of the future' (Jaggi 160). Yet, this gesture to the 'slightly positive' is equally evidence of Phillips's growing commitment to the utopian strategy: to realist visions that allow the reader to *think beyond current circumstance*.

Two years later, Kureishi published *The Black Album* (1995), with the same exuberance that characterized *Buddha*. Again a historical narrative, but of a more contemporary moment, concerning the Rushdie Affair of 1988 and its effect on young British Muslim males. The novel is a clear example of how optimism infused realist accounts of what, at the time, was seen as a bleak period in British history for race relations at the height of the Thatcher regime. Here, Kureishi gives more recognition to the harsh prejudice faced by British Asians, and the consequences of this for their sense of self, with tragic conclusions. There is much in the narrative that plays into the conventional, clichéd reading of British-born Asians as 'caught between cultures', with a cast of characters torn between an indulgent, Western culture and an Islam offering only stricture and intolerance towards difference. This, of course, was the decade of Homi Bhabha, whose most prominent essays were republished in *The Location of Culture* (1994). Kureishi's work embodies Bhabha's notion of vernacular cosmopolitanism: a harsher vision of hybridity than that rendered in Bhabha's earlier work, more conscious of the sociopolitical realities facing diasporic communities in favour of the awareness of hybridity as a necessary, and potentially fraught, space of identification for those in positions of often layered marginalities, encompassing gender, class and sexuality as well as race. In 'The Vernacular Cosmopolitan', Bhabha defines such a position as

> translating between cultures, renegotiating traditions from a position where 'locality' insists on its own terms, while entering into larger national and societal conversations. This is not a cosmopolitanism of the elite variety inspired by universalistic patterns of humanistic thought that run gloriously across cultures, establishing an enlightened unity. Vernacular cosmopolitans are compelled to make a tryst with cultural translation as an act of survival. Their specific and local histories, often threatened and repressed, are inserted 'between the lines' of dominant cultural practices. (139)

In this context, Kureishi presents a hope that is in many ways limited – the central protagonist, Shahid, can only triumph by fully embracing Western excess and abandoning any religious belief, choosing instead an alternative, liberal lifestyle embodied in his relationship with his literature tutor, the flamboyant Deedee Osgood. Yet, Shahid's ability to do this, whatever we think of it as a choice, does capture the sense of real possibility felt at a moment when Tory power was waning, and a new sea-change felt to be imminent. Still starkly utopian in that such change had yet to be secured, the final pages of *The Black Album* are the most explicit example of this possibility in evidence. Shahid asks:

> How could anyone confine themselves to one system or creed? Why should they feel they had to? There was no fixed self; surely our several selves melted and mutated daily? There had to be innumerable ways of being in the world. He would spread himself out, in his work and in love, following his curiosity. (Kureishi 274)

As in *Buddha*, this is not multiculturalism as much as endless cultural translation. Shahid and Deedee leave London for the coast; the final pages plot their lives from then on: Prince concerts, private parties, alcohol and adventure, that will go on 'Until it stops being fun' (276). Their mixed race, multi-generational relationship is unlikely to be permanent, but it is both possible and persistent.

Marketed as 'a story of triumph', Leone Ross's *All the Blood is Red* (1996) is an alternative example of this mid-decade possibility. Whilst one female protagonist, Alexandrea, is offended by the idea of dating anyone who isn't black, another, Nicola, a young actress, is in a long-term mixed-race relationship with a white director, Julius. The hope of Gilroy's planetary humanism is represented in the character of Jeanette, whose abandoned dancing in the aisle of a London bus is described thus:

> No-one could have denied the beauty of her movement. Every twist of her torso, shimmy of her hip made them all, for just one moment, forget. Forget all the things that we have been taught matter. Forget gender. Colour. Fashion. Morality. Religion. (36)

Ross's pointed direction here to *what we have been taught* matters speaks to a burgeoning political agenda to actively construct a multicultural society through social and educational reform. Against the stories of the women who survive and ultimately triumph is interwoven the story of an older woman, Mavis, whose mixed-race baby is rejected, finds herself driven into prostitution and who comes to England only to find her two daughters caught in the same suffering that plagued her own life. Yet, at the same time, this continued inequality only speaks to the utopianism of Jeanette's dancing, and the kind of planetary humanism it represents, resonant with Gilroy's argument in *Between Camps* that such a change 'entails the abolition of what is conventionally thought of as sexual division' (16). Whilst the last chapter of Ross's novel is an optimistic one, like all utopian realism, and strongly resonant with *The Black Album*, there is a disjunction between this conclusion – seemingly necessary – and what has gone before. In Ross's case, this optimism finds form in Jeanette's final words, celebrating the child she is carrying, conceived with her friend Michael, whose support after her rape develops into a relationship. Carried with no sign of the scars of her abuse, Jeanette's child is a promise of the new humanist world, a child who 'dances inside me' (246) just as Jeanette is introduced to us at the beginning of the novel, dancing on the bus.

By the time Phillips and Kureishi published their final novels of the decade, eighteen years of Conservative rule had come to an end, to be replaced with a Labour government offering in its rebranding as 'New Labour' the hope of positive movements towards an inclusive, tolerant and multicultural Britain. Emerging here, interestingly, is utopianism of a different character, defined not by the reworking of content and utopian conclusions as much as by the subject matter itself speaking to hopes for a transformed British society. At stake is both Phillips's and Kureishi's confidence that as authors they could be received in broader terms, producing fictions moving beyond their previous focus on subjects associated with their own ethnic backgrounds. Phillips's *The Nature of Blood* (1997) presents a series of centuries-divided voices, most members of the Jewish diaspora, but also including Shakespeare's Othello, connected to paint a haunting, tragic vision of the trauma of the mistreatment of the Jewish people. Kureishi's *Intimacy* (1998) is an autobiographical novel charting the breakdown of a marriage, bereft of the comic energy of his previous writings. Mark Stein, in his *Black British Literature: Novels of Transformation* (2004), refers to Kureishi's novel as 'post-ethnic', a term he defines as ethnicity 'displaced but not evaded, without entirely ceasing to be of concern' (142). Post-ethnicism in fact can be traced back to the late 1980s, where essays such as Fred D'Aguiar's 'Against Black British Literature' argued against the relevance of racial categorizing of literature, but these were picked up with more force in the 1990s (see Dawes 279).

It is more accurate, however, to see *Intimacy* as post-racial, in that it has little concern for identity at all in conventional terms: the only reference to ethnicity in the book comes through Jay's friend, Asif, whose dedication to his own marriage stands in contrast to Jay's own rampant individualism. In contrast, *The Nature of Blood* is very firmly a post-ethnic fiction. In *Crossing the River*, Phillips had already pointed to a post-ethnic direction in his writing, evading naming the race of the American GI whose story forms part three of the book (explicit reference comes on p. 223; before this, the only indication is a reference to the GI's hair on p. 167). *The Nature of Blood* continues this with its focus on the Jewish diaspora. If one considers Phillips's biography, then *The Nature of Blood* is concerned, like all his novels, with issues of identity connected in some way to the author's own life: Phillips discovered late in his life that his grandfather was a Jewish trader with Portuguese ancestry. Phillips unites this story with his own black British perspective as the repeated oppression of the Jews – herded, displaced, dehumanized, ghettoized – resonates with the recurring oppression of the black diaspora, first through the figure of Othello, and then at the end of the novel through the voices of a family of African Jews who have travelled to Palestine to settle (208–9). Yet, at the same time, the lack of 'obvious' connection to Phillips's black Britishness allows the novel to stand for the post-ethnic text, reflecting Phillips's own assertion by the end of the decade that race has only limited worth in an authorial context ('Introduction: The Burden of Race' 17).

Distasteful or not, the conclusion to *Intimacy* is hopeful, as its protagonist sees the end of his marriage as a liberation from the constraints of middle-class, familial conservatism. Given Kureishi's vocal dislike of the Thatcher regime, in its own tangential way, this *is* tied to the hope of a new future under Labour, as the novel presents the possibility of an old order falling away, which presumably would include a transformation of Britain's preoccupations with ethnicity. It is only in his final novel of the decade, however, that Phillips becomes the more explicitly hopeful in ethnic terms. Still resisting unrealistically happy endings, there is bleakness to the novel's perspective on cross-cultural encounter, defined by Othello's doomed love affair with Desdemona, echoed in the misunderstandings and miscommunications between other cross-cultural pairings such as Eva, the concentration camp survivor, and Gerry, the English soldier. And yet, within this context, the novel brings its disparate voices together in post-ethnic humanist desires, encapsulated in Eva's simple desire to be 'happy... a fine answer' (86). And, at the end of the novel, Stephan, Eva's uncle, offers hope. His sexual encounter with an African woman initially seems a story of intractable difference – 'people who belonged to another place' – but it is also a story of hope beginning again, and of renewal:

> And he understood that people are not made to live alone, neither when things are good, nor when they are bad. These inelegant attempts to heal the lesion in his soul... He did not want anyone to feel sorry for him. He, too, had lived. (212)

There is a stark contrast between the final image of Stephan, 'his arms outstretched, reaching across the years' (213) to his lost family, and Kureishi's celebratory closings. And yet, in the possibility of healing in such circumstances, there is a glimmer of a different future.

Tracing such a trajectory in relation to the British situation can only be done with an awareness of the broader contexts in which such optimism functions. For Phillips, hope lies not so much in the transformation of British politics as in the growing awareness of the healing power of a diasporic consciousness that might provide relief from national constraints and prejudices, drawing attention to the 'transnational' context of black British writing (see McLeod 'Fantasy Relationships'). By 2000, Philips was declaring his 'home' to be 'triangular in shape' with the points representing Africa, Britain, and North America and the Caribbean ('Conclusion' 305); his hope for the next millennium as outlined in his collection of essays *A New World Order* (2001) is not for a confident black Britishness so much as a confident diasporic consciousness of which an attachment to Britain would be an integral, but not singular, facet. This approach not only strongly appeals to Bhabha's critique of nationhood, but also to the other seminal piece of criticism of the decade, Gilroy's *The Black Atlantic: Modernity and Double Consciousness* (1993). Gilroy's argument that the focus on ethnic particularism and nationalism overlooks a diasporic 'circulation of ideas' (4) prompts its own unique form of utopianism. Indeed, Gilroy himself invokes the term in the service of his suggestion that black music forges a 'politics of transfiguration' that constructs 'both an imaginary anti-modern past and a postmodern yet-to-come' (37). For Gilroy, 'by posing the world as it is against the world as the racially subordinated would like it to be, this musical culture supplies a great deal of courage required to go on living in the present' (36). This leads to a 'politics of fulfillment: the notion that a future society will be able to realize the social and political promise that present society has left unaccomplished' (37). Black British literature speaks at the beginning of the decade from a position within neo-imperialist post-Thatcherite Britain, speculating hopefully on a possible future and forging a community with the confidence and strength to seize it; then by the end of the decade, it emerges as a voice of confidence and optimism that the 'yet-to-come' might realize the early promises of the New Labour administration.

Going against the grain

It would be inaccurate to suggest that utopian realism is *the* story of 1990s black British fiction. A number of literary fictions used realism without offering such hope; in Ferdinand Dennis's *The Last Blues Dance* (1996), racism and black on black crime coexist, and mixed race unions are rendered as false hopes; the latter point is picked up by Lucinda Roy's *Lady Moses* (1998), whose American mixed-race protagonist is far more classically alienated than Levy's triumphant young women. Likewise, returning to the Thatcherite 1980s, Joanna Traynor's Saga Prize winning *Sister Josephine* (1997) offers an ambivalent conclusion that, whilst upholding the decade's trend for strong black females, such as those presented in Atima Srivastava's *Transmission* (1992) and *Looking for Maya* (1999), also presents a bleak world of racism, sexual abuse, mental illness and racial division. Meera Syal's *Anita and Me* (1996) and Fred D'Aguiar's *Feeding the Ghosts* (1997) explicitly remind the reader that 'happy endings' are utopian. In the former, the protagonist, Meena, rewrites her own childhood as a self-conscious memoir which transforms the racism of 1970s Britain into a story of personal triumph, but the reader is only too aware of the fictional illusion by a framing text which announces the 'gap between what is said and what is thought, what is stated and what is implied' and situates Meena as an unreliable narrator. In the latter, the horrors of slavery experienced by the central protagonist Mintah are undercut by a romantic ending that reunites her with her lover, a cook's aid she meets on a ship that she comes to be thrown overboard from earlier in the novel, only for the narrative to reveal that this 'happy ending' is only a daydream. Some critics have mistakenly criticized the novel for its 'happy' conclusion, overlooking this twist (see, for example, Dawes 264).

Equally, the realist trend was powerfully resisted by Bernadine Evaristo, who followed her debut poetry collection *Island of Abraham* (1994) with an experimental verse novel, *Lara* (1997), by D'Aguiar's *The Longest Memory* (1994), by Biyi Bandele's *The Street* (1999), by Rukhsana Ahmad's *The Hope Chest* (1996), by the winner of the 1997 Saga Prize, Judith Bryan's *Bernard and the Cloth Monkey* (1998), and also, increasingly, by Leone Ross, whose *Orange Laughter* (1999) employs the use of modernist strategies to explore the complexities of mental illness, a subject taken up in equally bleak terms by Ifeona Fulani's *Seasons of Dust* (1997). Whereas novels such as D'Aguiar's, Bryan's and Ross's suggest a correlation between realism and utopianism as their movement away from the genre corresponds to a bleaker tone, Ahmad's novel is an uplifiting tale of female survival, whilst Evaristo's novel, equally, maintains the utopian spirit in experimental form: *Lara*'s final lines – 'I step out of Heathrow and into my future' (188) – celebrate the possibility of belonging in a text which has been riven by (un)belonging (see Velickovic).

There was, at the same time, an alternative popular black fiction in this period, more conventionally realist, with an intention to speak more directly to *what is*, rather than *what could be*. The X-Press, in particular, foregrounded popular black British writing with Victor Headley's *Yardie* (1992), the genre fiction of Peter Kalu, and Patrick Augustus's *Babyfather* series. Although X-Press became known for its hyper-masculine protagonists, it also published fiction targeted at women, and works such as Naomi King's *O.P.P.* (1993) and Yvette Richards's *Single Black Female* (1994) spoke for a new generation of strong black British women (see King, *The Oxford English Literary History* 236–42). At the same time, these 'positive' stories can be contrasted with an equally prevalent social realism of bleaker mood, reflected in texts that bridged the popular and the literary, such as Courttia Newland's *The Scholar* (1997) and *Society Within* (1999), Alex Wheatle's *Brixton Rock* (1999), Vanessa Walters's *Rude Girls* (1996) and *The Best Things in Life* (1998). Such narratives, with their focus on the continued racism experienced by blacks in British society, and the existence of an urban ethnic underclass, are referred to by Fatimah Kelleher as '"frontline" and council estate realism' and act as a corrective to the optimism of literary fictions, refusing the concept of a black Atlantic for specifically 'British' narratives. Wheatle's return to 1980s Brixton, for example, shows little revisionism despite being published at the very end of the 1990s.

Newland's contemporary-set fiction is the most pronounced example of this alternative realism. *The Scholar* is framed by an epigraph taken from Gilroy's *Small Acts* speaking of the black experience in England as possessing a 'certain uniqueness' (9). The story concerns two young black cousins, Sean and Cory, who grow up on the fictional Greenside council estate of West London. The novel presents a world in which educational aspiration and talent is thwarted by the relentless pull of crime and the social barriers of institutional racism, so that both boys, by the end of the narrative, have been 'lost to the darkness' (344), sucked into burglary, gun crime and gang violence. Newland offers a post-ethnic community, in which black and white youth mix freely together; yet, this positivity is overwritten by the powerlessness of young black men, without the knowledge needed to legally challenge police racism, denied the male role models to keep them on the right path, or the opportunities to physically remove them from the temptations of urban crime and its ability to correct the problems of overwhelming deprivation. Post-ethnic friendship groups and sexual relationships (46) have not eroded racial difference; rather, such connections merely represent a fluid movement between identity positions in which racial identification interweaves with economic status, national affiliation and, most prominently, geographical location and identification with 'the estate'. The tragedy of Sean, an intelligent, sensible and moral young man, is that honour and family loyalty keep him connected to a world that betrays his own potential, Newland making the point that black men cannot be saved by education unless this goes hand in hand with wider social regeneration and reform. Newland's message is explicit, not inferred:

> But he'd always prided himself on being different. Before today, he hadn't robbed, mugged, rioted or taken part in any of the numerous crimes people believed were natural for boys of his colour and age. He'd spent his whole life trying to prove to himself he was different. And now, circumstances and the environment he lived in, rather than a conscious decision had forced him to become a participant in an act completely against his nature. But had the white people noticed his difference, today, or at any other time in his life? ... Did they care if every black man in most TV police drama was a criminal, insane, or a drug pusher and that this negative image was put into homes the length and breadth of the country? ... he couldn't think of one single reason why he should be different, anymore. (170)

For Newland, these early fictions were about 'getting it right' when everyone else was 'getting it wrong': his commitment to unflinching social realism removes the possibility of him constructing a utopian fiction (Arana, 'Courttia Newland' 91). His sequel to *The Scholar, Society Within*, ends more ambivalently, as the young women Val and Elisha rise defiantly above their circumstances; but the Greenside Estate is still riddled with drug-use, crime, racial division and – in particular – sexual inequality. There is little sense of a 'New Labour' vision as the bulldozing of the estate's youth centre speaks instead to government cuts and increasing social inequality. Similarly, Joanna Traynor's *Sister Josephine* (1997), a hard-hitting story of a young mixed-race girl, stands in contrast to Kureishi's discourse of hybridity. In this respect, it is difficult not to focus on the backgrounds of the authors of these respective fictions: Traynor, raised in foster care, based her novel on her own traumatic childhood in the care system; Wheatle grew up in the care system and was imprisoned during the Brixton riots; Newland has remained fiercely connected to his local community, running writers' workshops in Shepherd's Bush where he grew up. Newland, in particular, has made comments which suggest a disjunction between his own location in London, and his own black-based fiction, and the work of 'distant' writers such as Phillips (see Benson).

To make these distinctions is not to suggest a false dichotomy between utopian, post ethnic 'literary' fictions and a realist, race-driven popular literature. In fact, a strong post-ethnic popular literature exists in the work, for example, of Mike Gayle, Nicola Williams and, most notably, in the successful crime novels of Mike Phillips: *The Last Candidate* (1990), *Point of Darkness* (1994), *An Image to Die For* (1995) and *The Dancing Face* (1997). If one wanted, however, to find a way to straddle such fictions and define utopian realism as it emerged in new writers of the decade, then one could turn to Diran Adebayo's *Some Kind of Black* (1996). Starkly realist in many regards, Adebayo's novel echoes the work of Newland and Wheatle in its exposure of the continued racism of British society, in particular the institutional racism of the British police force and the colour-class divide which prevents young black men from successfully resisting the lures of inner-city crime and escaping poverty. Like these authors, too, Adebayo cements the realism of the text in a meticulous attention to the detail of London's geography, and a dialect writing that captures the vibrancy of urban youth communication. Yet, the novel also draws in its model of black identity from poststructuralist influences and echoes the work of both Kureishi and Phillips in its rejection of essentialist claims for black identity. Adebayo's mediation of opposing positions, which includes Dele's claim to be 'some kind of black,' recognizes both the continued desire within the black community for ethnic identification, but also the need to end the notion of an essential black subject in order to prevent simplistic at best, racist at worst, imaginings of black cultures. The utopianism comes in the novel's elevation of the central character out of his inner-city circumstances, something which is rendered more believable given Adebayo's own attendance of Oxford University, although he comes from a much more privileged background than does his fictional character. *Some Kind of Black* ends humorously with Dele's evasion of his badly caricatured white girlfriend, and with a 'happy' resolution to his sister Dapo's situation as she awakes from her coma to hear stories of her brother's exploits. The parallels between Newland's and Adebayo's novels are striking; yet, whereas the police brutality that opens the former results in death and leads to a spiral of destruction, the latter ultimately counterbalances institutional racism with a focus on rebirth and regeneration.

Conclusion

Whilst it is simplistic to suggest that writers easily mirror the political circumstances of the production of their texts, nevertheless one can consider usefully how decades such as the 1990s, in which political change was dramatic and transformative, do offer insights into the sociopolitical relevance of literature, particularly when that writing is quite obviously politically engaged. This is not so much to see such fiction as reflective of political change, but rather to illuminate more distinctly how fiction might contribute towards such change, either through critiquing the political status quo, or gesturing towards alternate social possibilities. Of course, black British fiction is broader than the characteristics of its most well-known authors. Nonetheless, the popularity of particular authors in itself has significance, suggesting an appetite for their optimistic, but realistically positioned, vision, in contrast to the postcolonial magical-realism which dominated the market for ethnic fictions in the 1980s.

That this 1990s possibility has not been realized is the story of the fiction of the 2000s – reflective of Alison Donnell's belief that 'what may have seemed "optimistically probable" in terms of transforming national culture in the 1990s when Gilroy and Hall published many of their seminal essays on conceptualizing black identity, has now been relegated to the realms of the "hopefully possible"' (198). It is disheartening, for example, to read emerging writers such as Koye Oyedeji writing that a black British individual can never truly be British (370). In this context, the 1990s and the glow of optimism they brought to the early

2000s is the high point of an imaginative and speculative realism which began in the 1970s, and which struggles to survive in the new political contexts of twenty-first century Britain. As the decade went on, texts became less utopian, and more 'real'. Yet, paradoxically, looking back, these texts seem even more utopian in the early twenty-first century than they did in the context of their original reception, as the glow of 1990s optimism fails to be realized.

Works Cited

Adebayo, Diran. *Some Kind of Black*. London: Virago, 1996.
Ahmad, Rukhsana. *The Hope Chest*. London: Virago, 1996.
Antoine, Patsy. *Afrobeat: New Black British Fiction*. London: Pulp Faction, 1999.
Arana, R. Victoria. 'Courttia Newland's Psychological Realism and Consequential Ethics'. In *Write Black: Write British: From Post Colonial to Black British Literature*. Ed. Kadija George Sesay. London: Hansib, 2003, 86–106.
———. 'The 1980s: Retheorising and Refashioning British Identity'. In *Write Black: Write British: From Post Colonial to Black British Literature*. Ed. Kadija George Sesay. London: Hansib, 2003, 230–40.
———. 'Introduction: Aesthetics as Deliberate Design: Giving Form to Tigritude and Nommo'. In *Black British Aesthetics Today*. Ed. R. Victoria Arana. Newcastle: Cambridge Scholars Publishing, 2007, 1–13.
Baker Jr, Houston A., Manthia Diawara and Ruth H. Lindeborg (eds) *Black British Cultural Studies: A Reader*. Chicago: University of Chicago Press, 1996.
———. 'Introduction: Representing Blackness/Representing Britain: Cultural Studies and the Politics of Knowledge'. In *Black British Cultural Studies: A Reader*. Eds Houston Baker Jr, Manthia Diawara and Ruth H. Lindeborg. Chicago: University of Chicago Press, 1996, 1–15.
Bandele, Biyi. *The Street*. London: Picador, 1999.
Benson, Dzifa. 'Interview with Courttia Newland'. http://www.itzcaribbean.com/ courttia_newland_p1.php (accessed 10 December 2011).
Bhabha, Homi. *The Location of Culture*. London: Routledge, 1994.
———. 'The Vernacular Cosmopolitan'. In *Voices of the Crossing*. Eds Ferdinand Dennis and Naseem Khan. London: Serpent's Tail, 2000, 133–42.
Blair, Tony. Leader's Speech. Labour Party Annual Conference, Brighton, September 1997, http://www.prnewswire.co.uk/cgi/news/release?id=47983 (accessed 10 December 2011).
Brennan, Timothy. 'Writing from Black Britain'. *The Literary Review* 34.1 (Fall 1990): 5–11.
Bryan, Judith. *Bernard and the Cloth Monkey*. London: Flamingo, 1998.
Carr, Rocky. *Brixton Bwoy*. London: Fourth Estate, 1998.
D'Aguiar, Fred. *The Longest Memory*. London: Chatto and Windus, 1994.

———. *Feeding the Ghosts*. London: Chatto and Windus, 1997.
———. 'Against Black British Literature'. In *Tibisiri: Caribbean Writers and Critics*. Ed. Maggie Butcher. Sydney: Dangaroo Press, 1988, 106–14.
Dawes, Kwame. 'Negotiating the Ship on the Head: Black British Fiction'. In *Write Black: Write British: From Post Colonial to Black British Literature*. Ed. Kadija George Sesay. London: Hansib, 2003, 255–81.
Dennis, Ferdinand. *The Last Blues Dance*. London: Harper Collins, 1996.
Dennis, Ferdinand and Naseem Khan (eds) *Voices of the Crossing*. London: Serpent's Tail, 2000.
Donnell, Alison. 'Afterword: In Praise of a Black British Canon'. In *A Black British Canon*. Eds Gail Low and Marion Wynne-Davies. Basingstoke: Palgrave Macmillan, 2006, 189–204.
Evaristo, Bernardine. *Island of Abraham*. London: Peepal Tree Press, 1994.
———. *Lara*. 1997. Tarset: Bloodaxe, 2009.
Fulani, Ifeona. *Seasons of Dust*. New York: Harlem Rivers, 1997.
Gilroy, Paul. *There Ain't No Black in the Union Jack*. London: Hutchinson, 1987.
———. *The Black Atlantic: Modernity and Double Consciousness*. London: Verso, 1993.
———. *Between Camps*. 2000. London: Routledge, 2004.
Hall, Stuart. 'Frontlines and Backyards: The Terms of Change'. 1998. In *Black British Culture and Society: A Text Reader*. Ed. Kwesi Owusu. London: Routledge, 2000, 127–9.
Headley, Victor. *Yardie*. London: X-Press, 1992.
Huggan, Graham. *The Postcolonial Exotic: Marketing the Margins*. London: Routledge, 2001.
Jaggi, Maya. 'The Final Passage: An Interview with Writer Caryl Phillips'. 1996. In *Black British Culture and Society: A Text Reader*. Ed. Kwesi Owusu. London: Routledge, 2000, 157–68.
Kelleher, Fatimah. 'Concrete Vistas and Dreamtime Peoplescapes: The Rise of the Black Urban Novel in 1990s Britain'. In *Write Black: Write British: From Post Colonial to Black British Literature*. Ed. Kadija George Sesay. London: Hansib, 2003, 241–54.
King, Bruce. *The Oxford English Literary History, Volume 13: 1948–2000: The Internationalization of English Literature*. Oxford: Oxford University Press, 2004.
King, Naomi. *O.P.P.* London: X-Press, 1993.
Kureishi, Hanif. *The Buddha of Suburbia*. London: Faber, 1990.
———. *The Black Album*. London: Faber, 1995.
———. *My Beautiful Laundrette*. 1986. London: Faber, 1996.
———. *Intimacy*. London: Faber, 1998.
Lee, Robert. *Other Britain, Other British: Contemporary Multicultural Fiction*. London: Pluto, 1995.
Levy, Andrea. *Every Light in the House Burning*. London: Headline Review, 1994.
———. *Never Far from Nowhere*. London: Headline Review, 1996.
———. *Fruit of the Lemon*. London: Headline Review, 1999.

Lima, Maria Helena. '"Pivoting the Centre": The Fiction of Andrea Levy'. In *Write Black: Write British: From Post Colonial to Black British Literature*. Ed. Kadija George Sesay. London: Hansib, 2003, 56–85.

Maczynska, Magdalena. 'The Aesthetics of Realism in Contemporary Black London Fiction'. In *Black British Aesthetics Today*. Ed. R. Victoria Arana. Newcastle: Cambridge Scholars Publishing, 2007, 135–49.

Martin, S.I. *Incomparable World*. London: Quartet, 1997.

McCarthy, Karen. *Bittersweet: Contemporary Black Women's Poetry*. London: Women's Press, 1998.

McLeod, John. 'Fantasy Relationships: Black British Canons in a Transnational World'. In *A Black British Canon*. Eds Gail Low and Marion Wynne-Davies. Basingstoke: Palgrave Macmillan, 2006, 93–104.

———. 'Diaspora and Utopia: Reading the Recent Work of Paul Gilroy and Caryl Phillips'. In *Diasporic Literature and Theory – Where Now?* Ed. Mark Shackleton. Newcastle: Cambridge Scholars Publishing, 2008, 2–16.

———. 'Black British Culture and Fiction in the 1970s'. In *The 1970s: A Decade of Contemporary British Fiction*. Eds Nick Hubble, John McLeod and Philip Tew. London: Bloomsbury, 2014, 93–116.

Mercer, Kobena. *Welcome to the Jungle: New Positions in Black Cultural Studies*. New York: Routledge, 2004.

Newland, Courttia *The Scholar*. London: Abacus, 1997.

———. *Society Within*. London: Abacus, 1999.

Newland, Courttia and Kadija Sesay (eds) *IC3: The Penguin Book of New Black Writing in Britain*. Harmondsworth: Penguin, 2000.

Owusu, Kwesi (ed.) *Black British Culture and Society: A Text Reader*. London: Routledge, 2000.

Oyedeji, Koye. 'Prelude to a Brand New Purchase on Black Political Identity: A Reading of Bernadine Evaristo's *Lara* and Diran Adebayo's *Some Kind of Black*'. In *Write Black: Write British: From Post Colonial to Black British Literature*. Ed. Kadija George Sesay. London: Hansib, 2003, 346–71.

Phillips, Caryl. *The Final Passage*. London: Faber, 1985.

———. *Cambridge*. London: Bloomsbury, 1991.

———. *Crossing the River*. London: Bloomsbury, 1993.

———. *The Nature of Blood*. London: Faber, 1997.

———. 'Extravagant Strangers'. 1995. In *A New World Order*. Caryl Phillips. 2001. London: Vintage, 2002, 288–97.

———. 'The Pioneers: Fifty Years of Caribbean Migration to Britain'. 1998. In *A New World Order*. Caryl Phillips. 2001. London: Vintage, 2002b, 264–82.

———. 'Amistad'. In *A New World Order*. Caryl Phillips. 2001. London: Vintage, 2002c, 75–88.

———. 'Conclusion: The "High Anxiety" of Belonging'. In *A New World Order*. Caryl Phillips. 2001. London: Vintage, 2002, 303–9.

———. 'Following On'. In *A New World Order*. Caryl Phillips. 2001. London: Vintage, 2002, 232–40.
———. 'Introduction: A Little Luggage'. In *A New World Order*. Caryl Phillips. 2001. London: Vintage, 2002, 241–6.
———. 'Introduction: The Burden of Race'. In *A New World Order*. Caryl Phillips. 2001. London: Vintage, 2002, 9–17.
Phillips, Mike. *The Last Candidate*. New York: Dell, 1990.
———. *Point of Darkness*. London: Michael Joseph, 1994.
———. *An Image to Die For*. London: Harper Collins, 1995.
———. *The Dancing Face*. London: Harper Collins, 1997.
Procter, James. *Writing Black Britain 1948–1998*. Manchester: Manchester University Press, 2000.
Richards, Yvette. *Single Black Female*. London: X-Press, 1994.
Ross, Leone. *All the Blood Is Red*. London: Angela Royal, 1996.
———. *Orange Laughter*. London: Angela Royal, 1999.
Roy, Lucinda. *Lady Moses*. New York: Harper Collins, 1998.
Sesay, Kadija George (ed.) *Write Black: Write British: From Post Colonial to Black British Literature*. London: Hansib, 2003.
———. 'Transformations within the Black British Novel'. In *Black British Writing*. Eds R. Victoria Arana and Lauri Ramey. New York: Palgrave Macmillan, 2004, 99–108.
Sissay, Lem. *The Fire People: A Collection of Contemporary Black British Poets*. London: Payback, 1998.
Smith, John. Leader's Speech, Labour Party Annual Conference, Brighton, September 1993, http://www.britishpoliticalspeech.org/speech-archive.htm?speech=199 (accessed 10 December 2011).
Srivastava, Atima. *Transmission*. London: Serpent's Tail, 1992.
———. *Looking for Maya*. London: Quartet, 1999.
Stein, Mark. *Black British Literature: Novels of Transformation*. Columbus: Ohio State University Press, 2004.
Syal, Meera. *Anita and Me*. 1996. London: Flamingo, 2002.
Traynor, Joanna. *Sister Josephine*. London: Bloomsbury, 1997.
Velickovic, Vedrana. 'Melancholic Travellers and the Idea of (un)belonging in Bernardine Evaristo's *Lara* and *Soul Tourists*'. *Journal of Postcolonial Writing* 48.1 (2012): 65–78.
Walters, Vanessa. *Rude Girls*. London: Pan, 1996.
———. *The Best Things in Life*. London: Pan, 1998.
Wambu, Onyekachi. *Empire Windrush: Fifty Years of Writing about Black Britain*. London: Victor Gollancz, 1998.
Wheatle, Alex. *Brixton Rock*. London: BlackAmber, 1999.

5

Historical Representations
Between the Short and Long Twentieth Centuries: Temporal Displacement in the Historical Fiction of the 1990s

Nick Hubble

The end of history

Historical fiction has been one of the dominant forms of mainstream literary fiction over the contemporary period as indicated by the continued success of various examples of such novels – from John Berger's *G* (1972) and J.G. Farrell's *The Siege of Krishnapur* (1973) to Hilary Mantel's *Wolf Hall* (2009) and *Bring Up the Bodies* (2012) – in winning the United Kingdom's premier literary award, the Man Booker Prize. The 1990s was no exception in this respect with winners including A.S. Byatt's *Possession* (1990) and Pat Barker's *The Ghost Road* (1995), both of which are considered in more detail during the course of this chapter. However, what distinguishes this decade are the larger historical changes that occurred within it as outlined in the introduction to this volume. In particular, the fall of the 'Iron Curtain', which immediately preceded the 1990s, and the subsequent dissolution of the Soviet Union in 1991 marked the end of the global political order which had defined the post-war period. This seismic shift had immediate consequences for how history was understood by apparently legitimizing Francis Fukuyama's assertion of 'The End of History' and implicitly supporting various postmodern conceptions of history and historical fiction as advanced by theorists such as Fredric Jameson and Linda Hutcheon. This chapter will assess such conceptions by referring to books from the decade by writers such as Lawrence Norfolk and Mary Gentle. However, in retrospect, it is noticeable how much of the decade's historical fiction was set in the late Victorian and Edwardian periods. Aside from the work of Byatt and Barker, key contributions to this field came from writers who had established themselves in what we would have once considered to be non-literary genre fiction, such as Christopher Priest, Alan Moore and Kim Newman. Subsequently, the decade's close was bracketed by Sarah Waters's trio of novels set in Victorian London: *Tipping the Velvet* (1998), *Affinity* (1999) and *Fingersmith* (2002). On the face of it, it seems unclear why the collapse of Communism and the establishment of a postmodern age should have led to this outpouring of what has become known subsequently as Neo-Victorian fiction. By trying to answer this question, this chapter seeks to reconceptualize how one might understand both the 1990s in Britain historically and the decade's historical fiction.

Fukuyama's 'The End of History' began life as an invited lecture given at the University of Chicago in the 1988–9 academic year and was subsequently written up in 1989 as an article for the American journal *The National Interest*, before becoming extended into a longer book, *The End of History and the Last Man* (1992). The central thesis of his argument was that a global consensus had emerged recognizing the legitimacy of liberal democracy, which could now be regarded as the endpoint of ideological evolution and, therefore, of history. It is tempting to suggest that subsequent developments – such as 9/11, wars in the Balkans, the Gulf and Afghanistan and the financial crash of 2007–8 – have proved Fukuyama wrong but this would be to misunderstand his argument. Indeed, as he points out himself, even the short space of the three years between article and book was marked by the 'occurrence of events' including the fall of the Berlin Wall, the protests and crackdown in Tiananmen Square and the Iraqi invasion of Kuwait, but, his argument is, such events do not equate to 'History' understood as a 'single, coherent, evolutionary process' (xii). Rather, following the theoretical tradition of Hegel and Marx in arguing that history will end when humans have achieved a satisfactory form of society, Fukuyama claims that Western liberal democracy as constituted in the early 1990s is so well-suited to meeting human needs as to form such a historical end-state. The strength of his argument lies in the fact that it allows for 'events' of the type mentioned above and so therefore is not disturbed by their unceasing continuation:

> For the foreseeable future, the world will be divided between a post-historical part, and a part that is still stuck in history. Within the post-historical world, the chief axis of interaction between states would be economic, and the old rules of power politics would have decreasing relevance. That is, one could imagine a democratic Europe that was multipolar and dominated by German economic power, in which Germany's neighbours nonetheless felt relatively little sense of military threat and did not take any special efforts to increase their level of

military preparedness. There would be considerable economic but little military competition. The post-historical world would still be divided into nation-states, but its separate nationalisms would have made peace with liberalism and would express themselves increasingly in the sphere of private life alone. Economic rationality, in the meantime, will erode many traditional features of sovereignty as it unifies markets and production.

On the other hand, the historical world would still be riven with a variety of religious, national, and ideological conflicts depending on the stage of development of the particular countries concerned, in which the old rules of power politics continue to apply. Countries like Iraq and Libya will continue to invade their neighbours and fight bloody battles. In the historical world, the nation-state will continue to be the chief locus of political identification. (276–7)

With the European Union and the United States poised in 2014 to sign a new free trade agreement (after seven rounds of talks), while countries of the 'historical world' are involved in 'bloody battles', it might be argued that Fukuyama's position still retains its explanatory power with respect to understanding global politics at the time of writing. However, little remains of the optimism that pervaded liberal democracy in the early 1990s following the collapse of communism and the sense of release from the potential nuclear Armageddon that had haunted the post-war decades. Leaving aside the question of how mutually interdependent is the division between post-historical and historical countries that Fukuyama describes, or whether given the West's interests in the oil fields of the Gulf, it can even be described as post-historical, there remain other global phenomena, such as Climate Change, which cannot so easily be dismissed as merely outdated historical 'events'. If Western liberal democracy is based on a model of consumption that is unsustainable, then it cannot be the end-state of 'History'. At the moment, it is impossible to say how various technologies and developments will impact on this question of sustainability, but at the least, it does raise questions about the viability of Fukuyama's perspective, which is broadly speaking that of the ruling neoliberal ideology of the West. Therefore, it is worth considering alongside two different theories of history which also emerged at the same time in response to the same events that ushered in the 1990s, which is the concept of the 'short twentieth century'.

According to some historians, the period between 1914 and 1989 was a historical anomaly – at its most extreme, such a view entails seeing this 'short twentieth century' as coterminous with a world civil war between Bolshevism and the Liberal West with the latter emerging triumphant victors – so that the fall of the Soviet Union and the consequent global political realignments have allowed events to get back on the course they were following before the First World War. Indeed, a curious kind of consensus has developed around this notion of the 'short twentieth century' because it has also been endorsed by the Marxist historian Eric Hobsbawm, who agrees in his *Age of Extremes: The Short Twentieth Century 1914–1991* (1994) that 'The world that went to pieces at the end of the 1980s was the world shaped by the impact of the Russian Revolution of 1917' (4). Of course, Hobsbawm is trying to subvert the right-wing notion of the 'world civil war', by arguing that the success of capitalism was actually due to the long-term effects of the October revolution and the twin achievements in particular of defeating Nazi Germany and 'establishing the popularity of economic planning, [thereby] furnishing [capitalism] with some of the procedures for its reform' (7–8). Similarly, while he concedes the general charge of historical anomaly, he cleverly argues that what was truly anomalous about it was the socialist-inspired unprecedented period of economic growth and social transformation that characterized the 'Golden Age' of 1947–73. However, the trouble with this line of argument is that while it challenges right-wing ideas of history, it is equally conservative in its own way: seeking rather to close the twentieth century off as an idealized past than to continue further the struggles which characterized it. Such closure positively invites the neoliberal assertions of 'The End of History', to which Hobsbawm's text is ostensibly opposed.

An alternate historiography to that of the 'short twentieth century' can be found in Giovanni Arrighi's *The Long Twentieth Century* (1994), which develops Fernand Braudel's idea that finance capital is not the high point of global capitalism but a repeated stage marking the transition from one cycle of capitalist accumulation to another. Suggesting that this idea corresponds to Karl Marx's general formula of capital MCM', which represents the transition of fluid money capital (M) into fixed commodity capital (C) and back into (increased) fluid capital (M'), Arrighi identifies four overlapping systemic cycles of capitalist accumulation: respectively long fifteenth-sixteenth, seventeenth, nineteenth and twentieth centuries (6, 364). Periods of finance capitalism, when capital is released from the fixed commodity form, constitute the overlapping transitional phases between the cycles. For example, the financial expansion within the period 1870–1914 can be seen as both the final phase of a long nineteenth century and the opening phase of a long twentieth century, because it effectively began with capital flowing out from the fixed commodity form of nineteenth-century industry – typically associated with British global hegemony – and ended with capital flowing into twentieth-century mass production lines – characterized by Arrighi as the 'Fordist-Keynesian regime of accumulation' – typically associated with American global hegemony. According to Arrighi's model, the end of the 1947–73 'Golden Age' was not the collapse of a utopian ideal but merely the inevitable breakdown of the Fordist–Keynesian system as capital once again flowed out of the fixed commodity form in a new phase of financial expansion.

If the wider process of overlapping systemic cycles of capitalist accumulation were to continue, one might expect this latest phase of financial expansion to mark both the ending of the long twentieth century and the opening of a long twenty-first century. While this kind of specific periodization can only be dated convincingly in retrospect, an economic commentator such as Larry Elliott of the *Guardian* newspaper felt confident enough in Arrighi's thesis to use it as the basis for arguing in 2010 that the long twentieth century was clearly now on limited time:

> The financialisation of the American economy in turn can be traced back to the mid-1970s, so by this interpretation of history, the dotcom collapse of 2000–01 and the financial crisis of 2007–08 (with the military entanglements in Iraq and Afghanistan sandwiched in between) are part of a much longer term development. According to this thesis, the concentration of economic power on Wall Street, the stagnation of incomes for all but the rich, the structural trade deficit, the military overreach, the switch from being the world's biggest creditor nation to its biggest debtor add up to a simple conclusion: we are in the twilight years of the long American century (Elliott n.p.)

In retrospect, therefore, it can be argued contra Fukuyama that far from the 1990s representing the possibility of extending a 'new world order' of stability and satisfaction rooted in the global triumph of liberal democracy, they marked the first moment when people became aware that they were caught between the Short and Long Twentieth Centuries – that is to say, that they became fully aware that all the economic and political certainties that had held during the previous decades were now irrevocably in a state of flux. In this sense, however, evolutionary 'History' had indeed come to an end because it was no longer obvious which of many possible trajectories the 'right' one was.

Historiographic and biographical metafiction

The 1990s context of social flux and political uncertainty not only called our understanding of history into question but also one's understanding of historical fiction, and in this respect, Linda Hutcheon's discussion of postmodern historiographic metafiction, published at the end of the previous decade, was to prove influential with critics seeking new approaches in keeping with the times. Hutcheon defines historiographic metafiction as foregrounding the unreliability of historical narrative in opposition to the classic historical fiction of the nineteenth century, which she argues is 'motivated and made operative by a notion of history as a shaping force' (113). In particular, she focuses on what she takes to be the three defining characteristics of classic historical fiction as identified by the Marxist critic Georg Lukács in *The Historical Novel* (1981) and explains how historiographic metafiction differs. According to Hutcheon, Lukács is concerned with the universality of these novels within which the characters are types, but, in fact, their historical detail serves mainly to signify historicalness, and real historical personages occupy only secondary roles. In contrast, historiographic metafiction focuses on main characters who are not types and may well be real historical personages, who are represented self-reflexively in a manner which highlights both the lack of boundary that exists between fiction and fact, and the centrality of self-created narrative for making sense of facts.

For example, Lawrence Norfolk's *Lemprière's Dictionary* (1991) features John Lemprière, who was the author of the eponymous dictionary of classical history and mythology, as its main protagonist. The plot interlinks the nefarious dealings of a shadowy cabal with various real historical events spanning the foundation of the East India Company, the siege of La Rochelle and the French Revolution. The overall effect, rather like Thomas Pynchon's seminal postmodern novel, *The Crying of Lot 49* (1966), is to show 'history' as either a delusion or the product of an extended conspiracy. This possibility is highlighted by the way in which the classical myths Lemprière records alphabetically immediately manifest themselves in front of his eyes in real life causing him to question both causality and his own sanity before realizing that this is all part of an elaborate and cruel hoax being perpetuated upon him. Myth, history and fiction are shown as an entwined maze, which the protagonist has to negotiate individually before emerging blinking into the sunlight of the world of possibility.

However, such a set of circumstances is not as different from Lukács's analysis of the historical novel as Hutcheon's analysis would seem to suggest. While he argues that 'within capitalist society the class struggle of the proletariat gives birth to aims which directly unite the individual and the social' (175), he never simply equates history to a grand narrative of class struggle but recognizes it as the product of a heterogeneous interaction of social forces. For him, the strength of the classical historical novelists was their representation of the richness and complexity of popular life. Their characters may have been recognizable types but the achievement of novelists such as Walter Scott was 'to give living human embodiment to historical-social types' (34). In this sense, *Lemprière's Dictionary* is functioning as a Lukácsian historical novel because Lemprière is a recognizable type, a clerk with an enlightenment education, who is representative of the social impetus behind the French Revolution. However, the fact that he also simultaneously prefigures a modern London leftish sensibility is a product of the kind of postmodern self-reflexivity that Hutcheon describes. Therefore, *Lemprière's Dictionary* demonstrates that historical fiction and historiographic metafiction are not necessarily antithetical. Lukács would not have liked the novel for its bawdiness and irreverence, which he considered aspects of the development of the mass market in the later nineteenth century and the consequent pressure on writers 'to search for more and more exquisite, abnormal, perverse, etc., themes in order to escape monotony' (230). Lukács's attempt to isolate the materialist desires of the masses as the true revolutionary impulse by excluding sexual and consumer desires, led to his rejection of utopian dreaming as an alternative, and more inclusive, model for revolutionary desire and the driver of history: 'For the tendencies leading to the future are in fact more firmly and definitely contained in what really is than in the most beautiful Utopian dreams or projections' (421). Yet, in retrospect, it seems likely that it is the exclusion of utopian dreaming from the historical novel as naturalistic realism came to dominance in the later nineteenth century, rather than the impact of the market, that undermined the genre and led to its diminution as objected to extensively by Lukács in *The Historical Novel*. Viewed in this perspective, as this chapter will seek to demonstrate, 1990s British historical fiction was not so much a postmodern reflection on the collapse of the grand narrative of 'History', as a response designed to open up more diverse and heterogeneous forms of historical agency that addressed 'abnormal' and 'perverse' desires alongside social and materialist needs.

Not only did the historical fiction of the decade, such as the *Regeneration* trilogy and *Tipping the Velvet*, address such non-normative desires but also a significant amount of it was set in the 1870–1919 period in which the long nineteenth century had broken apart and the long twentieth century had been born: the nearest analogue to the final phase of the long twentieth century which was now discernible. Max Saunders's *Self Impression: Life Writing, Autobiografiction, and the Forms of Modern Literature* (2010) describes this long turn of the nineteenth to twentieth century, which he extends from the 1870s to the 1930s, as being dominated by the emergence of an awareness of an inner life that was inconsistent with mid-Victorian certitude and which manifested itself in the widespread appearance of 'autobiografiction', a term dating from 1906. His examples of this phenomenon include books such as *The Autobiography of Mark Rutherford* (1881) and H.G. Wells's *Boon* (1915), which are not just fictional versions of autobiography but texts which consciously set out to present 'identity and the project of self-representation as problematic' (142). In other words, they foreground the complex non-identity at the core of subjectivity: that, on the one hand, the 'I' has to be somehow other than the self it speaks for in order for it to have the perspective to speak of itself as a discrete self, while, on the other hand, there is a gap between the conscious self and its unconscious motivations. This is a similar problematic to the one foregrounded by historiographic metafiction: the fact that narrative representation can never be identical with the actual events of the past. The intermediate form between autobiografiction and historiographic metafiction is what Saunders calls biographical metafiction in which the foregrounded problematic is the non-identity between the actual (imagined) subject of the fictional biography and their representation within the text. Saunders suggests this form can be traced back well before the conventional dating of the postmodern period to at least 'say, 1941 – the year of Nabokov's *The Real Life of Sebastian Knight*' (497), but he goes on to describe Byatt's *Possession*, published right at the beginning of the 1990s as the prime example of the form.

Byatt's novel concerns two contemporary scholars, Roland and Maud, and their involvement with two Victorian poets, Randall Henry Ash and Christabel Lamotte – the story being supplemented by poems, letters, journals and extracts from biographies that have been created by Byatt but which are presented as the reproduction of actual texts. The result is that the satisfaction of the mutual desires that the Victorian couple could not lastingly fulfil are eventually realized by their present-day counterparts. The structure is similar to the 1981 film version of John Fowles's *The French Lieutenant's Woman* (1969), adapted by Harold Pinter, in which the alternate endings of the novel are transposed to the film-within-the-film and the relationship between the fictional actors playing the parts in that film. Superficially, *Possession* appears to be imposing a happy ending on the template of viewing the Victorian past through a contemporary focus that both versions of *The French Lieutenant's Woman* refuse. However, as Saunders demonstrates convincingly, the interplay between biography and literature in *Possession* functions in a much more sophisticated manner than the above summary might suggest (although it is difficult not to suspect that part of the book's popularity was nonetheless due precisely to its happy ending). According to Saunders, there are two ways in which the framing of the novel structures the fictional writings within it. First, the two contemporary scholars find out as much about themselves through their study as about their objects; most importantly, that they love each other: 'Their literary work turns out to matter to them as biography rather than as literature' (498). Second, they find that the texts – poems, journals and other writings – which they think they know as scholars transpire to have had quite different personal meanings to their subjects: 'the literary works they are studying turn out to have mattered to their writers more as biography than as literature' (498). This reconnection of texts with lives, implicit to the 'biographical turn' identified here by Saunders, reinscribes the historical novel with a Lukácsian agency.

In general terms, what becomes apparent from these metafictional forms of historical writing that became paramount in the 1990s is that at the same time as history was being exposed as not having a single unified meaning, it was also being revealed as something whose meaning could not be contained in any way either. As the sense of universal meaning closed down, new possibilities opened up for those prepared to accept the multiple meanings of a fragmented, heterogeneous world.

The beginning of historics

This model of biographical metafiction is also followed by another neo-Victorian novel, Christopher Priest's tale of feuding turn-of-the-century stage magicians, *The Prestige* (1996). There are a number of similar elements to those found in Byatt's narrative: notably severely alienated contemporary characters who are the descendents of the two stage magicians, the disrupting of fake séances, and the story being advanced through the reproduction of extracts from memoirs and diaries. The unreliability of these accounts is foregrounded by a passage from the journal of one of the magicians, Alfred Borden: 'Already, without once writing a falsehood, I have started the deception that is my life. The lie is contained in these words, even in the very first of them. It is the fabric of everything that follows, yet nowhere will it be apparent' (38). The 'very first of these words' is 'I' (35). As discussed above, 'I' can never be identical with the self being described; it is a grammatical fiction. In this case, this non-identity is highlighted in the text by the fact that Borden is actually both of a pair of identical twins who share the personal pronoun between themselves without distinction. The fact that there are two of them/him is the secret behind his most celebrated illusion, 'The New Transported Man'. The trick begins with Borden standing on the stage in front of a wardrobe playing with a ball before bouncing it across the stage and stepping back into the wardrobe and shutting the door. As the door shuts, the door on an identical wardrobe placed at the other side of the stage opens and Borden steps out and catches the ball as it comes past.

It is a trick which Borden's rival Rupert Angier, the Great Danton, finds understandably difficult to replicate despite his use of an out-of-work actor as a double. The drunken unreliability of the actor, whom Angier comes to suspect of deliberately sabotaging his tricks, is a reminder of the non-identity between our unconscious and conscious selves and the fact that the latter does sometimes work against what we perceive to be our best interests. Angier eventually solves this problem only after travelling to the United States and hiring the electrical experimenter, Nicola Tesla (a real historical person), to invent a machine that will project a human being through space. This is done, but the result is not quite what Angier bargained for because while he finds himself projected a distance of fifty years or so, which is enough for him to work the trick of disappearing from the stage of a theatre and instantaneously appearing balancing on the rim of the circle in the audience to rapturous applause, a lifeless doppelgänger of him is left at the point of departure. This problem can be solved for the purposes of the show by an ingeniously placed trapdoor and a puff of smoke, but stagecraft is no help for the implied possibility that Angier is in fact killing himself every time he performs the trick and only continuing in the shape of a newly formed clone. This element of the novel is intensified by the 2006 film adaptation, directed by Christopher Nolan, in which the doppelgänger is alive; a problem which Angier solves by placing an open tank of water underneath the trapdoor every time he performs the trick so that one of him is drowned and his identity therefore preserved. In effect, in both book and film, Angier's trick is dependent on the notion of 'quantum suicide', a hypothetical thought experiment assuming the existence of parallel universes, which is a reworking of the equally hypothetical Shrödinger's cat experiment.

This latter conundrum was described by Erwin Shrödinger in 1935 to illustrate what he perceived as a problem with the 'Copenhagen Interpretation' of quantum mechanics. According to quantum mechanics, particles can exist in superposition, which is to say in more than one place or state at the same time, and this can be mathematically described by equations that represent what is known as the 'waveform' state. This discovery raised obvious problems for the basis of classical physics in the laws of cause and effect. The solution devised to this problem, known as the Copenhagen Interpretation, was the idea that if something is not being observed, then it behaves as a waveform, but if it is being observed, then its waveform collapses so that we see things in only one place at a time. The point of Shrödinger's example of a cat placed in a box with a quantum trigger that might or might not lead to it being killed in some way – for example, by releasing poison – was to illustrate that according to the logic of the Copenhagen Interpretation the cat must be simultaneously both alive and dead as long as the box is not opened and observation has therefore not occurred. The idea was intended as a refutation of the Copenhagen Interpretation on the grounds that it would be absurd to insist that a cat could be both alive and dead, but the signification of the analogy has subsequently taken on a further life of its own. Specifically, since the development of the 'Parallel Worlds' hypothesis by Hugh Everett in the 1950s, the idea of the experiment can be used to illustrate how after the first second of the experiment, there will be two parallel universes in one of which the cat will be alive and in the other of which it will be dead. The physicist Max Tegmark devised the quantum suicide paradigm as a hypothetical version of the experiment that would convince someone of the existence of parallel worlds:

> Surprisingly, this experiment requires only rather low-tech equipment that's readily available. However, it also requires you to be an unusually dedicated experimentalist, since it amounts to a repeated and faster version of Shrödinger's cat experiment – with you as the cat. The apparatus is a 'quantum machine gun', which fires depending on the outcome of a quantum measurement. Specifically, each time the gun is triggered, it places a particle in superposition where it's equally in two states at once (spinning clockwise and counterclockwise, say), then measures the particle. If the particle is found to be in the first of the two states, the gun fires, otherwise it merely makes an audible click [...] you'll predict that you'll hear a seemingly random sequence of shots and duds such as *bang-click-bang-bang-bang-click-click-bang-click-click*. Suddenly you do something radical: you place your head in front of the gun barrel and wait. (2014: 216)

What happens next depends on whether Everett's parallel universes are real or not. If they are not, the 'dedicated experimentalist' might hear one or two clicks but would be dead within seconds. However, if they are real:

> There will be two parallel universes after the first second: one where you're alive and one where you're dead and there's blood all over the place. In other words, there's exactly one copy of you having perceptions both before and after the trigger event, and since it occurred too fast to notice, the prediction is that you'll hear *click* with 100% certainty. Wait a little longer, and you'll find this quite striking: as soon as you put your head in the firing line, the seemingly random

sequence of bangs and clicks gives way to just *click-click-click-click-click-click-click*, etc. (217)

Under such (hypothetical) circumstances, the laws of probability simply would not hold and the consequence would be the equivalent of magic. Thinking about *The Prestige* in these terms allows us to perceive of Angier as exactly such a 'dedicated experimentalist' whose commitment to the logic of quantum suicide allows him to break the rules of probability to real magical effect, as opposed to Borden who is merely performing a good trick.

However, there is a catch to quantum suicide and this is that the experiment works because the subject is also the object. Once you have a second observer, then they are just going to see the participant get their brains blown out very quickly in millions of universes. As Tegmark observes, 'you might experimentally convince yourself that the quantum parallel universes are real, but you can never convince anyone else!' (217). The waveform, therefore, might be going on across the parallel universes as a whole, but in any particular one, it would still be subject to 'collapsing' back into the conventional laws of physics and probability when observed. Therefore, because Angier is being observed by an audience of hundreds, his playing with probability should automatically collapse. The reason this does not happen is because like all stage magicians he relies upon misdirecting his audience so that they are looking the wrong way. Misdirection, at its most basic level, functions simply by placing an object close to another apparently more interesting object that distracts the attention of onlookers. By use of lighting, set design and smoke effects, Angier distracts his audience so that his own particular version of quantum suicide is not subject to waveform collapse. In highlighting this through depicting the extremes of Angier's performance, Priest implies that all stage magic is dependent on preventing waveform collapse and allowing superposition of objects to exist within the audience's consciousness.

Moreover, through his use of journals and diaries to reveal the thoughts of both magicians, it is evident that Priest is using the example of the stage magician's use of misdirection, to postpone waveform collapse long enough for the trick to be enacted, as a metaphor for the writer's use of suspension of disbelief. This metaphor, however, is double-edged because while, on one level, it simply suggests that the writer needs readers to be aware of the flux of probability inherent to the waveform in order for them to enjoy a story that is contrary to the laws of cause and effect, it also raises the subversive possibility that the waveform is the deeper reality and our notions of cause and effect merely a story that simplifies the complex process of actually living in the world. If we think of the nature of reality according to quantum physics as a kind of dream, the waveform is equivalent to the latent content of the dream, and the manifest content is the product of waveform collapse. However, while physicists pretend the waveform has collapsed, so that they can pretend that things are in only one place at a time and that the classical laws of physics hold so that they can do experiments and make measurements, they are actually perfectly aware that the waveform never collapses. Basically, people choose the manifest content of reality to impose order on life. Consensus reality is a product of waveform collapse; a partial fixing of randomness that allows an individual to reconcile their subjective, internal modelling of the world around them with an external physical reality that is always radically random and unknowable. A writer like Priest alerts his readers to this situation and implicitly poses the question as to whether they should be accepting the partial truth of consensus reality, whether that be of history or the contemporary society reflected in the framing narrative of *The Prestige*, or embracing the complex world of multiple possibilities that lay hidden underneath; a world full of the promise of new beginnings.

Looking again at Norfolk's *Lemprière's Dictionary*, it is possible to see similar themes in evidence. For example, Shrödinger's cat experiment is implicitly referenced in a passage involving the Imperial Internuncio of the Hapsburg Empire who has been imprisoned by the Turks. The Turks find themselves in a quandary as neither decapitation, implying a hard-line insistence on fighting, nor returning him home, implying appeasement, represents the message they wish to send, and therefore, they compromise by leaving him shut up in a crate: 'If the Internuncio survived, all well and good. If not, well, he was the enemy after all' (405). More generally, the novel equates a malign binary automatism with the conspirators trying to impose a 'Zero State' (363) on humanity and history. Against this, the attempt to hoax Lemprière, into believing that the classical myths he is recording in his dictionary are coming true, misfires by raising the possibility that 'all his dreams came true' (269) and, therefore, shifting the terrain of the novel from the manifest content of consensus reality towards the latent mutability of a dream-world, consistent with the multiple possibilities of parallel worlds. In such a world where dreams come true and babies can turn into seagulls, Lemprière can see the alternatives to being trapped by his ancestor into taking up his role in patriarchal history and therefore escapes from the destiny that has been set down for him. However, in general, this contestation of history in the name of new possibilities which became the most significant form of historical fiction in the 1990s was particularly prevalent in the work of writers, such as

Priest (for whom, see also Hubble 2005, 2007), who had developed their careers by writing science fiction and other forms of genre fiction. In *Archaeologies of the Future* (2005), Fredric Jameson argues that science fiction emerged as a modern genre in the late nineteenth century by superseding historical fiction and registering a sense of the future in the space formerly occupied by a sense of the past (see 284–6). Therefore, it is not surprising that by the 1990s, when history was in a state of flux comparable with that at the end of the nineteenth century as described in the first section of this chapter, science fiction should prove itself to have been a form of secret history all along.

Secret histories

The title of *The Prestige* comes from the three stages of an illusion, as described in the novel: the setup, the performance and the prestige: 'the product of magic. If a rabbit is pulled from a hat, the rabbit, which apparently did not exist before the trick was performed, can be said to be the prestige of that trick' (73). The point is that the aim of magic is not simply to access the multiple possibilities of the waveform and promote chaos but, rather, to change a rather mundane form of consensus reality – an empty hat, for example – into something more exciting – by pulling a rabbit out of it, for example – that forms part of a new stable consensus reality that the audience can accept. This transformative function of illusion has been identified by critics as central to how literature functions; indeed, it might even be seen as the purpose of literature if one wanted to be didactic about it. For example, in *Illusion and Reality* (1937), Christopher Caudwell argues the case that it is poetry's capacity for illusion that enables social change:

> In the collective festival, where poetry is born, the phantastic world of poetry anticipates the harvest and, by so doing, makes possible the real harvest. But the illusion of this collective phantasy is not a mere drab copy of the harvest yet to be: it is a reflection of the emotional complex involved in the fact that man must stand in a certain relation to others and to the harvest, that his instincts must be adapted in a certain way to Nature and other men, to make the harvest possible ... It is a real picture of man's heart. (81)

In other words, by presenting the world changed in imagination, literature allows people to adapt mentally to the projected new possibilities, which, in turn, allow them to adapt to the change when it actually happens. Change, itself, is always potentially unsettling and unstable; the key element here, however, is not the change *per se* but the fact that such a changed set of conditions is presented as a stable reality with which people will feel secure. The reason why Jameson links science fiction with historical fiction is that they both serve precisely such a purpose of allowing people to deal with change. The *Waverley* novels of Walter Scott provided a retrospective coming to terms with the shift in Scottish history from the feudalism of the Highland clans towards the dominance of the capitalist classical economics of Adam Smith and the rationalism of the Scottish Enlightenment. By the late nineteenth century, the pace of technological change in Britain shifted the focus of popular anxiety from the need to adapt to changes that had already happened to fear of the future changes that were inevitably coming. A writer such as H.G. Wells, in books ranging from *The Time Machine* (1895) to *The Shape of Things to Come* (1933), provided a framework for contemplating that change, which even if it included unpleasant features such as wars, suggested that at least there were various evolutionary stages for a society to progress or regress through and, therefore, that not just anything and everything could happen. In this manner, science fiction, like the historical fiction whose function it began to usurp in the 1880s and 1890s, actually functions by mapping the limits of possible change and showing how people might adjust to that, rather than simply celebrating unknown futures.

As the 1990s progresses, despite the attempt of those such as Fukuyama who posited the future as simply contemporary Western liberal democracy spread globally, *fin-de-siècle* uncertainty began to spread – even if it mainly manifested itself in overblown 'scare' stories such as the so-called millennium bug or Year 2000 problem – as it became clear that the future was uncertain in comparison to the relatively stable earlier decades of the post-war period. In this context, science fiction and related fantastic genres began to gain a cultural centrality due to their capacity to provide a framework for coming to terms with unknown change. Moreover, works such as Mary Gentle's *Ash: A Secret History* (1999), which was shortlisted for the Arthur C. Clarke Award in 2000, foregrounded how the genre could function as a realist intervention against potential chaos. During its 1,100 pages of alternate history, this novel revolves around characters who, like magicians, collapse the waveform of quantum randomness in order to create an understandable world; a safe space that ensures continued human existence in the face of the threat of hostile radical indeterminacy. The eponymous heroine, Ash is a fourteenth-century mercenary captain involved in the desperate defence of the Duchy of Burgundy against a Carthaginian Empire. Carthage is ruled by 'Wild Machines' – artificial intelligences – created in antiquity, who are sending forth a perpetual darkness which is spreading slowly across Europe. Eventually, only the Duchy of Burgundy, which is figured in a familiar trope of mythology as the 'golden country', remains light and thus stands between Carthage and global denomination. However, once the Duke, Charles, is mortally injured, the light begins to fade, and the Burgundians institute a hunt in the middle of the artificial winter now surrounding their city, to find his successor. The common-born mercenary, Ash, finds this ludicrous but takes part nonetheless, accompanying her mercenary company's Burgundy-born surgeon, the womanizer Florian, who by now readers know to be a lesbian, Floria, disguising herself as a man. The hunt through stunted countryside quickly turns into a chase through a mythical 'wild wood' in which Ash tracks down a beast but cannot decide whether it is real or not:

> Ash could not tell which she saw: a hart with muddy, bloodstained sides, and red rolling eyes; or a beast with a coat like milk, and eyes of gold. She froze.
> Someone tugged her hand.
> She felt it, dimly; felt someone unpeeling her fingers in her gauntlet from the grip of her sword.
> The weight of the weapon left her hand. That jolted her into full alertness.
> Floria del Guiz strode forward in front of her, the sword held awkwardly in her right hand. A woman in doublet and hose, with her hood thrown back to the cold air. She circled right. Ash saw her expression: intent, frustrated, determined. Brilliant eyes, under straw-gold hair: all her tall, rangy, body alert, moving with old reflexes – *of course, she's from a noble Burgundian family, she will have hunted as a girl* – and as Ash opened her mouth to protest the loss of her sword, the black alaunt feinted left, and Floria stepped in. (773)

Floria, who by killing the hart has now become Duchess of Burgundy and the protector of humankind against the forces of darkness, observes to Ash: 'You hunted a myth. I made it real' (776). However, Ash still doesn't understand the full import of what has happened and tries to laugh it off:

> 'That's a pretty shabby looking miracle for a royal miracle.'
> 'No you've got it wrong. The Burgundian Dukes and Duchesses don't perform miracles. They prevent them being performed.'
> 'Finding a hart, out of season, in a wood with no game; this *isn't* a miracle?'
> Olivier de la Marche came a few steps closer to the hart. His battle-raw voice said, 'No, Demoiselle-Captain, not a miracle. The true Duke of Burgundy – or, as it now seems, the true Duchess – may find the myth of our Heraldic Beast, the crowned hart, and from it bring this. Not miraculous, but mundane. A true beast, flesh and blood, as you and I.' (776)

The decisive attribute of the ruler of Burgundy is precisely the capacity to collapse the waveform and enable a condition of stability as demonstrated by successfully hunting a mythic hart and reducing it to the state of reality by killing it. The idea that this ability to reinforce a liveable consensus reality is a rare human attribute is not merely a consequence of the plot but a central aspect of the novel's logic, which is critically concerned with the collective capacity of humanity for creating chaos. Indeed, it transpires that the reason why the Wild Machines are attacking Burgundy is not because they are evil or power-hungry but because they perceive Burgundy, or rather its ruler, as the exception among a humanity who are randomly unstable and prone to generate reality-destroying weapons from nuclear bombs to whatever destructive possibilities quantum physics may one day enable. As the Wild Machines say:

> IN THE END, YOU WILL ALL BE WONDER-WORKERS. YOU WILL BREED YOURSELF INTO IT. WE HAVE RUN THE SIMULATIONS A BILLION, BILLION TIMES: IT IS WHAT WILL BE, THERE IS NO WAY TO PREVENT IT EXCEPT BY PREVENTING YOU. WE WILL WIPE OUT HUMANITY, MAKE IT AS IF IT HAD NEVER EXISTED, SO THAT THE UNIVERSE WILL REMAIN COHERENT AND WHOLE. (1083)

It can be seen here how the inclusion of this alien – in this case, machine – intelligence in the novel subverts human-centric history and historical fiction. From the point of view of the Universe, history looks different and maybe humanity is the problem which must be overcome. This extra-human perspective originates in the genre of science fiction, dating back to Wells's *The War of the Worlds* (1898) and his creation of Martians with 'intellects vast and cool and unsympathetic' (1) as a means of decentring the British viewpoint of colonialism by depicting them as the colonized rather than the colonisers. Gentle may even be directly referencing Wells's Martians when she describes the Wild Machines: 'Their perception more vast than human; their power inorganic and endless, tapping into the fabric of the universe' (1111). This tradition of writing from an extra-human perspective has been carried through the twentieth century by writers such as Olaf Stapledon and Doris Lessing as a contestation of the human-centric norms of mainstream literary fiction, which demonstrates the capacity of humanity in general, and the British in particular, to switch adherence from one consensus reality to an opposing one in a very short period of time with destructive consequences. As discussed in the 1970s volume of this book series, Lessing's *Shikasta* (1979) represents an expansion of Orwell's argument in *Nineteen Eighty-Four* (1949) in this respect, by revealing the thorough embeddedness of the ideology of bourgeois individualism in these unstable collective mind states (see Hubble 2014). Such perspectives often draw from religious or philosophic traditions, and *Ash* is no exception in this respect as can be seen from the sequence of passages towards the end of the novel which assume the dialogic form of classical philosophy as two of the present-day protagonists from the framing narrative discuss the implications of the relationship between humanity and the instability of reality in a quantum universe:

> Burgundy exists among, and governs the shape of, the Real. It is – or has been – the one true reality, of which we are the imperfect shadows. Good lord, man, does nobody read Plato any more? ... The species-mind will continue to collapse the probable into a predictable real. But eventually, without Burgundy, enough random chaos will filter through, we'll become able to manipulate the Real again consciously – or technologically. There will be wars. Wars in which the Real is the casualty. (1099–1100)

Moreover, Burgundy functions in the novel as a kind of persistence of the Garden of Eden before the Fall, which means that the overall logic of *Ash* is very similar to the argument advanced by Walter Benjamin in 'Theses on the Philosophy of History' in his discussion of the angel of history:

> His face is turned towards the past. Where we perceive a chain of events, he sees one single catastrophe which keeps piling wreckage and hurls it in front of his feet. The angel would like to stay, awaken the dead, and make whole what has been smashed. But a storm is blowing from Paradise; it has got caught in his wings with such violence and the angel can no longer close them. This storm irresistibly propels him into the future to which his back is turned, while the pile of debris before him grows skyward. This storm is what we call progress. (1992: 249)

In this view, progress is the problem because it takes us ever further away from the utopian past possibility of a stable liveable consensus reality by trapping us in the permanent revolution of proliferating possibilities. On the other hand, simple nostalgia for the past does nothing to halt this progress and simply adds to the number of possible realities competing for people's attention. Benjamin argues that this circle can be broken only by bringing the historical trace of the past 'as it flashes up at the moment of danger' (247) into dialectical constellation with the present, so that it shapes a stability that allows humanity to live in tune with the extra-human world. Such a possibility is fictionally realized at the end of *Ash*, when Floria and Ash come to an accommodation with the Wild Machines by which they find themselves transported to the novel's present in the year 2009, along with Ash's company, as members of a UN-style military force encamped in Belgium but shortly to depart for peacekeeping duties on the Chinese border. This particular 'new world order' is stable because the Wild Machines have taken over the role of Burgundy and become a processing force outside time – in the same sense that Edenic utopias are outside time – from where they are 'monitoring the probability wave, keeping the possibility of miracle-working out of the Real' (1110–1). *Ash* is an illustration of how the alternate history subgenre of science fiction makes it easier to highlight temporal perspectives that are not so readily available to mimetic realist literary fiction. However, the quest for Benjaminian resolutions to the question of historical flux and instability can also be detected in other fiction of the decade, including arguably the most significant work of British 1990s historical fiction, Pat Barker's *Regeneration* trilogy, which is discussed in the following section of this chapter.

The ghosts of history

As I have discussed in 'Pat Barker's *Regeneration* Trilogy' (2006), moments in which a character becomes conscious of repressed elemental forces straining against the constructed meanings of 'reality' occur throughout Barker's fiction:

> In her first novel, *Union Street* (1982), eleven year-old Kelly Brown is scared by the appearance of a man in black on a fairground ghost train: simultaneously the lingering impression of a man she had met in the park earlier and the harbinger of her impending rape. Similar uncanny experiences occur in Barker's other early novels, including descriptions of séances in both *Liza's England* (originally published as *This Century's Daughter* in 1986 before being republished under Barker's original choice of title in 1996) and *The Man Who Wasn't There* (1989). This tendency has developed since the *Regeneration* trilogy – *Regeneration* (1991), *The Eye in the Door* (1993) and *The Ghost Road* (1995) – into a fully-realised psychosocial landscape, in which different planes of existence overlap and interact with different forms of class, gender and sexual consciousness. The wider transition in Barker's work, therefore, has been from the supernatural marking the imminent onset of unavoidable fate to it marking a series of human possibilities, which haunt the present but do not always come to pass. (153)

As this suggests, the *Regeneration* trilogy represents a key stage in Barker's work in which the concern with class and gender foregrounded in her first novels *Union Street* and *Blow Your House Down* (1984) becomes fully intersectional through the application of a temporal perspective that, if not itself science fictional, nonetheless paves the way to the 'generic turn' apparent in *Double Vision* (2003), which combines elements of crime fiction and Ballardian overtones to produce a 'fictional excavation of the future' (see Hubble 2011). At one point in

Double Vision, Barker uses the metaphor 'an infestation of ghosts' to describe the aftereffects of a forensic examination of a crime scene (250). This description recalls the various ghosts of the past which inhabit the *Regeneration* trilogy, ranging from those that the military psychologist, W.H.R. Rivers, remembers from his anthropological fieldwork on Eddystone in the Soloman Islands, to the visitations of dead soldiers who appear regularly to the traumatized officers that Rivers is treating at Craiglockhart War Hospital in the opening novel. The most famous of these officers are the two War poets, Siegfried Sassoon and Wilfred Owen, who in a memorable scene from *Regeneration* (83–4) discuss how the skulls in the trenches invoke for them both earlier dead soldiers from wars past and the sense that they will become the ghosts of the past for future generations. On one level, this serves to highlight not only how the repeating patterns of history entrap otherwise modern societies in cycles of destructive behaviour. The trilogy ends with Rivers half asleep in a hospital ward, following the military engagement in which Owen dies, remembering an exorcism performed on Eddystone by the healer Njiru, in which the unhappy spirits of the dead were allowed to depart. The implication, on one level, is the need to exorcise the repeating patterns of history that permeate modernity. However, the structure of the trilogy is much more sophisticated than this simple message would suggest.

The ghosts that infest the books are not just those of the past but also those of the future, particularly that of Billy Prior, a fictional creation of Barker's who is not only working-class and bisexual but also the source of an ahistorical contemporary sensibility that slowly comes to dominate the tone of the books. As Pat Wheeler demonstrates, Prior serves to explore a fault-line of '"moral" masculinity and sexual degeneracy' exposed by wartime conflation of 'masculinity and heterosexuality ... [with] national identity' (54–5). Like characters from throughout Barker's oeuvre, Prior's function at one level is to relive certain archetypal working-class experiences, but, because he is free from the contextual boundaries of the period where he has been located and is – in the words of his father as expressed in the novel – 'neither fish nor fowl' (57) in terms of class, sexuality and gender, he is able to represent possibilities of living that were not open to people at the time. For example, his sexual liaison with fellow officer, but social superior, Charles Manning in *The Eye in the Door*, subverts a number of assumptions of the period:

> Realising that Charles Manning cannot 'let go sexually with a social equal', Prior removes his uniform jacket, lights a cigarette, roughens his accent and transforms himself 'into the sort of working-class boy Manning would think it was all right to fuck' [Barker 1994: 11]. The potential antagonism of the situation

is then exacerbated by Manning taking Prior into what is obviously a servant's bedroom.

The hierarchical ordering seems obvious but events confound the reader's expectations as it is Prior who proceeds to take the active role and Manning who subsequently admits that 'I needed that ... I needed a good fucking' [Barker 1994: 14]. (Hubble 2006: 160)

As Wheeler notes, Prior performs working-class queerness, but this is not his self-image, and while it is a position he adopts from his own sexual need, he does not consider himself subordinate to Manning. Through the agency that this objective understanding gives him, Prior transforms the sexual encounter into a genuine mutual recognition between the two men that deconstructs their false equality as fellow officers by highlighting 'inequality and difference to the point that they become desired by, and thus fully interchangeable between, both participants' (Hubble 2006: 160). As Wheeler concludes, 'what is most evident in this episode of the novel is the idea that masculinity is transmutable and that hegemonic masculinity can be transformed and regenerated' (2011: 57).

One way to consider Prior's overall role in the trilogy would be to think of him as giving expression to all the repressed latent potentialities of the period. Rivers's role as a psychologist leads to an emphasis within the texts on the interpretation of dreams, a process which functions differently to how we have come to understand it by focusing on conflict resolution because 'the historical Rivers rejected Freud's insistence that hidden trauma of the kind involved in dreams was almost inevitably sexual' (Alden 2014: 60). As Natasha Alden notes, Barker invents dreams for Rivers rather than restricting herself to those he actually recorded in real life, and the first of these in *Regeneration* reflects the conflict stemming from 'River's sense of guilt about treating soldiers in order to return them to the front' (60). It is notable, however, that when Prior discusses one of his own dreams with Rivers in *The Eye in the Door*, in which he stabs an eye, he denies that there is any conflict because he identifies with the struggle of home front dissidents against surveillance: 'I mean it might be very inconvenient in real life but in the dream there was no doubt whose side I was on. Theirs.' (75). In performing the acts that would have been 'inconvenient' in real life, the fictional ghost-from-the-future Prior enables Barker to perform the Benjaminian task of bringing the present into dialectical constellation with the past and suggesting new possibilities of non-hierarchical living.

Each of the three volumes of the trilogy ends with an author's note outlining the historical basis of the elements within each novel. The first of these notes, from *Regeneration*, begins: 'Fact and fiction are so interwoven in this book that it may help the reader to know what is historical and what is not' (251). As Philip Tew comments, this is somewhat disingenuous when applied 'to what has appeared to be a fully fictionalized narrative with reconstructive ambitions' (167). As we have seen, it is not that difficult to distinguish between the invented escapades of Prior and the events rooted in the actual biographies of Owen, Sassoon and Rivers (for an in-depth analysis, see Alden 2014: 52–116). Yet, as Tew goes on to argue, the salience of Barker's notes lie in their highlighting of the mix of elements within the novels, which stem from the Benjaminian trans-historical perspective outlined above that brings into focus the extent of the asymmetries of the various class, gender and sexual relationships that were concealed within the apparently monolithic hierarchical society of the imperial British state in the run-up to, and during, the First World War. By re-invoking 'the past to reinforce its sense of crisis and instability', Barker, according to Tew, exposes 'the imperial illusion of social cohesion' (167). Of course, Barker's fictional interventions in British history were not merely concerned with setting the record straight but also functioned as a challenge to the political hierarchy of 1990s Britain in which she was writing. Margaret Thatcher might no longer have been Prime Minister but the ideas she espoused, such as the need to reclaim imperial Britain's 'greatness' and the superiority of so-called Victorian values, remained very much part of the ruling ideology.

Alternative Victorian values

In a 1983 television interview, Thatcher, the then prime minister, alleged – after prompting from the interviewer Brian Walden – that 'Victorian values' were the values that had made Britain great and the phrase became a hallmark of Thatcherism, denoting an emphasis on the self-reliance of individuals as opposed to the collective values that had characterized post-war British society up until the end of the 1970s. Within the interview, Thatcher related Victorian values to a politics rooted in conviction rather than the value of consensus (Thatcher 1983). Over time, Victorian values became associated with another of Thatcher's famous proclamations made in 1987: 'There is no such thing as society'. This broader conception encompassed, especially in the wake of the onset of AIDS, the endorsement of traditional family structures, morality and religious views as norms to be upheld. These values were to become subject to vigorous cultural contestation throughout the 1990s, and historical fiction was to become one of the principle forms that this took.

The fictional template for satirizing Victorian values long predated Thatcher's rise and fall. Beginning in 1969, the same year as Fowles published *The French Lieutenant's Woman* and only three years after Jean Rhys's *Wide Sargasso Sea* (1966) instituted the idea of rewriting Victorian literature, George Macdonald Fraser had been publishing his *Flashman* series which savagely satirized Victorian imperial adventures and morality in particular. As discussed by Sam Goodman in *The 1970s* volume of this series published in 2014, in common with J.G. Farrell's *The Siege of Krishnapur* (1973), Fraser's cynical historical parodies marked a subversion of both traditional historical novels and the mimetic realism of mainstream post-war literature (132–7). However, in their blending of historical figures and pre-existing literary characters – Flashman, himself, is the bully from Thomas Hughes's *Tom Brown's School Days* (1857) – Fraser's novels prefigured what would become known as the 'mash-up', a term applied to books such as Seth Grahame-Smith's *Pride and Prejudice and Zombies* (2009) which blend genre elements into classic literary texts. In fact, Fraser's own output in the 1990s increasingly became more self-conscious in its reference to fictional as well as historical sources. For example, the title story of *Flashman and the Tiger* (1999) features an encounter between Flashman and Sherlock Holmes, who attempts to deduce the origins of the former in his characteristic manner and is hopelessly wrong:

> ... this is a nautical, not a military man; he is not English, but either American or German – probably the latter, since he has certainly studied at a second-rate German university, but undoubtedly he has been in America quite lately. He is known to the police, is currently working as a ship's steward, or in some equally menial capacity at sea – for I observe that he has declined even from his modest beginnings – and will, unless I am greatly mistaken, be in Hamburg by the beginning of next week... (310)

However, by the time this amusing pastiche was published, a younger generation of writers had begun employing the mash-up to much sharper political effect.

Notably, Kim Newman, a journalist and film critic who started publishing fiction at the end of the 1980s, wrote *Anno Dracula* (1992), a sequel to Bram Stoker's 1897 novel *Dracula*, set in an alternate 1888 in which not only has Dracula survived but he has also married Queen Victoria and become in all practical respects the effective ruler of the British Empire. The plot revolves around the Jack the Ripper murders, which were also the subject of *From Hell*, the collaboration between Alan Moore, the author of graphic novels such as *Watchmen* (1987) and *V for Vendetta* (1990), and the comics artist Eddie Campbell, which ran as a serial between 1989 and 1996 before being first collected in 1999. *From Hell* is an intricately plotted and densely worked retelling of the murders drawing on multiple sources, which are discussed in an extensive set of annotations written by Moore in 1996. Although he does not employ mash-up techniques here (as he would in his subsequent series, *The League of Extraordinary Gentlemen*, begun in 1999), he does weave historical facts together in the manner of a novel, so that, for instance, the action cuts from London in the run-up to the murders to include the contemporaneous conception of Adolf Hitler (Chapter Five, 1–3). Moore states clearly that he perceives the period of the killings as a direct precursor to twentieth-century and contemporary concerns:

> In many ways, it seems to me that the 1880s contain the seeds of the twentieth century, not only in terms of politics and technology, but also in the fields of art and philosophy as well. The suggestion that the 1880s embody the essence of the twentieth century, along with the attendant notion that the Whitechapel murders embody the essence of the 1880s, is central to *From Hell*. (Appendix I, 14)

Newman was aware of these historical connections, but he chooses to highlight them in a different way by presenting the murders as being committed by Stoker's Dr Seward, who has been driven mad by the staking of Lucy Westenra and now preys on the vampire prostitutes of Whitechapel. *Anno Dracula's* cast is a mixture of Stoker characters, other fictional creations such as Henry Jekyll, Sherlock Holmes and Raffles, and historical personages – especially writers – such as Oscar Wilde, Arthur Morrison and Stoker, himself, who has been incarcerated in a concentration camp at Devil's Dyke by the repressive vampire regime. In fact, there is a huge range of esoteric literary reference – as opposed to Moore's range of historical reference – involved in the novel, much of which is acknowledged in the 'Annotations' section of the 2011 edition of the novel (427–42). Many of the characters have become vampires, although some of these are opposed to Dracula's reactionary politics, including Geneviève Dieudonné, an earlier fictional creation of Newman's taken from a novel set in the Warhammer Fantasy world written under the name of Jack Yeovil.

While, as the 'Afterword' to the novel explains, the roots of *Anno Dracula* lay in a 1978 Sussex University module called 'Late Victorian Revolt' and an interest in the invasion narratives of that period, Newman also admits to a desire 'to overlay the actual 1980s on the imaginary 1880s' (436). In particular, he wanted to juxtapose Government sloganizing about Victorian values 'with the real and imagined 1880s, when blood was flowing in the fog and there was widespread social unrest' (455). One example of this is Dracula's decision to outlaw 'unnatural vice' and punish sodomy by the stake (65), which functions as a correlative to Section 28 of the 1988 Local Government Act which banned local authorities from promoting homosexuality or representing it as a form of family relationship. However, more generally, the increased presence of vampires in London allows the novel to critique a society in which self-interest has become culturally dominant. As Geneviève reflects, the Ripper case is about more than the murders:

> It was about Disraeli's 'two nations', it was about the regrettable spread of vampirism among the lower classes, it was about the decline of public order, it was about the fragile equilibrium of a transformed kingdom. The murders were mere sparks, but Great Britain was a tinderbox. (109)

As a self-reflective vampire, Geneviève is like Barker's Billy Prior in her ability to recognize that inequality and difference can be the basis for a much more lasting state of mutual recognition than the implied normative homogeneity of 'Victorian values'. Her analysis of vampire couples and families can be read as a critique of the notion of monogamous marriages central to such normative values: 'After centuries together, they tended to meld into one creature with two or more bodies, leeching off each other so much they lost their original individualities' (363). In the novel's climactic scenes, set in Buckingham Palace, Queen Victoria is finally encountered in her shift and stockings kneeling 'by the throne, a spiked collar around her neck, a massive chain leading from it to a loose bracelet upon Dracula's wrist' (411). This powerful and disturbing image is suggestive as to the true regard in which 'Victorian values' were held by the Conservative Government of the 1980s and 1990s.

Newman turned *Anno Dracula* into a series of which the latest instalment has just appeared in 2013. The first sequel, *The Bloody Red Baron* (1995) shifts forward to the time of the First World War and is able to deploy its vampire metaphors effectively again in exposing the shortcomings and hypocrisies of that period. However, it also develops some interesting literary ideas through having Edgar Allen Poe, turned vampire, as one of the protagonists, who at one point encounters Franz Kafka. Through combinations such as this, and the central project of using standard genre conventions to write sophisticated historical fiction, Newman not only contributed to the trend within the 1990s that saw the sharp division between popular and literary fiction being challenged in contemporary writing but he also challenged the conventional view of literary history which locates such divisions across the twentieth century. One of the reasons that writers, who had studied English Literature at university, such as Newman or Norfolk, apparently wrote historical fiction was to intervene within, and rewrite, the literary history they had been subjected to. Another such writer whose work appeared towards the end of the decade was Sarah Waters, who had gained a PhD in 1995 for her thesis *Wolfskins and Togas: Lesbian and Gay Historical Fictions, 1870 to the Present*.

By 2007, the paperback edition of Waters's *Tipping the Velvet*, which had first appeared in 1999 following the novel's hardback publication the previous year, was already on its fifteenth reprinting. While this success was partly due to the popularity of the BBC television adaptation first shown in 2002, it still needs to be considered as something of a cultural phenomenon given that the novel – a picaresque lesbian coming-of-age story of a young woman called Nancy Astley, set against a cross-section of 1880s London life from music halls to the socialist movement – was initially hard to place with a publisher. Mark Wormald has discussed how the novel utilizes Waters's academic research into *fin de siècle* homosexual culture, and how it forms a decisive period for subsequent homosexual definition and organization (see Wormald 2006: 186–97). In particular, he highlights how Waters's intervention is not so much based on a reproduction of historical research as an imaginative reconstruction of the male homosexual discourses surrounding Victorian representations of Antinous, who was an attendant of the Roman emperor Hadrian. Waters utilizes her knowledge of such circles to invent a lesbian culture of the period, in the sequence in which Nancy is living with Diana Lethaby, for which there is no direct historical record. However, in the overall schema of the novel, this is only one of a number of roles that Nan takes on as she progresses from Whitstable oyster girl to music hall act to cross-dressed rent boy and so on to the point where, as Wormald indicates, she becomes able 'to reflect variously with ironic self-consciousness and with bitter plangency on the roles she finds herself playing' (191).

This capacity for ironic self-consciousness – again similar to that of Barker's Billy Prior – is revealed in the final section of Waters's book when Nancy is living in the same house with Florence, a social worker, and her brother, Ralph. The slow-build-up of her relationship with Florence reaches an unbearable intensity just at the moment of the great Socialist rally at Victoria Park in which Ralph is to speak. When he forgets his speech, Nancy, who had been helping him try to learn it, steps in to deliver it for him and is able to employ all the tricks of working a crowd that she has learnt. In a different book, this would be a triumphant finale, but Nancy's adeptness, in conjunction with other climactic events, causes Florence to question whether she ever means what she says or just repeats her speeches 'like a – like a dam' parrot' (461). This leads to a final moment of full self-recognition for Nancy: 'Oh! I feel like I've been repeating other people's speeches all my life. Now, when I want to make a speech of my own, I find I hardly know how' (471). However, of course, she does manage to find the words to say that she loves Florence and then kiss her 'careless of whether anybody watched or not' (472). Commenting on this closing passage to the novel, Stefania Ciocia figures Nancy's overall trajectory as a 'carnivalesque theatrical apprenticeship' in which she eventually moves beyond role-playing in order to participate in the carnivalesque London crowd 'which makes no difference between actors and spectators, where it does not matter whether one watches or is being watched' (n.p., paragraph 16).

Tipping the Velvet, therefore, is much more than a sexy romp, but a book which shows an individual learning how to achieve the balance of interaction with the world that enables agency. As Ciocia notes, 'Nancy claims for herself what Bakhtin would call the "third-person" or outsider status of the protagonist of a picaresque narrative (Bakhtin, 1990), a character who lives at the periphery of society and therefore can look onto its conventions and norms for what they are, unmasking their hidden ideological bias' (paragraph 17). In this respect, the novel realizes the qualities which Lukács located in the classical historical novels of the nineteenth century and represents a positive culmination of the trends that this chapter has identified in 1990s historical fiction, by which the postmodern recognition of the collapse of the grand narrative of 'History' became superseded by the realization that this enabled the birth of new histories reflecting multiplicity and diversity. It is true that Waters's next two novels were not so upbeat in this respect, partly due to the author's determination not to repeat the same story, but they do similarly end with the protagonists gaining self-knowledge, albeit especially painfully in *Affinity*. In some respects, the difference in tone is due to the fact that *Affinity* and *Fingersmith* are closer to the mash-up form than their predecessor, more obviously drawing on the models of Wilkie Collins and Charles Dickens. As Wormald suggests, Waters's combination of cultural research with 'a mischievous and notably self-conscious series of allusions to canonical literature' (192) can sometimes sit uneasily. However, these works also have a deeper literary resonance which lies in their performing the processes they describe. For example, there is a passage in *Affinity* which essays a thought experiment requiring the protagonist and the reader to imagine that nine-tenths of the population of England have an eye condition preventing them from seeing red. Those afflicted with such a condition would see blue skies, yellow flowers and think the world fine place while dismissing those who spoke of another marvellous colour as fools:

> 'Then,' he went on, 'a morning comes and you awaken – and your eye has corrected itself. Now you can see pillar-boxes and lips, poppies and cherries and guardsmen's jackets. You can see all the glorious shades of red –crimson, scarlet, ruby, vermilion, carnation, rose... You will want to hide your eyes, at first, in wonder and fear. Then you will look, and you will tell your friends, your family – and they will laugh at you, they will frown at you, they will send you to a surgeon or a doctor of the brain. It will be very hard, to become aware of all those marvellous scarlet things. And yet – tell me, Miss Prior – having seen them once, could you bear ever to look again, and see only blue, and yellow, and green?' (226)

Ostensibly, the speaker is making the case for spiritualism as adding an extra dimension to people's interaction with the world around them. Because of the way spiritualism is coded in the novel, we also read this as a description of how someone who has become self-aware that they are a lesbian or queer might view the world differently ever after. However, this rewriting of nineteenth-century literature also functions at another level. In common with the other neo-Victorian novels of the 1990s discussed here (most definitely including the work of Moore and Newman) and subsequent additions to the genre, such as Michel Faber's *The Crimson Petal and the White* (2002), the act of reading *Affinity* has the consequence that it will be no longer possible for the reader to return to Victorian novels of the actual period without awareness of the full spectrum of possibility within them. In response to the ideological Conservative espousal of Victorian values in the 1980s, British writers rewrote those values in the 1990s to opposite effect.

Conclusion: The return of agency

In conclusion, the terms of debate concerning historical fiction in the 1990s were set right at the beginning of the decade by Byatt's *Possession*, which emphasized the importance of biography over literature, of lives over texts. As Byatt's protagonist, Roland, comes to understand in an epiphanic passage towards the end of the novel, in which he considers a photograph of Ash on his death bed:

He had been taught that language was essentially inadequate, that it could never speak what was there, that it only spoke itself.

He thought about the death mask. He could and could not say that the man and mask were dead. What had happened to him was that the ways in which it *could* be said had become more interesting than the idea that it could not. (513)

The understanding here, contrary to much of the flow of literary theory over the preceding two decades, is that rather than literature seeking to reflect the pre-existing meanings of things, and inevitably failing, it is literature – narrative, poetry – that constitutes the meaning of things. It was this reversal, apparent in the historical sense of the possibility of a new beginning that stemmed from the collapse of communism and the sense that the long twentieth century was finally starting to draw to a close, that gave the writers of the 1990s, and particularly the historical writers, a renewed sense of purpose. Whereas the political, social and moral certainties of the preceding decades had become increasingly hollow, inviting writers to deconstruct their fragility and emptiness; the explicit condition of fluidity that marked the 1990s freed them once more to concentrate on their primary function, that of creating meaning and the possibility of agency. This agency may be considered historical agency, in the sense that Lukács envisioned, because the ironical self-consciousness of characters such as Barker's Billy Prior and Waters's Nancy Astley, which enables free interaction with the world, is itself a product of their authors' choices to bring the past into dialectical constellation with the present.

Works Cited

Alden, Natasha. *Reading Behind the Lines: Postmemory in Contemporary British War Fiction*. Manchester: Manchester University Press, 2014.
Arrighi, Giovanni. *The Long Twentieth Century*. London: Verso, 1994.
Bakhtin, Mikhail. 'Forms of Time and Chronotope in the Novel'. In *The Dialogic Imagination*. Trans. Caryl Emerson and Michael Holquist. Ed. Micheal Holquist Austin: University of Texas Press, 1990, 84–258.
Barker, Pat. *Regeneration*. Harmondsworth: Penguin, 1992.
——. *The Eye in the Door*. Harmondsworth: Penguin, 1994.
——. *The Ghost Road*. Harmondsworth: Penguin, 1996.
——. *Double Vision*. London: Hamish Hamilton, 2003.
Benjamin, Walter. *Illuminations*. Trans. Harry Zohn. Hammersmith: Fontana, 1992.
Byatt, A.S. *Possession*. New York: Random House, 1990.
Caudwell, Christopher. *Illusion and Reality: A Study of the Sources of Poetry*. London: Lawrence and Wishart, 1997 [1937].

Ciocia, Stefania. '"Journeying Against the Current": A Carnivalesque Theatrical Apprenticeship in Sarah Waters's *Tipping the Velvet*'. *Literary London* 3.1 (March 2005): http://www.literarylondon.org/london-journal/march2005/Ciocia.html

Elliott, Larry. 'America's Century Is Over but It Will Fight On'. *Guardian* 23 August 2010: http://www.theguardian.com/business/2010/aug/23/us-economy-unemployment-property-market

Faber, Michel. *The Crimson Petal and the White*. Edinburgh: Canongate, 2002.

Fraser, George MacDonald. *Flashman and the Tiger*. Hammersmith: HarperCollins, 1999.

Gentle, Mary. *Ash: A Secret History*. London: Gollancz, 2001.

Goodman, Sam. '"This Time It's Personal": Reliving and Rewriting History in 1970s Fiction'. In *The 1970s: A Decade of Contemporary British Fiction*. Eds. Nick Hubble, John McLeod and Philip Tew. London: Bloomsbury, 2014, 117–44.

Hubble, Nick. 'Priest's Repetitive Strain'. In *Christopher Priest: The Interaction*. Ed. Andrew M. Butler. Cambridge: Science Fiction Foundation, 2005, 35–51.

———. 'Pat Barker's *Regeneration* Trilogy'. In *British Fiction Today*. Eds Philip Tew and Rod Mengham. London: Continuum, 2006, 153–64.

———. 'Virtual Histories and Counterfactual Myths: Christopher Priest's *The Separation*'. *Extrapolation* 48.3 (Winter 2007): 450–61.

———. 'Historical Psychology, Utopian Dreams and Other Fool's Errands'. *Modernist Cultures* 3.2 (2008): 192–207. http://www.js-modcult.bham.ac.uk/articles/issue6_hubble.pdf

———. 'The Fictional Excavation of the Future in *Double Vision*'. In *Re-Reading Pat Barker*. Ed. Pat Wheeler. Newcastle: Cambridge Scholars, 2011, 113–29.

———. 'The Ordinariness of the Extraordinary Break-Up of Britain'. In *The 1970s: A Decade of Contemporary British Fiction*. Eds Nick Hubble, John McLeod and Philip Tew London: Bloomsbury, 2014, 43–67.

Hutcheon, Linda. *A Poetics of Postmodernism: History, Theory, Fiction*. London: Routledge, 1988.

Jameson, Fredric. *Archaeologies of the Future: The Desire Called Utopia and Other Science Fictions*. London: Verso, 2005.

Lukács, Georg. *The Historical Novel*. Harmondsworth: Pelican, 1981.

Moore, Alan and Eddie Campbell. *From Hell*. London: Knockabout, 2006.

Newman, Kim. *Anno Dracula [1992]*. London: Titan, 2011 [1999].

———. *Anno Dracula: The Bloody Red Baron*. London: Titan, 2012 [1995].

———. *Anno Dracula: Johnny Alucard*. London: Titan, 2013.

Norfolk, Lawrence. *Lemprière's Dictionary*. London: Vintage, 1999 [1991].

Priest, Christopher. *The Prestige*. London: Touchstone, 1996.

Saunders, Max. *Self-Impression: Life Writing, Autobiografiction, and the Forms of Modern Literature*. Oxford: Oxford University Press, 2010.

Tegmark, Max. *Our Mathematical Universe: My Quest for the Ultimate Nature of Reality*. London: Allen Lane, 2014.

Tew, Philip. *The Contemporary British Novel*. London: Continuum, 2004.
Tew, Philip and Rod Mengham (eds) *British Fiction Today*. London: Continuum, 2006.
Thatcher, Margaret. TV Interview for *Weekend World*, London Weekend Television, 16 January 1983. http://www.margaretthatcher.org/speeches/displaydocument.asp?docid=105087 (accessed 29 May 2014).
———. Interview with *Woman's Own* 23 September 1987. http://www.margaretthatcher.org/document/106689 (accessed 29 May 2014) (see fo29 and fo30).
Waters, Sarah. *Tipping the Velvet*. London: Virago, 1998.
———. *Fingersmith*. London: Virago, 2002.
———. *Affinity [1999]*. London: Virago, 2008.
Wells, H.G. *The War of the Worlds*. London: Pan, 1975 [1898].
Wheeler, Pat (ed.) *Re-Reading Pat Barker*. Newcastle: Cambridge Scholars, 2011a.
———. '"Where Unknown, There Place Monsters": Reading Class Conflict and Sexual Anxiety in the *Regeneration* Trilogy'. In *Re-Reading Pat Barker*. Ed. Pat Wheeler. Newcastle: Cambridge Scholars, 2011b, 43–61.
Wormald, Mark. 'Prior Knowledge: Sarah Waters and the Victorians'. In *British Fiction Today*. Eds. Philip Tew and Rod Mengham. London: Continuum, 2006, 186–97.

6

Generic Discontinuities and Variations
Experimental Enunciations in 1990s British Fiction

Mark P. Williams

Experimentalism in the 1990s

The organizing principle behind experiment is dissatisfaction. All the diverse sub-traditions, avant-garde-inflected anthologies, aesthetic resistances and anti-traditions share a fundamental desire to negate. In this chapter, I am drawing on Christine Brooke-Rose's *Rhetoric of the Unreal* (1983), Pierre Macherey's *A Theory of Literary Production* (1996) and Felix Guattari's work 'On the Production of Subjectivity' (1995), to argue that experimentation constitutes a materialist attempt to relate what Macherey calls the 'conditions of literary production', that is, the unconscious of the text, to the desires of producers of fiction. Because experimental work examines the terrain of production in terms of the exchanges between the author and reader, this chapter will consider the production of fiction as a process that takes place in the shared territory between subjects and as an interaction through social matrices. Experimental texts examine the intersubjective character of fiction; whether it is Christine Brook-Rose's characteristic refusal to differentiate between speech and thought, or Kim Newman's second-person 'Choose Your Own-Adventure Novel', *Life's Lottery* (1999) which changes genre according to readerly decisions, or the collective authorship of Seaton Point (1998), the primary focus of experiment is the social subject. The readerly relationship to the text forms a shared fantasy within the experimental text, a place of uncertainty concerning perception which Rosemary Jackson terms the 'paraxial point' (19) – that space where reflection and reality seem to meet and your eyes tell you that you can almost touch the fingers of your reflection in a mirror.

Christine Brooke-Rose's collection *Stories, Theories, Things* (1991) summarizes and recapitulates the trajectory of her own career, and previous novels, through condensed 'metastories' (6) of literary theory and (anti-)narrative practice which can act as a useful coordinate point to begin from, both chronologically at the beginning of the decade and thematically in terms of presenting a moment of departure and a radical experience of doubt. The multiplying ways in which these interact she provisionally calls 'complex experiences':

> Chapter 1 (draft). Once upon a time, in 1968, there appeared a novel called *Between*, by Christine Brooke-Rose, hereafter in this metastory or story-matter referred to as the author, author of *Out*, *Such*, and earlier novels. *Between* deals with (?), explores (?), represents (?), plays around with (?), makes variations on (?), expresses (?), communicates (?), is about (?), generates (?), has great fun with the theme/complex experience (?) story/of bilingualism. (6)

It is the central tenet of the work of Christine Brooke-Rose that habits of perception produce limitations through the exercise of form. Her writing is perhaps the most extreme form of anti-novelistic examination of technique which this chapter will deal with, since her work restlessly deconstructs all possible angles of critical approach to the basic, root act of Fantasy-making while in the process of constructing 'story'. Although I describe her as a Literary experimenter, her work actually functions far more like the work of anti-novel writers in that it mounts a fierce critique of the enunciative act of fiction writing. In this way, although her style appears utterly incomparable to the transgressive work of Stewart Home, Steven Wells and Bill Drummond and Mark Manning, it mounts a similar challenge to literature as that presented by the contemporary anti-novel.

At its root, the desire to experiment is a desire to push against the limits. Certain limits are obvious, while others are so subtle and insidiously pervasive that we fail to recognize them as such: experimental fiction then encompasses those things which push against habits of expression, the 'habitus' (Bourdieu) of the literary as the dominant tendency, whether regulated by taste and sensibility, marketing or censorship, which characterizes a particular set of assumptions about subjectivity. Experimental fiction concerns resistances of 'form' and resistances of 'content', which attempt to express or create new ways of engaging with the world. In reaching towards new modes of expression through existing forms, they reveal the central problematic of identifying distinctions between form and content. Felix Guattari (1995) chooses to employ the term 'enunciations' to denote the way 'form' and 'content' operate together.

Each set of experimental enunciations that constitutes a text creates an argument about contemporary subjectivity in the 1990s: whether this is the anti-novel, as practised by Stewart Home, Bill Drummond and Mark Manning; the postmodernist literary novel as written by Martin Amis and Will Self; the club novel, which might encompass Q, Jeff Noon, Two Fingers and James T. Kirk; the cyber novel, including Indra Sinha's *The Cybergypsies* (1999) and Steve Beard's *Digital Leatherette* (1999) and *Perfumed Head* (1998); the genre novels of practitioners such as Kim Newman; the philosophical novel, which might include Christine Brooke-Rose; the psychogeographical novels of Iain Sinclair; or the graphic novels of Alan Moore and Grant Morrison. All of these can be placed alongside other, less readily defined forms: the Decadent Surrealist fiction of David Britton versus the populist post-punk DIY novels of Steven Wells, Simon Strong and Tommy Udo; even the radical collective novel *Seaton Point*, written by seven authors and published with a 'No copyright' statement, encouraging piracy and adaptation. Bearing in mind Derrida's writing on the logic of the example as it applies to objects which are definitionally unique and distinct, or indeterminate, such as the continent of Europe in *The Other Heading* (Derrida, 1992), any attempt to find commonality between avant-garde works must be contingent. Despite this, there are clear common threads at work between these diverse writers. The techniques and narrative strategies used by such works alternate between those borrowed from or inspired by Modernism, Surrealism and subsequent avant-garde art movements, and those which are attempting to engage with the popular cultural expressions of contemporary media, music, the internet and club culture, as well as the more diverse strands of multicultural Britain's heritage, both positive and negative. Experimentalism reformulates existing relationships between reader, writer and fiction through play with our understandings of 'form' and 'content' by precipitating a sense of crisis. In *Literature, Politics and Intellectual Crisis in Britain Today* (2000), Clive Bloom observes that the essence of experiment, of the avant-garde, is an opposition to present 'regimes of thought'. The writers here are all oppositional: several are making conscious attempts to create highly politicized, socially engaged postmodernisms, while others reject 'postmodernism' as a recapitulation of the social and political status quo. The texts this chapter analyses raise important questions about authenticity and identity, and about how politics finds its expression in British culture.

The postmodernist literary novel

To investigate experimentalism in 1990s postmodernist literary fiction, this chapter will consider Martin Amis and Will Self. The work of both writers during the 1990s seemed an attempt to create controversy while still maintaining contact with literary postmodernism through the use of language-games and by playing with narrative structure. Amis's novel *Time's Arrow* (1991) writes the life story of a man called Tod T. Friendly in reverse, from the convulsive unbirth of his death bed through his career as a doctor in the United States, and back to his previous life as a Nazi in the concentration camps. The story unfolds in reversed dialogue and reversed narrative, a defamiliarization effect which is essentially cinematic and indicates moral reversal. This reversal of time allows Amis to play multiple literary games. First is the constant invocation of shock or surprise as all those around the narrator continually forget their past and remember their future only until it coincides with the present. This seems to be an allusion to Walter Benjamin's description of history as an angel facing backwards into the catastrophe of history while being 'irresistibly propelled forward' by the storm of progress (249). Reverse dialogue offers opportunities for humour as light relief and black comedy, counterpointed by the reverse logic of happy patients visiting Dr Tod Friendly only to be sent away unhappy and complaining of illness. Second, and in an interaction with this, is the reversal of moral positions in an extended game with the reader's sense of narrative cause and effect: the reader knows where things are going – the reversal of the narrator's name already hints at it: Friendly, Tod. T; it may be read as friendly dead (*todt*) or death (*tod*) in German, and also puns on the *Organisation Todt* (named after Fritz Todt) which ran the concentration camps in Nazi Germany, foreshadowing the narrative to come.

In this inverted world, the narration forms a kind of internal split, implying a split self born of trauma or denial, so that the narrative commentaries on the world constantly reiterate the implied defamiliarized position of the reader but with the dramatic irony of the reader's knowledge of forward-time history. Its most extreme manifestation is found in the relationship the narrative draws between cause and effect in the extermination camps, where the split narrative voice says 'The world, after all, here in Auschwitz, has a new habit [,] it makes sense' (138). This new sense suggests that the only way Auschwitz can make moral sense is through the lens of inverted moral and causal logic. This argument is counterpointed further with the explosive flaring into life of the inevitable ovens and gas chambers, mended by explosions when the Nazis arrive:

> Ours was a human enterprise, but the animal kingdom played its part in the new order of being. Cartfuls of corpses were shoved from the burial pits by mules and oxen [...] Cows did not look up from their grazing, their indifference seeming to say, *This is all right. This need not be remarked,* as if it wasn't unusual to conjure a multitude from the sky above the river. (139)

Amis's reader must keep up their own counter-narrative logic in this text, inverting each statement's causes or implications, as later (earlier) when the narrator says after (before) Auschwitz, that his 'position on the Jews has always been without ambiguity [,] I like them', describing himself as a 'philo-Semite' whose 'only wish' is for 'them to exist, and to flourish, and to have their right to life and love' (160). Problematically, the seriousness of this subject matter and Amis's inverse approach to 'seriousness' here may cause dissatisfaction due to the in-built predictability of the language games and the fact that the text operates from a premise of absolute inevitability in respect of the concept of the death camps. It may be interpreted as Amis's answer to Theodor Adorno's famous dictum that there can be no poetry after Auschwitz, but as a text, it leaves the reader with a scene of utter powerlessness when the split narrative voice has a vision of an arrow flying 'wrongly', 'point-first' and is left to conclude 'And I within, who came at the wrong time – either too soon, or after it was all too late' (173).

My Idea of Fun (1993), arguably Self's first novel, exhibits its formalism with an obsessiveness that matches the obsessions and perversions of its central character Ian Wharton. Wharton introduces himself as a young man with a highly developed photographic memory and a disturbed mind; he defines himself by a Freudian set of sexual concerns with his absent father and oppressive view of his mother. This is then reinforced by the appearance of a physically and mentally overbearing surrogate father known as Mr Broadhurst or Mr Northcliffe, but who also insists on being called The Fat Controller and appears to be either supernatural or imaginary. The text is split into two 'books' of five chapters; these books are subtitled 'the First Person' and 'the Third Person' respectively and are bracketed, or bookended by a prologue and an epilogue. This splitting is intended to reflect the internal split of Self's central character as he gives us his unreliable narrative in first person before his delusions are introduced to us in third person. Self overemphasizes the technical textual detail in this way in order to draw attention to the formal overdetermination of his fiction: it pantomimes its postmodernism before the reader. The prologue introduces the question 'So what's your idea of fun then, Ian?' in the first line of text (3). The narrator, Ian Wharton, then goes on an internal migration from the questioner, and the bourgeois space of the party he is attending, to fantasize or relive a surrealistically violent encounter where he decapitates an 'old dosser on the Tube' and 'penetrates the still seeping stem' of his neck (4). The opening tension of the text, given in the prologue, is the question of whether someone who thinks or fantasizes in this way will ultimately carry out violence against his wife and their unborn baby, which is apparently possessed by a malignant being called The Fat Controller.

The two narratives, and narrative approaches, allow Self to comment on the subject-position of his lead character in their relationship with the people who are apparently controlling his mind. In 'The Third Person' the reader is presented with the most concretely grotesque sequences, including the living grotesques of The Land of Children's Jokes. Its hallucinary sequences and prose excesses seem to borrow from William Burroughs's *Naked Lunch* (1959) and Hermann Hesse's *Steppenwolf* (1927) but inflected through an obsession with lost or underused vocabulary that characterizes many of Self's fictions. The novel is subtitled 'A Cautionary Tale' and set in a world of drugs and violent excesses in advertising and media culture. Similarly, Self returns to this milieu in his late 1990s novel, *Great Apes* (1997). *Great Apes* is an extended riff on Pierre Boule's *Planet of the Apes* (1963), combining it with appropriations from the 'Yahoo' section of Swift's *Gulliver's Travels*. In the novel, the character Simon Dykes wakes up after a night of excess to find himself in a world where chimpanzees have taken on all the social roles while humans live much as chimps do in 'our' world. This central device allows the novel to operate as a satire on white-collar work, therapy culture, contemporary British modernity and perhaps the chemical-generation fictions that Self's literary postmodernism knowingly flirts with.

My Idea of Fun can also be interpreted as a broad-ranging commentary on the evolution of avant-garde experiments in shock tactics into the standard fare of 1990s media culture. To the extent that it becomes, perhaps deliberately, unclear where the target of the 'cautionary tale' really lies, chapter ten concludes with an address to the reader that implicates them in what has gone before. It returns to the scene from the prologue:

> Time for bed now, isn't it? Time to climb the angled stair and settle my accounts with my destiny. What's the line – 'ripped untimely from its mother's womb'? That's it. [...]
>
> I also happen to know that it's a particular private anxiety of my wife. Neat, eh?
>
> You what? Oh yes, your opportunity to participate, silly me, I was forgetting... Well of course you may, if that's what you want but give it plenty of thought, don't rush into anything. Remember that I may have killed, I may have tortured, I may have done all sorts of terrible things but it hurts me too. I do have feelings, as you know. (304)

Ultimately, the 'idea of fun' question from the opening, applies to the reader: the 'entertainment' value of the fiction, is integral to its violence and vice versa, an attitude shared with the work of Irvine Welsh.

The chemical generation and the club novel

Chemical-generation fictions present a dual life of the white-collared worker classes: subjectivity illuminated by psychedelia from last thing on a Friday until the inevitable comedowns of Sunday, in a pattern alleviated by occasional sneaky mid-week binges and washed-out mornings of play-acted labour. The milieu is exemplified in the anthologies *Disco Biscuits* (1997) and *Disco 2000* (1998), both edited by Sarah Champion, which demonstrate ambiguities and intersections with club novels. Their one similarity with the nineteenth-century 'club novel', exemplified by texts like H.G. Wells's *The Time Machine* (1895) and Joseph Conrad's *Heart of Darkness* (1899), is that they too suggest that the heart of the contemporary metropolis is also defined by an overweening darkness, in this case one illuminated by psychotropic substances, lasers, strobes and fast, heavy drumbeats. The glamour of this environment counterpoints or disguises the crime and degradation which helps create that environment. Contemporary club novels of the 1990s are, for all their emphasis on 'gritty' experience and 'street culture', fictions which are charged with fantasy and which aspire to new modes of expression in both narrative style and form.

Deadmeat by Q and *Junglist* by Two Fingers and James T. Kirk

This is particularly clear in texts like *Deadmeat* (1997) by Q (Kwabena Manso) and Junglist (1997) by Two Fingers (Andrew Green) and James T. Kirk (Eddie Otchere). These novels are formulated by mixing cinematic registers. On one hand, the action and events are defined by fast cuts and an emphasis on the visual surface lives of their protagonists. As a counterpoint to this, the interior lives of characters are expressed through free associations in textual terms which mix minimalist language. These novels incorporate intertextual references to music into characters' lives via lyrics from hip hop, RnB and Drum n Bass, which are juxtaposed without introduction or explanation into the prose. Sometimes, artists and track titles form interruptions on their own as points of reference for the reader to imagine as either soundtrack or music on the character's minds. *Junglist* tends to use track titles as accompanying mood while *Deadmeat* creates its own lyrical associations between Clarkie, the protagonist and famous songs by rappers and singers. Clarkie's life is defined by club culture, and the sampling of lyrics in the text is coupled to rhyme, which he then riffs on, mixing rhyme into his first-person prose. Q then builds several different forms of sampling into his text as central themes to further accentuate the cultural stance of the novel. Q juggles subplots involving international crime-rings, paedophiles and the art world through the connectedness of the Internet. All of his characters are aspirational, attempting to take elements of the harsh world around them and transform them into something uniquely expressive. Along the way, they fall prey to the manipulations and greed of others, and although Q does not balance all of the subplots in narrative terms, making some feel more developed than others, as a mosaic, the whole forms a sequence of strongly resonant cultural intersections.

A central trope is the upward narrative trajectory that might be said to define both club novels and chemical-generation fictions in general: the narrative is directionally vague but boundless in its desire for release. Similarly, the styles employed can vary tremendously over a few pages or from character to character, emulating classic stream of consciousness but interrupting it with bursts of quoted or paraphrased lyrics which are shared between different characters and, by implication, between author and reader.

Junglist and *Deadmeat* draw very heavily on popular culture in cinematic and musical forms, splitting paragraphs with chorus lines or repeated refrains. This strategy has complex effects, reaching towards visual equivalences for the incommensurable realms of music and text. It is the creation of a vernacular modernism which exists in a dialogic exchange with the culture it is reporting and commenting on. Q's novel in particular, although published as a complete text in 1997, had in fact been circulating in episodic form since 1991 as Q offered it for sale outside of London clubs and on market stalls accompanied by mix tapes to help cement the mood. The overlap and intersection between writing and music is not only essential to understanding how these diverse experimental fictions define themselves outside the traditions of both literary Modernism and literary postmodernism, but also important for understanding more conventional popular novels.

Irvine Welsh: *Marabou Stork Nightmares* and *Filth*

Welsh's novels *Marabou Stork Nightmares* (1995) and *Filth* (1998) evince a level of theoretical play with the textual surface which possesses unusual unity of visual style and emotional and thematic content. The subjective, interior life of characters is both expressed and commented upon by Welsh's use of typographical play and visual interruption in these novels. Some popular reviews of *Filth* were somewhat dismissive of the sentient tapeworm, which appears in it, as gimmicky or a mixed effect which did not form a satisfying unity with the narrative of the protagonist, corrupt copper Bruce Robertson. As an experiment with textual convention, I suggest that we can read this aspect of the text as the most important: it is this sustained attack on the novelistic mode, represented by the narrating voice of Robertson, which defines the central tension of the novel as one between reader and form rather than between characters.

The tapeworm voice is a stylistic and textual intrusion. It physically intrudes across lengthy passages of prose written from the perspective of the anti-hero Robertson. As a character, Robertson indulges in the kind of repetitive, self-centred rants that recall Bret Easton Ellis's *American Psycho* (1991). The intestine-shaped speech bubbles of the tapeworm voice render these rants secondary, making what is virtually unreadable indulgence literally unreadable. The tapeworm obliterates Robertson's narrative flow to give commentary on his character defects, both those which are already plainly on show to the reader and those which are concealed in Robertson's past. Through this near-omniscient tapeworm, Welsh is ironically bringing fundamental truths to the surface from inside Robertson's fundament: by enacting a complex pun on surface and depth, interior and exterior life, the novel contrasts readerly expectation and literary form by concealing the textual surface to reveal 'character'. But, Welsh is doing more with his play on form than this; the tapeworm speaks in something closer to a standardized English than Robertson, allowing Welsh to formulate a perspective on the relationship between Robertson and the tapeworm which can also be read as a caricature of that between critic and author as parasitism. *Filth* parodies academic analysis while employing its conventions to help structure its primary tension. The lead character is shown to have layers by the literal manner in which contrary subtext is overlaid on primary text. Interiority is the key to the exterior life because it grants access to the meanings of Robertson's many dismissive and derogatory remarks regarding colleagues and women.

Through the tapeworm narrative, the reader is given access to the latent content of Robertson's personal history, immanent within his own story. The tapeworm relates the tale of Bruce's long-lost love, who suffered bullying from other youngsters because of leg callipers she was forced to wear. The intestinal flashbacks to the formative experiences of Robertson's sexuality offer the reader a classically psychoanalytic explanation for both Robertson's casual misogyny and his habit of describing colleagues he dislikes as 'spastics', while his hyper-masculine rhetoric is countered by the eventual revelation of his cross-dressing. Welsh's dark humour in this novel twists what would otherwise function as a parody into a more serious subversion of readerly expectation and generic determinism. This takes the form of a metaphorical turn towards allegory which toys with the possibility of metafiction but never performs a metafictional break with the 'reality' of the world constructed by the fiction. Robertson's superior officer is secretly writing a manuscript based on his colleagues, and, in particular, he is focusing on the extra-legal and more outrightly unlawful abuse of his position carried out by Robertson. Robertson steals the manuscript and reads enough of it to realize it is based on him but, out of bloody-mindedness and spite, destroys it without reading any more: a supreme act of denial from a psychoanalytically constructed character. This unread fiction haunts the rest of *Filth* as an unrealized subplot which refuses to confirm to readers the degree to which it would reflect upon the story with which they have been presented.

What is at stake in Welsh's text is the idea of characterization itself, through its dissection of the presumed bourgeois-centred subject, and of the anticipated relationship between textual convention and the ideas of 'surface' and 'depth'. *Filth* demonstrates to Welsh's audience that the expectations of a contrasting relationship are a pantomime performed by textual surface, by exaggerating the relationship between manifest and latent characterization through the voices of Robertson and his critical-parasitical tapeworm. Welsh's play with form and surface is taken further by the thematic and structural interplay of the novel. Schematically, the novel presents a number of surface narratives which must each be accepted on their own terms, and which together create a radical confusion of textual expectation by playing with cliché. Robertson is an archetypically corrupt police officer – early reviewers cited Abel Ferrara's film *Bad Lieutenant* (1992) as an obvious cultural precursor. The narrative of the corrupt police officer, the moral guardian who leads a double life, breaks down into a Gothic paradigm – which, given Welsh's self-conscious relationship with Scottish literary and cultural traditions, suggests James Hogg's *The Private Memoirs and Confessions of A Justified Sinner* (1824) and Robert Louis Stevenson's *Strange Case of Dr Jekyll and Mr Hyde* (1886), revelling in the disparity between public and private presentations of the individual. This is particularly compounded by Robertson's personal health and hygiene problems: he is physically corrupted, and the surface of his skin in the most private regions is constantly sore, itching and bleeding. It is crucial that these physical markers of corruption are, during the daylight hours of his job, concealed under his work clothes. It also works as a pun: he is quite literally a dirty cop.

Welsh then collapses the narrative distinction of stable identity, and the barrier between criminal and police still further. Robertson's narrative is infrequently intersected with that of a female streetwalker and murderer. At the end of the novel, playing again on cliché and expectation, Welsh reveals that this other voice is an alter-ego of Robertson, and Robertson takes his own life. This invites further comparisons with Hogg and Stevenson's Gothic texts but, in its nastiness and emphasis on sexual politics, suggests Derek Raymond's *I Was Dora Suarez* (1990) and *He Died With His Eyes Open* (1984) and Alan Parker's film *Angel Heart* (1997) as more immediate points of cultural reference. In killing himself, Robertson also causes the death of the only redemptive voice in his life, that of the tapeworm, which has provided his social conscience. The connection between parasite and reader is marked and intriguing, and again, it is through the structural relationship between them that Welsh's novel performs its most radical gestures. If Robertson were not so 'dirty', he would not harbour the tapeworm, and by extension, if he were not such a dirty cop, he would not be narratively interesting to his superior officer as a potential character and, by further implication, would not be interesting to Welsh's popular readership. The reader is made complicit in Welsh's narrative construction of Robertson by the ostensibly defamiliarizing voice of the tapeworm. Welsh implies that the desires of the reader are desires for corruption, abuse, violence, degradation, sex and drugs and murder. The voice of the tapeworm, by functioning as a kind of moral commentator, is doubly ironic: it depends on Robertson's corruption, the subject of its critique, in order to survive. Without Robertson's filthy habits, it could not survive physically or textually.

The ambiguity Welsh is presenting through these nested conflicts of surface and depth, interiority and exteriority, are a kind of restatement of the debates which surrounded Welsh's earlier novel *Trainspotting*, as filtered through the media debates about representation and glorification in writing narratives of 'low life'. *Filth*, again, literally leaves the problem hanging with Robertson's suicide, because the problem is not one which can be effectively resolved from within the form of the novel: *Filth* exteriorizes the potential conflict of readers between their own position as consumer and parasite upon such 'low life' narratives.

Perhaps one of the lowest of Welsh's low-lives is the voice of Roy Strang, narrator of his most formally experimental novel *Marabou Stork Nightmares* (1995). Strang's narrative is an estranged life story of a man in a coma, a mixture of bildungsroman and confessional. Strang, who insists he not be called 'Strange', has had a harsh, violent life split between Scotland and South Africa. He has been both abused and abuser; suffering the repeated sexual predations of his expatriate uncle while ostensibly watching wild birds, including the predatory Marabou Storks, he eventually takes part in a gang rape and succumbs to depression. His failed suicide attempt leaves him stranded in a hospital bed, reliving and revisiting his memories as flashbacks and hallucinatory sequences of stark viciousness and occasionally coming close enough to consciousness to hear the voices of his visitors. The final revenge scene where his former victim castrates and stabs him is lived as a whirling psychedelic sequence of intercutting memories where his sublimated guilt for his own abuse leaves him transformed into a predatory Marabou Stork staring down the barrel of a memory of a gun as his body dies. Welsh evokes this extraordinary scene with a cinematic sense of the relationship of textual surface, juxtaposing the reading space and the reading time, the imagery of the African landscape slipping in and out of affective communication and symbolism; he makes evocative phrases function as motifs of character and small spatial interruptions within the flow of the reader's left-right progression. Welsh changes font size and text direction using the motif of a 'Z' for 'Zero Tolerance' that has haunted Roy Strang and ultimately marks both his own ending at the hands of his former victim and the end of the novel itself with a symbolic alphabetical finality.

Welsh's place in media culture is distinctive: he is, as a voice of the chemical generation, a writer very much embedded within 'style culture'. By comparison, Martin Amis's experimentation with 'low life' culture is always held at a critical remove; it does not enter into dialectic with the culture but presumes a higher position for its implied reader. Contrastingly, Will Self's play with forms slips much more comfortably into the chemical-generation milieu. This was perhaps aided in the 1990s by reprints of Hunter S. Thompson, Jack Kerouac and William S. Burroughs, which were all held up alongside Self and Welsh and their contemporaries in popular magazines. The rise of new magazine cultures during the 1990s, spearheaded by *iD* and *The Face*, and then by *Loaded* and *FHM*, dovetailed with the rise of popular writing devoted to the subjective experience, particularly the attenuated sense of social cohesion and aggrandized individualism envisaged in fictions dealing with the social matrices of drugs, sex and clubbing. The rediscovery of the American Beat writers coincided with the popularity of writers inspired by them. The bloom of 'laddism' is one manifestation of this, but the threads it brings together are the social extension of the growth of aspirational individualism as the pinnacle of modernity, which was promoted by late 1980s culture.

'Lad culture' is tied to specific constructions of authenticity and maleness, of hedonism as titillation, which is an extension and intellectual justification of tabloid culture. In *Filth* and *Marabou Stork Nightmares*, Welsh was demolishing the codes of aggressive, active masculinity, showing instead fragmentary, divided and wounded men whose relationships with women are brutish symbolism, ultimately projections of their own self-destructiveness. Welsh's fictions thus punctuate constructions of 'Laddism' and tabloid culture; his characters and narratives always contain far more varied takes on gender politics and subjectivity than the magazines of the period, as demonstrated in the novellas of *Ecstasy* and even in *Trainspotting*. If style culture and laddism were complicit in constructing Welsh as a controversial author, then, in fact, they were actually promoting his resistance to becoming the poster child of their values.

In Welsh, the 'experiment' is an engagement with his own populist reception as much as it is with the form of the novel. In *Filth*, Bruce Robertson's story could have functioned effectively as a crime story in the tradition of Derek Raymond's 'Factory novels' (which mix elements of Chandler and Hammett with uniquely English environs), adapted to Welsh's own vision of contemporary Scotland. Introducing the tapeworm forces the reader into a position of reading their own relationship with the text as object of consumption and their own choices to interpret it within its crime genre framework: text-as-low-life-glorified versus text-as-moral-lesson; a literary study of the crime genre versus a revelling in the excesses of cliché and convention. In this light, Welsh's text displays a critical self-consciousness which distinguishes it from its apparent contexts. *Filth* might be considered as performing similar self-analytical gestures to Christine Brooke-Rose in *Remake* (1996), in which she interrogates the concept of autobiographical fiction while telling her own story: *Filth* is both a play with and a serious commentary upon form. This takes the reader beyond the social utility of the novel as balance between maintenance/defiance of expectation and enters into a dialectical relationship with the social function of the form.

Like *Deadmeat*'s play with hip hop and RnB lyrics to demonstrate interiority, it is a gesture which reveals that the external is already in a dialectical exchange with internality in the preconditions of the text: the culture that it draws upon. Club novels and chemical-generation fictions, and Welsh's take on crime fiction, all entertain this relationship structurally within themselves. They manifest the conditions of textual production as the emergence of a textual unconscious.

Indra Sinha: *The Cybergypsies*

Indra Sinha's *The Cybergypsies* (1999) marks another distinctive development: the Internet confessional novel as a textual model, which may now be a historical genre. Although it is primarily a confessional text, it necessarily incorporates fiction and hyperrealism to establish its setting and its milieu as a historically specific mode. It has a realist epistemology, but the activities within the novel are centred around and concern purely textual worlds which are 'lifestyle fantasies' (Stableford, 247–8) lived as if they are Real – it stretches literary categories and might be regarded as a uniquely post-postmodernist mode, a kind of hyper/Realist meta(non)fiction. For these reasons, I argue that it constitutes an experiment in fictive writing. Consider Sinha's account of the central shared fantasy world of Shades:

> Shades is a multi-user game, a place where unusual folk come to escape 'reality' (Eve, note the ass's ears I affix to that vulgar word) and to enact agonies and ironies upon one another. A place, I say, but the cave, landscape castle and underlying labyrinth of Shades are no more than words on a screen, descriptions to be navigated solely by the compass of the imagination. They are, nonetheless, completely real to the characters who inhabit them. (24)

As Peter Guttridge explains in the postscript, one of Sinha's defining, guiding impressions for the text is Thomas De Quincey's *Confessions of An English Opium Eater* (1821). *Cybergypsies* charts a similar relationship with subjectivity and time, determined by the demands of experiential coordinates. In this way, it is very much a non-linear narrative and an assemblage of linkages between twilight text-worlds and real ones. It is a methodological experiment in testing Realist epistemology against the realities of everyday life within network society for a very specific, idiosyncratic subculture. As such, it transgresses several stylistic and categorical distinctions.

The first-person protagonist of Sinha's autobiographical novel, Bear, lives a second life through online text-based fantasy worlds that is more important to him than the mundane life of the 'Real' world. Perhaps most unusually in this novel, when the world of shared fantasy is reported in the text, it is actually being reproduced in its original form, that is, as text (Sinha confirms that he is mostly using the real tags of those he met through this subculture). The result is a highly specific mode of writing which is hyper real in its attention to exteriority as an externalized expression of internal life. In reproducing the hypertext mark-up language and chat-room conventions of its originary milieu with a confessional mode, it produces a series of apparently metafictional affects: a fantastical world within a set of Realist conventions; self-conscious textuality; constant ambiguity and uncertainty about the gender, identity, and reliability of other characters; a co-mixing of different registers as nested forms of produced language; and a fundamental challenge to the distinctions and hierarchies between interior and exterior life as online lifestyle Fantasy produces real-world bills, debts and relationship tensions.

As a fantasy form, it writes a self-reflexive analogue between the subconscious world of the net, where normal rules of socialization are routinely transgressed but still have concrete affects. We get a clear demonstration of this in the opening page where we are introduced to a character whose attitude towards women (and their corresponding relationship problems) is foregrounded in their chosen net handle:

> It's 3 a.m. and I'm online to Jesus Slutfucker. JS informs me that he's typing one-handed, knuckling open a beer with the other. Needs a drink, he tells me. He just got home to find his girlfriend throwing her clothes into a case. She said she was sick of being shackled to a sleazeball, his lifestyle was doing unspeakable things to her head, she was leaving. To emphasise the point, on the way out she stuck a knife in his arse. JS is a nurse, so he knows he's barely scratched, but in any case, it's not the knife that hurt.
>
> i ' m b etter off w i tho t t he bitch ...
>
> He's trying to tough it out but the bugger's clearly had a sock. I can tell he's upset by the way he's typing, characters detonating on my screen in bursts of venom (1)

Character is inferred through attention to text in 'real time'; how people utter words in time being represented by space on the page. The reader, revisiting the roamers of the 'pre-internet net' (2), has to reconstruct these characterization modes constantly with the narrator's qualifying asides: 'ARiSToTLE is a flamboyant virus collector from Virginia' (6).

Early on Sinha samples 'Tristram Shandy's Quixote-inspired Uncle Toby' reproducing his gestural flourish within his own prose, setting the scenes of his internetizens by intertextuality even in the 'Real' world. A castle conjures up 'Fata Morgana's cloudy keep', 'Macbeth's castle-"heaven's breath smells wooingly here"' and 'Monty Python's castle of the Holy Grail from whose ramparts enemies were pelted with tandoori'd chicken-legs' (21). This play with cliché and construct is particularly telling, and reflexive, in the description of the female character of Lorelei, real name Laura Hunter:

> A cynic might say that Lorelei lives out a set of clichés. Hers is exactly the sort of life you'd imagine for a girl as smart, intelligent and attractive as she appears. She's bright, a double-first from Cambridge in Eng. Lit., and naturally she's attractive–twenty-three, slim, a natural blonde–men's jaws plummet past their balls at her very description. (20–21)

What is particularly notable about this 'description' is that it takes place primarily through projection and is described as a form of projection; Lorelei's character is a simulacrum designed to manipulate the reader into the position of being caught between the personas of social cynic and the romantic (in the senses of generically fantastic and of gendered fantasizing) occupied by his narrator, Bear. This reflects the central theme of the text, which questions the Reality of attitudes such as cynicism and romanticism by questioning the extent to which internal and external realities can be separated meaningfully within a networked society.

A monstrous collection of texts: Decadents, surrealists and the experimental baroque

Savoy Books emerged directly out of *New Worlds SF* magazine. As edited by Michael Moorcock between 1964 and 1971 (consultant editor thereafter), *New Worlds* was a forum for unifying science fiction as the literature of ideas with the countercultural penchant for stylization. The co-founders of Savoy, David Britton and Michael Butterworth met through their association with *New Worlds* writers; at the time Britton was an illustrator-designer and book publisher who owned and ran SF bookshops with Charles Partington, who was a contributor to *New Worlds*. Butterworth was a writer and associate of writers such as J.G. Ballard who were part of the 'New Wave'. In the 1970s, Britton and Butterworth co-edited a special edition of *New Worlds* based on shared interests, and in 1978, they published a collection of fiction and artwork called *The Savoy Book* which featured contributions from 'New Wave' legend Harlan Ellison, up-and-coming writer of the fantastic, M. John Harrison, and an imaginary interview with the deceased Jimi Hendrix by rock'n'roll critic Lester Bangs, all packaged in a distinctive decadent style with a cover illustration of William Holman-Hunt's *Lady of Shallot*.

Savoy's aesthetic grows out of unifying the interests of Modernism with those of the 1960s libertarian counterculture. Their own take on this eventually took a peculiarly eccentric turn as a result of clashes with the police. David Britton ran bookshops which were raided by Manchester police forty times between 1976 and 1981, where police seized, among other things the Savoy publications, *The Gas* (1970) by Charles Platt and *The Tides of Lust* (1973) by Samuel R. Delany, two satirical SF novels by respected writers in the field. Britton was then imprisoned for selling remaindered, out-of-print erotic novels that, when in print, had been available from high-street booksellers. All of these experiences appear in Savoy's subsequent novels, starting with stories and articles in *Savoy Dreams* (1984), and coming to a head with Britton's writing of *Lord Horror*, which was published in 1989 despite being dated 1990.

Lord Horror concerns a British fascist and Nazi, Horace Joyce or Lord Horror, loosely based on Lord Haw-Haw. Set in an SF-Fantasy universe which revolves around extermination camps, it is a politically and morally unsettling monochrome vision of the twentieth century from within the mind of its British fascist protagonist. The original book was prosecuted under the Obscene Publications Act in 1991 for anti-Semitism, the last novel to be banned for obscenity in Britain. The nature of Savoy's real offence is that of appropriation. The novel includes scenes of anti-Semitic ranting in form of a lampoon of a radio speech delivered by Manchester's fundamentalist Christian Chief Constable, James Anderton. *Lord Horror* changed the word 'homosexual' to the word 'Jew' and attributed it to a fictional Mancunian Chief Constable named Appleton. When combined with the Nazi politics and razor-wielding attacks on minorities of the eponymous anti-hero, the novel was found to be obscene, leading to a short jail term for Britton. 'New Wave' authors Brian Stableford and Michael Moorcock both gave evidence for the defence at the trial of *Lord Horror*; Moorcock called the book 'one of the most authoritative indictments of the Holocaust and our moral responsibility to it' (cited in Jones 235). Savoy overturned the conviction on appeal in 1995 backed by Geoffrey Robertson QC and Article 19 (the legal team which defended *The Satanic Verses* from blasphemy charges).

Britton expanded the multiverse of Lord Horror in an even more transgressive novel *Motherfuckers: The Auschwitz of Oz* (1996) and the highly experimental comic book series *Reverbstorm* #1-7 (1994-2000) which was finally concluded with the addition of *Reverbstorm*#8 in the collected hardback *Lord Horror: Reverbstorm* (2013). This novel focuses around mutant twins, Meng and Ecker, experimental project of Dr Mengele, who travel through time and space with a sentient, flying Volkswagen called Herbie Schopenhauer telling vicious jokes and having surrealistic encounters with historical and fictional figures – Savoy submitted this novel to the Booker Prize that year. All Britton's Lord Horror fictions are notable for their use of a disjointed chronotope, but in *Motherfuckers*, Britton has one of his dubious characters muse more explicitly: 'A work of fiction that would do justice to the Holocaust must take as its first principle the shattering of chronology' (86). This phrase evokes Amis's *Time's Arrow*, but Britton has taken a further step: not just reversal, leaving the historical narrative intact, but complete dislocation of time and morality, suggesting that fascism is not consigned to history but travels with us. As the title of the novel suggests, Britton's transgressive use of 'appropriate' and 'inappropriate' representation remains hotly contested and problematic, but its direction remains consistent: Lord Horror's politics is destructive and ultimately destroys him as the 2013 conclusion of the *Reverbstorm* makes clear by having the physically decaying and mentally dissolving Lord Horror consume himself. Britton's fictions produce a dark counter-narrative of mainstream consensus politics which reveals the latent, suppressed content of contemporary British society: they suggest that consensus liberalism is in denial about the presence of racism and fascism in Britain. Savoy publish analyses of their work dealing with these issues constantly (See Noys, Petley, 1995; Petley, 1996).

The Starry Wisdom: A Tribute to H. P. Lovecraft

The Starry Wisdom (1994) is an anthology from Creation Books edited by D M Mitchell. Mitchell went on to set up his own Lovecraftian imprint, Oneiros Books, now Creation Oneiros. Oneiros published John Coulthart and Alan Moore's *Haunter of the Dark and Other Grotesque Horrors* (2006), Grant Morrison's *Lovely Biscuits* (1998), and David Conway's *Metal Sushi* (1998) – which I argue are precursors of the 'New Weird' (See Williams 2011a). I will briefly explore two stories which appear in *The Starry Wisdom*, Alan Moore's 'The Courtyard' and Grant Morrison's 'Lovecraft in Heaven'.

'The Courtyard' is based on hard-boiled American detective fiction. Narrated by a jaded FBI agent named Sax, the story is an investigation into a series of murders. Sax discovers that all of the murderers were users of 'Aklo'. He assumes Aklo to be a drug but the trick of the tale (foreshadowed for those familiar with Lovecraft or Arthur Machen) is that Aklo is a language. The city is a textual landscape of Realist horrors defamiliarized through Lovecraftian metaphor. New York is symbolically a sunken city, the atmosphere of repellent inhumanity as subject-dependent is evoked by '[v]ile centipedal graffiti that covers the tenement steps in its writhings' (151-2) and by the suggestion of other-worldliness found in a wall mural 'a *trompe l'oeil*-effect landscape that seems to stretch into the wall with a shape in the foreground I hope is a tree' (151). Inverting the racist metaphorical treatments of foreigners in Lovecraft, Moore creates an unsettling vision of an urban nightmare in which the 'Abhuman' horrors are reinvented as symbols of the dehumanizing aspects of urban modernity:

> An inverted whirlpool of concrete and shadow, the tenement stairwell is dragging me up from the lampless sea-bed of the ground floor (unoccupied:

nothing can live with those terrible pressures), through wife-beatings, bad food and babyscreams fathomed above. (152)

From Johnny Carcosa, Sax receives his three 'hits' of Aklo – three phrases – and the prose begins to take in ever more abstract concepts and attach to them various Aklo phrases, implying the altered state of Sax's subjectivity outside of English and into a 'new continuity' composed of 'dissociate clusters of data in pregnant, post-linear arrays' (152), the verbal equivalent of the unknown dimensions of Cthulhu and Yog-Sothoth:

> 'wza-y'ei'. A mental floor gives way beneath me. I realise I know what the word means; I've known all along [...] 'Dho-Hna'[...] A force which defines; lends significance to its receptacle as with the hand in the glove; wind in mill-vanes; the guest or the trespasser crossing a threshold. (153)

These alien syllables both enable and disable appropriate definitions and discussions; the text presents a conceptual vocabulary for Lovecraftian 'unknowables' which obfuscates while giving the illusion of explicating: Lovecraftian pseudostructuralism. Moore's version of Aklo is almost a parody of Derrida's conception of *différance*; it creates spaces whose boundaries are untranslatable except in their own terms. The familiar crime-story description of murder is expressed through alien combinations of syllables and letters (which are only a human approximation of how Aklo should sound) which in turn express the negative concepts; the 'outside' of what is being done. The text becomes the unknowable alien entity of the piece, disguising the dimensions of a distinctly human monstrosity from the gaze of the reader:

> I know you're still worrying over your hands, but please don't. They're quite safe, I assure you. The thing is to focus yourself on the Wza-y'ei; the concept of not-hands. No. No, don't black out. There. That's better.
>
> I want you to watch this part closely. This is the unfolding, from Glaaki to Lloigor. We make the first cut, the y'nghai, just here. Now, gnh'gna equalling y'nghai are tekel'd to mhhg-gthaa, uguth and Y'golonac. (154)

Although the reader knows what must be happening, this knowledge too is deferred, it refers to an earlier point in the text and to earlier murders. The voice of the first person is itself breaking down in the concluding paragraph, denying the reader access to the traumatic moment, the event of murder, making it a site of trauma for the reader.

Grant Morrison's short stories form condensed anti-narratives. Morrison's Lovecraft stories may be productively considered as 'anti-horror' writing, in the sense meant by Linda Badley in *Writing Horror and the Body* (1996). Badley designates Clive Barker's early horror fiction in this way, describing the kind of double-bind common to avant-garde writing. Morrison's approach to the writing of H.P. Lovecraft gets to the hub of these meshings of pulp and avant-garde, which subsequently manifest in his more popular comic book work through his symbolic figures:

> The mirror is dying.
>   'Cancer of the glass', Lovecraft is told.
>   […]
>   The mirror fluxes, alive with uncanny tides and the odours of pure creation. Sweet rotten scent of biological mystery. He stares into the depths as something stirs far below, wakens and begins to rise. Storms and rain wrack the mirror's surface. The thing is coming up from the deep, getting bigger and bigger. It is vast and primitive and he knows its name. (13)

Morrison here draws on Lovecraft's story 'The Outsider'. The storms are those of Lovecraft's own textual mirror-world, where physical depth is the corollary of all unknowns, from the space between the stars to caverns in the earth and the ocean floor. In this reconstruction of the Lovecraftian, Lovecraft's own internal bodily dimensions correspond to textual concepts, all unseen and unknown. In this case, Lovecraft's cancer is both a metaphor for and manifestation of the unspeakable in his stories, but also the textual content of the stories themselves: 'Inside him, in the dead cell, he can feel what he knows to be words, like maggots, eating at him. Words giving birth to words and more words; all the things he dared not say. […] He is becoming a thing of words, a word-crab built for descent into the dark (13–14).

Morrison emphasizes the textual aspect in his fiction as a way of plugging Lovecraft into his own avant-garde interests by taking his work beyond that of a single authorial identity and into the group-authored corpus it has been growing into since its inception. Read alongside the other stories in *The Starry Wisdom*, particularly 'Meltdown' by D.F. Lewis – a brief satire which takes Lovecraftian beings as concrete metaphors for the fantastical worlds of international commerce and the stock markets; specifically trading in futures markets – it becomes a coherent metaphoric system, a subgenre all its own, which can be turned towards many interlocking social spheres. It is a *détourned* Lovecraft we are presented with, the horror story of a mind forced to self-psychoanalyse on the cusp of death so that Lovecraft's repugnance for physical sexuality becomes his fear of a descent into 'the cuntworld that is KUTULU's kingdom' (17). The unknown horror is the relentless self-examination which carefully destroys and re-destroys the constructed barriers of personality, confidence, faith in yourself, hope:

> Stories disintegrate and fill the room like flying ash. Ash in his head. A blizzard of atomic debris, stories tearing themselves apart, reconfiguring, creating new stories endlessly. A carrion storm of words eating him from within, descending upon him from outside. (14)

This is almost a description of Morrison's practice of quotation, appropriation and recontextualization in his other short fictions, collected in *Lovely Biscuits*, such as 'The Room Where Love Lives', a mash-up of Conan-Doyle and Lovecraft via Wilhelm Reich's 'orgone' theory, and 'I'm A Policeman', which mixes Moorcockian characters with a parodic cyberpunk stylization. Morrison makes versions of other writers' creations which self-annihilate and rewrite their originals, getting his own stories 'inside' the corpus of other writers' work to extend them outward to implicate the world of the reader; he is a maker of intertextual babushka dolls. In the introduction to *Lovely Biscuits*, Stewart Home describes this as a 'blurring of boundaries between fiction and non-fiction, critical insight and satire, narrative and cyclical return, [which] destabilise[s] every category that conventional literary criticism is struggling to uphold' (iv–v). Home observes that Morrison has in this regard been very successful at spreading avant-garde ideas like *détournement* to a mass audience; he goes on to say that he considers Morrison's 'psychogeography' more internationally significant than, say, Iain Sinclair, who is generally taken to be emblematic of psychogeography in Britain (Home, 2008).

Alan Moore: *Voice of the Fire* (1995)

Magician, performer and best-recognized name in British and American comic books, from his post-industrial midlands home town of Northampton, Alan Moore has helped define modern comics. He is a modern antinomian in terms of his aesthetic thought. Drawing on visionary writers from Margaret Cavendish to Abiezer Coppe, he enfolds the mundane, working-class provinces of England within the immaterial, subjective realms of the collective imagination. *Voice of the Fire* is a mosaic novel of place built up from a collection of historical narrative centred on Northampton from 4000BC through to AD 1995. Characters are tied to locations by either building or violence; constructions, both physical and emotional, and specific images and roles recur between the chapters: black dogs and severed limbs, fools and outcasts and wise men. Various themes and historically specific events form the backdrops to each: the end of Roman Britain in 'The Head of Diocletian: AD 290', a witch trial of two lesbian lovers in 'Partners in Knitting: AD 1705' and a brief episode from the life of poet John Clare in 'The Sun Looks Pale Upon the Wall: AD 1841'. Each chapter is marked in some way by a traumatic event corresponding to a physical construction or land mark, building steadily towards the status of Northampton as it is in 1995. In 'Confessions of a Mask: AD 1607', it is both, the story being narrated by the severed head of Francis Tresham, executed and placed on a spike for his association with 'Bob Catesby, Guido Fawkes, Tom Winter and the others' who plotted against James the First (175).

In concluding this crescendo of time and place, Moore ends with his own authorial voice in a chapter entitled 'Phipps' Fire Escape: AD 1995'. The location, built in the previous century to house the town's workers, is used in the present to symbolize everything which Moore places at the door of contemporary society; it is a symbol for historical class division, aspiration and the sometimes precarious perching of the present generations on the markers of previous lives:

> The final act: no more impersonations. No more sleight-of-voice or period costume. [...]
>
> On stage, although the set remains the same, the scenery is somewhat modified. Some of the buildings on the painted nineteen-thirties backdrop have been whited out and new ones added: Caligari hulks against the slate November sky. It's 1995. The lights go down. The empty rows wait for the final monologue. [...]
>
> History is heard. Zanib Badawi nightly holds aloft the blackened crucible for our inspection. (259)

Moore's meta-report on the news media here then moves, as Moore-as-narrator moves, towards descriptions of the local histories of Northampton. His 'authorial' exposition of Northampton shows echoes of psychogeographers Peter Ackroyd and Iain Sinclair – writers he knows and reads – and reverberates with the macrocosm of violence to space and subjectivity suggested by the news.

Perhaps the most famous of Moore's texts to deal with the occasionally brutalizing relationship of space to subjectivity is the graphic novel *From Hell* (1989–1996; collected 1999) about Jack the Ripper, which draws upon Peter Ackroyd's novel *Hawksmoor* (1985), together with Iain Sinclair's *White Chappell, Scarlett Tracings* (1987). Both texts are extensively referred to in the appendix to

Knockabout Books' collected edition of *From Hell*, where Moore explains that it was the aspect of people and place in connection with the murder sites rather than the detective fiction aspect which interested him most. Having explored certain books on the Ripper's identity, most notably Stephen Knight's *Jack the Ripper: The Final Solution* (1976), Moore uses *From Hell* to undermine the significance of the 'real' Ripper. Using a grand conspiracy theory, he explores the different responses of the social strata to the phantom presence of the Ripper in their midst. Moore's text takes the constant focus of 'Ripperology' away from the identity of the mysterious murderer, choosing instead to explore and explode the myths surrounding the case. *From Hell* reminds its readers from the very start that the study of the Ripper's crimes consistently ignores a central issue in its analysis: the brutal murders of five women.

From Hell is infamous for its unstinting portrayal of the graphic violence of the crimes against bleak social realist backgrounds but around the moments of the murders the imagery becomes expressionist. The scar-like greyscale lines and deep blacks of Eddie Campbell's meticulous illustrations cut and ooze respectively across the pages to striking effect, particularly in the most brutal murder scenes where they suggest a subjective time frame surrounding the event of murder. In the murder scenes, the murder seems to take place in a space wholly filled by the killer and victim where no landmarks or physical features of the surroundings are visible. Only the frenzied lines of the killer's movement and the gouts of blood have a solid expression. We cannot skip past the murder by missing a panel, and it takes place over two pages; seconds are rendered visible as if in film stills. After these scenes, we are granted access to the subjective experiences of Moore's Ripper, who is no longer a man but becomes a narrative linked forward and backward in time to the 'Monster' of 1788 and to the Yorkshire Ripper, the Moors Murderers and the Krays. The Ripper as a figure straddling the impulses of myth and modernity becomes a device for linking the so-called psychogeography of London with an obsessive psychosis; the grandiloquent monologues he delivers on occult systems of cosmic signification are the justifications by which he elevates himself above the sordid reality of his crimes.

Elizabeth Ho takes Moore's relation to Ripperology and Ripperature as a problematic engagement with the cultural legacies of Thatcher, as recuperated by Tony Blair, in her essay on 'Post imperial Landscapes: "Psychogeography" and Englishness' in *From Hell*. She writes that 'Jack the Ripper speaks both to and against Blairite cultural policies. Jack is the epitome of modernity' and goes on to argue that 'Moore's graphic novel is an intervention ... in what seems to be an uninterrupted and at times uncritical expression of Englishness' (109).

The local is the most visible concrete manifestation of global ideologies in Moore. Where these ideologies are harsh or rapacious to individuals globally, this is reflected in their social and physical architecture locally. To Moore, industrial and post-industrial landscapes are intimately connected to their ideational structures as expressed in the critical visions of *From Hell* and *Voice of the Fire*.

Iain Sinclair: *Downriver* and *Radon Daughters*

The writing of Iain Sinclair is similarly recalcitrant in its relationship to contemporary modernity. Sinclair's prose style fuses registers between the supposed conventions of postmodernism with a sort of Beat generation rhythmic pacing. His characters are formed from utterances of quotation and impressionistic collections of phrases. His approach to the language of fiction writing can move from imagery of a surrealistic clarity to intimations of emotional noumena. Where his friend Alan Moore's psychogeographies remain anchored to clearer narrative structures, Sinclair draws elliptical linkages from which story emerges by duration.

His most memorable characters, like the misanthropic Todd Sileen (whose name partially echoes Louis Ferdinand Celine) in *Radon Daughters* (1994), think and act through an assemblage of texts. Sileen is defined by an obsession with text, collecting the ultimate Joseph Conrad assemblage and chasing after a phantasmatic sequel to William Hope Hodgson's apocalyptic *House on the Borderland* (1908).

Sinclair's characters frequently occupy extremely gothic social roles, which are formulations of spectral living: they parasitize ruins or dead writers or walk around the sites of murders. Here, in *Radon Daughters*, Sinclair returns again to the haunted sites of the Ripper murders, this time via the perambulations of a tour guide. The streets are 'Tributaries of risk':

> She walked them incessantly with her tight flocks of whitecoat Japanese murder buffs, leasing them the sacrificial sites, coaxing them to sniff the stones, place their palms against the heat retained in the walls. Click/click/click. They activated instant memory triggers, fumetti; converting their grubby trek into a viable photo-romance. Dr Jack was an honorary Samurai. The visiting Americans were heavier, talking loudly to ward off ghosts they refused to acknowledge. For them, Whitechapel existed in dry ice and cheap yellow paper. *A Study In Terror*. Reality did not travel beyond their own shores. (49–50)

In these texts, character traits and habits emerge from collections of cultural critique and observation; Sinclair's characters both stand in and for their place in the environment of contemporary Britain. Sinclair's fictional prose is more a comment on 'psychogeography' than an enunciation of it: his literal walks, such as those detailed in *London Orbital* (2002) and *Lights Out for the Territory* (1997), are the concrete psychogeographical activities that his novels emerge from as a counterpoint rather than extension. We might consider Sinclair's work to work around the edges of the forms identified with postmodernism: they are quasi-fictions more than metafictions, which obsess over their textuality as a concrete corollary of the texture of the world. In a sense, Sinclair's dominant principle partakes in *too* rigorous an attention to the principles of realism, overburdening fiction to the point where it ceases to really function as fiction at all.

Experiments in method: Interactivity, collaboration and collectivism

Even at the point where those of us who studied literature in 1990s and early 2000s were being taught that literary postmodernism constituted an important set of critical attitudes and techniques towards representation employed by contemporary writers, we were already surrounded by texts which proposed radical reconceptions of literary form while rejecting postmodernism. For the reader of alternative 'cult' and 'genre' fiction, of avant-garde and fantastic texts in Science Fiction and Fantasy traditions, there was another set of critical languages which already revisited their own conventions and histories with irony, critical distance and through thought-experiments. Some have now been embraced as fellow-travellers to literary postmodernism; terms such as 'slipstream' situate these texts on the shared borderlines of established formal or generic modes and literary postmodernism, while some remain separate and distinct.

Kim Newman's *Life's Lottery*

Kim Newman's *Life's Lottery* (1999) is a unique interactive novel which borrows from the form of the 'Fighting Fantasy' novels published by Steve Jackson and Ian Livingston. Jackson and Livingston's series of Choose-Your-Own Adventure novels began in 1980 with *The Warlock of Firetop Mountain*. The form is often that of a second-person narrative, it is divided into numbered sections and the end of each section presents the reader with a choice that will affect the nature of their fantasy quest. Newman takes these conventions and applies them to the literary novel of character, producing a series of diverse but interconnected stories which form a multiverse within a single text. You are Keith Marion, depending on which choice you make, you will end up living a very different life: some narratives see you committing murder, fighting for survival against your old school bully, encountering supernatural or extradimensional events or simply living a mundane life which ends with 'And so on'. The demands this novel places on the reader are extreme: Newman's novel makes an implicit comparison between the competitive play of the Role Playing Game (RPG) reader and the irony of the metafiction reader; in *Life's Lottery*, there is no functional difference between dying ('*Go to 0*') and living a normal life ('*And so on*'); since both equal 'Game Over', both are implicitly a loss. What he offers are the alternatives of refusing to read the text according to the rules (which reveals another narrative which cannot be accessed any other way). The reader is tempted by Newman's Mephistophelean character, Derek Leech, who appears in his earlier fictions as a media mogul. Leech offers the reader a seemingly infinite array of choices:

> Go back to any earlier choice.
>   If all else fails, go back to 1.
>   You'll be here again. You've probably been here before. (147)

The one thing that the narrative voice constantly demands of the reader, activity over passivity, investment in (fictive) life, which it also hints, tauntingly, is beyond the character/reader – postmodernist play is paralysis. In a supreme irony to this riff on postmodernism, the most fantastical narrative, an inter-dimensional invasion, is the elusive 'Real' narrative (inaccessible by playing the game) which is echoed in all the other narratives. This fantastic 'Real' can be accessed only by taking the text most seriously, literally reading against the form.

Seaton Point (1998) by Rob Colson, Martin Cooper, Ted Curtis, Robert Dellar, Keith Mallinson, Emma McElwee and Lucy Williams

The collective novel *Seaton Point* (1998) is one which stands as a distinctive intervention, outside of postmodernism's purview. *Seaton Point* is more than just a novel; it is also a politico-aesthetic manifesto on the role of the writer in contemporary fiction which makes an explicit opposition to postmodernism as a representation of the culture of the ruling classes, the novel's introduction says 'we are notpostmodern or ironic [...] we mean it' (5). The seven authors of *Seaton Point* open their text with a polemical introduction where they make it clear that their story is as important to them on a methodological and practical level as it is on the level of story, and that it represents a unity of theory and praxis. The introduction defines the novel as a practical experiment in opposing the cult of alienated authorship in contemporary life which supports mythic ideals and heroic narratives of 'the great and the good'; it describes itself instead as being about 'the survival struggles of the not so great and the downright bad' (6). They state their case forcefully:

> We have created an urban myth, an inner-city tale of magic, mayhem and gratuitous sex scenes. Occasionally beautiful, mostly repulsive, the characters and plot came into being and from seven minds was born one novel. Far from hindering the text as each different bit is taken on by a different voice, the contrasting styles complement and enrich each other, as in traditional storytelling where a body of countless imaginations is added to in each rendition. We do not seek to disguise the multi-authorship: there is no conscious attempt to harmonise conflicting styles. The tensions and conflicts are central to the novel, the catalyst through which many of us have produced some of our best work it was the only way that such an enterprise could have succeeded. This is a living work which we feel compelled to disseminate to the wider world. (5-6)

For the seven authors of this book, collaborative storytelling produces effects which have specific subjective value in themselves, generated socially through interaction and creative play; the shared immaterial labour of producing an affective narrative based on their own lived experiences enriches that lived experience. They argue the case for a new creative praxis of fiction writing based on the model of orature and community. As an extension of this, they also refuse the protection of copyright, which places them into the same tradition of avant-garde resistance to cultural regulation as the collaborative exercises of the Luther Blissett Project and Wu Ming Foundation (see Williams, 2012).

By choosing to assert 'No Copyright' in the CIP page, the novel refuses the distinctiveness and uniqueness accorded to the literary text, refusing even the uniqueness that the avant-garde text often represents; not only does it suggest that anyone could have produced this text, it gives everyone permission to copy or rewrite it to their own purposes – we can all play with the text. Unlike the example of Borges' Pierre Maynard (re)writing *Don Quixote*, anyone producing a *Seaton Point* of their own is simply contributing to the spirit of the original's collaborative praxis.

Christine Brooke-Rose: *Textermination* and *Next*

Seaton Point's intersubjective openness extends itself to the same realms of cultural collaboration as Christine Brooke-Rose's *Textermination* (1991), which borrows (although from within the limits of the Berne convention) from a large array of contemporary and classical texts to tell what she might term a 'metastory' of characters interacting at a vast conference. It reaches levels of intertextually far over and above the unity of a novelistic structure, creating instead a trans- or meta-novelistic framework that is as transgressive in its own collectivism as *Seaton Point*. Her acknowledgements list is instructive:

> The dialogue and the descriptive or narrative sentences by or about the literary characters in the novel are always by its author except for occasional quotations, both from classics and modern authors. The modern quotations, all under the regulation three hundred words, are from the following texts: Elias Canetti, *Auto da Fe*; Angela Carter, *The Magic Toyshop*; Carlos Fuentes, *Terra Nostra*; Ismail Kadaré, *Avril Brise* (translated by me from the French translation, permission obtained from the author); Lars Gustafsson, *La Mot d'um Apiculteur* (translated by me from the French translation); Toni Morrison, *Beloved*; Milorad Pavic, *Dictionary of the Khazars: A Lexical Novel in 100,000 Words*; Thomas Pynchon, *The Crying of Lot 49*; Philip Roth, *The Counterlife*; Salman Rushdie, *The Satanic Verses*; Chrisa Wolf, *Kassandra*. (Brooke-Rose, CIP, n.p.)

The breadth of the list indicates that *Textermination* can be seen as a miscellany of other writing, particularly other experimental or transgressive writing, from historiographic metafiction to the mosaic novel. In that sense, it is an attempt to formulate a summation of the novelistic form which, by crossing so many textual boundaries, and having characters blurring into and back out of one another's identities, suggests that the collaboration of the reader with the essential fantasy of the text, the subjective investiture of reader in text, constitutes the social value of any and all of these diverse fictions. To that extent, Brooke-Rose's texts are rigorously anti-novelistic and orientated towards the reader as social subject. This is further accentuated by the alphabetical structure and central linguistic device of *Next* (1998), a crime story set among the homeless whose 26 voices have alphabetized names. Brooke-Rose deliberately omits any variations of the possessive verb 'to have' from any of the voices in the text to emphasize the material deprivation of the homeless and point towards the still wider social crime of impoverishment and disempowerment throughout the novel.

The anti-Novels

Brooke-Rose's texts can be compared to those of avant-gardist and 'anti-novel' writers. Among these, one of the most significant is Stewart Home. Home has carved out a niche for his work using combinations of dense theory and aggressively avant-garde positioning in respect of culture (he wants to transform world culture in its entirety) and literature (which he wants to collide with non-literary conventions to create 'something unprecedented' from the two). Home is also a performer, artist, prankster, activist, prolific (obscurantist) essayist, online and in print, and not just a novelist; his cultural interests are manifold and his frame of reference frequently bridges many fields.

An important facet of Home's fictions is their engagement with the actually existing conditions of social life, something that seems to be at odds with his highly theoretical stance in other areas and his (post)modernist narratives. This habit too is part of his critique of literature: it reinserts the question of social values into the question of literary value; he makes this explicit in novels like *Slow Death* (1996), which offer fierce critique of the Art world and 'culture' in general. In other texts, Home refuses narrative order or consistency in favour of cyclical return, as in *Come Before Christ and Murder Love* (1997) to attack the novelistic conventions of structure and characterization. Fellow anti-novel writers like Bill Drummond and Mark Manning offer techniques of collaboration and contradictory parallel narratives, as in *Bad Wisdom* (1996). Drummond and Manning also utilize extreme bad taste and transgression, including sexual violence and racism, to attack more mainstream forms. This places them closer to the work of David Britton than to Home, whose fictions take clear political positions in opposition to right-wing ideologies, but the focus of their offensiveness is to question contemporary liberalism. Using moral ambiguity to do so is also a trait of post-punk texts like Simon Strong's *A259 Multiplex Bomb "Outrage"* (1995), which creates a music, beer and drug-fuelled Maldororian environment where dead musicians and pornographers meet through hallucination and time travel. It borrows styles and techniques from a number of other writers, among them, Lautréamont, JG Ballard and Stewart Home, all acknowledged at the end as DIY inspiration. Steve Beard's *Digital Leatherette* (1999) describes itself as 'an ethno-techno cyberpunk novel about sex, drugs and dum'n'bass, consisting of text fragments pulled down from invented internet web-sites by an imaginary intelligence agent'.

Punk's DIY aesthetic is important to the interrogations of liberalism's relationship with postmodernism, nowhere more so than in the deliberately millennial Attack! Books edited by Steven Wells. This series of novels, to which both Stewart Home and Mark Manning contributed in their characteristically transgressive styles, constitute a fin du siècle assault on British cultural politics. The Attack! novels include titles like *Get Your Cock Out* (1999) by Mark Manning and *Raiders of the Low Forehead* (1999) by Stanly Manly. It includes a strong anti-religious and anti-Royalist element: Stewart Home contributes *Whips and Furs: My Life as A Bon-Vivant, Gambler and Love Rat by Jesus H. Christ* (2000) and Tommy Udo adds *Vatican Bloodbath* (2000), about a secret war between the Vatican and the British Royal Family. Wells's own Attack! novel is called *Tits-Out Teenage Terror Totty* (1999) and is a sequence of increasingly wild routines which critique the British Armed forces, Police, Politicians and ruling classes, as well as novelists and the Royal family, and God (See Williams 2011b).

In all these texts, the common points of contact are those of the intersubjective and intra-subjective: they invite the reader to enter into specific, active positions. They act as a lure to draw out something of the fictive unconscious, the preconditions from which the act of fiction-making is formed. What they play upon is the capacity of the reader to enter into, or invest themselves within, the central fantasy (the virtual world) of fiction, and encourage or demonstrate or attack, the social assumptions which make this a passive act. These texts all argue, implicitly and explicitly, that reading a text is a process of active engagement, and furthermore this quality – this mutual investiture – has a much wider potential because it applies to other fictive relationships. Ideology, politics, class, race, gender and other permutations of social relationships are all placed within the sphere of the fictive in these texts. By manipulating the conventions of enunciation, to force the reader to realize their complicity, and express the unconscious of the texts on their manifest surfaces, these texts offer ways of reconsidering our perception of our relationships with all forms of social enunciation. In offering highly diverse, alternating responses, they demonstrate some of the rich veins of potential in British experimental fiction which subsequent generations of writers can return to, and/or explore, and/or depart from.

The experiment has already been staged; we are constantly collecting new and surprising results.

Works Cited

Amis, Martin. *Time's Arrow; Or, The Nature of the Offence*. London: Jonathan Cape, 1991.

Badley, Linda. *Writing Horror and the Body: The Fiction of Stephen King, Clive Barker and Anne Rice*. Westpoint, Connecticut and London: Greenwood Press, 1996.

Benjamin, Walter. *Illuminations*. Trans. Harry Zohn. Hammersmith: Fontana, 1992.
Bloom, Clive. *Literature, Politics and Intellectual Crisis in Britain Today*. Basingstoke: Palgrave, 2000.
Bourdieu, Pierre. *The Field of Cultural Production*. Ed. Randal Johnson. Cambridge: Polity, 1993.
Britton, David. *Lord Horror*. Manchester: Savoy, 1990.
———. *Motherfuckers: The Auschwitz of Oz*. Manchester: Savoy, 1996.
———. *Reverbstorm* #1-7 illustrated John Coulthart with additional art by Kris Guidio. 1994–2000.
———. *Lord Horror: Reverbstorm*. illustrated John Coulthart with additional art by Kris Guidio. Manchester: Savoy. 2013.
Brooke-Rose, Christine. *Textermination*. London: Carcanet, 1991.
———. *Next*. London: Carcanet, 1998.
———. *Stories, Theories, Things*. Cambridge: Cambridge University Press, [1991] 2009.
Colson, Rob, Martin Cooper, Ted Curtis, Robert Dellar, Keith Mallinson, Emma McElwee and Lucy Williams. *Seaton Point*. London: Spare Change Books, 1998.
Derrida, Jacques. *The Other Heading*. Translated by Pascale Anne-Brault and Michael B. Naas. Bloomington: Indianna University Press, 1992.
Drummond, Bill and Mark Manning. *Bad Wisdom*. Harmondsworth: Penguin, 1996.
Guattari, Felix. 'On The Production of Subjectivity'. In *Chaosmosis: An Ethico-Aesthetic Paradigm*. Trans. Paul Bains and Julian Pefanis. Bloomington and Indianapolis: Indiana University Press, 1995, 1–33.
Ho, Elizabeth. 'Post Imperial Landscapes: "Psychogeography" and Englishness in Alan Moore's Graphic Novel *From Hell: A Melodrama in Sixteen Parts*'. *Cultural Critique* 63 (2006): 99–121.
Home, Stewart. *Slow Death*. London: Serpent's Tail, 1996.
———. *Come Before Christ and Murder Love*. London: Serpent's Tail, 1997.
———. 'Introduction'. Grant Morrison, *Lovely Biscuits*. Swansea: Oneiros Books, 1998.
———. 'Book: *Pocket Essentials Psychogeography* by Merlin Coverly' *Stewart Home* [website] 4 Feb. 2008, n.p.: http://www.stewarthomesociety.org/sp/psycho.htm.
Jackson, Rosemary. *Fantasy, the Literature of Subversion*. London and New York: Methuen, 1981.
Jones, Stephen (ed.) *Clive Barker's A – Z of Horror*. London: BBC Books, 1997.
Moore, Alan. 'The Courtyard'. In *The Starry Wisdom*. Ed. D.M. Mitchell. London: Creation Books, 1994.
———. *Voice of the Fire* [1995]. Atlanta/Portland: Top Shelf, 2003.
Moore, Alan and Eddie Campbell. *From Hell* [1999]. London: Knockabout, 2006.
Morrison, Grant. 'Lovecraft in Heaven'. In *The Starry Wisdom*. Ed. D.M. Mitchell. London: Creation Books, 1994, n.p.
———. *Lovely Biscuits*. Swansea: Oneiros Books, 1998.
Newman, Kim. *Life's Lottery: A Choose-Your-Own Adventure Book*. London: Simon & Schuster, 1999.

Noys, Benjamin. 'Fascinating (British) Fascism: David Britton's Lord Horror'. *Rethinking History* 6.3 (Winter 2002): 305–18.
Petley, Julian. 'Savoy Scrapbook'. *Index on Censorship* 24.6 (1995): 23–32.
———. 'Lord Horror's Defence'. *The New Statesman* (30 August 1996).
Q. *Deadmeat*. London: Sceptre, 1997.
Self, Will. *My Idea of Fun*. London: Bloomsbury, 1993.
———. *Great Apes*. London: Bloomsbury, 1997.
Sinclair, Iain. *Downriver*. London: Granta Books, 1991.
———. *Radon Daughters*. London: Jonathan Cape, 1994.
———. *Lights Out for the Territory*. Illus. Marc Atkins. London: Granta Books, 1997.
Sinha, Indra, *The Cybergypsies*. London: Scribner, 1999.
Stableford, Brian. 'The Adventures of Lord Horror across the Media Landscape.' In (Ed.) Brian Stableford. *Slaves of the Death Spiders: Essays on Fantastic Literature*. Rockville: Wildside Press, 1998, 43–56.
Two Fingers and James T. Kirk. *Junglist*. London: Boxtree, 1997.
Wells, Steven. *Tits Out Teenage Terror Totty*. London: Attack! Books, 1999.
Welsh, Irvine. *Marabou Stork Nightmares*. London: Jonathan Cape, 1995.
———. *Filfth*. London: Jonathan Cape, 1998.
Williams, Mark P. 'The Superheated, Superdense Prose of David Conway: Gender and Subjectivity Beyond the Starry Wisdom'. In *Gothic Science Fiction 1980–2010*. Eds. Sara Patricia Wasson and Emily Alder. Liverpool: Liverpool University Press, 2011a. 133–48.
———. 'In Defence of Literature: The Counter-Cultural Critique of Steven Wells' Attack! Books'. *Critical Engagements* 2.2 (September 2011b): 15–45.
———. 'Literature of Resistance as Literal Resistance: The Seven-Author Novel *Seaton Point*'. *Werewolf* 34 (September 5 2012). http://werewolf.co.nz/2011/08/literature-of-resistance-as-literal-resistance/.

International Contexts 1
Whatever do the Germans Want? 1990s British Fiction and the Condition of Germany

Anja Müller-Wood

Introduction

In the *London Review of Books* of 18 November 2010, Andrew O'Hagan writes somewhat dismissively about the tendency (which he claims began in the twentieth century) to 'forc[e] a character on decades' (22) so as to impose a distinct, comprehensive mood on what were in fact diverse and diffuse experiences. He concedes that some periods, the 1970s for example, are prone to be given such an identity but maintains that 'the 1990s don't yet have a mood' (22) (other than seeming, in retrospect, slightly less troubling than the decade that followed). Not least because this contention contradicts the underlying premise of the present collection of work about the 1990s, it needs to be put to the test. What is more, however, for someone like me, writing from a German perspective, to deny this particular decade a specific mood strikes me as an oddly blinkered, if not insular, stance to take. This stance is of course nothing new: O'Hagan's view echoes the United Kingdom's distance from and disinterest in the tectonic shifts taking place in mainland Europe at the time in question, an unperturbed Anglocentrism which observers such as Buckley had identified already at the time (147–8). Still, this continuity does not make O'Hagan's assessment any less flawed. For however undefined the 1990s might have seemed (and might continue to seem) from a British perspective, in most continental European countries, the more immediate experience with the end of the Cold War had more decisive, noticeable and (arguably) mood-defining effects. In Germany, the period was crucial to the country's self-perception and marked the rise to prominence of a discomforting concern: the question of national identity, suppressed by the doctrine of 'normalisation' through Western integration expounded by Germany's then Chancellor Helmut Kohl.

The starting point for my research for this chapter was my own subjective recollection of a distinct 1990s mood manifesting itself in a general bewilderment about the end of the GDR and the unexpected prospect of a (re-)unified Germany.[1] Daunted by the shadow cast by the past, many Germans looked to Britain for a model of a society that was open, ethnically diverse and culturally exciting, but also stable and confident, for their new, reunified identity – an orientation which also allowed them to avoid thinking too much about the issues on their own doorsteps. British fiction, by extension, seemed to provide a medium of this society's parameters. These personal hunches were corroborated when my research into the reception of British fiction in the 1990s unearthed a wealth of critical commentary of which I had hardly been aware at the time, corroborating my personal hunches and enabling me to place my own experiences in a larger context (whose scope had previously not been entirely apparent to me).

Before I begin to focus on the role of British fiction in 1990s Germany, however, a few words about the general popularity of fiction by English-speaking authors in Germany would seem to be in order. Literature originally published in English is read as a matter of course in Germany; in fact, there seems to be a consensus that literature by Anglo-American authors is more entertaining and accessible than that of German-speaking writers. On average, about 14 per cent of first editions published on the German market are translations from other languages (as opposed to 5 per cent in the United Kingdom), of which around 70 per cent are translations of books originally published in English. According to Börsenverein des deutschen Buchhandels, fiction has the largest share of these translations (70). As Gisa Funck explains, it is a cliché amongst those in the publishing sector that in German bookshops Anglo-American bestsellers are used as a marketable and readable bait to sell German classics (n.p.), and although the last decades have seen a surge of popularity of contemporary *German* fiction – with as Liebenstein argues a concomitant decrease in translations of fiction first published in English into German (33) – in the period in question, Anglo-American writing appears to have exuded a particular attraction for German readers.

These figures become even more meaningful if one considers the representation of fiction translated from English on German bestseller lists. The bestseller lists published by the German weekly magazine *Der Spiegel* and *buchreport*, the trade journal for the publishing sector, show that most bestsellers on the German market in the period between 1974 and 2002 were translations of books originally published in English. In fact, as Liebenstein points out, 1990 was the first year in which a majority of books on German bestseller lists had originally been published in English-speaking countries (36). This trend peaked in 1996, when 64 of the 100 books on the annual list of best-selling titles were originally English-speaking (32–3). These figures do not distinguish between books by British and American authors, and of course, one has to bear in mind that these lists are populated by the likes of Rosamunde Pilcher, John Grisham and Donna Leon (the most popular Anglophone authors in Germany in the 1990s).[2] Still, such data is indicative of the breadth of market presence of books from English-language sources in Germany in the 1990s and of their success. As such, they offer a map of a general trend of such fiction's popularity that provides a backdrop also for our understanding of the reception of different kinds of British fiction in Germany, from perhaps more 'sophisticated' mainstream authors (Salman Rushdie, Hanif Kureishi, Ian McEwan, Julian Barnes and Tim Parks) and more popular genre writers like Iain Banks and Nick Hornby, to authors on the fringes of the literary mainstream, such as Scottish authors like James Kelman (before the Booker), A.L. Kennedy and Jeff Torrington.

The immense appreciation of British fiction in Germany illustrated by these figures alone is supported by the reception of the work of such writers in the German national press. Much of this chapter is based on a qualitative analysis of a broad range of press sources: reviews of individual novels translated into German, features about individual authors and genres and commentaries about British culture and literature in general, published in the weeklies *Der Spiegel* and *Die Zeit* and the national dailies *Süddeutsche Zeitung, Frankfurter Allgemeine Zeitung, Die Tageszeitung* and *Der Tagesspiegel*. I neither claim that these materials are exhaustive, nor that this sample is fully representative; still, they meaningfully capture the mood of an important section of the German population during the period (and provide the basis for further, more systematic empirical research). What they certainly show is the status of British fiction in Germany, the overall admiration with which such writing is seen by a significant cross section of the literary opinion makers in the popular press. They depict British fiction as narratives that possess depth, zest, sexiness and overall insist that they are inherently funny. Again and again, reviewers emphasize the seemingly natural skill of British authors in wrapping deep truths about life in what might be labelled 'rippingly good yarns'. Although critics sometimes take British authors to task for their tendency to eschew theory and experiment, on the whole critics praise them for their worldly wisdom and wit, their courage to tackle the mundane and everyday and their ability to channel or incorporate postmodern concerns without being overly theoretical. In fact, the admired accessibility of British fiction is presented as a solution to what is perceived as an integral problem of German literature, and indeed, the obverse was offered as a reason for the 'crisis' in which German literature was seen to be in the period in question (see Bußmann 20 ff.): its reputed seriousness and excessive intellectualism. This notion has resulted in compliments that at closer consideration can but be considered backhanded. Somewhat patronizingly, the German publisher Arnulf Conradi views Anglo-American writers as 'historically immune' to the kind of intellectualizations to which German authors are traditionally prone, praising them instead for their storytelling abilities and courage to express 'powerful emotions' (anon., 'Große Gefühle' n.p.). British authors not only appear to be unperturbed by such platitudes, but also seem to embrace them gladly. Graham Swift, for instance, is quoted as suggesting that English authors fulfil a desire for stories that continental European authors appear 'unwilling' to satisfy (quoted in Funck n.p.). Swift's willing submission to cliché comes as no surprise when one considers that in 1997 Georg Reuchlin, publishing manager with German publishers Bertelsmann and Goldmann, suggested that London had replaced New York as the world's publishing capital and that 'the most interesting literature at the moment comes from the UK' (quoted in Meyhöfer 160).[3]

Although one might take the popularity of British fiction in Germany as a gauge of its objective superiority over German literature, this phenomenon nevertheless needs to be placed within its historical context. The following is an attempt to explain why British fiction (and, by extension, British culture at large) was received particularly positively during the last decade of the twentieth century, that is, during a particular (and particularly momentous) period in German history. The domestic response to the collapse of the GDR and the subsequent reunification of the two German states was far less triumphant than the Thatcherite anti-German propaganda of those years might have led people in the United Kingdom to believe, as Brockmann explains (43),[4] and the sense of uncertainty or 'disorientation' identified by Geyer (355) by which Germany was characterized throughout most of the 1990s manifested itself in the immense attractiveness of a culture apparently blissfully untouched by the changes and challenges that confronted continental Europe. For many Germans, myself included, Britain appeared to be a clearly demarcated cultural haven where an unperturbed national self-confidence coexisted with its casual subversion, where tradition and innovation joined in a fruitful and creative symbiosis that manifested itself on all levels of culture. Philip Oltermann echoes my own recollections when he remembers himself thinking of London in the 1990s as a place which 'more than any other city in Europe, seemed to embody a dream of personal freedom and intercultural harmony' (xx). The confrontation with Britain provided many Germans with an appealing 'imagined community' by proxy while allowing them to skirt the more challenging task of imagining such a community at home.

This is not to say that German attitudes vis-à-vis Britain in the 1990s were monolithic; indeed, in retrospect, German attitudes towards British culture in the 1990s appear to take two directions that coexist throughout the decade in an uneasy relationship. Especially, in the early years of the 1990s, the emphasis of literary and cultural critics writing about Britain is on authenticity, subversion and resistance, often harking back to the Thatcher era as if to invoke the kind of fighting spirit needed to blast the perceived entropy of Chancellor Helmut Kohl's conservative government. New Labour's success of 1997 marked a watershed, presenting Germans with an officially sanctioned sense of 'cool' (cf. Smith passim) that – to avail myself of an iconic Britpop anthem – had abandoned the need to look back in anger. Many Germans were quite happy to embrace this stance of cheerful self-confidence, which the German press helped to disseminate. In May 1997, *Der Tagesspiegel* printed Tony Blair's views on culture in translation; in the wake of 'Cool Britannia' articles about British art exhibitions, fashion shows and music journalism abounded in German newspapers, and the phrase 'felix Britannia' was used in more than one review to suggest the superiority of the British way of life. Indeed, whatever cultural advances Germany appears to have undergone in the late 1990s have often been associated with British influences. Arguably, as Brockmann says, a 'less tortured attitude towards German national identity' (15) manifested itself in the 1998 election of social democrat Gerhard Schröder as German chancellor, who not only sought to set in train a process of renewal in Germany, but together with Tony Blair sought to 'modernise' European social democracy at large (Blair and Schröder n.p.). The new sense of 'lightness' that is often ascribed to contemporary Germany, as Olterman specifies usually in connection with the United Kingdom (235), had already begun to make itself felt in the 1990s. For instance, in his 1997 response to Bernd Ulrich's essay *Deutsch, aber glücklich* ('German but happy'), Reinhard Mohr asserts that Germany at the end of the 1990s had achieved a long-desired state of Westernized normality (and finally acknowledged this achievement). This understanding is reflected not least by the impression that the country had become 'more Mediterranean and British' at the same time – that is, both 'more light-hearted and joyful, but also more sober and relaxed' (45). By extension, voices such as Thomas's were critical of the aggressive self-promotion of the Blair era (35) and may be seen as expressions of this greater self-confidence and a sign, according to Berger, that Germans finally had come to terms with their national past (467). In fact, it could be argued that the politics of normalization pursued by Helmut Kohl had been achieved by his successor Gerhard Schröder (cf. Taberner 6).

How does the reception of British literature interact with these changing attitudes? Here, I take my cue from Stephen Brockmann, who sees German literature from the post-reunification period as 'a privileged sphere for reflection on German national identity' (19). Extending this insightful assessment, I argue in this chapter that it is not only literature by German authors that holds the mirror up to Germany, the German reception of foreign literature in Germany may also have a share in this self-reflective project. Accordingly, the German reception of British fiction allows us to gain insight into the condition of 1990s Germany – its 'need state', as it were – albeit in a roundabout way. At first sight, one might be tempted to see the admiration of British literature accompanied by an almost masochistic dismissiveness towards Germany and its cultural products. The scant scholarly work relevant to my topic only supports this stance: on the whole, it tends to idealize British fiction as both aesthetically and thematically having the upper hand over its German counterpart. However, as I will suggest, the pervasive admiration of British culture is ambiguous in so far as it is strategic, allowing Germans to explore their otherwise tabooed desire for a normal relationship with their own national identity in another, positively connoted cultural context.

The context: Post-reunification Germany

Germany occupies a singular position in the chain of revolutions that collectively made up the fall of the Eastern bloc. While Poland, Hungary and, somewhat later, Czechoslovakia embraced Mikhail Gorbachev's ideas of glasnost and perestroika and engaged in a slow but steady development of democratic principles, East Germany was one of the last steadfast defenders of communism (second only to Ceaucescu's Romania). It was too steadfast even for the USSR's reformist leader, who allegedly told Erich Honecker during the fortieth anniversary celebrations of the GDR that 'he who arrives late will be punished by life' (cf. Plog 16). Ultimately, the breakdown of the East German State was caused by a number of related developments: the internal political and economic collapse of the regime, revolutionary decisions by some fellow Warsaw Pact nations (especially Hungary, where the dismantling of border installations led to a massive exodus of citizens of the GDR to Austria) and the persistent peaceful pressure put on the government by ordinary citizens. Collectively, these factors meant the end of the GDR – albeit not with the bang of a revolution, but in a whimpering chain of embarrassing accidents and political and communicative blunders as Meyer explains.

But, the case of Germany was different not only because of East Germany's delayed entry into the wave of revolutions, the collapse of the country also had fundamentally different structural implications for both Germanys. Whereas other former communist states broke apart into the individual entities from which they had originally been constructed, Germany was the only state that *merged* with another. In Tony Judt's astute formulation in *Postwar: A History of Europe since 1945*, 'German re-unification [was] a unique case of fusion in a decade of fission' (638) – a 'fusion', moreover, that involved two countries conjoined by their shared Nazi past (that they had been dealing with in very different ways). Reunification therefore, rather than fostering an instant and all-embracing sense of national pride, led to an identity crisis that was played out differently on different levels of society and in different parts of the country. According to Berger, this crisis brought the 'elusive search for national normality' (451) that had overshadowed post-war German history to a climax by confronting Germans once again with the discomforting question that they had managed to avoid since 1945: how to establish a sense of national identity in the face of the past.

The first free elections in East Germany after the fall of the old regime in March 1990 led to a somewhat counter-intuitive result. Its winners were not the parties linked to the human and civil rights groups whose peaceful protest had been instrumental in the gradual collapse of the GDR, but conservative parties modelled on (and associated with) Chancellor Helmut Kohl's Christian Democratic Union (CDU). This success was clearly related to Kohl's promises, in the run-up to the elections, of a swift reunification, a painless and cost-free introduction of the Deutschmark and the creation of 'blossoming landscapes' ('blühende Landschaften') in the East. Intellectuals on the Left both in East and West Germany were frustrated by this result, which they saw as a betrayal of the revolutionary spirit that had made these elections possible for a cowardly embrace of promises of comfort, security and normalcy in the fold of a CDU-style paternalism. The conservative triumph was echoed by the first federal elections of the reunified Germany in December of the same year, which essentially cemented the supremacy of the existing conservative government – reinforcing Kohl's self-image as 'chancellor of reunification' and the general drift of his cautious, provincial conservatism.

The sense of left-wing resentment in the wake of the first joint elections might have appeared mean-spirited at the time (see Ash 15); in hindsight, it seems less far off the mark, as the dream of overnight prosperity did not materialize and, with a few remarkable exceptions, landscapes in the 'new' (Eastern) states failed to blossom (Geyer 361–2). Lives in the 'old' and 'new' states continued to differ markedly. Many Westerners felt (and continue to feel) that it was they who had to foot the bill (to this day, a 'solidarity levy' is collected from taxpayers in the 'old' federal states); numerous others lost huge sums in rogue investments in the former GDR. Although many East Germans profited economically from reunification, the great majority felt that they had lost out in the process and soon wallowed in what came to be known as 'Ostalgie' – 'Eastalgia'. In its most harmless guise, this nostalgic mood expressed itself in a fashion for GDR brands (some of which have in the meantime been rescued or reinvigorated by Western firms) and cultural fixtures (such as the East German 'Ampelmännchen' – the characteristic image on traffic lights in the GDR) (Berger 479–80); with the foundation of the PDS ('Partei des Demokratischen Sozialismus') as the successor party to the SED ('Sozialistische Einheitspartei Deutschlands'), which styled itself as the political party defending the interests of those who had lost out in the reunification process, it also took a (sometimes troubling) political form.

A sense of 'But not only those on the left were disappointed and disillusioned' was not restricted to the Left, however, and in other contexts, it took the disturbing form of nationalist aggression. The first traces of such sentiments had announced themselves soon after reunification as Ignatieff indicates (2) in the form of an increasingly vociferous racism against anyone perceived as non-German. This led to a spate of racist assaults in the early 1990s, both in the old and new German states, resulting in an overall sense that the Nazi spectre had risen from the grave: Germany, it seemed, was unable to reinvent itself but in the most horrific guises. In other words, in Germany, the revolution of 1989 not only fell short of its transformative potential, it also led to the rise of sentiments that Germans on both sides of the iron curtain had hoped to have overcome.[5]

These events seemed to confirm fears voiced by anti-nationalists since the collapse of the GDR. Already in 1989, observers were baffled by the sudden rephrasing of the slogan of the East German protesters that accompanied the fall of the Wall: 'We are the people' had suddenly, long before anybody had begun to speak of reunification, become according to Ignatieff 'We are *one* people' (45). Although on the whole commentators across the political spectrum welcomed reunification, voices on both left and right spoke up against it – be it out of concern that a presumably authentic GDR would be corrupted by Western influences, be it out of fear that Germany would abandon its post-war achievements and fall back into nationalistic posturing, if not worse, arguments well summarized by Berger (453–5). In 1990, Günter Grass – one of the most eminent and outspoken critics of reunification – depicted himself as a 'knave without fatherland' in an open letter published in *Die Zeit*. Reminding his readers that it was a 'centralised Germany' that was responsible for the genocide of the European Jews, he warned against an overhasty unification, as it could lead to the repetition of history, and imagined the kind of Germany that he would want to live in: 'my fatherland would have to be more diverse, colourful, neighbourly, it would have learnt from its mistakes and be more compatible with Europe' (61).

Granted, Grass here does not invoke Britain as the model for his imaginary fatherland; yet, some of the qualities that he ascribes to this future Germany – notably its diversity and colourfulness – were persistently associated with Britain by other commentators on British culture and British fiction. For the reminder of my essay, I will specify the rules of attraction determining the perception of British fiction in the 1990s, and the way they are revealing about the way Germans saw themselves. Here, too, the response is not uniform: while the left-wing *Tageszeitung* appears to fashion itself as a mouthpiece of British cultural politics, the liberal *Spiegel* and the conservative *Frankfurter Allgemeine Zeitung* provided a more toned-down, at times even ironic counterpoint to developments in Britain and British cultural products. The academic context in the 1990s, too, contributes to an idealizing image of Britain, although its recourse to the parameters of postcolonial criticism entails significant contradictions and ironies that deserve to be investigated further.

The rules of attraction

The German admiration for superior British storytelling notwithstanding, many reviews in the early 1990s emphasized the traditionalism and commercialism of British fiction and suggested that it was in dire need of rejuvenation (anon., 'Schale' 232; Robben '(Nichts) Neues' n.p.); on reflection, however, this stance appears to be strategic, emphasizing the innovative force of the authors discussed. In 1996, *Die Tageszeitung* published an article in translation in which

Neil Belton, then editor of *Granta* magazine, complained about the uniformity of British fiction, which he put down to the specifics of British publishing, which is both commercial and unprofessional (that is, nepotistically dominated by the cultural elites) at the same time. Two years later, *Granta* was publicized once again, this time (with a new editor) during the so-called 'Tea Time Lectures' organized in connection with the *Berliner Festwochen* of 1998, whose focus was on Britain (in itself an interesting fact affirming the international success of Blairite cultural politics). Although these lectures appear to have gone unnoticed by the national press published outside of Berlin, they resulted in a number of interesting responses in papers published in the capital. While Karen Fuchs in *Der Tagesspiegel* described *Granta* as a 'joyous bulwark against the perpetual nagging about the death of the English novel', Martin Hager, in a brief item in *Die Tageszeitung*, emphasized that one of the strengths of *Granta* is to combine stylistic sophistication with the ability to depict 'the foreign'. In short, British fiction is so interesting because it brings together enjoyable writing and with a concern with cultural otherness.

This equation is pervasive in the decade in question, when many German critics were intrigued by the United Kingdom's ethnic diversity and its impact on literary production. Throughout the 1990s, the complexity of an author's cultural identity served as a mark of literary quality. In 1991, Michi Strausfeld argued in *Die Zeit* that the ethnic and cultural in-betweenness of authors like V.S. Naipaul, Nadine Gordimer, Kazuo Ishiguro and Jamaica Kincaid is their forte. Whatever 'lack' their uncertain origins might entail, these authors are able to turn it into a 'surplus' in creative terms: 'narrating with admirable vividness and vivacity, fascinating their readers with everyday topics drawn insouciantly from all areas of human experience – as if there never had been a crisis of literature'. Some years later, also in *Die Zeit*, the doyen of German literary criticism Ulrich Greiner was inspired by Pico Iyer's seminal 'The Empire Writes Back' article from 1993 to entitle a brief item of his own on Anglophone 'World Literature' 'Amphibians' ('Amphibien'); he lists Naipaul, Ishiguro, Kureishi and Brodsky as examples of this amphibious cultural identity. The idea that traditional, canonic literature can be rejuvenated from the margin is also at the centre of a long survey article from 1993 in *Der Spiegel* entitled 'Die Schale wird zum Kern' ('The shell becomes the core') about 'ethnic literature' published in the United Kingdom and the United States. The title encapsulates what the anonymous author sees as the programme of this literature, the subversion of the mainstream from the margin, which in many ways is an aesthetic issue: ethnic authors have managed to 'spice up' the staid and predictable fare of (white) British fiction, not least by enriching it with a hefty dose of non-Western irrationality (anon. 'Die Schale wird zum Kern' 236).

Despite the admiration and openness that these responses reveal, they also document the writers' susceptibility to what Graham Huggan has called 'the postcolonial exotic' (413): the semiotic system enabling and sustaining the circulation of notions of marginality, authenticity and resistance as cultural commodities in a late-capitalist world. In endorsing such notions as their ideals and values, the postcolonial programmes of Western cultural and educational institutions become complicit in the very political economy that they seek to subvert. A similar process is also at work in Christa von Bernruth's 1995 self-castigating article about the 'boom' (in Germany and beyond) in ethnic literature in *Süddeutsche Zeitung*. For von Bernruth (herself a writer of crime fiction), Germany has become a 'prosaic' culture, whose fundamental needs are no longer addressed: it is therefore particularly responsive to the magic of the intuitive orality that much ethnic writing displays. For Bernruth this has wider, social dimensions: Westerners, she claims, live in individualized societies; what they need are big plots and convoluted stories to provide vicarious encounters with a world they have lost (903). Ethnic literature, then, heals a widespread Western malaise.

Comforting (and common) though such home-grown diagnoses about the status quo of Western culture and the therapeutic quality of 'ethnic fiction' might be, they are also exceedingly simplistic. What underpins them is a monolithic notion of culture, with labels like 'ethnic literature' serving as convenient but unwieldy umbrella terms for writers from a variety of entirely different cultural backgrounds (Indigenous Americans, those from Latin America and Africa) to be juxtaposed with an equally undifferentiated notion of 'the West'. In this apparently subversive process, the latter's cultural values ultimately remain intact. Still, the appeal of an all-ecompassing (if ultimately vague) multiculturalism in 1990s Germany is obvious: the undifferentiated ethno-stew invoked by von Bernruth and others provides a pleasant and exotic alternative to the more daunting question of how Germans can relate to and interpret their own national identity.

Other writers eschew the fraught label of multiculturalism and instead have recourse to the more sophisticated (but no less troubled) category of 'World Literature'. This category is based on the assumption that authors writing from the margin do not merely exemplify a subversive influence upon the centre, their presence unsettles the centre in such a way that it does away with traditional notions of literature and literary value – including such an essentialist concept as 'national literature' – altogether (anon. 'Die Schale' 236). For Ulrich Greiner, therefore, Michael Ondatjee is a 'modern cosmopolitan who, deracinated, finds his home in his homelessness'; a non-European whose external perspective is predestined to shed light on European history, in a lingua franca adopted from the colonial power. To be understood globally, a 'World Literature' requires a 'World Language'. This insight is particularly significant for Germany, which as Greiner reminds his readers somewhat nostalgically provided the literary lingua franca for authors like Franz Kafka, Joseph Roth and Arthur Koestler at the beginning of the twentieth century – a cosmopolitan epoch to which the Second World War put an abrupt and absolute stop.

The need for a cosmopolitan perspective is made even more emphatically by Bernhard Robben in an article in *Die Tageszeitung* about a British Council symposium entitled 'At Home in England' in 1990, which brought together authors Angela Carter, Anne Devlin, Christopher Hope, Amryl Johnson and Caryl Philipps and German academics and publishers. With unabashed admiration for the openness of the British debate about cultural and national identity, Robben proposed the British confrontation with the postcolonial reality as a model for Germany. The best and most complex contemporary British authors, he claims, are engaged in a process he calls 'coasting' – exploring the world while keeping one foot on the island; all others (among whom he counts Margaret Drabble, Iris Murdoch, Kingsley Amis and Anita Brookner) are no longer even credible. But, while the literary foreigners that challenge this exhausted literary mainstream betoken the collapse of the British Empire, they have also contributed to a rethinking of the concept of 'home'. And this, he claims, has specific resonances for a post-Cold War continental Europe. Quoting a prophetic Salman Rushdie, who claims that the experience of migration not only changes the individuals undergoing this experience, but also enables them to rejuvenate the countries which they have joined, Robben suggests that German authors, too, ought to define the term 'Heimat' in a positive way, by taking that which is other, foreign, 'fremd' in it into account.

Following on from Robben's argument, the kind of cosmopolitanism embodied in British literature is seen to provide a solution of sorts to Germany's anguished search for a post-1989 national identity precisely by reintroducing a category that in Germany was tabooed. By abandoning the notion of nation, Germans can once again think about their country as a 'home'. British cultural institutions have been happy to further such ideas. The seminar attended by Robben was one of the legendary meetings the British Council had been organizing since 1986 in Walberberg near Cologne. Founded by Malcolm Bradbury, the

'Walberberg Seminar' was one particularly prestigious means of furthering the British Council's educational mission; it was also a way of reaching academics, the group that mainly frequented this event (some might cynically add that it was always the same group of grey-haired academics frequenting this event) (Harms and Luig).[6] From that perspective, the Walberberg Seminars defined an ideal of British fiction that would be of relevance not least in German academic circles, from where it would percolate down to other areas of society. In the 1990s, the seminar repeatedly addressed issues of cultural identity, subverting any essentialist notion of identity by inviting Caryl Phillips as chair twice (1994 and 1995) and dealing with topics such as 'Balance Between Diverse Cultures', 'I am an English Writer' and 'Roots and Routes'; among the invited writers were Wilson Harris, Timothy Mo, Pauline Melville, Amit Chauduri and Abdulrazak Gurnah.

The Walberberg Seminar had a not inconsiderable influence on the academic debate about British fiction. As in other European countries, postcolonial studies became an established field in German universities in the 1990s; however, because of the delayed publication of academic research, much of this only began appearing in the 2000s. Drawing on the parameters of postmodernity, critics reinterpreted the broadening of horizons ('Horizonterweiterung') resulting from the new voices within the traditional canons, as a deconstruction of both the individual and collective identities associated by critics such as Reckwitz with the Western bourgeoisie and its cultural products (210). This is the perspective adopted by Korte and Müller in their 1998 exploration of contemporary British fiction based on a toned-down postmodernism that takes British culture to be defined by a combination of unity and diversity. Modelling their view of Britain on the 'dynamic' cultural unity of Canada, 'in which differences are contained and negotiated, in which diversity and unity can be reconciled' albeit 'only in a strange and contradictory relationship' (19), they claim that a traditional concept of white Britishness (as endorsed by Daniel Defoe and T.S. Eliot) has in recent years been challenged by an array of different critical and (subcultural perspectives) (15):

> [t]oday it is widely accepted that Britain is in the process of re-defining itself along flexible terms that derive from modern and contemporary identity concepts, concepts of a pluralized self, and this is increasingly expressed in contemporary writing. Thus the protagonists of Hanif Kureishi's fiction and screenplays... have highly flexible identity concepts that are not only determined by ethnicity, but also by fluid sexual orientation and affiliation with various subcultures in contemporary urban Britain. (16)

However, while terms like 'flexibility' and 'fluidity' may be appealing in the realm of representations, they are less fruitful to reality (even of the academic kind); where agency is required, flexibility can be a hindrance and individuals need to take decisions. The limits of such ideas become apparent when we consider another area where they are played out: in the German fascination with the non-English regions of the United Kingdom, notably Scotland. The lure of Scotland has a long pedigree in Germany, reaching back to early nineteenth-century German Romantic nationalism, whose celebration of authentic cultural expression manifested itself in an interest in the indigenous 'margins' of larger, artificial political constructs. Because of their specific sense of authenticity, these margins were also predestined to become sites of resistance, notably against English power and influence. Inevitably, Scottish authors are often evaluated in terms of how conflicted their relationship with England is, and in the 1990s, even well into the Blair era, this conflictedness is again and again associated with the figure of Margaret Thatcher and the Tories as one finds in Peter Zenzinger's 'Contemporary Scottish Fiction' (218). In 1999, a gleeful Hauke Goos describes Iain Banks mischievously translating an acronym used by a fashion label as 'Fuck the Tories' (37). Ironically, this presumed subversive marginality also made Scotland attractive in the eyes of the GDR, which during the 1980s, in an attempt at self-marketing, steeped up its attempts to make contacts in the West. It seems that people in Scotland were not averse to these kind of links as explained by Howarth: 'for Scotland, the attraction of the GDR derived principally from a shared sense of otherness, an ingrained community of alternative and socialist identities and approaches, a bond which was perceived to have been lost as the socialism came to an end' (123).

The German rediscovery of Scotland in the 1990s was no less entangled with the question of national identity than the Romantic cult of the Brothers Grimm and Herder (or dyed-in-the wool socialists in the GDR) but had to find new ways of addressing this topic. The style of 1990s Scottish fiction, with its focus on urban decay and working-class disaffection, facilitated the distinction from the nationalist tradition of 'Scotticism'. In Germany, 'Scottish Studies' tried to shed their folkloristic reputation by reinventing themselves along the postcolonial model that began to be proposed for the study of Scottish literature in the 1990s (Bell). Even scholars adhering to the idea of what Mahlzahn labels a Scottish 'national psychology' (16) and Zenzinger calls the 'distinctiveness of Scottish fiction' (216) ultimately emphasized the diversity of cultural expression and literary styles. Such gestures are fully in line with the attempt of an increasingly assertive Scottish nationalism to found a new nationalist narrative within the broader multicultural framework of 1990s Britain. Gustav Klaus draws an analogy between postcolonial literatures in the Commonwealth and an indigenous Scottish literature (186), while Jürgen Neubauer views contemporary Scottish fiction as 'a contested terrain on which conflicting visions of the future clash' (16).

Yet, where is the difference between such notions of 'productive' conflict and the 'apocalyptic mood' detected around the same time in 1990s Scottish fiction by Franziska Augstein? In her ironic article in *Frankfurter Allgemeine Zeitung*, the term 'apocalypse' is used (appropriately) in a double sense: spurred by the prospect of political independence and cultural innovation, 1990s Scotland evinces both an atmosphere of departure and an anarchic self-destructiveness. In turn, Scottish fiction – with its helpless, disorganized and passive characters, the urban wastelands of its settings and its open-ended plots – records similar emotional and experiential contradictions. It is this apocalyptic quality, however, that might explain why German readers – many of whom saw themselves and their country as going through a major crisis as Geyer explains (363–4) – were so attracted to Scottish fiction. Once again, it seems that Germans reflected best upon themselves by looking at others.

Authenticity and its discontents

The reception of Scottish fiction in Germany accentuates the growing fascination with the foreign, but it also crystallizes the problems relating to the dogma of difference with a no less important ideal of authenticity and resistance. This goes for Germany's view of Britain in general, which is both praised as a model for multi-ethnicity (and a relaxed, rootless – if spicy – cosmopolitanism) and associated with struggle (usually connected with a vague memory of the Thatcher years). It seems that German readers in the 1990s came to expect a certain thematic quality in British fiction:[7] a writing that expressed a gritty, realistic view of the world and social problems – at least if one believes the press. The aforementioned articles on *Granta* emphasized the 'dirty realism' on which the magazine prides itself: for the *Tageszeitung* reviewer, the magazine is 'without illusions, hard-boiled, life itself' ('Illusionslos, hard-boiled, das Leben selbst'), while *Der Tagesspiegel* glosses: 'Not revolutionary, but good' ('Nicht revolutionär, dafür gut'). Author and journalist Sky Nonhoff is no less sensationalist in the Introduction to his 1997 anthology *Off Limits*, which contains, among others, stories by Amis, Doyle, Ishiguro, Swift and Welsh. Nonhoff writes somewhat pompously: 'Reality can only belong to those who grab it by the lapels and interrogate it' (7).

From these perspectives, the more hard-boiled an author presents herself or himself to be, the better. This formula may help to explain the success of Hanif Kureishi in Germany. Kureishi – whose books are listed on German school and university curricula and are reviewed extensively in the German press – seems to encapsulate what Germans like best about British fiction: a wholly acculturated second-generation Briton with Pakistani roots and charming rogue without pretensions, Kureishi incorporates both the cosmopolitan promise of multiculturalism and a robust sense of working-class anger. Strausfeld's review of *The Buddha of Suburbia* links the novel's depiction of events causing 'understandable rage, resistance and vengefulness' (n.p.) with the reality of racism in Britain. Small wonder that he is referenced by German academics such as Korte and Müller and is, to his own bewilderment, the subject of doctoral dissertations written in Germany (Böhner 15).

Outside of academia, criticism of Kureishi in Germany has been mixed. The same critic Stein that found the language of *The Black Album* 'plain and uninspired' applauded him for the plot of this 'wonderful, picaresque novel' (B5). Another reviewer, Allmeier, in the conservative *Frankfurter Allgemeine Zeitung*, was appreciative of his absence of pretentiousness in *In a Blue Time*, but also detected a certain lack of stylistic care (L6). Yet, another reviewer of the same book in *Süddeutsche Zeitung*, Draesner, was reminded of *Trainspotting* but found it smoother and more superficial, wavering 'between coolness and kitsch' (905). If, on the whole, critics in the 1990s treated Kureishi with great benevolence, things began to go awry when he departed from the traditional pattern and abandoned his postcolonial concerns and social anger. In his review of *Intimacy*, Lothar Gorris expresses his disappointment that an author whose former claim to fame had been 'funny and provocative film scripts and novels about the lives of Pakistani migrants in London' had discovered, at the age of 44, 'the drama of modern man' ('Die Welt' 212) as a topic – thereby becoming banal. In the same year, Jörg von Uthmann bemoans that Kureishi – having 'climbed up the social ladder and leaving the discomforts of his background behind' – has written a play, *Sleep With Me*, that does not feature a single black character. If Kureishi had once been applauded for being provocative, then his conscious and justified alignment with new, mainstream topics was seen as a provocation that was too much to bear – even if, as Gorris acknowledges, provocation may no longer be necessary when there are no enemies left to antagonize ('Die Welt' 215).

But, von Uthmann makes an important point when he draws attention to the potentially counterproductive effects of the autobiographic element in Kureishi's later work. The possibility that the representation of the mundane qualities of 'life itself' may ultimately be as potentially prosaic and trite as life as it is actually sometimes lived might also explain the German press's love-hate relationship with Nick Hornby. In the late 1990s, Hornby was omnipresent across the press spectrum, whether as a reference point to assess other authors or as a topic in himself. Kolja Mensing opened an article about an academic symposium on the topic of 'German Literature on the threshold to the twenty-first Century' (organized and funded in 1999 by the conservative Konrad-Adenauer-Stiftung) by invoking Hornby. Thomas Groß saw in *High Fidelity* 'traces of an *éducation sentimentale*' whose significance is less psychological than philosophical; the unidentified reviewer of *About a Boy* likens the novel to *The Catcher in the Rye* ('Außenseiter' 118). Uwe Wittstock applauded Hornby for focusing on the narrow world of his characters in the same novel, which he deems 'funny, smart and an impressive storyteller' (15). Lothar Gorris, in a longer portrait of Hornby in *Der Spiegel*, credited him with having returned humour to British contemporary fiction ('Liebe ist nur ein Sport' 230), while Gisa Funck associated him with a postmodern blurring of high and low culture. Even the most dismissive critics such as Jacobs suggested that German literature had something to learn from a 'recorder of our mediocrity' like Hornby. For Steinert, he is a 'popular writer with a fresh and straightforward language' who is ambitious 'to hit the bestseller lists also as an accomplished stylistician'.

Some reviewers have suggested that Hornby's 'charmingly-laconic' (Berger, 'Verloren' 13) stories have provided the models for younger German writers in the 1990s, notably according to Plowman the 'pop literature' which 'exploded aggressively onto the scene in the mid-1990s' (50); other commentators reach different conclusions, however. The decade saw a string of reviews drawing comparisons between the styles of young British and German writers – an odd competition in which the German authors usually lost out. Birgit Weidinger juxtaposed the lad-lit writers Simon Nolan and William Sutcliffe with young German authors of the period, applauding the formers' interest in character, their sense of humour and general entertainment value with the latters' tendency to 'bicker, be argumentative and long-winded'. In a similar vein, Funck juxtaposed young English and German authors, suggesting that even authors of the 'pop literature' often associated with British influences appeared to her dire, self-pitying and oddly elitist. Such commentaries appeared to have been influenced by the call for 'unencumbered storytelling' in German literature that began to be heard in the middle of the decade and sometimes went under the label, as Plowman describes matters, of 'new storytelling' (50). It is therefore hardly surprising that there was considerable suspicion on the part of German authors towards these ideals and their Anglo-American provenance. Although Benjamin von Stuckrad-Barre's novel *Soloalbum* (1998) draws on Hornby's *High Fidelity* thematically (a disappointed love story told from a male perspective, suffused with pop references), structurally (the novel is organized like a record, each chapter given a song by *Oasis* as a title) and in its use of everyday language, Stuckrad-Barre (the poster boy of pop literature) was less appreciative of other authors. In 1999, he thrashed Salman Rushdie's novel *The Ground Beneath her Feet* for its contrived pop cultural references and artificial nonchalance in a review that probably was meant to appear as an act of iconoclastic resistance against a literary godfather. I am uncertain whether Rushdie ever heard about this review (let alone about its author). Still, I am inclined to read Stuckrad-Barre's review as a gesture of self-confidence that is meaningful both in a literary and a wider cultural and political sense. It may in fact have marked the beginning of the new German writing of the 2000s which, although clearly influenced by British models, also appears distinctly 'German'. Writers like Karin Duve and Frank Goosen quite deliberately echo authors like Nick Hornby and Helen Fielding and cultivate a 'distinctly British voice' marked by irony and self-deprecation, while at the same time managing to reinscribe a sense of 'Germanness', and elements of the 'German cultural tradition' in their novels (Plowman 57). In that way, they appear to fulfil in a literary context a task that on the political level still needs to be completed: the shaping of a 'national self-confidence' independent of the broader framework of the EU (Müller, 'What do Germans Think About' 18).

British fiction may have influenced German writing in the 1990s in another extra-literary sense. Thomas Brussig and Ingo Schulze are both authors that were born in the GDR who came to fame in the 1990s with unconventional novels that were manifestly indebted to the Anglo-American tradition. Schulze's first published novel, *Simple Stories*, was compared to Anglo-American writers like Raymond Carver, and Brussig's funny novels about emotionally challenged men and football were thought to echo those of Nick Hornby. In a well-known and oft-cited interview in *Die Tageszeitung*, both novelists discuss the position of writers and the future of literature in Germany. In this conversation, Brussig speaks of a change in attitude in mid-1990s German literary culture that manifested itself in writers' 'wish to have readers' – a desire, he maintains, that can only be fulfilled in a changed literary culture in which authors no longer lived by grants and prizes but needed to market their books. While it is ironic that it should be an East German author who defends notions of 'new storytelling' with capitalist models of production and consumption for aspiring authors, it seems particularly so as Brussig embraces a market economy view of publishing in the same German newspaper in which *Granta*-editor Neil Belton, only two years earlier, had dismissed the commercial nature of British publishing.

That authenticity and/or authentic resistance potentially breed strange fruits can also be seen in other contexts. Both the extreme left and the extreme right looked to England for reference points and iconography. Working-class resistance in the United Kingdom not only served as a role model for young punks in the former East Germany (anon., 'Da braut sich was zusammen' 106), but also for young people on the right. Michael Ignatieff recounts an interesting encounter with neo-Nazis in Leipzig wearing braces decorated with Union Jacks; his claim that 'skin culture may just be Britain's most enduring contribution to Germany and the new Europe' (61) is affirmed by Timothy Brown's recounting of how the Nazi rock rooted in late 1970s skinhead culture spread from the United Kingdom into Germany (seen by some British neo-Nazis as a venerated spiritual home), where, as Brown says 'it has served as an accompaniment to a rising tide of racist and anti-immigrant violence in Germany' (157). As these examples demonstrate, Britain has been serving as a model for various kinds of ideals, not all of them tolerant, multicultural and subversive, and as such presents a model to be overcome as much as imitated.

Conclusion

During the time when disorientation constituted a key element of the 1990s as a sociopolitical and aesthetic period in Germany, Britain provided an attractive model for a national self-image that was not nationalistic, or whose national self-confidence resulted from its potential for multicultural tolerance and authentic subversion. Literature produced in Britain similarly represented these ideals. However, already in the final years of the decade a change began to announce itself, as Müller notes in 'Triumph', with fewer books from Britain translated and turned into bestsellers and not every novel shortlisted for the Booker or the Whitbread making it onto the German market any longer. This declining interest might have to do with the awareness that the tried and tested patterns of Hornby, Kureishi and others simply had become too formulaic for German readers; it might also have to do with the fact that these authors themselves found them too familiar and replaced them with new forms and topics, thereby frustrating readers who merely expected more of the same. It is mirrored by a concomitant new interest in German-speaking authors, not least in German-speaking authors whose background lies outside of Germany or the German-speaking world. As such, it can be read as a sign that the British model that German readers had been admiring from afar during the 1990s had finally arrived in Germany. In 2010, the German Book Prize (Deutscher Buchpreis), itself established in 2005 along the lines of the Man Booker, was awarded to Melinda Nadj Abonji – a Swiss-Hungarian author born in Serbia – for her novel *Tauben fliegen auf* (*Doves Ascend*). Told from the (initially) naïve perspective of Ildiko, the daughter of a family of Hungarian Serbs setting up a restaurant in provincial Switzerland, the novel fulfils the parameters of a postcolonial Bildungsroman. Whether or not one likes the novel (and the decision was controversial), it certainly illustrates a shift in attitudes, both on the part of the publishing industry (which awards this prize) and authors.

To substantiate my claims about the popularity and the significance of British fiction during the period in question, much further research would have to be undertaken. Although I believe that my chapter might be the basis of a larger interdisciplinary and international project that could result in a systematic and comparative evaluation of book reviews, a statistical assessment of author popularity and a study of the marketing considerations that might have contributed to the awareness of British authors in Germany (for example, the influence of the British Council on the marketing on British fiction in Germany), it provides only a beginning. What I can say for now is that the German reception of British literature in the 1990s is more revealing about Germans in the period than an astute assessment of what British literature was. In that sense, what I have undertaken in this chapter might be fruitfully applied also to other cultural contexts and other literary encounters.

Notes

1   The discussion around the question of whether to speak of a 'unification' or 'reunification' divided critics on the left and right in the 1990s. The former term was used mainly by left-wing commentators, 'to indicate that what was in the making was not something that had existed previously, least of all a reincarnation of Bismarckian Prussian Germany' (Berger 450).
2   For example, in week 41 in 1992, 9 of 15 titles on the *Spiegel* bestseller list were titles originally published in English, three of them by Rosamunde Pilcher alone. In week 39 in 1998, 6 of the 15 titles had come from the United Kingdom or the United States.

3   This translation from the German, as are all others in this chapter, is my own.
4   According to Wittlinger, the prospect of reunification put a 'severe strain' on the up to that point peaceful relationship between the United Kingdom and Germany (454). The notorious Chequers meeting in July 1990 resulted in a memorandum by Charles Powell, Thatcher's private secretary for foreign affairs, in which he listed the characteristics attributed to the German national character during this meeting: 'angst, aggressiveness, assertiveness, bullying, egotism, inferiority complex, sentimentality' (quoted in Ash 49). These attitudes were echoed in a statement by Nicholas Ridley, then secretary of state for trade and industry, who famously called the proposed European monetary union 'a German racket designed to take over the whole of Europe' and equated accepting the authority of a Commission of the European Communities with giving Europe 'up to Adolf Hitler' (quoted in Ash 48).
5   The GDR's official line had been that state socialism had eradicated fascism within its own borders, and the sudden eruption of neo-Nazi violence after reunification in the East was sometimes explained as an effect of Western corruption or an expression of culture shock. However, commentators soon suggested that neo-fascism in the 'new' German states was home grown (Poutrus, Behrends and Kuck), and it has since been established that the government of the GDR had been aware of neo-Nazi activities (see Reinhard). These suspicions have been confirmed most recently after the accidental discovery that a small group of neo-Nazis (the 'Nationalsozialistische Untergrund' aka the 'Zwickau cell') had systematically murdered eight Turkish citizens and one Greek citizen over a period of six years in a string of attacks the authorities had falsely put down to intra-ethnic squabbles (http://de.wikipedia.org/wiki/Nationalsozialistischer_Untergrund).
6   http://www.britishcouncil.de/e/walberberg/index.htm.
7   Though this fascination can also help explain the popularity of 'In Yer Face Theatre' (in particular the work of Sarah Kane) in Germany (Haas 7).

Works Cited

Allmaier, Michael. 'Dauerkicker im blauen Labyrinth'. *Frankfurter Allgemeine Zeitung* 2 December 1997, p. L6.
Anon. 'Wenig Respekt'. *Der Spiegel* 37 (1988): 207–10.
———. 'Da braut sich was zusammen'. *Der Spiegel* 46 (1991): 106–19.
———. 'Die Schale wird zum Kern'. *Der Spiegel* 48 (1993): 232–8.
———. 'Außenseiter mit Happy-End'. *Der Spiegel* 10 (1998): 118.
———. 'Gefeit vor Utopien: Interview with Thomas Brussig and Ingo Schulze'. *Die Tageszeitung* 5 October 1998. Online version, n.p. http://www.taz.de/digitaz/1998/10/05/a0179.archiv/textdruck (accessed 23 October 2010).

———. 'Wir brauchen große Gefühle: Gespräch mit dem Verleger Arnulf Conradi'. *Der Tagesspiegel* 14 February 1999. Online version, n.p. http://www.tagesspiegel.de/kultur/wir-brauchen-grosse-gefühle/71422.html (accessed 19 February 2012).

Ash, Timothy Garton. *History of the Present: Essays, Sketches, and Dispatches from Europe in the 1990s*. London: Vintage, 2001.

Augstein, Franziska. 'Ewiger Herbst jenseits des Tweed'. *Frankfurter Allgemeine Zeitung* 21 March 1998, 1.

Baringhorst, Sigrid. 'Multikulturalismus und Anti-Diskriminierungspolitik in Großbritannien'. In *Multikulturalität – Interkulturalität: Probleme und Perspektiven der multikulturellen Gesellschaft*. Ed. Caroline Y. Robertson-Wensauer. Baden-Baden: Nomos, 2000, 233–52.

Bell, Ian A. 'Scotticism: Textual Attitudes and National Characters'. *Southern Review* 23 (1990): 127–36.

Belton, Neil. 'Trauriger Hang zum Familiären'. *Die Tageszeitung* 27 March 1996. Online version, n.p. http://www.taz.de/digitaz/1996/03/27/a0155.archiv/textdruck (accessed 23 October 2010).

Berger, Jan. 'Verloren im Faselland'. *Süddeutsche Zeitung* 30 November 1998, 13.

Berger, Stefan. 'Quo Vadis Germany? National Identity Debates after Reunification'. *Ab Imperio* 2 (2004): 449–86.

Bernuth, Christa von. 'All die Geschichten, die in euch schlummern'. *Süddeutsche Zeitung* 17 June 1995, 903.

Blair, Tony. 'Die Kultur bricht durch die Fenster'. Trans. Peter von Becker. *Der Tagesspiegel* 8 May 1997. Online version, n.p. http://www.tagesspiegel.de/kultur/die-kultur-bricht-durch-die-fenster/11000.html (accessed 23 November 2010).

Blair, Tony and Gerhard Schröder. 'Europe: The Third Way/Die neue Mitte'. Labour Party 19 August 1999. Online version, n.p. http://web.archive.org/web/19990819090124/http://www.labour.org.uk/views/items/00000053.html (accessed 25 February 2012).

Böhner, Ines Karin. *My Beautiful Laundrette und Sammy and Rosie Get Laid: Filmische Reflextion von Identitätsprozessen*. Frankfurt/Main: Lang, 1996.

Börsenverein des deutschen Buchhandels. *Buch und Buchhandel in Zahlen*. Frankfurt: MVB Marketing, 2001.

Brockmann, Stephen. *Literature and German Reunification*. Cambridge: Cambridge University Press, 1999.

Brown, Timothy S. 'Subcultures, Pop Music and Politics: Skinheads and "Nazi Rock" in England and Germany'. *Journal of Social History* 38.1 (2004): 157–78.

Bußmann, Carla. *Deutschsprachige Erfolgsautoren – ein aktueller Trend auf dem Buchmarkt? Eine Analyse der belletristischen Bestsellerlisten der Jahre 1987–2008*. Unpublished M.A. thesis, Johannes Gutenberg-Universität Mainz, 2010.

Buckley, William F. *The Fall of the Berlin Wall*. Hoboken: Wiley, 2004.

Cuevas, Susanne. *Babylon and Golden City: Representations of London in Black and Asian British Novels since the 1990s*. Heidelberg: Winter, 2008.
Draesner, Ulrike. 'Große Lügen und kleine'. *Süddeutsche Zeitung* 15 November 1997, 905.
Fuchs, Karen. 'Nicht revolutionär, dafür gut'. *Der Tagesspiegel* 14 September 1998. Online version, n.p. http://www.tagesspiegel.de/kultur/nicht-revolutionaer-dafuer-gut/58270.html (accessed 23 November 2011).
Funck, Gisa. 'Hautnah und leicht verdaulich'. *Süddeutsche Zeitung* 30 April 1999. ROM 2.
Geyer, Michael. 'The Long Good-Bye: German Culture Wars in the Nineties'. In *The Power of Intellectuals in Contemporary Germany*. Ed. Michael Geyer. Chicago: University of Chicago Press, 2001, 355–80.
Goos, Hauke. 'Heimat on the Rocks'. *Spiegel Extra* 4 (1996): 36–8.
Gorris, Lothar. 'Liebe ist nur ein Sport'. *Der Spiegel* 39 (1998): 230–3.
———. 'Die Welt: ein Weiberrock'. *Der Spiegel* 19 (1999): 212–15.
Grass, Günter. 'Kurze Rede eines vaterlandslosen Gesellen'. *Die Zeit* 9 February 1990, 61.
Greiner, Ulrich. 'Als Kip lernte, die Bombe zu hassen'. *Die Zeit* 41, 8 October 1993. Online version, n.p. http://www.zeit.de/1993/41/Als-Kip-lernte-die-Bombe-zu-hassen (accessed 15 Nov 2010).
———. 'Amphibien'. *Die Zeit* 12 January 1996. Online version, n.p. (accessed 3 February 2012).
Groß, Thomas. 'Das Große Jungensding'. *Die Tageszeitung* 24 February 1996. Online version, n.p. http://www.taz.de/digitaz/1996/02/24/a0170.archiv/textdruck (accessed 23 October 2010).
Haas, Birgit. *Modern German Political Drama 1980–2000*. Rochester: Camden House, 2003.
Hager, Martin. 'Illusionslos, hard-boiled, das Leben selbst'. *Die Tageszeitung* 12 September 1998. Online version, n.p. http://www.taz.de/digitaz/1998/09/12/a0261.archiv/textdruck (accessed 23 October 2010).
Harms, Ingeborg. 'Wal und Wurm'. *Frankfurter Allgemeine Zeitung* 28 January 1998, 35.
Howarth, Marianne. 'The Pipes of Peace: Projecting "Scottishness" to the GDR'. In *The Other Germany: Perceptions and Influences in British-East German Relations, 1945–1990*. Eds Stefan Berger and Norman La Porte. Augsburg: Wißner-Verlag, 2005, 107–22.
Huggan, Graham. 'Prizing 'Otherness': A Short History of the Booker'. *Studies in the Novel* 29.3 (1997): 412–33.
Ignatieff, Michael. *Blood and Belonging: Journeys into the New Nationalism*. London: Chatto & Windus (BBC Books), 1993.
Jacobs, Steffen. 'Als sie mich nicht wollte'. *Frankfurter Allgemeine Zeitung* 5 August 1996, 36.
Judt, Tony. *Postwar: A History of Europe since 1945*. London: Penguin, 2005.

Klaus, Gustav H. 'New Bearings in Scottish Writing: Alasdair Gray, Tom Leonard, James Kelman'. In *Anglistentag 1992 Stuttgart: Proceedings*. Eds Hans Ulrich Seeber and Walter Göbel. Tübingen: Max Niemeier, 1993, 186–95.

Korte, Barbara and Klaus Peter Müller (eds) *Unity in Diversity Revisited? British Literature and Culture in the 1990s*. Tübingen: Narr, 1998.

Kröncke, Gerd. 'Aus dem Leben eines Habenichts'. *Süddeutsche Zeitung* 12 March 1993, 3.

Liebenstein, Karina. *Bestsellerlisten 1962–2001: Eine statistische Analyse*. Erlangen-Nürnberg: Buchwissenschaft Universität, 2005.

Luig, Judith. 'Konfus, aber schön'. *Die Tageszeitung* 4 February 2008. Online version, n.p. http://www.taz.de/1/archiv/digitaz/artikel/?ressort=ku&d ig=2008/02... (accessed 15 February 2012).

Malzahn, Manfred. *Aspects of Identity: The Contemporary Scottish Novel (1978–1981) as National Self-Expression*. Frankfurt/Main: Peter Lang, 1984.

Mensing, Kolja. 'Der harte Beat der Hochkultur'. *Die Tageszeitung* 8 November 1999. Online version, n.p. http://www.taz.de/digitaz/1999/11/08/a0120.archiv/textdruck (accessed 23 October 2010).

Meyer, Michael. *The Year That Changed the World: The Untold Story behind the Fall of the Berlin Wall*. New York: Scribner, 2009.

Meyrhöfer, Annette. 'Der Swing der harten Jahre'. *Der Spiegel* 26 (1997): 160–2.

Mohr, Reinhard. 'Deutsch, aber glücklich'. *Der Spiegel* 43 (1997): 41–5.

Müller, Annette. 'Der Triumph der Erwartung über die Realität: Über den Status zeitgenössischer englischer Literatur in Deutschland und den Buchmarkt in England'. *literaturkritik.de* 6 (June 2002), n.p. http://www.literaturkritik.de/public/ rezension.php?rez_id=5044 (accessed 13 September 2010).

Müller, Jan-Werner. 'What do Germans Think about When They Think about Europe?' *London Review of Books* 34.3 (9 February 2012), 18–19.

Neubauer, Jürgen. *Literature as Intervention: Struggles over Cultural Identity in Contemporary Scottish Fiction*. Marburg: Tectum, 1999.

Nonhoff, Sky (ed.). *Off Limits*. München: Goldmann, 1997.

O'Hagan, Andrew. 'Short Cuts'. *London Review of Books* 32.22 (2010): 22.

Oltermann, Philip. *Keeping Up with the Germans: A History of Anglo-German Encounters*. London: Faber, 2012.

Plog, Ulla. 'Wer zu spät kommt, den bestraft das Leben'. *Frankfurter Allgemeine Zeitung* 6 October 2004. http://www.faz.net/aktuell/politik/15-jahre-danach-wer-zu-spaet -kommt-den-bestraft-das-leben-1191290.html (accessed 19 February 2012).

Plowman, Andrew. '"Was will ich als Westdeutscher erzählen?" Globalisation and the "Old" West in Recent German Prose'. In *German Literature in the Age of Globalisation*. Ed. Stuart Taberner. Birmingham: Birmingham University Press, 2004.

Poutrus, Patrice G., Jan C. Behrends and Dennis Kuck. 'Historische Ursachen der Fremdenfeindlichkeit in den neuen Bundesländern'. *Aus Politik und Zeitgeschichte* 39 (2000). http://www.bpb.de/publikationen/OKZ5MW.html (accessed 20 February 2012).

Reckwitz, Erhard. '"Britain's Other Islanders": Multikulturalismus im Englischen Roman'. In *Radikalität und Mäßigung: Der Englische Roman seit 1960*. Eds Annegret Maack and Rüdiger Imhof. Darmstadt: Wiss. Buchgesellschaft, 1993, 208–29.

Reinhard, Oliver. 'Wotansbrüder und Weimarer Front'. *Die Zeit* 16 February 2012. Online version, n.p. http://www.zeit.de/2012/08/DDR-Nazis (accessed 17 February 2012).

Robben, Bernhard. '(Nichts) Neues aus England'. *Die Tageszeitung* 14 October 1989. Online version, n.p. http://www.taz.digitaz/1989/10/12/a0054.archiv/textdruck (accessed 5 December 2010).

———. 'Fremde Heimat'. *Die Tageszeitung* 8 February 1990. Online version, n.p. http://www.taz.de/digitaz/1990/02/08/a0134.archiv/textdruck (accessed 13 September 2010).

Smith, Chris. *Creative Britain*. London, 1998.

Stein, Hannes. 'Heilige Auberginen'. *Frankfurter Allgemeine Zeitung* 21 October 1995, B5.

Steinert, Hajo. 'Fußball, Platten, Gameboys'. *Die Zeit* 17 September 1998. Online version, n.p. http://www.zeit.de/1998/39/Fussball_Platten_Gameboys (accessed 15 September 2010).

Strausfeld, Michi. 'Mitten dazwischen'. *Die Zeit* 26 April 1991. Online version, n.p. http://www.zeit.de/1991/18/mitten-dazwischen (accessed 23 February 2012).

Stuckrad-Barre, Benjamin von. 'Der Zettelkasten des Rock'n'Roll'. *Der Spiegel* 16 (1999): 250–3.

Taberner, Stuart. *German Literature in the Age of Globalisation*. Birmingham: Birmingham University Press, 2004.

Thomas, Gina. 'Cool Britannia: Tony Blair und die Regierungskunst der Selbstanpreisung'. *Frankfurter Allgemeine Zeitung* 2 May 1998, 35.

Uthmann, Jörg von. 'Gute Nazis, schlechte Männer'. *Der Tagesspiegel* 13 June 1999. Online version, n.p. http://www.tagesspiegel.de/kultur/gute-nazis-schlechte-maenner/80130.html (accessed 23 November 2010).

Weidinger, Birgit. 'Im Wechselbad der Befindlichkeiten'. *Süddeutsche Zeitung* 27 November 1999, ROM 2.

Wittlinger, Ruth. 'Perceptions of Germany and the Germans in Post-War Britain'. *Journal of Multilinguial and Multicultural Development* 25.5&6 (2004): 453–65.

Wittstock, Uwe. 'Reicher, glücklicher Single sucht …' *Süddeutsche Zeitung* 20 October 1998, 15.

Zenzinger, Peter. 'Contemporary Scottish Fiction'. In *Scotland: Literature, Culture, Politics*. Anglistik & Englischunterricht. Ed. Peter Zenzinger. Heidelberg: Winter, 1989, 215–39.

8

International Contexts 2
National Identity and the Immigrant

Paoi Hwang

From the early twentieth century, there has been a continual Western influence in Taiwan's literary production, and the proliferation of Internet media and globalization has only ensured that Western tastes, styles and thoughts infiltrate every aspect of life faster and more completely. As in Britain, cultural theory and identity politics became an important focus in Taiwan in the 1990s. What Nick Bentley observed in Britain can also be applied to Taiwan: 'Identity became the main concept by which individuals mapped out their relationship with society and often provided a way of producing narratives of empowerment across a variety of marginalized subject positions' (8). According to Bentley, the central issues of the 1990s that British writers, especially novelists, picked up on were gender, sexuality, race and nation. This is also true for writers in Taiwan. For example, while British writers such as Jeanette Winterson and Helen Fielding focused on the female body and women's empowerment, Taiwanese writers such as Ang Li and Shuching Shih explored similar themes connected to women's liberation through experimentation and by challenging the social expectations that Chinese society, in particular, placed on women. While Hanif Kureishi and Alan Hollinghurst explored bisexuality and gay cultures, writers such as Tienwen Zhu also questioned the gender breakdown of gay men and their views on identity. While writers such as Salman Rushdie and Caryl Phillips concentrated on race and the meaning of the nation, writers such as Yaode Lin and Dong Nian asked questions concerning the aboriginal, Japanese and Chinese presence in Taiwan, and how this was affecting the idea of Taiwanese nationhood and identity.

These ideas and debates precipitated a fierce debate on postmodernity and postcoloniality amongst writers and academics. While for some postmodernity became a focal point, for others it was postcoloniality and decolonization, but both were used to reflect on the question of nationhood in Taiwan. Postmodernity and its influences on the literary and art scenes in Taiwan not only raised the question of Western influence in Taiwanese cultural life but also illuminated the ongoing process of decolonization, as Taiwan sought its own identity and recognition from the world as a nation. Writers and artists alike asked the fundamental question: What would be the consequences of embracing a very different cultural identity if one was already confused by one's own cultural ambiguity and undergoing an identity crisis? Indeed, globalization and consumer culture has allowed Taiwan, as a relatively wealthy country, to compete equally with Western nations, but in terms of political security and cultural identity, can Taiwan gain the recognition that it desires? The arguments and discussions leading back to national identity confirm that Taiwan's struggle to find a cultural and political stance is a constant one. As Bentley points out:

> The politics of identity were particularly influenced by a politics of difference during the 1990s. The decade saw the increasing importance of postcolonial theory, which in turn offered new ways of interpreting Britain's relationship with its colonial past, and the make-up of contemporary ethnic, racial and religious identities. (9)

As decolonization, diaspora and even devolution came to the fore, the question of immigration, integration and cultural hybridity was highlighted. While Britain considered devolution as a more 'democratic' option to nationhood for its Scottish, Welsh and Irish components, Taiwan after the lifting of martial law in 1987 also moved towards democracy in permitting the formation of new political parties. For postcolonial Britain, the 'immigrant' voices of African and Asian writers took on a new legitimacy and breathed new life into its literature. For Taiwan, 'native' writers were finally able to present their own views of what Taiwanese literature meant and add their voices to those of the Chinese 'immigrant' writers who had received preferential treatment by the Chinese Nationalist government. As Britain's empire 'wrote back' to hasten the process of decolonization and postcoloniality, Taiwan began to examine its experiences with Japanese colonialism and question its relationship with the Chinese Nationalist regime that took over in 1949.

Applying these questions of identity to individual writers gives them a specificity. Hanif Kureishi is a British writer. But what does that mean? Does he write about Britain, or is he simply a writer with British citizenship? Kureishi was born in 1954 to a Pakistani father and an English mother; his writing is often based around the Indian and Pakistani communities in Britain. Although

Kureishi is British and indubitably has a place in British literature, his cultural influences and affiliations are not always regarded as 'conventionally' British. Tachun Chang was born in 1957 to parents who had moved to Taiwan from China. His works are usually set in Taiwan, depicting the contemporary Taipei scene in particular, but they are categorized as 'Chinese literature from Taiwan' as opposed to 'Taiwanese literature', which is usually taken to refer to literature produced by the native people of Taiwan. 'Literature from Taiwan' is the term used to include writers from China who do not always regard themselves as Taiwanese, but who write about Taiwan. In fact, many second-generation immigrant writers, in other words those who have parents that arrived with the Chinese Nationalists, often still refer to China as their 'motherland' and regard their works as part of Chinese literature.

While Kureishi and Chang grew up in two very different places and have different backgrounds, they belong to the same generation and both published semi-autobiographical novels exploring very similar issues in the 1990s. Kureishi's Karim Amir in *The Buddha of Suburbia* (1990) and Chang's protagonist in *Wild Kids* (1996) suffer similar problems of rootlessness and identity crises. This chapter focuses on the postcolonial question and explores national identity in literature according to these two 'immigrants' in Britain and Taiwan.

National identity in Britain and Taiwan

The constitutional birth of Great Britain can be dated to 1707, when Scotland joined England and Wales under the Act of Union. The creation of an 'official' Britain occurred in three stages with Wales joining England in 1536, Scotland in 1707 and Ireland in 1800. Bhikhu Parekh notes the changes in the title with each addition:

> Constitutionally, it was only after the Union with Scotland (1707) that England, Scotland and Wales became known as *Great Britain*. From 1801 to 1922 Ireland was joined to Great Britain and the state's name changed to the *United Kingdom*. After Partition (1922) the state's name changed again. It was now the *United Kingdom of Great Britain and Northern Ireland* (emphasis added). (15)

However, Parekh suggests, it was through performing the role of 'mother country' to the British Empire that the Scots, Irish, Welsh and English came to overlook their internal differences and forge a common British identity (see 21–2). If the Viking invasion in the ninth century encouraged the various British kings to unite for the first time, the rebellions in the colonies similarly encouraged the English, Irish, Welsh and Scottish to identify themselves as British in order to maintain imperial power. However, Scottish and Welsh devolution and Irish independence have inevitably called into question the feasibility of both the British state and the idea of British nationality. The meaning and unity of Britain has undergone many changes over the years, but as a nation, it has relied on definitions of an 'us' and a 'them' because, as Eric Hobsbawm states in *Nations and Nationalism since 1780* (1991), 'there is no more effective way of bonding together the disparate sections of restless people than to unite them against outsiders' (91).

Ernest Renan has stated that 'a nation is a soul, a spiritual principle' that is made up of the past and present, a shared history or memory which the present consents to perpetuate as a heritage (see Renan 1990). A nation is not made of one language, one race or one religion but one decision to 'live together' with a 'common will' to share a 'common glory' and have a common history/ancestry that means out 'of all cults, that of the ancestors is the most legitimate, for the ancestors have made us what we are. A heroic past, great men, glory... this is the social capital upon which one bases a national idea' (Renan 1990: 19). Ernest Gellner believes that cultural homogeneity is responsible for creating a centre from which a nation can form its identity (see Gellner 1990). For Gellner, the nation operates on many levels and may be regarded as a cultural storehouse as well as a species of political thought and social movement. Next to the nation's administrative and economical aspects, cultural ideologies occupy a significant part of national representation. The concept of national identity is based as much on a shared, collective communal identity as it is enforced by the existence of difference in others. Nationality emerges through cultural awareness, its main ideas centred on a core, dominant ethnic community that is embraced by the bureaucratic state, which is given the authority to incorporate or dissolve smaller communities through law reinforcement. Communities that form a nation can be seen to be bound both intrinsically to each other – through accumulation of shared characteristics, shared history, myths and linguistic traditions – and also by external governing bodies and their laws. Unions forged under such circumstances, however, are subject to the possibility of fragmentation because of the uneven distribution of power that inevitably results. Some form of cultural hierarchy is to be expected in any society. The need to maintain power in any situation means the dominant party has to downplay the other's merits. This is especially true of the colonial situation as can be seen in the European portrayal of 'New World' cultures. Not only was it important to distort the cultural contents of foreign communities, but their portrayal had to be restricted to lower forms of style to ensure that it did not vie for attention with the 'superior' home-myths. For a more comprehensive reading of cultural representation, see Richards 1994.

Similarity can bring people together, but there are also degrees of dissimilarity within similarity, thus the question arises as to how much dissimilarity is acceptable before a particular community no longer fits in the nation? Since there is constantly a need for difference from an external other to clarify the existence of the self, there will always be the need to draw a line between the two. The question then is where the line is drawn, how much difference can be accepted within the idea of the similar. If there are non-members who practice dissimilar patterns that do not belong to any community within the nation, they are expected either to be subsumed over a period of time or to be integrated successfully as an additional community. And this 'pattern of similarity-cum-dissimilarity' plays an important role in the national formation of an identity (Smith 75). For individuals who belong to any community in a nation two questions can be asked: How will they perceive their community's relationship with other communities? And, if they all belong to one nation, when does intra-community cohesion end and true foreignness begin?

Terence Ranger in his introduction to *Culture, Identity and Politics* argues that the Celts, and not the people from Africa, Asia or the Caribbean, were the original 'other' who first brought national awareness to Britain:

> There certainly were blacks in early modern England and they were certainly the object of prejudice. But from the mid-sixteenth century onwards, the essential marker of first English and then British identity was not whiteness but Protestantism. The significant Other for the construction of English and British identity was not the black but the Celts. (6)

Looking at the history of Britain, it is possible to discern that 'Celtic speech was the prime marker of the outsider; Celtic societies, whether in Gaelic Ireland or in the Scottish Highlands, were relegated to the backwardness of tribalism' (Ranger 6). Despite being the earliest inhabitants of Britain, they became the Other in the eyes of the governing body. It is this 'foreigner within' who produced a national identity that also threatens to fragment that British nationality. Ranger believes that the search for a British identity actually stemmed from the search for an English identity, and for a long period of time Britishness was synonymous with Englishness. This relation between Englishness and Britishness has remained problematic.

Ron Ramdin argues that it was the improved communications network formed in the nineteenth century that was responsible for exposing Ireland, Wales and Scotland to English political influence. However, the relationships were subtly different between the communities.

> Ireland was less of an issue in English national politics [in the latter part of the nineteenth century] than it was in 1850, while Wales and Scotland were constituent parts of the class politics of the rest of the kingdom. With time, Ireland proved to be more susceptible to outside influences than Wales and Scotland, its Irish-born Gaelic speakers declining drastically in the latter part of the nineteenth century. However, although the southern English culture would come to dominate the British Isles, the years from 1860 to 1914 would see the rise and proliferation of ethnic consciousness within the region. (38)

Although the Scottish, Welsh and Irish people have related to England and have been treated by the British government in different ways, it is the Catholic Irish in particular who most readily conform to the 'foreign' presence in British identity formation. They were early victims of racism: they were despised, dispossessed, disenfranchised, crudely stereotyped and exploited when the need for manual labour brought hundreds of thousands of them to industrial England. It is Declan Kiberd's belief that the Irish take pleasure in the fact that 'identity is seldom straightforward' and that 'Ireland was pressed into service as a foil to set off English virtues' (1). As he puts it, '[e]ach nation badly needed the other, for the purpose of defining itself' (2). In more recent times, the Gaelic other has been superseded by new 'foreign' others, but all such cases serve to highlight the role of the 'foreigner' in the ongoing processes of British nationality formation.

In many ways, the aborigines of Taiwan are like the Celtic inhabitants of Britain. They are of Malayo-Polynesian origin and are the earliest settlers in Taiwan. However, they were driven into the mountains by successive waves of new settlers. The Portuguese who 'discovered' the island in the early sixteenth century called it *Ilha Formosa* or 'Beautiful Island'. The Dutch, who colonized Taiwan from 1624 to 1662, continued to call it Formosa but also referred to it as Zeelandia after one of the fortresses that they built (Hong 22). From 1626 to 1642, the Spanish occupied the north of Taiwan and effectively divided the island in two. In 1662, Cheng Chengkung or Koxinga (who was half-Japanese) led a Chinese invasion of Taiwan and managed to defeat the Dutch. Although from very early on Chinese people have continually migrated across the Taiwan Strait, it was during Dutch settlement and Cheng's takeover that these settlers arrived in significantly large numbers. Whereas the Dutch encouraged Chinese settlement for labour purposes, Cheng set up a military colony where the families of his soldiers were ordered to move to Taiwan to develop the land and support his troops. Cheng regarded Taiwan as a part of China and most of the Chinese immigrants already in Taiwan did not resist his rule, even though the aboriginal tribes did and continued to rebel against the Chinese presence as they had the Dutch and the Spanish. Similar to the Anglo-Saxons that the English can be traced from, the majority of Taiwanese people have Chinese ancestry, but their ancestors left China in the seventeenth century. Hence, the Japanese colonization in 1895 and the arrival of the Chinese Nationalists (also known as the Kuomingtang or KMT) in 1949 can be portrayed as new and 'foreign' presences.

The Japanese colonized Taiwan for fifty years. The Japanese government established a north-south transport structure that brought all the different parts of Taiwan together. In addition, they published an island-wide newspaper that helped to create an information platform for the whole island. These set the conditions for the formation of a Taiwanese consciousness that was further consolidated by the unequal treatment of the colonizer and the colonized.

> The Japanese referred to all Taiwanese as 'people of Taiwan', while the title 'people of the homeland' was used for Japanese. Taiwanese went to public schools, while Japanese were educated separately. This highlighted the unequal treatment of the local people... No matter whether one was Minnanese, Hakka, or aborigine, all were treated as 'people of Taiwan'. Over time, this gradually blurred the previous differentiations of Minnanese and Hakka as well as the different identities of the aboriginal tribes. Instead, clear lines were made between the Taiwanese and Japanese, which helped to foster a group awareness among the people of Taiwan. (Hsueh, Tai and Chow 114)

The Japanese encouraged native literary development in a way that would present Taiwan as a separate entity from China. Indeed, Japanese colonialism is responsible for reorienting and de-sinicising Taiwan. As Leo Ching has so succinctly put it, 'the triangulation between colonial Taiwan, imperial Japan and nationalist China formed the terrain where contradictory, conflicting and complicitous desires and identities were projected, negotiated and vanquished' (Ching 8). Even as the world wars pushed Japan into stricter and more oppressive policies of assimilation regarding its colonies, the spirit of a Taiwanese identity had taken root and there are countless articles from this period that, albeit being published in Japanese, clearly argue for a Taiwan that is independent of Japan and China. For example, journals such as *Taiwanese Literature* published works by writers of the Taiwanese New Literature Movement. Authors not only focused on local customs, rural life and folk traditions but also vigorously argued against colonial biases and voiced their resentment of Japanese imperialism (see Davison 72). In fact, Taiwan was the first country in Asia to attempt to establish a republic. When the Manchu government ceded Taiwan in perpetuity to the Japanese in 1895, the Taiwanese intelligentsia tried to declare its independence in a document entitled 'Autonomy Declaration of the Taiwan Democratic Republic' (Hsueh, Tai and Chow 140). However, without external support and true internal cohesion, the people of Taiwan were unable to fend off the Japanese invasion and achieve independence.

The Japanese colonization of Taiwan, similarly to the later Chinese colonization, remains a problematic and much debated topic. It has been argued that Japanese expansionism, like Chinese imperialism, is not the same as Western colonialism. The Japanese were non-Western and non-white, hence they were regarded as racially inferior by Western imperialist nations; they were considered to be culturally and racially similar to those they colonized; and, being latecomers in the colonial game, they did things differently. According to Bruce Cumings, the Japanese were not only interested in colonial development but also metropolitan industrialization; they 'were imperialists but also capitalists, colonisers but also modernisers' (73). Because the Japanese brought modern technology and infrastructure to Taiwan which elevated the overall living standards of the population, opinions and sentiments on Japan have remained divided. Furthermore, when Japan was defeated after the Second World War, it simply left Taiwan without anything comparable to the decolonization processes that happened in, say, India or other former Western colonies:

> The abrupt dissolution of the Japanese Empire by an external mandate instead of through prolonged struggle and negotiation with its colonies has enabled Japan to circumvent and disavow its colonial question and, in turn, quickened its economic recovery. In Taiwan the sudden void left by the Japanese coloniser after 'liberation' was filled not by the Taiwanese but by the takeover army from mainland China. (Ching 20)

The Chinese Nationalists who took over had a very different agenda and view of Taiwan. First, they were retreating from the Communists in China and had not willingly moved to Taiwan. Second, Chiang Kai-shek had every intention to 'retake' China once he had obtained the power to do so; hence, their stay in Taiwan was meant to be temporary. Third, the KMT government occupied Taiwan as enemy (Japanese) territory on behalf of the Allied Forces (see Chow 86). Despite calling Taiwan the Republic of China (ROC) after itself and perceiving it as an 'inalienable part of China', the new ruling elite did not see themselves as equals with the 'natives', nor did they consider the people of Taiwan as ROC citizens (Chow 26). Hence, the nationalist ideology that the KMT forced on Taiwan was highly problematic because it did not openly incorporate the populace and because Taiwan had only recently been colonized by another nation. It can be seen that the 'cultural reconstruction' that the KMT government undertook was done so in order to overturn the previous Japanese nationalism as well as to suppress the Taiwanese native and indigenous voices. Mandarin became the official language and mainland Chinese literature was promoted over local literature. According to Taiwanese scholar, Fangming Chen:

> The introduction of Chinese nationalism into Taiwan can be seen as a fictional and even factional dissemination. In particular, the Nationalist government's raising of the Nationalist flag constituted a welcome to only those literary works favourable to its own position. [...] This censorship testifies to the fact that the Nationalist government's 'nationalism' was actually a divisive political ideal, based on considerations of what was advantageous to the 'part', rather than what was actually best for the 'whole' national populace itself. (31)

Hence, the national identity that the Chinese Nationalists enforced should rightly be seen as a form of *recolonization* (see Chen 32). These issues with nationhood, colonization and identity have persistently plagued Taiwan in its quest for independence; they have also created many problems for writers seeking to portray Taiwan as a separate entity from China.

Taiwan's ambiguity regarding the People's Republic of China is twofold. On the ethnic level, many view Taiwan and China as sharing the same cultural and historical ties. However, the Taiwanese are culturally and even genetically different from the Chinese. It has been argued that the culture and the genes of the Taiwanese people constitute a unique fusion of Indonesian, Portuguese, Spanish, Dutch, Fukienese, Cantonese and Japanese elements (see Hsueh, Tai and Chow 121–2). In other words, the Taiwanese people are as Chinese as the English are Danish or the Belgians are Dutch. On a political level, the KMT government have indirectly given China the opportunity to lay claims to Taiwan and suppress its voice internationally. However, not only is the KMT governance of Taiwan questionable but even if it were legalized, it would still be insufficient to justify China's claim on Taiwan. Because the KMT occupied Taiwan in 1949 but Japan did not relinquish Taiwan until 1951, when it signed the Treaty of San Francisco but did not designate a successor, under international law, Taiwan remains 'unclaimed territory' and by the mandate of self-determination should be returned to its people. Furthermore, the Chinese Nationalists made a point of differentiating themselves from the Communists, and when they settled in Taiwan they were an immigrant minority:

> The new immigrants who arrived in Taiwan with the KMT government... were unwilling exiles. From the very beginning they held a different mindset than other Chinese immigrants. The new immigrants regarded themselves very much as temporary residents, and they saw themselves as being culturally superior. (Hsueh, Tai and Chow 83).

Therefore, it is unreasonable for China to automatically claim Taiwan and for the world to assume that they are one entity. Historically, in terms of political and cultural development, the two have had very different experiences. While China remains a communist country, Taiwan has been electing its own presidents since 1988.

What is most interesting about the role and situation of the immigrant in Britain and Taiwan, despite these very different histories, is their contribution to the idea and the identity of a nation. Although both Hanif Kureishi and Tachun Chang assume 'immigrant' voices by mobilizing their own differences to comment on and distance themselves from the society that they write about, there are subtle differences in their treatment of nationhood and identity. While Kureishi may be seen to use a postcolonial approach in his construction of a British identity and contributes to British literature as an 'insider' who uses the voice of an 'outsider', Tachun Chang is ambiguously silent on postcoloniality, and his literary voice is like that of an 'outsider' assuming the rights of an 'insider'.

The question of belonging

Hanif Kureishi's *The Buddha of Suburbia* is a partly autobiographical novel narrated by a boy, Karim Amir, from an interracial marriage, growing up in the London suburbs in the 1970s. Karim declares, at the start of the novel:

> I am an Englishman born and bred, almost. I am often considered to be a funny kind of Englishman, a new breed as it were, having emerged from two old histories. But I don't care – Englishman I am (though not proud of it), from the South London suburbs and going somewhere. (3)

The first sentence prepares the stage for a cultural conflict since Karim Amir is clearly not a traditional English name, although birthplace and upbringing have given him indisputable ties. His defiant claim to place and confident assertion of identity are undermined by a tone of uncertainty. He calls himself a 'funny' type of Englishman and a 'new breed' because he is a hybrid that is made up of two very different cultures. He clearly claims his English identity, even though he is not proud of it. *The Buddha of Suburbia* is about Karim's exploration of Eastern and Western cultures, his attempts to be himself as well as his negotiation of what others expect of him and finally his experimentation with sexuality by sleeping with men and women. By tackling the basic binaries of East-West, self-other and male-female differences, Kureishi's work reflects Rosi Braidotti's suggestions for a society of infinite possibilities:

> To think constructively about change and changing conditions... one needs to emphasise a vision of the thinking, knowing subject as not-one but rather as being split over and over again in a rainbow of yet uncoded and ever so beautiful possibilities. (158)

The type of equality that Karim embodies does not depend on the marginal superseding the dominant, neither is it about creating groups so that each can obtain its equal share, but it is about breaking down all the barriers of difference so that all entities overlap to become one and many.

Bart Moore-Gilbert has remarked on Kureishi's unusual Anglo-Pakistani/Indian parentage as the belonging of a 'minority within minorities' (13). As a British writer who is half English and identifies, for different reasons, with both Pakistan and India, Kureishi truly straddles cultures and is in a position that is at once inside and outside, native and immigrant and black and white. Therefore, as he writes with an intimate understanding of the 'immigrant' experience, he is also positioning that discourse within his equally intimate understanding of the 'dominant' English experience. All his works are composed of a variety of characters from different backgrounds, and he is able to write about black characters as convincingly as white characters. Ruvani Ranasinha even argues that Kureishi cannot be seen as a 'migrant' since he has never physically relocated (13). As improved transport allows people from very different places and cultures to meet each other, the boundaries of nations and the concept of national identity become increasingly destabilized. The immigrant's presence results in two possible effects. The first is oversensitivity about difference and paranoia about the problems that may be created, which results in xenophobia; the second is a fear of homogeneity, which leads to a competition to be unique and individual. These can affect both the immigrant and the host.

As a second-generation 'immigrant', born in England and half English, Kureishi feels justified in his right to remain. One of the first things that he makes clear in *The Buddha of Suburbia* is that 'coloured people' in Britain cannot all be labelled 'blacks' or all categorized as 'immigrants'. The trouble with British identity in Karim's experience is that it is divided into the 'whites' or 'natives' and the 'blacks' or 'immigrants'. Karim's conversation with a famous director, who refuses him a Western part, makes this point:

> 'We need someone from your own background', he said. 'Someone black'.
> 'Yeah?' I didn't know anyone black; though I'd been at school with a Nigerian. But I wouldn't know where to find him. 'Who do you mean?' I asked.
> 'What about your family?' Pyke said. 'Uncles and aunts. They'll give the play a little variety. I bet they're fascinating'. (170)

Kureishi uses this incident to show how white people are often undifferentiating in their conception of 'difference', generally lumping all that is non-white under the word 'black'. Earlier on, Karim had shown that he knew perfectly well what the term 'black' meant and had declared: 'Two of us were officially "black" (though truly I was more beige than anything)' (167). Karim understands that he is not 'white', but he is clearly not 'black' either. In the novel, there are at least three distinct types of Asian 'immigrants'. There are those like Haroon and Anwar, the first generation who travelled from India in the 1950s to study in England. Then there is the second generation, those born and bred in England like Jamila and Karim, who have not travelled anywhere. Finally, there are those like Changez, who arrived in the 1970s for various reasons. These are not the only differences that set each group apart, for even between Haroon and Anwar there are differences that affect their progress in England and their methods of settling into the community. Haroon marries an Englishwoman, Margaret, and brings his two sons up in the suburbs. Anwar marries an Indian princess, Jeeta, and their daughter grows up in a flat above their grocery store in outer London. The different methods of settling in England endorsed by Haroon and Anwar greatly affect the status of their children and also create a whole new set of problems.

How long does a person have to stay in one place before they can call it home? What do they have to do before they are accepted by the society? There is a common fable of migration, as Yasmin Alibhai-Brown describes:

> [T]he first generation works inhumanly hard, expects little, longs and plans for back home. The second generation learns to squander time and money a little more, partly because ease is setting in and back home is just a faraway dream resort. Their values shift; they get into terrible battles with the deepest values so carefully imported by their parents, but some kind of understanding is reached by both sides, partly because the older generation is also having to change in spite of itself. By the third generation, acceptance is complete, the problems are over. (84)

Salman Rushdie's description of the same process omits the three stages but arrives at a similar conclusion:

> All migrants leave their pasts behind, although some try to pack it into bundles and boxes – but on the journey something seeps out of the treasured mementoes and old photographs, until even their owners fail to recognize them, because it is the fate of migrants to be stripped of history, to stand naked amidst the scorn of strangers upon whom they see the rich clothing, the brocades of continuity and the eyebrows of belonging. (1983: 63)

First-generation immigrants such as Rushdie and V. S. Naipaul exhibit signs of cultural contestation, in which a 'home' culture can be seen to vie with the British culture, but this does not unduly disturb Kureishi's main characters and seems only of secondary importance to his minor characters. First-generation immigrants also tend to apply themselves to perfecting a language in the hopes of integrating with the new society. Kureishi's second-generation characters no longer have this problem, and they feel that they have their own contributions to make to the British identity.

When Karim meets Eva Kay, an ambitious, middle-class woman, he is yet again confronted with another aspect of his immigrant status. Eva, who becomes Haroon's lover and later second wife, wears multicoloured kaftans, uses oriental perfumes, enjoys yoga and bowing in the Japanese fashion. She enjoys organizing get-togethers in the houses of the bourgeoisie, which are decorated with souvenirs bought from all over the world and perceived as signs of 'culture'. In such a society, Haroon finds himself reclaiming and exploiting his cultural difference to humour his 'hosts': 'He was hissing his s's and exaggerating his Indian accent. He'd spent years trying to be more of an Englishman, to be less risibly conspicuous, and now he was putting it back in spadeloads' (21). Instead of trying to be an imitation Englishman, he has become a pastiche of the Indian.

This is most problematic for Karim, since even his mother confuses him with her attitude towards his identity. She tells him:

> 'But you are not an Indian. You've never been to India. You'd get diarrhoea the minute you stepped off the plane, I know you would'.
> 'Why don't you say that a bit louder', I said. 'Aren't I part Indian?'
> 'What about me?' Mum said. 'Who gave birth to you? You're an Englishman, I'm glad to say'.
> 'I don't care', I said. 'I'm an actor. It's a job'.
> 'Don't say that', she said. 'Be what you are'.
> 'Oh yeah'. (232)

Because she gave birth to him and he has never left England, Margaret believes her son is an Englishman through and through. In the passage above, she considers the English identity a birthright, as if by virtue of the *ius soli* or citizenship by birth: Rushdie points out that the Nationality Act of 1981 removed this right when it installed partiality (see Rushdie 1992: 136). Despite being married to an Indian, Margaret does not want her son to have anything to do with India and tells him to be who he is – meaning that he should ignore his Indian half. Karim's reply that he is an actor points to his intention of being everything and anything, no matter how different.

Eva, on the other hand, can only see Karim's Indianness ('you are so exotic, so original'), thus showing her appreciation and acceptance as something superficial and misconceived (9). Others, like his girlfriend's father, who says he's 'with Enoch', call Karim a 'blackie', a 'coon', a 'nigger', a 'wog', and provide him with a clear reminder of his unwelcome presence (40). Helen tries to redress and justify the Indian presence in Britain, in contrast to her father: 'But this is your home... We like you being here. You benefit our country with your traditions' (74). But, she makes it sound as if immigrants need to serve a useful purpose before they should be recognized. When Karim lands a coveted part in Pyke's play, his co-actor, Terry, declares that talent will get people nowhere, and it is only the disadvantaged minority who are going to succeed in 1970s England (165). Ironically, Terry does not see himself as a Welshman and another kind of minority in England, too. The irony of the black immigrant in Britain is best summed up by what occurs to Karim on his return from America. On a visit to the dentist, he overhears the dentist asking the nurse, in a South African accent, whether the patient spoke any English. Karim laconically replies, 'A few words' (258). This situation indicates clearly the different sense of belonging between black and white immigrants. The dentist's white skin allows him to ask impertinent questions of someone with a darker skin, while his South African accent indicates that he is actually the immigrant. The white immigrant can hide inside his skin, but there are other ways to expose his difference.

Tachun Chang's *My Kid Sister* is also a partly autobiographical novel. It is narrated by a twenty-seven-year-old man growing up in Taipei in the 1970s. The protagonist is known as Big Head Spring, which is also a pen name used by Tachun Chang for his own publications, being a play on his real name, Big Spring Chang. In the novel, Big Head is a successful writer and has won a literary award for a short story called 'The General's Monument', which is a story that Chang has written in real life and won an award for. However, while Chang writes for a newspaper in real life, in the story this role is given to the narrator's father.

Unlike Chang, who is a second-generation Chinese immigrant, Big Head is of the third generation. However, the story begins with him remembering his early life in the *juancun*. A *juancun* is a makeshift housing community that the KMT government set up for those who fled with them to Taiwan. Although Big Head's grandparents were considered a minority within a minority that were insulated and living in poverty, like an underclass of the one million Chinese immigrants, they received special treatment from the government which set them apart from the Taiwanese majority. As a result, they associated with the ruling elite and felt culturally superior (see Fan 417). According to Bennett Yuhsiang Fu, the KMT government attempted to relocate the soldiers and their families within

> an enclosed 'Chinese' community for cultural remembrance and patriotic education. The soldiers and their dependents from different provinces or regions of China constructed temporary shelters in the hopes of returning to mainland China soon. However, in the new settlement, the Chinese expatriates faced the linguistic estrangement of speaking Mandarin unintelligible to local Taiwanese speakers... [which] confined them culturally as well as physically to the spatial enclosure. (276)

Although the insularity of this community was partly inflicted, it was also willingly perpetuated. Big Head's grandparents preferred to befriend those in their own community, to eat food that they were familiar with and sing nostalgic Chinese songs with other expatriates. However, Big Head compares this life to that of an ant:

> I often had the delusion that I was a tiny ant forced to carry a cotton blanket as thick and heavy as a bed down a long corridor... Carrying that blanket, I had been crawling for God knows how long when a woman came over. She removed the cumbersome burden from my back, but just as I was enjoying the happiness of freedom from the blanket, she stuck out her index finger, snatched me up, and popped me into her mouth. (75)

It is possible to read this feeling of confinement and liberation in several ways. On the one hand, Big Head feels suffocated by his grandparents, not only literally in that he is ill and under their care, but also by their seemingly self-imposed insularity and subservience to poverty; just like their commitment to a dysfunctional marriage, they have never considered moving out of the dilapidated *juancun*. Although he is a third-generation Chinese immigrant, Big Head cannot escape his connection to the *juancun*, even when he feels that it affects his own sense of identity adversely. Symbolically, he imagines that having relationships with women who may be outside his own ethnic minority and possibly having offspring with them might offer a way out, but he is also afraid that women might consume him altogether in a different way. He becomes very promiscuous and, inevitably, all his relationships are greatly dissatisfying because they accentuate the aridness of his heart and his self-loathing. He finally admits that what he desires is his own sister. Ultimately, like his penchant for Jiangsu and Zhejiang cuisine, the food from China that his grandparents have taught him to enjoy, he cannot really escape his heritage and its insularity. Furthermore, if we borrow his Freudian interpretations, we can see the incest as reflecting a desire for inbreeding which is the ultimate form of insularity.

Throughout the novel, we sense a cultural uncertainty within the protagonist. Although Big Head does not dwell on the different cultural groups in Taiwan, he is too preoccupied with his own ethnic discomfort; his fleeting acknowledgements of their presence accentuate the insularity within him. An obvious example of this is Big Head's recollection of his grandfather's opinion of the Japanese. The Chinese Nationalists regarded both the Communists and the Japanese as enemies; thus when they arrived in Taiwan, they were unsure of the loyalty of the Taiwanese people. Big Head's grandfather displays this enmity towards the Japanese by scorning Dr Zhong who, albeit being a vet, cures both his son and grandson of very serious illnesses. He refuses to let his wife take their grandson to see Dr Zhong, not because he has a better doctor in mind but because Dr Zhong is married to a Japanese woman. As he pointedly asks his wife while blocking her path, 'Do you realise that he married a Japanese? What's so great about marrying a Japanese?' This ridiculous reasoning is further compounded by the fact that Dr Zhong like Big Head's grandfather is also a Christian.

Big Head does not make any real distinctions between Chinese immigrants like himself and the local Taiwanese. However, he does clarify that the KMT government is not the same as the Chinese Communist government. In fact, he refers to Taiwan as 'a small island country' with a 'national leader' and a 'president'. In *Wild Child*, the sequel to *My Kid Sister*, the problematic line between the Chinese immigrants and the Taiwanese is more clearly delineated. In *My Kid Sister*, references are made to 'old-timers' who have 'thick accents', and we are not sure which accents these are, but it is likely that they refer to the various provincial accents of the Chinese immigrants. In *Wild Child*, a few of the characters are said to speak Taiwanese, and there is a character called Little Xinjiang who speaks 'Taiwanese Mandarin'. In fact, there is a paradoxical term for the Mandarin spoken in Taiwan that can be literally translated as 'Taiwan National Language' (台灣國語). The 'Taiwan National Language' is actually Mandarin spoken with a Taiwanese accent. The term indicates that there are two competing dominant languages in Taiwan; hence, if the 'national language' is Mandarin it is nevertheless a version that has been altered by the Taiwanese language. This problematic representation of Taiwan is best conveyed by another second-generation Chinese writer called Tienwen Zhu. In her novel *Notes of a Desolate Man*, her protagonist struggles with the concept of a National Language.

> The accent of the Fido generation sounded much like the National Language spoken by those born in the 1970s. No, no, a more accurate name for their language would be Pekingese or Putonghua. Nowadays, in the Republic of Taiwan, the so-called National Language is no longer the one we used to know. But Fido couldn't care less about these differences. Several decades from now, we will mourn the disappearance of the mother tongue of the Republic of Taiwan. At that time, the National Language in circulation will be the one used and continuously transformed by the Fido kid sitting across from me. It will be the language heard on every variety show on every channel when you turn on the TV. At that time, the language used by my generation, a relic from the previous century, will die off amid either derision or nostalgia. Our accent will disappear from the face of the earth forever. (Zhu 69)

Who does the 'we' refer to and what accent did the generation born in the 1970s have? Did they *all* speak the same language with the *same* accent? Furthermore, why does the 'National Language' that is the 'mother tongue' of the 'Republic of Taiwan' sound like 'Pekingese'? If the Fido generation is going to change everything, as the protagonist laments, how come they still sound like his generation? The excessive sentimentality of the protagonist is not only confusing but also insincere. The 'generation' of speakers that he alludes to and the 'mother tongue' that 'we' are going to mourn for are, in fact, a very select group of people who think they represent a whole generation and a whole nation. Ultimately, if 'Pekingese' is going to disappear in Taiwan, will it really change in Peking? Or does the protagonist suggest that he and his generation represent all the Pekingese?

This presumptuous attitude towards what represents Taiwan is typical of the early generations of Chinese immigrants to Taiwan. As time passed, second- and third-generation immigrants exhibited a more confused loyalty. The emphasis on their Chineseness – the nostalgia for a lost motherland, the sense of uprootedness, the desire to return to a place they have never been – begins to fade and subsequently this identity conflicts with their view of Taiwan as a possible home. Again, Zhu depicts this very succinctly:

> As for the other side of the Taiwan Straits... I have never there, not once. The dark mountain roads are heavily travelled. But I have never been there. Yes, on

my map of the world, I skipped only that vast piece of land. Now it was there, like a sloughed-off skin of my youth, like the remains of a love, cast into a heap. I walked by it indifferently, sensing it to be more alien than all the distant countries of the world. I had no intention of ever going there. I use its language. I am using it right now. It, it is here. It is here, containing everything about it that language represents, still flowing at this very moment, after tens of thousands of years. No chance, no chance at all. I can only be here. I finally realized that the place I'd longed to visit, the place I'd dreamed about, does not, cannot actually exist. It is an unattainable place that has always existed only in the written word. (150–1)

Although Zhu's protagonist awakens to the circumstances of his reality, he nevertheless dreams of and continues to write about this 'unattainable place'. Chang's protagonist deals with this nostalgia in a less sentimental fashion. In one of his letters written during his military service, Big Head mentions his sister eating her own faeces the day before Chiang Kai-shek died and was almost court-martialled for 'defiling our national leader' and sentenced to death: 'The security officer cared about only one thing: why I mentioned the death of Chiang Kai-shek and a disgusting incident like eating faeces IN THE SAME SENTENCE' (23). In a comical fashion, Big Head crawls on his knees to beg for forgiveness and then reflects on his actions: 'Was I using the irresistible power of an ethical rite, which human nature makes us susceptible to, in order to deceive an old fool who deeply loved our country's leader? Was I so weak that I could not even admit just how much of a coward I really was? Was I going insane?' (23).

Even in the twenty-first century, over ten years after the elections of two native Taiwanese presidents who spoke 'Taiwanese Mandarin', the Taiwanese accent still carries derogatory connotations. Like anyone belonging to a colonial or foreign governing body, who is aware of and accepts that their language is spoken with various accents back home, the Chinese immigrants saw their own accents as superior to that of the Taiwanese. This sense of superiority is underscored in Chang's novels. Little Xinjiang is an interesting amalgamation of the different cultural groups in Taiwan: he looks like an American hence his name, Xinjiang, a reference to a province in China where the people have Western features, but he speaks Mandarin with a thick Taiwanese accent. The protagonist notes that these multicultural affiliations act like a curse that make Little Xinjiang a 'foreigner' from birth. Unlike Kureishi's Karim, who embraces his differences and sees it as a trait that allows him to belong anywhere, Little Xinjiang is ostracized by all and is looked down upon as a 'mongrel' and a 'half-breed'.

Another culturally distinct group that is not mentioned in the novel is that of the aborigines of Taiwan. Big Head may have indirectly made references through his father's discovery of the Dobuan people of New Guinea. Big Head remembers his father's 'fairly extensive journey through cartography' and how he forced his whole family to share his 'delirious fantasy of a magnificent voyage' (98). As Big Head claims, it was the first time he discovered that 'such a thing as the Dobuans' existed. His father's obsession with the acquisition of maps, and his anthropological studies into the customs and habits of other peoples, conveys an admiration for great imperial conquests and travel-writing. He takes his family on cartographic journeys of territorial acquisition, and by far, the rarest and most precious of his discoveries was that of the New Guinea Island territories. This may be an inadvertent reference to Taiwan. Of all the Dobuan customs, one of them stands out for Big Head's mother. According to Big Head's father, in the Dobuan tradition if a parent dies or gets divorced, the children will be exiled from that parent's village. When Big Head's mother hears this, she is mentally shaken and Junxin, Big Head's sister, falls about laughing hysterically. We are left to ponder the implications of this custom and its impact on women. Big Head furtively concludes that sometimes laughter hides an unmentionable pain.

Although *My Kid Sister* is humorous and jubilantly irreverent, the destructive self-loathing and incestuous musings are all signs of an identity crisis. Big Head sums up the state of his life in one sentence. 'Your dad is having an affair, except for playing her violin your sister doesn't understand shit, and your mother is insane' (57). And, when he is on the brink of madness himself, says: 'I felt the filth within myself. That was also when I realised that everything was pointless' (25). Big Head has no friends and even though he has many girlfriends, he does not love them and is really a misogynist. He says he seeks out others like himself who are 'shells of flesh that don't even like themselves' (84). All the women he sleeps with are just 'chicks' and 'babes' that he discards when sex with them is no longer exciting or enjoyable. This inevitably happens to all his relationships because he cannot possess what he truly desires which is his sister. He describes her as a 'taboo': something that exists but cannot be touched (58). He admits that his favourite chat-up line is 'Your smile is just like my sister's' and is seemingly so obsessed with her that one of his girlfriends tells him: 'Why don't you go fuck your sister!' (99). He eventually does, in a dream:

> The night after my sister came to visit, I dreamed of her riding on a statue of a strange monster... Then I realised she was actually straddling me. What were we doing? Don't ask – I don't believe that I could have such a dream. But my sister indeed said, 'Let's go!' Just as the distant wake-up call was pressing near, from within the mosquito net I murmured, 'Actually, you can fall in love with your sister'. (103)

Junxin interprets her brother's promiscuity as another form of incest: men 'play around with a whole bunch of women just because they can't screw their own mothers' (101). Big Head admires his sister's perspicacity and enjoys incorporating her views into his own writing. He sees her as his other half, a muse who shares his blurred identity but sacrificed her own creativity in order to enhance his.

Big Head sees his writing as a form of self-dissection, self-treatment and escape. His father and his psychiatrist friend, Dr Shen, interpret his novels as vehicles for escape. The latter asks him about his fears and what he is trying to escape from. Big Head realizes that writing is his way of negotiating between the truths and untruths of daily life, a way to live with his father's lies and his mother's illness. He tells his sister that writing is his way of fighting against the insanity that his mother had succumbed to so helplessly. His mother's insanity was not only exacerbated by his father's infidelity, but also by his manipulation and distortion of her voice. Big Head recalls how his father's publication of his mother's spontaneous photos of a school-bus accident caused her so much pain that she quit medical school and was forever haunted by the ghosts of children. Because her story was taken out of her hands and used in a manner that she had not intended, she shunned the tool that had facilitated this and never picked up a camera again. Language and storytelling became weapons with which his father tortured her and kept her captive. From very early on, Big Head discovers that storytelling can be terrifying because 'It can make the true nature of events clear or hazy, stronger or weaker; it can make them right or wrong' (93). Indeed, language and writing has been shown to be a very powerful colonial tool. Big Head, and his creator, may both be suffering from a sense of guilt. How have they suppressed and usurped the existence of other voices? And, when they speak, who do they really speak for and what untruths do they utter?

Conclusion

Both Kureishi's and Chang's protagonists are searching for their identity and both their lives reflect some aspect of their authors' lives. As Bentley notes:

> The abundant use of self-reflexive narratives in contemporary fiction reveals a concern to question the relationship between fiction, reality and the construction (or writing) of identity. The role of narrative and storytelling thereby becomes crucial in how identities are communicated to us and to others. (10–11)

In the process, the purpose of writing is questioned. While homosexuality brings an alternative perspective to Karim's explorations of identity, it is incest that provides this perspective for Big Head. Both use unorthodox sexuality to challenge their identities and locate it within a wider context. Experimenting with sexuality is one of the methods Kureishi uses to break barriers and question boundaries. According to Ranasinha: 'His male and female characters deploy sex to contest prescribed gender roles and oppose reductive attempts to categorise them according to ethnic boundaries' (17). There are many examples of homosexual relationships in *The Buddha of Suburbia*: Jamila and Joanna, Karim and Pyke/Charlie, Richard and his interest in black men, Eleanor and the performance artist. There are also many interracial relationships – for example, Haroon and Margaret, Karim and Helen, Eleanor and Gene, Allie and his black girlfriend, Jamila and Simon, Changez and Shinko. Through these relationships, classes also intermix: Haroon from the upper class marries Margaret from the working class; Karim is from the lower middle class and Charlie the middle class; Eleanor is from the upper class and Heater is from the working class. From such promiscuous mixing, it is very difficult to tell who has the power and where exploitation begins and victimization ends, hence everything boils down individual preference, in which everyone gains or loses in some ways. Karim wants a bit of everything; he is a mixture of races but he is also a carrier of difference. He collects little bits of his identity throughout his life and is constantly putting this collective self to the test. His method of experimenting with everything, before trying to find a balance for his emotions, points to his desire for a more pluralistic understanding. In his effort to contain both Englishness and Indianness equally, Karim is able to successfully adopt a chameleon-like identity that he is finally comfortable with in the end.

In contrast, all of Big Head's relationships are portrayed as meaningless except for the one he fantasizes about with his sister. His existence is one of emotional aridness and mental insularity. Despite being born in Taiwan and having lived there for almost three decades, he cannot move beyond the barriers of the *juancun*. Unwilling to let go of his past, he cannot incorporate the cultural differences around him and embrace the future. Hence, his incestuous tendency and fear of procreation all point to future sterility, which is vicariously realized by his sister's abortion. The intensity of Big Head's self-loathing and destructiveness is reflected in his revenge on his father. The novel concludes with Big Head and Junxin gate-crashing their father's first art exhibition to discredit him by announcing in front of his audience that Junxin has had an abortion at nineteen and their mother is in a mental hospital. This self-destructive streak runs throughout the novel and gives it a deep undercurrent of guilt and despair. For Big Head, the act of writing is a selfish form of self-treatment, an opportunity to offload his problems on unwary readers. It is ultimately a vengeful act where the author serves up a deceptively tantalizing dish to fool his readers.

> Since I began writing, I have also learned the art of slicing pork. I take people's experiences, words, my own impressions, illusions, and those tidbits of knowledge that appear to be brimming with wisdom and scramble them together. Then I chop and fry, presenting a dish brimming with hidden anger and malice. It is a meat dish: a Holy Communion saturated in jealousy. There is no need for me to say that my cooking skill was inherited from my grandfather. Actually its origin is much earlier; you could even trace it back to the beginning of the universe. (124)

At no point does Big Head show any interest in the differences and the opportunities for change that surround him; he remains self-centredly obsessed with his own thoughts and menial issues. In contrast to a *bildungsroman* such as The *Buddha of Suburbia*, the protagonist of *My Kid Sister* does not truly grow and proudly declares, 'I have yet to grow old' (100).

With migration being a large part of our lives today, we are bound to be confronted by each other's cultural differences. Whether these meetings become sources of antagonism or renewal depends as much on the immigrant as it does on the host community. Kureishi and Chang assume 'immigrant' voices to comment on and distance themselves from the society that they write about, but there are subtle differences in their treatment of nationhood and identity. It is clear that despite Britain being a hostile place for Karim to be sometimes, he accepts the larger British identity even when he is adamant about retaining a sense of his own identity. On the other hand, Big Head clings to his Chineseness and overlooks the existence of other identities. The Taiwanese identity does not figure in his world view; not because he is integrated into it or because he feels comfortable in assuming his Chinese identity in Taiwan, but because it is of little interest to him. His preoccupation with the *juancun* defines him and serves as evidence that the identity he relates to is constrictive and unnatural. Hence, it is surprising to find the minority immigrant status that binds and constricts his grandfather still so strong in this third-generation immigrant. While Kureishi believes in a postcolonial approach and contributes to the British identity as an 'insider' using the voice of an 'outsider', it seems that Chang's lack of interest in postmodernity rather than postcoloniality is the result of an 'outsider' who believes in claiming the rights of an 'insider'. Whether we acknowledge as hosts or as immigrants or other identities, will we, as Julia Kristeva puts it in *Strangers to Ourselves*: 'be, intimately and subjectively, able to live with the others, to live *as others*, without ostracism but also without levelling?' (1). Further comparative study of such novels, dealing with second and third generation immigrants in different contexts around the globe, may help us realize more clearly exactly what is at stake in Kristeva's question of how we should live in this world of increasingly permeable borders.

Works Cited

Alibhai-Brown, Yasmin. *Who Do We Think We Are? Imagining the New Britain*. London: Penguin, 2000.
Bentley, Nick. *British Fiction of the 1990s*. Oxon: Routledge, 2005.
Braidotti, Rosi. *Nomadic Subjects*. New York: Columbia University Press, 1994.
Chen, Fangming. 'Postmodern or Postcolonial? An Inquiry into Postwar Taiwanese Literary History'. In *Writing Taiwan*. Eds David Der-wei Wang and Carlos Rojas. Durham & London: Duke University Press, 2007, 26–50.
Ching, Leo. *Becoming Taiwan: Colonial Taiwan and the Politics of Identity Formation*. Berkeley: University of California Press, 2001.
Chow, Meili (ed.) *Taiwan's International Status: History and Theory*. Taipei: Taiwan Advocates, 2005.
Cumings, Bruce. *Parallax Visions: Making Sense of American-East Asian Relations at the End of the Century*. Durham: Duke University Press, 1999.
Davison, Gary Marvin. *A Short History of Taiwan*. London: Praeger, 2003.
Fan, Luoping. *The Historical Criticism of Contemporary Taiwan Female Fiction*. Taipei: Taiwan Shengwu Inshua Guan, 2006.
Fu, Bennett Yuhsiang. 'The Interlocution between Two (National) Solitudes'. In *L'Echo de Nos Classiques*. Ed. Agnes Whitfield. Ottawa: Les Editions David, 2009, 271–88.
Gellner, Ernest. *Nation and Nationalism*. Oxford: Blackwell Press, 1990.
Hobsbawm, Eric. *Nations and Nationalism since 1780*. Cambridge: Cambridge University Press, 1991.
Hong, Chien-chao. *A History of Taiwan*. Rimini: Il Cerchio Iniziative Editoriali, 2000.
Hsueh, Hua-yuan, Pao-tsun Tai and Meili Chow. *Is Taiwan Chinese? A History of Taiwanese Nationality*. Taipei: Taiwan Advocates, 2005.
Hutchinson, John. *Nations as Zones of Conflict*. London: Sage, 2005.
Kiberd, Declan. *Inventing Ireland*. London: Jonathan Cape, 1995.
Kristeva, Julia. *Strangers to Ourselves*. New York: Harvester Wheatsheaf, 1991.
Kureishi, Hanif. *The Buddha of Suburbia*. London: Faber and Faber, 1999.
Moore-Gilbert, Bart. *Contemporary World Writers: Hanif Kureishi*. Manchester: Manchester University Press, 2001.

Parekh, Bhikhu. *The Future of Multi-Ethnic Britain*. London: Profile Books, 2000.
Ramdin, Ron. *Reimaging Britain: 500 Years of Black and Asian History*. London: Pluto, 1999.
Ranasinha, Ruvani. *Writers and Their Works: Hanif Kureishi*. Devon: Northcote House, 2002.
Ranger, Terence, Yunas Samad and Ossie Stuart (eds) *Culture, Identity and Politics*. Aldershot: Avebury, 1996.
Renan, Ernest. 'What Is a Nation?' In *Nation and Narration*. Ed. Homi K. Bhabha. New York & London: Routledge, 1990, 8–22.
Richards, David. *Masks of Difference: Cultural Representations in Literature, Anthropology and Art*. Cambridge: Cambridge University Press, 1994.
Rushdie, Salman. *Shame*. London: Jonathan Cape, 1983.
———. *Imaginary Homelands*. London: Granta, 1992.
Smith, Anthony D. *National Identity*. Reno: University of Nevada Press, 1991.
Zhu, Tienwen. *Notes of a Desolate Man*. New York: Columbia University Press, 1999.

Timeline of Works

1990

David Britton *Lord Horror*
A.S. Byatt *Possession*
Jonathan Coe *The Dwarves of Death*
Hanif Kureishi *The Buddha of Suburbia*
Christopher Priest *The Quiet Woman*

1991

Martin Amis *Time's Arrow*
Iain Banks *The State of the Art*
Pat Barker *Regeneration*
Christine Brooke-Rose *Textermination*
Lawrence Norfolk *Lemprière's Dictionary*
Caryl Phillips *Cambridge*
Will Self *The Quantity Theory of Insanity*
Iain Sinclair *Downriver*

1992

Iain Banks *The Crow Road*
A.S. Byatt *Morpho Eugenia*
Mary Gentle *Grunts*
Kim Newman *Anno Dracula*
Will Self *Cock and Bull*
Adam Thorpe *Ulverton*
Jeanette Winterson *Written on the Body*

1993

Iain Banks *Complicity*
Pat Barker *The Eye in the Door*
Caryl Phillips *Crossing the River*
Will Self *My Idea of Fun*
Irvine Welsh *Trainspotting*

1994

Jonathan Coe *What a Carve Up!*
James Kelman *How Late it Was, How Late*
Andrea Levy *Every Light in the House Burnin'*
Bernard MacLaverty *Walking the Dog & Other Stories*
Alan Moore 'The Courtyard'
Grant Morrison 'Lovecraft in Heaven'
Will Self *Grey Area*
Iain Sinclair *Radon Daughters*
Irvine Welsh *The Acid House*
Jeanette Winterson *Art & Lies*

1995

Diran Adebayo *Some Kind of Black*
Martin Amis *The Information*
Iain Banks *Whit*
Pat Barker *The Ghost Road*
Nick Hornby *High Fidelity*
Hanif Kureishi *The Black Album*
Alan Moore *Voice of the Fire*
Kim Newman *The Bloody Red Baron*
Adam Thorpe *Still*
Irvine Welsh *Maribou Stork Nightmares*

1996

David Britton *Motherfuckers: The Auschwitz of Oz*
Bill Drummond and Mark Manning *Bad Wisdom*
Stewart Home *Slow Death*
John King *The Football Factory*
Andrea Levy *Never Far from Nowhere*
Lawrence Norfolk *The Pope's Rhinoceros*
Christopher Priest *The Prestige*
Will Self *The Sweet Smell of Psychosis*

1997

Martin Amis *Night Train*
Iain Banks *A Song of Stone*
A.S. Byatt *Babel Tower*

Eugene Byrne and Kim Newman 'Teddy Bear's Picnic'
Jonathan Coe *The House of Sleep*
Stewart Home *Come Before Christ and Murder Love*
John King *Headhunters*
Bernard MacLaverty *Grace Notes*
Courttia Newland *The Scholar*
Caryl Phillips *The Nature of Blood*
Q *Deadmeat*
Will Self *The Great Apes*

1998

Pat Barker *Another World*
Julian Barnes *England England*
Christine Brooke-Rose *Next*
Rob Colson, Martin Cooper, Ted Curtis, Robert Dellar, Keith Mallinson, Emma McElwee and Lucy Williams *Seaton Point*
Nick Hornby *About a Boy*
John King *England Away*
Hanif Kureishi *Intimacy*
Grant Morrison *Lovely Biscuits*
Kim Newman *Dracula Cha Cha Cha*
Christopher Priest *The Extremes*
Adam Thorpe *Pieces of Light*
Sarah Waters *Tipping the Velvet*
Irvine Welsh *Filth*
Jeanette Winterson *Gut Symmetries*

1999

Iain Banks *The Business*
Andrea Levy *Fruit of the Lemon*
Alan Moore and Eddie Campbell *From Hell* (collected edition)
Mary Gentle *Ash: A Secret History*
Courttia Newland *Society Within*
Kim Newman *Life's Lottery*
Kim Newman 'Further Developments in the Strange Case of Dr Jekyll and Mr Hyde'
David Peace *Nineteen Seventy Four*
Indra Sinha *The Cybergypsies*
Sarah Waters *Affinity*
Steven Wells *Tits Out Teenage Terror Totty*

Timeline of National Events

1990

A huge demonstration against the 'Poll Tax' was held in London on 31 March representing the culmination of civil unrest in the face of the introduction of the Community Charge, which attempted to fund Local Government by placing a flat-rate tax on all adults regardless of income.

20 July Provisional IRA attack on the London Stock Exchange.

Foundation of the satellite broadcast and telecommunications company BskyB, now known as Sky, effectively controlled by Rupert Murdoch's News Corporation.

After more than eleven years in power, Margaret Thatcher resigned as Prime Minister on 22 November following a challenge for leadership of the Conservative Party from Michael Heseltine. Although Thatcher won the resultant ballot, Heseltine gained enough votes to trigger a second ballot, and after initially intending to fight on, Thatcher was persuaded by supporters to withdraw. Her supporters now backed John Major who won the second leadership ballot and became Prime Minister.

The World Wide Web/Internet protocol (HTTP) and WWW language (HTML) were created by Briton, Tim Berners-Lee.

1991

The convictions of the Birmingham Six were quashed by the Court of Appeal, and the men who had been in prison since 1975 for the November 1974 Birmingham pub bombings, carried out by the Provisional IRA, were released. Following the release of the Guildford Four in 1989, who had been wrongly jailed for carrying out the Guildford pub bombings in October 1975, and in conjunction with the subsequent release of the Maguire Seven, also falsely imprisoned for involvement with the Guildford bombings, this case reinforced the impression that the British criminal justice system had been corrupt in the 1970s.

Damien Hirst's *The Physical Impossibility of Death in the Mind of Someone Living* (1991) was first exhibited in Charles Saatchi's gallery in Boundary Road, London. The work consists of a 13-foot tiger shark suspended in a tank of formaldehyde, and it quickly becomes the most well-known work of the so-called Young British Arts associated with Saatchi.

The Internet first became available to the British public.

1992

- In April, the Conservative Party won their fourth consecutive General Election, defying the exit polls which predicted a slim Labour majority by winning over 14 million votes – still the highest for any political Party in a UK election. John Major would continue as Prime Minister for another five years.
- The start of the football season in August saw the inauguration of the Premier League comprised by teams from the former First Division, who had split from the Football League. The income generated from television rights sold to BskyB, who now broadcast live matches to their subscription satellite channels, no longer had to be shared with clubs in the lower divisions, and allowed the Premier League to attain its current status of being the most-watched league in the world with the highest revenues. Football would henceforth be a commodity and match tickets would become priced out of the range of its traditional working-class male support.
- On 'Black Wednesday', 16 September, Britain was forced out of the European Exchange Rate Mechanism (ERM) under the pressure of currency traders' short selling sterling. This eventually allowed the high interest rates necessary to keep Britain in the ERM to relax and arguably paved the way for Britain to emerge from its economic recession during the middle years of the decade.
- On 3 December, the first ever SMS text message in the World, 'Merry Christmas', was sent in the United Kingdom.

1993

- The short-lived Community Charge was replaced by the Council Tax, which included a range of exemptions ensuring greater fairness and thus a general acceptability to the public.
- In April, Stephen Lawrence, an 18-year-old black school student, was murdered at a bus stop in a racist attack. Five suspects were quickly arrested by the police, but the subsequent trials and a private prosecution by the Lawrence family all broke down due to a lack of evidence, leading to national outrage and the 1998 Macpherson Inquiry in to how the Metropolitan Police conducted the investigation, the proceedings of which were published in 1999 (see below). As a result of consequent changes to the law of double jeopardy, two of the original suspects were successfully convicted of Lawrence's murder in 2012.
- In December, Prime Minister John Major and the Irish Taoiseach Albert Reynolds jointly made the Downing Street Declaration stating that the people of Ireland would have the sole right to determine the relationship between the North and the South of the island, but that the North would join the Republic only if the majority of its population was in favour.

1994

The Provisional IRA announced a ceasefire in response to the previous year's Downing Street Declaration.

The National Lottery was introduced with a potential weekly first prize in the millions. The funds raised were available to support charitable causes and national sports bodies.

Tesco launched Clubcard, the first major UK-wide supermarket loyalty card scheme.

The Channel Tunnel was opened as a passenger, car shuttle and freight rail link with mainland Europe. High-speed rail travel was available to Paris and beyond, but the equivalent for London was only completed in 2007 with the opening of the new terminal at St Pancras.

The *Daily Telegraph* launched the first online daily newspaper in Europe.

1995

The oldest investment bank in the United Kingdom, Barings Bank, was declared insolvent after 'rogue trader' Nick Leeson lost hundreds of millions of pounds in unauthorized speculations. Leeson was subsequently jailed.

On 22 June, John Major resigned as leader of the Conservative Party, while continuing as caretaker Prime Minister, inviting his critics to stop criticizing and stand against him if they wanted different policies. He easily won the subsequent contest with challenger John Redwood and resumed his leadership; the critics also resumed their criticizing.

Seamus Heaney won the Nobel Prize for Literature.

1996

The IRA ended its ceasefire in February due to dissatisfaction with the progress of the Peace Process and let off a huge lorry bomb in London Docklands which caused two fatalities and millions of pounds worth of damage. The armed struggle was to continue for the next fifteen months and included high-profile actions such as the bomb exploded in Manchester City Centre on 15 June, which injured over 200 people and caused well over half a billion pounds worth of damage.

Sixteen children and one teacher were killed by gunman Thomas Hamilton on 13 March in a primary school in Dunblane, near Stirling in Scotland. Hamilton went on to kill himself. This was one of the worst ever shooting incidents in the United Kingdom. A subsequent report, the Cullen Report, recommended tougher controls on handgun ownership. Two subsequent laws (one under John Major and the other under Tony Blair in 1997) effectively banning the private ownership of handguns in the United Kingdom.

The first mammal was cloned from an adult somatic cell by scientists at the University of Edinburgh. The cloned sheep, which was named Dolly, was born in July and lived for six and a half years.

The import of British beef was banned by the European Union due to the threat of Bovine Spongiform Encephalitis, or 'mad cow disease' as it was more commonly known. The ban would last for ten years with consequent effects on British farming.

Charles and Diana, the Prince and Princess of Wales, divorced. Diana retained her title but lost the right to be addressed as Her Royal Highness.

1997

The Conservatives lost power after seventeen years as Tony Blair's New Labour won a landslide election victory. While it later transpired that the jubilant crowds in Downing Street were not spontaneous but in fact supporters bussed in by the Labour Party, there was a genuine widespread sense of relief throughout the country with strangers expressing joy to each other at the change of government.

The IRA resumed their ceasefire in July.

On 31 August, Diana, Princess of Wales, her companion Dodi Fayed and their driver Paul Henri died in a car crash in a Paris road tunnel. The subsequent scope and emotion of mourning by the British public was unprecedented and forced the royal family to rethink an initial frosty response in favour of a more fulsome tribute.

Sensation, an exhibition of the works in the collection of Charles Saatchi, took place at the Royal Academy of Art in London between September and December. A number of pieces in the exhibition provoked much controversy, in particular Marcus Harvey's *Myra*, a huge portrait of the child murderer Myra Hindley. The show also caused controversy when it moved to New York. A showing of the exhibition in Australia was cancelled, the gallery's director saying that Saatchi's financial investment in it made it 'too close to the market'.

In September, in accordance with pledges in the Labour Party Election Manifesto, referenda were held in both Scotland and Wales resulting in majorities – a large one in the former and a much narrower one in the latter – for devolution.

As part of a Joint Declaration between the United Kingdom and the People's Republic of China (signed by Margaret Thatcher and the Chinese president Deng Xiaoping) signed in 1984, Britain had agreed to handover the territory of Hong Kong on 1 July 1997 following 150 years of control. The British flag was lowered over government house on that date, and Hong Kong's final British governor, the Tory peer Chris Pattern, took part in the handover ceremony, along with Prime Minister Tony Blair, Foreign Minister Robin Cook and Prince Charles. The handover was seen by many in the United Kingdom as finally bringing the British Empire to an end.

J.K. Rowling's *Harry Potter and the Philosopher's Stone*, the first of the series, was published with a print run of 500. The novel won many prizes within the first two years of publication, and by the end of 1999, it had sold 300,000 copies in the United

Kingdom. In the summer of 1999, the novel was top of the *New York Times* list of best-selling fiction and stayed there until 2001, by which time it had sold over 5 million in hardback and over 6 million in paperback. The Harry Potter series has been credited with starting a reading revolution among children in the United Kingdom.

1998

The Good Friday Agreement, which was signed on the bank holiday from which its name derived, formalized the process inaugurated by the earlier Downing Street Declaration by agreeing a number of structures to deal with North/South issues and outlining the formation of a Northern Ireland Assembly and Executive. In May, the Agreement was put to the populations of both parts of the island in respective referenda which both return positive majorities. In July, elections were held for the new Northern Ireland Assembly.

15 August Omagh bombing by dissident republicans in the Real IRA killed twenty-nine civilians.

A subsequently discredited research paper in *The Lancet* suggested that the Measles, Mumps and Rubella (MMR) vaccine was causally linked to autism. This allegation was indiscriminately reported in sections of the tabloid press with the consequence that vaccination rates fell sharply over the succeeding years to the point where measles became once more endemic in the United Kingdom and the cause of occasional fatalities.

1999

The Macpherson Report of the previous year's enquiry into the handling of the Stephen Lawrence murder case was published and concluded that the Metropolitan Police was institutionally racist.

During April, a series of nail bombs exploded in various multicultural areas of London such as Brixton and Brick Lane, as well as in a Soho pub well known for being frequented by gay clientele. These attacks, which left three people dead and injured many others, were the work of David Copeland, a former member of the far-right British National Party and Neo-Nazi. Copeland is currently serving five consecutive life sentences in prison.

From 24 March to 10 June, Britain participated in a full-scale NATO bombing of Yugoslavia to prevent the claimed atrocities by Serb forces in Kosovo.

On the 19 April, BBC newsreader Jill Dando was shot and killed outside her house in Fulham. A local man was subsequently tried and convicted of her murder but subsequently released on appeal and the crime remains unresolved.

In May 1999, elections were held for the first time for both the Scottish Parliament and the Welsh Assembly. It was now the case that all the constituent nations of the United Kingdom apart from England had an elected body of representatives.

The online edition of the *Guardian* was launched.

UK mobile phone networks allowed customers to start sending texts to people on other networks and texting culture takes off.

Timeline of International Events

1990

Nelson Mandela was released from prison and entered into negotiations with President F.W. de Klerk concerning the abolition of the apartheid system.

Mikhail Gorbachev was elected President of the Soviet Union; he introduced an era of radical change that would lead to the end of Communist Party rule.

Iraqi troops invaded Kuwait.

The German Democratic Republic and the Federal Republic of Germany were united into one combined Germany. At the same time, Berlin was reunited into an undivided capital, although the Government did not actually relocate there from Bonn until 1999.

Microsoft introduced Microsoft Office and Windows 3.0, both of which quickly became dominant across the IT sector.

1991

In January 1991, US, British and other allied planes started bombing Iraq before allied ground troops invaded in response to Iraq's invasion of and annexation of Kuwait in August of 1990. The allied Coalition was the largest military alliance since the Second World War. The conflict was the first from which live news broadcasts were sent from the front lines, leading the French theorist Jean Baudrillard to claim that the Gulf War, for the west, did not really take place but was rather merely a set of TV images. Ceasefire terms were established by the United Nations Security Council in April.

Following an unsuccessful coup attempted by Communist hardliners, the Soviet Union was dissolved and restructured as the Russian Federation without many of its former peripheral constituent regions – including Latvia, Estonia, Lithuania, the Ukraine, Armenia, Georgia and Kazakhstan – which had all declared independence. Dissolution occurs on 26 December.

Former trade union leader and activist Lech Walesa was elected as the First President of post-communist Poland.

In August 1991, the World Wide Web, which depended on a system of interlinked hypertext that had been principally developed by Tim Berners-Lee since he wrote a proposal for it in 1989, became publicly accessible for the first time.

The Socialist Federal Republic of Yugoslavia broke up, leading to ongoing disputes about whether its formerly constituent republics of Bosnia and Herzegovina, Croatia, Macedonia, Montenegro, Serbia and Slovenia should be more loosely federated or achieve full independence. Following this dissolution tensions around minority ethnic groups resident in each republic, particularly in Croatia and Bosnia, became increasingly fraught.

1992

The Maastricht Treaty was signed by the member states of the European Economic Community, setting out the parameters of the Exchange Rate Mechanism and charting the pathway to economic and political convergence in what would henceforth be known as the European Union.

Fifty-three people died and over 2000 were injured in the Los Angeles riots that followed the acquittal of police officers for assaulting the African-American Rodney King the previous year. US Marines had to be deployed.

Publication of Francis Fukuyama's *The End of History and the Last Man*, an extension of his influential 1989 essay 'The End of History' which had argued that the twentieth century had ended in victory for economic and political liberalism, and thus, historical struggle was over.

The Bosnian War began in April between the forces of the Republic of Bosnia and Herzegovina and those Bosnians of Serb or Croat descent who wished to establish separate states. The latter were supported by the governments of Serbia and Croatia. Ethnic Bosnians were mainly made up of Muslims, Orthodox Christian Serbs and Catholic Croats. The war was bitterly fought and marked by the use of widespread shelling of civilian populations, ethnic cleansing and mass rape of women.

Citizens of Czechoslovakia voted to divide the country into two nations, Slovakia and the Czech Republic, which occurs in the following year.

Bill Clinton was elected the forty-second president of the United States.

Official end of the Cold War was declared.

1993

The European Union was formally established when the Maastricht Treaty came into effect on 1 November 1993.

A bomb was detonated in February beneath the North Tower of the World Trade Center with the failed intention of destroying both towers. However, six people were killed and over a thousand were injured. A group of men linked to Al-Qaeda were believed to have planned and carried out the attack. Four men were convicted of carrying out the bombing in March 1994.

The development of the Mosaic Browser allowed the World Wide Web to become the most popular Internet protocol.

The first Pentium processor was developed by Intel and went on to give personal computers a performance edge over rivals such as the Apple Macintosh.

Between February and April, the compound of a religious sect, the Branch Davidians, near Waco in Texas, was besieged by US federal agents who suspected the group of violations of weapons laws. The siege, initiated and run by the FBI, followed an attempt to raid the compound by the Bureau of Alcohol, Tobacco and Firearms and violent resistance to this on the part of its inhabitants. On 19 April, the FBI launched a tear-gas attack in an attempt to force the Davidians out. A fire broke out in the compound and seventy-six members of the sect (the majority of those still inside), including its leader, David Koresh, and many children, died.

Russian president Boris Yeltsin and American counterpart George H. Bush signed the START II nuclear weapons treaty; they pledged a reduction of missiles held by both superpowers.

Bill Clinton elected President of the United States, with Al Gore as his Vice-President.

In September, the Russian Federation's first president, Boris Yeltsin, dissolved parliament, ordering new elections and a referendum on a new constitution. When parliament resisted, Yeltsin's tanks surrounded their 'White House' building and rebellious parliamentarians capitulated.

1994

Nelson Mandela was elected President of South Africa by its National Assembly.

War broke out between the Russian Federation and one of its federal subject, the Chechen Republic of Ichkeria, which lasted for two years. The Chechens had declared independence from the Russian Federation in 1993, and the war was one of the most violent effects of the break-up of the USSR. Thousands of civilians died, as well as Chechen fighters and Russian soldiers, mostly made up of young conscripts, particularly during the Battle of Grozny in the winter of 1994/5, drawing much criticism of Russia both domestically and internationally. Islam is the dominant religion of Chechnya, and the claim that the war was jihad against Orthodox Christian Russia drew many non-Chechen Muslims into the conflict. Following the war, the Republic asserted *de facto* independence from the Russian Federation.

Over the course of a hundred-day period between April and July, an estimated 500,000 to 1 million people were murdered in the Republic of Rwanda in central Africa. The genocide was planned by the members of the Hutu political elite, and perpetrated against both members of the Tutsi tribe and moderate Hutus, murdered by members of the armed forces, the National Police (*gendarmerie*), and government-backed militias after the previous President and Prime Minister had both been assassinated. The slaughter was the most violent period in an ongoing conflict between Hutus and Tutsis which had begun in 1990. In part, in response to the genocide, the International Criminal Court was created in 2002 to prosecute perpetrators of genocide, of crimes against humanity and war crimes.

O.J. Simpson was arrested on 12 June for murdering of his wife, Nicole Brown Simpson, and her friend Ronald Goldman. A frenzy of media coverage ensued until Simpson's controversial acquittal on 3 October 1995.

In Japan, on 3 December, the original PlayStation console was first launched.

1995

The World Trade Organization was established.

A bomb destroyed a Federal Building in Oklahoma City, in the United States, killing 168 people and injuring over 600, as well as severely damaging hundred of other buildings. Although first reports suggested the work of foreign terrorists, those responsible were quickly arrested and charged, all were US citizens. Principal perpetrator, Timothy McVeigh, was a Gulf war veteran who sympathized with anti-federal government militia groups. He had timed the attack for the second anniversary of the storming of David Koresh's compound in Waco, Texas. McVeigh was found guilty in 1997 and executed in 2001.

The NATO bombing campaign against Bosnian Serb positions, known as Operation Deliberate Force, was begun in August. It lasted into September, when Bosnian Serbs complied with conditions set out by the United Nations. This effectively ends the Bosnian War which had begun in 1992, whose end came officially on 14 December.

Microsoft introduced Windows 95 and the web browser Internet Explorer, further extending their market dominance and setting the pattern for personal computing in the years ahead.

Amazon.com was launched as an online bookseller and grew steadily over the rest of the decade as computing and Internet use expanded, but it did not start to turn a profit until 2001.

Auction Website eBay was founded in San Jose, California, on 3 September by French-born Iranian-American computer programmer, Pierre Omidyar.

DVDs (digital video/versatile disc) were invented and developed by Phillips, Sony, Toshiba and Panasonic.

Yitzhak Rabin, Prime Minister of Israel, was assassinated in Tel Aviv on 4 November.

1996

Osama Bin Laden, living in Afghanistan, issued a declaration of war on Americans, entitled 'Declaration of war against the Americans occupying the land of the Two Holy Places'. It received very little attention, as he was not yet known as the leader of Al-Qaeda.

In April, the so-called Unabomber, Theodore John 'Ted' Kaczynski, was arrested.

In July, the first public HDTV broadcast occurred in the United States involving WRAL-HD television station in Raleigh, North Carolina.

The summer Olympic Games in Atlanta, Georgia, were disrupted by a bomb. Two died as a result of the bomb and nearly 200 were injured. Eric Robert Rudolph was arrested for the bombing, and several others, in 2003 and convicted in 2005. The bomb had been part of his protest against federal laws sanctioning abortion.

By the end of the year, the Taliban were in control of the majority of Afghanistan.

1997

The Asian financial crisis, beginning in Thailand in July, swept through the region, particularly affecting Thailand, South Korea and Indonesia.

Formal peace treaty signed between Boris Yeltsin, President of Russian Federation, and the elected president of Chechnya, Aslan Maskhadov.

Stock markets crashed around the world on 27 October in response to the financial crisis in Southeast Asia. It marked the beginning of the end of the 1990s economic boom in the United States and Canada.

Kyoto Protocol agreement to the United Nations Framework Convention of Climate Change was signed in Japan, setting out obligations on industrialized countries to reduce the emissions of greenhouse gases. It was signed by 191 states (including all those in the United Nations with a few exceptions) and the European Union. The United States signed the treaty but did not ratify it.

1998

In February, Osama Bin Laden's second declaration of war on Americans issued, signed by Bin Laden plus four others.

The war in Kosovo began in February, fought between the army of the Federal Republic of Yugoslavia (Serbia and Montenegro), who had been in control of Kosovo, against the Kosovo Liberation Army and the Albanian Army.

On 19 December, US President Bill Clinton was impeached by the House of Representatives on charges of perjury and obstruction of justice in relation to his conduct with the White House intern Monica Lewinsky. He was acquitted by Senate in the following February.

In August, the US embassies in Nairobi and Dar es Salaam, both in east Africa, were destroyed by bombs, killing hundreds. The bombings brought Osama Bin Laden to the attention of the West for the first time, and following the bombings, he was placed on the FBI's ten most wanted list.

Google, who would introduce unique sorting algorithms for Internet searches, was founded in California.

1999

On 1 January, the Euro was introduced by the European Union in electronic form to replace the notional European Currency Unit (ECU) as an accounting currency. Actual coins and banknotes were first issued three years later.

Hugo Chavez was elected president of Venezuela.

Two American school students murdered thirteen people and committed suicide at the Columbine High School massacre in Colorado.

NATO bombed the Federal Republic of Yugoslavia between March and June in an operation that went ahead without UN approval. It was the first time that NATO used military force without the approval of the United Nations and the aim was to end the war in Kosovo begun the year before.

The Second Chechen War was begun by the Russian Federation in response to the invasion of Dagestan by the Islamic International Brigade.

A coup attempt brought General Pervez Musharraf to power in Pakistan.

Biographies of Writers

Born Oludiran Adebayo in London in 1968 to Nigerian parents, **Diran Adebayo** attended Malvern College in his teens and read law at Oxford University. On graduating, he worked as a journalist for *The Voice* and the BBC, among others. In 1995, his first novel, *Some Kind of Black*, won the inaugural Saga Prize for unpublished Black novelists born in the United Kingdom. The novel was published by Virago in 1996 and went on to win the Writers Guild of Great Britain New Writer of the Year Award, the Author's Club First Novel Award and a Betty Trask Award. It was longlisted for the Booker Prize. The novel follows its protagonist, Dele, through his attempts to reconcile his Nigerian background, his experiences at Oxford and his life in London. His second novel, *My Once Upon a Time* (2000), is a fable set in the London of the near future. In 2003, Adebayo co-edited, with Blake Morrison and Jane Rogers, the British Council's *New Writing 12*, an annual anthology of new writing by British and Commonwealth writers. He is currently working on his third novel, *The Ballad of Dizzy and Miss P*.

Born in 1949 in Swansea, South Wales, **Martin Amis** is the son of the novelist Kingsley Amis. After graduating from Oxford in 1971, where he studied English, Martin Amis worked as a literary journalist until 1979. During this time, he worked on his first four novels: *The Rachel Papers* (1973), *Dead Babies* (1975), *Success* (1978) and *Other People: A Mystery Story* (1981). In 1984, he published his most acclaimed novel, *Money: A Suicide Note*. After publishing a collection of essays, *The Moronic Inferno and Other Visits to America* (1986) and a collection of stories, *Einstein's Monsters* (1987), he published the second of an informal trilogy of novels, *London Fields* (1989) (the first being *Money*). His other works include *Time's Arrow* (1991), *The Information* (1995) (the third novel of his trilogy), *Night Train*, a pseudo-detective story (1997), *Yellow Dog* (2003), *House of Meetings* (2006) and *The Pregnant Widow* (2010). His other published work includes a collection of stories, *Heavy Weather and Other Stories* (1998), a highly original memoir, *Experience* (2000), a collection of his journalism, *The War Against Cliché: Essays and Reviews, 1971–2000* (2001) and a political essay about Stalin's years of terror, *Koba the Dead: Laughter and the Twenty Million* (2002).

Pat Barker was born in Yorkshire in 1943. She studied at the London School of Economics, graduating in 1965. She began to write in her mid-20s. Her first novel, *Union Street*, was published by Virago Press in 1982, after being rejected by many publishers as too depressing. This novel and the next two, *Blow Your House Down* (1984) and *Liza's England* (1986) (originally published as *The Century's Daughter*) depict the lives of working-class women in the north of England. *Blow Your House* down alludes to the serial killer Peter Sutcliffe, known as the Yorkshire Ripper, who murdered thirteen women around Leeds between 1975 and 1980. In the 1990s, Barker published the Regeneration Trilogy – *Regeneration* (1991), *The Eye in the Door* (1993) and *The Ghost Road* (1995) – which explores the history of the First World War. The final novel in the trilogy won the Booker Prize. Other works include *Another World* (1998), *Border Crossing* (2001), *Double Vision* (2003), *Life Class* (2007) and *Toby's Room* (2012).

Born in Leicester in 1946, **Julian Barnes** grew up in two London suburbs, Acton and Northwood, and attended City of London School. During his degree at Oxford, Barnes spent his second year in France, which led him to become a Francophile, as is reflected in several of his books. After graduating in Modern Languages in 1968, he moved to north London and became a lexicographer for the Oxford English Dictionary Supplement. He then worked in various editorial positions from 1971 to 1979 and from 1979 to 1986 as a television critic. Barnes's first novel, *Metroland* (1980), is set in the London suburbs in which he grew up. It won the Somerset Maugham Award and was made into a film in 1998. Barnes also published *Duffy* in 1980, the first of four detective novels under the name of Dan Kavanagh. The other three are *Fiddle City* (1981), *Putting the Boot In* (1985) and *Going to the Dogs* (1987). In 1982, he published his second novel, about a man's descent into insane jealousy, *Before She Met Me*, followed by *Flaubert's Parrot* (1984). After *Staring at the Sun* (1986), a more realist novel began before *Flaubert's Parrot*, he reverted to the innovative mode of the latter with *A History of the World in 10 ½ Chapters* (1989). His subsequent novels are: *Talking It Over* (1991), *Love, etc.* (2000), *The Porcupine* (1992), *England, England* (1998), *Arthur and George* (2005) and *The Sense of an Ending* (2011), which won the Booker Prize. He has published three collections of stories and four books of non-fiction: *Letters from London* (1995), *Something to Declare* (2002), *The Pedant in the Kitchen* (2003) and *Nothing to Be Frightened Of* (2008).

David Britton is an illustrator and writer, and the co-founder with Michael Butterworth of the publisher, Savoy Books, and best known as the creator of the Lord Horror books and comics. Britton and Butterfield met in the circles surrounding *New Worlds* magazine in the 1960s and, following their respective involvement with independent small press magazines, founded Savoy in Manchester in 1976. Britton ran bookshops stocking counter-cultural publications that were frequently raided by the Manchester Police, under then Chief Constable, James Anderton. Britton's *Lord Horror* (published in 1989 but dated 1990), which had editorial and creative input from Butterworth, features the eponymous British fascist living in an alternate universe. Scenes in the book satirized Anderton – thinly disguised as Chief Constable Appleton – by quoting from his speeches and substituting the word 'jew' for every time he had said 'homosexual'. *Lord Horror* was subsequently prosecuted and banned under the Obscene Publications Act and Britton spent four months in prison, of which he later commented: 'Prison just reinforced everything I already believed about society's lack of judgement – 40% of the people in there shouldn't be there. Mostly they're there for misdemeanours like soft drugs, traffic offences, non-payments of fines, or because they're poor or mentally, badly parked.' Britton continued the Lord Horror series with *Motherfuckers: The Auschwitz of Oz* (1996) and *Baptised in the Blood of Millions* (2001).

Christine Frances Evelyn Brooke-Rose (16 January 1923–21 March 2012) was a British writer and literary critic, known for experimental novels which are considered playful and intellectually demanding. She published sixteen novels, five collections of criticism and several collections of short stories and poems. After four traditional yet satirical, comic fictions, inspired by Nathalie Sarraute's *The Age of Suspicion*, Brooke-Rose began to experiment with the novel's form. Labelled a *nouveau romancier*, a term which she rejected, nevertheless she accepted Alain Robbe-Grillet's influence upon her, even translating his fiction. Born in Geneva, Switzerland, to an English father and American–Swiss mother, Brooke-Rose was brought up and educated in Brussels. During the Second World War, she worked in intelligence at Bletchley Park as a WAAF. Later a literary journalist in London, initially she studied for a BA in English (1949) at Somerville College, Oxford, and then a PhD in Middle English (1954) at University College London. She became an academic at the newlyfounded University of Paris, Vincennes, teaching linguistics and English Literature from 1968 to 1988, at which point she retired, spending the remainder of her life resident in the south of France. Her fiction included *The Languages of Love* (1957), *The Sycamore Tree* (1958), *Out* (1964), *Such* (1966), *Between* (1968), *Thru* (1975), *Textermination* (1991), *Next* (1998) and *Subscript* (1999). Among her critical works were: *A Grammar of Metaphor* (1958), *A ZBC of Ezra Pound* (1971) and *Stories, Theories, and Things* (1991). She completed two autobiographical novels: *Remake* (1996) and *Life, End of* (2006).

A.S. Byatt was born in Sheffield in 1936 as Antonia Susan Drabble. Her father was a barrister, her mother was a scholar of Robert Browning and her younger sister is the novelist, Margaret Drabble. Byatt graduated from Newham College, Cambridge, and went on to study at Bryn Mawr College, Philadelphia and Somerville College, Oxford, before subsequently worked as an academic from 1962 to 1983. Her first novel, *The Shadow of the Sun* (1964), was the story of a girl growing up in the shadow of a dominant father. Other novels include *The Game* (1967), which concerns the relationship between two sisters, *The Virgin in the Garden* (1978), *Still Life* (1985), *Babel Tower* (1996), *The Biographer's Tale* (2000) and *A Whistling Woman* (2002). *Possession* (1990), the story of two academics uncovering the relationship between two nineteenth-century poets, won the Booker Prize and was filmed in 2002. *Angels and Insects* (1992) was set entirely in the Victorian period and was filmed in 1995 and *The Children's Book* (2009) was shortlisted for the Booker Prize. Byatt was awarded a CBE in 1990 and made a Dame in 1999.

Mary Gentle was born in Sussex in 1956, left Hastings Grammar School at 16 and undertook various jobs before becoming a full-time writer in 1979. She has gained various degrees as a mature student including an MA in Seventeenth Century Studies at Goldsmith's College and an MA in War Studies at King's College, London. She has also published erotic fiction under the name of Roxanne Morgan. Gentle published her first novel, *Hawk in Silver*, a fantasy for young adults, in 1977. She established her science fiction credentials with *Golden Witchbreed* (1983) and its sequel *Ancient Light* (1987), which involve an Earth woman who goes to the planet Orthe in order to open it up for exploitation but finds the situation there more complex than she imagines. The *White Crow* sequence (1990–4) revolves around a multiverse which includes alternative versions of seventeenth-century England. *Grunts* (1992) is an amusing parody of epic fantasy in which the orcs are heroes. *Ash: A Secret History* (1999) is a huge complex work of science fiction concerned with how the struggles of a fourteenth-century woman mercenary captain to save the Duchy of Burgundy impinges on the present of the novel's framing narrative. It was shortlisted for the Arthur C. Clarke Award and a further novel, *Ilario* (2006), is set in the same timeline, although featuring different characters. *1610: A Sundial in A Grave* (2003) is another alternate history set in England and France, involving sword play, cross dressing and a plot to kill King Charles I. Her most recent novel is *Black Opera* (2012).

Niall Griffiths was born in Toxteth, Liverpool, in 1966 into a family with Welsh roots. In 1976, the family emigrated to Australia only to return three years later. His non-fiction book, *Ten Pound Pom* (2009), records his experiences returning to Australia and reflecting on his childhood memories. After gaining a degree in English, Griffiths worked in a number of short term jobs before starting a PhD at Aberystwyth University. However, he ended up dropping out and accumulating experiences around the town, which fed into his first novel, *Grits* (2000). His second novel, *Sheepshagger* (2001), was a compelling account of the revenge that Ianto from the West Wales mountains takes on those he sees as desecrating his homeland. *Kelly + Victor* (2002), set in Liverpool, describes how a passionate sexual relationship tips into destruction with visceral detail and was subsequently filmed in 2012. His fourth novel *Stump* (2003) tells the intersecting stories of a one-armed man from Liverpool hiding out in a Welsh seaside town and two men on the way from Liverpool hunting for a one-armed man somewhere in Wales. *Stump* won both the Welsh Books Council Book of the Year and the Arts Council of Wales Book of the Year Award. After two more novels *Wreckage* (2005) and *Runt* (2007), he wrote the travel guides *Real Aberystwyth* (2008) and *Real Liverpool* (2008). *The Dreams of Max and Ronnie* (2010) was Griffith's take on *The Dream of Rhonabwy*, a contribution to the Welsh publishing imprint Seren's series *New Stories of the Mabinogion*, in which modern authors rewrote the stories from that Welsh classic. Griffiths's most recent novel is *A Great Big Shining Star* (2013).

Born in Redhill, Surrey, on 17 April 1957, **Nick Hornby** is an English novelist, essayist, lyricist and screenwriter, best known for the novels *High Fidelity* (1995) about an obsessive record-shop owner and *About a Boy* (1998), a 2002 film version of which starred Hugh Grant and Nicholas Hoult. Hornby's parents divorced when he was eleven. He was brought up in Maidenhead, attending the local grammar school and subsequently read English at Jesus College, Cambridge. His early work details the aimless and obsessive natures of his protagonists; their narratives include cultural references to music, sport and other adolescent past-times that divert these male characters facing their thirties from perhaps achieving social acceptance or full emotional maturity. His first book was *Fever Pitch* (1992), an autobiographical account of his fanatical support for Arsenal Football Club, to whose matches his father first took him in adolescence and for which work Hornby received the William Hill Sports Book of the Year Award. In 1997, the memoir was adapted for a British film starring Colin Firth, screenplay adapted by Hornby. A 2005 remake for the American market, starring Drew Barrymore and Jimmy Fallon, directed by the Farrelly brothers, featured its protagonist's obsession with the Boston Red Sox baseball team. Much of Hornby's writing is semi-autobiographical, although the novel *How to Be Good* (2001), which won the W.H. Smith Award for Fiction in 2002, features a female protagonist, Katie Carr, who explores contemporary morals, marriage and parenthood. His style is colloquial, the kind of quasi-demotic Estuary favoured by middle-class metropolitans trying to be urban, generally comic and whimsical. However, his narratives are essentially romances, and by 2009, his books had sold more than 5 million copies worldwide.

James Kelman was born in Glasgow in 1946. After leaving school at the age of fifteen, he undertook a six-year apprenticeship in the printing industry and worked as a bus-driver, before beginning his writing career. In 1971, Kelman joined a creative writing evening class under the direction of Philip Hobsbaum, where he met Alasdair Gray. His work is committed to a complex and politically engaged representation of working-class life. His first novel was *The Busconductor Hines* (1984) and his second *A Chancer* (1985). He won the Cheltenham Prize for his short story collection, *Greyhound for Breakfast* (1987), and the James Tait Black Memorial Prize for his third novel, *A Disaffection* (1989) (also shortlisted for the Booker Prize). His fourth novel, *How Late It Was, How Late*, won the Booker Prize in 1994. Other works include *Translated Accounts* (2001), *You Have To Be Careful in the Land of the Free* (2004), *Kieron Smith, Boy* (2006), which won Scotland's most prestigious literary award, the Saltire Society's Book of the Year Award, and *Mo Said She Was Quirky* (2012). He has published two collections of essays and numerous short story collections.

John King was born in Slough in 1960. His first novel, *The Football Factory* (1996), made an immediate impact on publication for its hard-hitting story of working-class football 'hooligans' in London. It was followed by two loosely linked sequels, *Headhunters* (1997) and *England Away* (1998), which intercut scenes following fans to an England football match in Berlin with those of a pensioner's memories of the First World War. His fourth novel, *Human Punk* (2000), drew on his memories of growing up in Slough as it switches between scenes set in the present and in 1977 at the height of the punk rock era. It is regarded as the first volume of *The Satellite Cycle*, which also includes *White Trash* (2001) and *Skinheads* (2008). King's other novel, *The Prison House* (2004), has a more existential feel being set in a prison outside England but is nonetheless intense and impassioned as all his work is. In 2006, King set up independent publisher London Books with fellow author Martin Knight, and they have since republished a number of out-of-print working-class novels in their London Books Classics series. King has contributed introductions to two of these: Gerald Kersh's *Night and the City* (2007) and John Sommerfield's *May Day* (2010).

Hanif Kureishi was born in Bromley, Kent, in 1954. He dropped out after his first year on a philosophy degree at Lancaster University and later went on to complete a degree in philosophy at Kings College, London. He moved to London after graduating and began to write plays, becoming writer in residence at the Royal Court in 1982. His screenplay, *My Beautiful Laundrette*, was made in to a film, directed by Stephen Frears, in 1985. Kureishi has continued his involvement in films, writing the screenplays for *Sammy and Rosie Get Laid* (dir. Stephen Frears, 1987), *The Mother* (dir. Roger Michell, 2003), *Venus* (dir. Roger Michell, 2006) and *Le Week-End* (dir. Roger Michell, 2013), and writing and directing *London Kills Me* (1991). Kureishi's first novel, *The Buddha of Suburbia*, was published in 1990. It won the Whitbread Prize for the Best First Novel and was adapted for television in 1993. This was followed by the novels *The Black Album* (1995), *Intimacy* (1998), *Gabriel's Gift* (2001), *Something to Tell You* (2005) and *The Last Word* (2014). Much of Kureishi's fictional work has provoked questions and the relation between fiction and the autobiographical. He has also published three short-story collections, and three works of non-fiction, including the memoir, *My Ear at His Heart* (2004). Kureishi was awarded a CBE in 2008 and is Professor of Creative Writing at Kingston University.

Born in London on 7 March 1956 to Jamaican parents who sailed to England on the *Empire Windrush* in 1948, **Andrea Levy** is an English author whose novels are often related to the concerns of those from the Jamaican diaspora peoples in England and their experiences in terms of ethnicity, culture and national identity. Not an overly enthusiastic student at school, she studied Design and Weaving at Middlesex University, followed by part-time work in a variety of costume departments at the Royal Opera House and the BBC. Inspired by issues of civil rights she began reading avidly and attempted fiction in her mid-thirties, producing a quasi-autobiographical novel, *Every Light in the House Burnin'* (1994), followed by *Never Far from Nowhere* (1996) and *Fruit of the Lemon* (1999). After modest success, her career took off with *Small Island* (2004), which brought prizes, including the Orange Prize, the Whitbread Novel Award and the Commonwealth Writers Prize, and prestige and sold over a million copies worldwide. *Small Island* focuses on four main characters: its narrative told from the differing perspectives of Hortense, Queenie, Gilbert and Bernard. Its chief setting is mostly in 1948 and concerns Jamaican immigrants, who have escaped economic hardship at home, moving to the Mother Country, for which the men have fought during the Second World War. Levy's story is concerned with the various adjustments and difficulties to a new life at a time of national hardship, and the interracial relationship between Queenie and Michael. In her fifth novel, *The Long Song* (2010), which won the 2011 Walter Scott Prize and was shortlisted for the Man Booker Prize, Levy tells the life story of July, a slave on a sugar plantation in 1830s Jamaica just as emancipation is about to occur. Levy still resides in London, with graphic designer and husband, Bill Mayblin, stepmother to his two daughters.

Bernard MacLaverty was born in Belfast in 1942. Following various jobs and studying at Queen's University as a mature student, he moved to Scotland with his wife and four children in 1975. Since then, MacLaverty has published a number of volumes of short stories culminating in a volume of *Collected Stories* (2013). However, he is best known for the novels *Lamb* (1980) and *Cal* (1983), both of which were subsequently filmed from his own screenplays in 1985 and 1984, respectively. *Lamb* was the story of a priest working in a boys' home on the West coast of Ireland and his struggles with faith. *Cal* was set in the contemporary Northern Ireland of 'the Troubles' and told the story of a young IRA member who became involved with the catholic widow of an IRA victim. *Grace Notes* (1997), the story of a Northern Irish woman living in Scotland, was shortlisted for the Booker Prize.

Alan Moore was born in Northampton, where he still lives, in 1953. Moore began writing comics for various independent outlets in the late 1970s before progressing to writing serials for British comics, such as *Warrior*, in which *V for Vendetta* (1982–9; collected 1990) first appeared, and *2000 AD*, for which perhaps his best work was *The Ballad of Halo Jones* (1984–6; first collected 1991), the story of a fiftieth-century mall rat who manages to find her way into the wider galaxy, gaining a political education in the process. Moore spearheaded the British invasion of American comics and made his reputation through his 1984–7 run on *Swamp Thing*, which was later credited by Neil Gaiman as inspiring him to write his own comics. This was followed by *Watchmen* (1986–7; collected 1987), illustrated by Dave Gibbons, a groundbreaking story of superheroes with very human problems set in the context of post-Vietnam America. The completion of the dystopian *V for Vendetta*, which had been interrupted when *Warrior* closed down, compounded his status. From the late 1980s onwards, Moore started to consciously step back from the limelight, concentrating on writing for independent outlets again and producing work such as *From Hell* (1989–96; collected 1999) a retelling of the Jack the Ripper story, the sexually explicit *Lost Girls* (1991–2006) and *The League of Extraordinary Gentlemen* (1999–2012). His novel, *Voice of the Fire*, was first published in the mid-1990s but did not appear in a commercial edition until 2004. It is set in Northampton over the period of several millennia. In 2014, the *Guardian* newspaper reported that Moore had finished the first draft, over a million words long, of a novel, provisionally entitled *Jerusalem*, which is set once more in Northampton.

Grant Morrison was born in Glasgow in 1960. He spent the late 1970s and early 1980s playing with a band and writing comic strips for various outlets, before getting his first continuing serial, *Zenith*, with co-creator Steve Yeowell, in *2000AD* in 1987. As a result of *Zenith*, DC comics asked Morrison to pitch an idea for them, which they then commissioned as *Animal Man*. Morrison also took over writing *Doom Patrol* and then, in 1989, published a Batman story, *Arkham Asylum: A Serious House on a Serious Earth*, which was illustrated by Dave McKean. The story and Mckean's sumptious artwork showcased Morrison's surrealist and anarchic worldview to devastating effect, leading *Arkham Asylum* to become one of the best-selling graphic novels of all time. During the course of the 1990s, Morrison was involved in various comic projects including revamping the *Justice League of America*. Between 1994 and 2000, he wrote the series for which he is arguably best known, *The Invisibles*, which was subsequently collected into seven volumes. The plot is complex, involving time paradoxes, hallucinations and random chaos, interspersed with a wealth of cultural allusions, but the central theme of resistance to oppression provides a unity and a point of identification for readers. In 1998, Morrison published *Lovely Biscuits*, a collection of short stories and plays. Since 2000, he has continued to write many comics projects, and in 2011, he published the non-fiction, *Supergods*, which combined elements of his autobiography with a personal history of comics from the 'Golden Age' of the 1940s to the present. Morrison was awarded an MBE in the 2012 Birthday Honours List for services to film and literature.

Courttia Newland was born in London in 1973 to Jamaican and Bajan parents and grew up in Shepherd's Bush. He worked in music as a rapper and producer and published his first novel *The Scholar* in 1997, and this was followed by *Society Within* (1999) and *Snakeskin* (2002). In 2006, he published *The Dying Wish: A James and Sinclair Mystery*, and he was shortlisted for the Crime Writers' Association Dagger in the Library Award in 2007. He has written numerous short stories, including those collected in *Music for the Off-Key* (2006), and co-founded the Tell-TalesCollective in 2003. He co-edited *Tell-Tales 4: The Global Village* in 2009 and *IC3: The Penguin Book of New Black Writing in Britain* (2000). He has also written numerous plays, most recently *Look to the* Sky (2011). He has been writer-in-residence at Trinity College, Dublin, and at Georgetown University, Washington DC.

Kim Newman was born in London in 1959 but grew up in Somerset before leaving to study English at the University of Sussex in the late 1970s. He became a journalist and film critic in the 1980s and remains a regular contributor to film magazines such as *Empire* and *Sight and Sound*. After co-writing a book with Neil Gaiman, *Ghastly Beyond Belief: The Science Fiction and Fantasy Book of Quotations* (1985), Newman wrote *Nightmare Movies: A Critical History of the Horror Film, 1968–88* (1988), which was revised, expanded and updated as a new edition in 2011. Other works of film criticism include *Wild West Movies: Or How the West Was Found, Won, Lost, Lied About, Filmed and Forgotten* (1990), *The BFI Companion to Horror* (1996) and *Millennium Movies: End of the World Cinema* (1999). His first published novel, *The Night Mayor*, appeared in 1989, the same year, as he began contributing under the name of Jack Yeovil, to a series of novels set in the world of the *Warhammer* role-playing games. In 1992, he published *Anno Dracula*, a version of the Jack the Ripper story set in an alternate 1880s England, in which Dracula has married Queen Victoria and vampires have become common throughout society. Subsequent novels in the series are set in progressively more recent times: *The Bloody Red Baron* (1995) is set in the First World War and *Dracula Cha Cha Cha* (1998) in the 1950s. Since 2011, Titan Books have reissued the series with copious annotations and added a fourth volume, *Johnny Alucard* (2013). Other novels include *Bad Dreams* (1990), *The Quorum* (1994) and *Life's Lottery* (1999), in which readers' choices determine the story. Newman is also a prolific short story writer and has published a number of collections. For example, *Unforgivable Stories* (2000) brings together various alternative histories including 'Further Developments in the Strange Case of Dr Jekyll and Mr Hyde' and 'Teddy Bear's Picnic', a story in which Britain fights in the Vietnam War and most of the characters are taken from television sitcoms.

Lawrence Norfolk was born in London in 1963 and then spent time as a small child in Iraq before growing up in the West of England. He took his degree in English and American Literature at King's College, London. His first novel, *Lemprière's Dictionary* (1991), which links the writing of the famous Classical dictionary with a complex plot concerned with the foundation and legacy of the East India Company, won the Somerset Maugham Prize. In 1993, he was included among *Granta's* ten-yearly list of the best young British novelists. *Lemprière's Dictionary* was followed by other two long, complex, historical novels: *The Pope's Rhinoceros* (1996) and *In the Shape of a Boar* (2000). However, the next novel Norfolk began to write, which was provisionally entitled *The Levels*, proved impossible for him to complete. The problem was that the structure was so complex with three interacting time periods – Britain at the end of the Roman era, the Second World War and 1981 – in which anything that happened in the first period had knock-on effects for the second period, which exponentially increased for the third, that the project just proliferated and was impossible to control. By 2007, Norfolk had abandoned *The Levels* and begun to write a new novel about a chef in the seventeenth century whose fate gets bound up with the Civil War and the Restoration, which was published in 2012 as *John Saturnall's Feast*.

Caryl Phillips is a British novelist, playwright and essayist whose Black Atlantic writing fiction often focuses on or features people from the African diaspora in England, the Caribbean or the United States. Born in St. Kitts on 13 March 1958, at four months old Phillips's family settled in Leeds, Yorkshire, where he was schooled locally. He read English at Queen's College, Oxford University, from 1976 to 1979, after which he lived in Edinburgh and London. Aged twenty-two a first return to St. Kitts inspired Phillips's first novel, *The Final Passage* (1985). Moving to America in 1990, he worked as an academic variously at Amherst and Barnard Colleges; later, he was appointed Professor of English in 2005 at Yale University. He was made an elected fellow of the Royal Society of Literature in 2000 and of the Royal Society of Arts in 2011. His novels include *A State of Independence* (1986), *Higher Ground* (1989); *Cambridge* (1991), *Crossing the River* (1993), *The Nature of Blood* (1997) and *A Distant Shore* (2003). He has published four essay collections: *The European Tribe* (1987), *The Atlantic Sound* (2000), *A New World Order* (2001) and *Colour Me English* (2011). His diasporic vision explores the tensions of migration, resettlement, attempted return and the daily events which are the lived coordinates of cultures defined by multicultural and ethnic tensions. He has received numerous awards, including the Martin Luther King Memorial Prize, a Guggenheim Fellowship, the 1993 James Tait Black Memorial Prize for *Crossing the River* and the 2004 Commonwealth Writers' Prize Best Book award for *A Distant Shore*.

Christopher Priest was born in 1943 and grew up in Cheshire; he left school at 16 when his family relocated to Essex. For the next seven years, he worked unhappily with a firm of chartered accountants in Central London but found consolation when a colleague introduced him to science fiction. Priest began writing his own stories from the mid-1960s and published his first novel *Indoctrinaire* in 1970. *Fugue for a Darkening Island* (1972), *Inverted World* (1974), *The Space Machine* (1976), *A Dream of Wessex* (1977) and *The Affirmation* (1981) followed before his inclusion among 'The Best of Young British Novelists 1983'. Priest's characteristically acerbic memoir of the photo shoot and launch party marking the announcement of this list, 'Where Am I Now?' (2008), mercilessly condemns the whole process as a charade and is scathing about the behaviour of some of his peers. Priest's ninth novel *The Prestige* (1995), winner of both the James Tait Black Memorial Prize and the World Fantasy Award, was filmed by Christopher Nolan in 2006. *The Separation* (2002) won the Arthur C. Clarke Award. His most recent work includes *The Islanders* (2011) and *The Adjacent* (2013).

Will Self was born in London in 1961. He graduated from Exeter College, Oxford, moving back to London to do a variety of jobs, including working for the Greater London Council. Self's first short story collection, *The Quantity Theory of Insanity*, was published in 1991 to considerable critical acclaim. The collection won the Geoffrey Faber Memorial Prize, and Self was included on Granta's 'Best Young British Novelists' list in 1993. Self's first novel, *My Idea of Fun*, was published in 1993 and received less critical acclaim. Through the 1990s, Self became an increasingly familiar voice in the press, writing columns for, among others, the *Observer, The Times* and the *Independent on Sunday*. In the early twentieth-first century, Self's fame spread, and he became a regular guest on television shows, including the comedy panel show *Shooting Stars*. In the 1990s, Self published three more short story collections, an illustrated novella – *The Sweet Smell of Psychosis* (1996) – and another novel, *Great Apes* (1997). Into the twenty-first century, while Self left behind the reputation most obviously gained by doing drugs on John Major's campaign plane just before the 1997 general election, Self's writing continued to construct strange and powerful versions of the contemporary world. His *Dorian, an Imitation* (2002) rewrote Oscar Wilde's *The Picture of Dorian Grey* set in the 1980s and 1990s, and *Umbrella* (2012), which was shortlisted for the Booker Prize, is an engagement with *Ulysses*. He has also published three more short story collections, and a number of collections of his writing for newspapers and magazines.

Born on 11 June 1943 in Cardiff, Wales, **Iain Sinclair** is a British writer and filmmaker whose work has been largely focused on London, and much influenced by his interpretation of psychogeography. Educated at Trinity College, Dublin, he edited its literary magazine, *Icarus*; subsequently, he attended the Courtauld Institute of Art and the London School of Film Technique. Originally a poet, his verse largely published by his small press, Albion Village Press; Sinclair is still associated with the 1960s and 1970s British avant-garde scene. Early books such as *Lud Heat* (1975) and *Suicide Bridge* (1979) interweave essays, fiction and poetry; the later novel, *White Chappell, Scarlet Tracings* (1987), details two parallel stories, one concerning disreputable book-dealers hunting for a priceless copy of Arthur Conan Doyle's *A Study in Scarlet* and the other the Jack the Ripper murders (attributed to the physician William Gull). His novel *Downriver* (1991), winner of the James Tait Black Memorial Prize and the 1992 Encore Award, offers twelve interconnected stories about mostly the East End, concerning Britain under the rule of the Widow, a grotesque depiction of Margaret Thatcher. Sinclair addresses the demonic energy of that period, drawing on the past for concepts of resistance. The river dominates, and each narrative is affected variously by the sinking of the pleasure boat *Princess Alice* after its collision with the *Byewell Castle*. Granta's publication of the nine essays comprising *Lights Out for the Territory* (1997) secured Sinclair a broader readership. *London Orbital* (2002) describes a series of trips around the M25 on foot, while *Edge of the Orison* (2005) reconstructs poet John Clare's walk from Dr Matthew Allen's private lunatic asylum at High Beach, at the heart of Epping Forest in Essex, to his home in Helpston, near Peterborough. Other significant works by Sinclair include the novels, *Radon Daughters* (1994) and *Landor's Tower* (2001) and the non-fiction book, *Rodinsky's Room* (1999) with Rachel Lichtenstein.

Born in 1950 in Colaba, Mumbai in India, **Indra Sinha** is a British writer. Son of an Indian naval officer and an English writer, Irene Elizabeth Phare, Indra Sinha was educated at Mayo College, Ajmer, India, Oakham School in Rutland, and Pembroke College Cambridge where he studied English literature. Together with a wife, Vickie, with whom he has three grown-up children, he lives in south-west France. Formerly, a copywriter for London-based Ogilvy & Mather and Collett Dickenson Pearce & Partners, Sinha was voted one of the top ten British copywriters of all time. *Animal's People*, his most recent novel, was shortlisted for the 2007 Man Booker Prize and winner of the 2008 Commonwealth Writers' Prize for Europe and South Asia. Written between 2001 and 2006, the novel reworks the Bhopal disaster in an imaginary city Khaufpur (from *khauf*, an Urdu word meaning terror). A dark and at times comic fable, its narrator is a 19-year-old orphan, born just days before the disaster, his spine so twisted he walks on all fours, spouting obscenities, obsessed with sex. *The Cybergypsies* (1999) is a confessional text which incorporates fiction and hyperrealism, while *The Death of Mr. Love* (2002) draws upon a 1959 Indian court case in which a Naval Commander was tried for the murder of his wife's lover. Among Sinha's earlier published works are translations of ancient Sanskrit texts into English, *The Love Teachings of Kama Sutra* (1980), *Tantra: The Search for Ecstasy* (1993) and *The Great Book of Tantra: Translations and Images from the Classic Indian Text* (1993).

Sarah Waters was born in Pembrokeshire in 1966 and grew up there until leaving school and going to study English Literature at the University of Kent. Following an MA from Lancaster University, she gained a PhD from Queen Mary's, University of London, in 1995 for her thesis *Wolfskins and Togas: Lesbian and Gay Historical Fictions, 1870 to the Present*. Although she did work for a while as an associate lecturer for the Open University, she went more or less straight from writing her thesis to writing her first novel, the 1880s-set picaresque lesbian coming-of-age story *Tipping the Velvet* (1998). Her next two novels *Affinity* (1999) and *Fingersmith* (2002), which was shortlisted for the Booker and Orange Prizes, were also lesbian-themed and set in the Victorian period. In 2003, Waters was included among *Granta's* ten-yearly list of the best young British novelists. Her fourth novel, *The Night Watch* (2006) is set during, and in the aftermath, of the Second World War. However, the sections of the novel appear in reverse chronological order, running backwards from 1947 to 1941. *The Little Stranger* (2009), a ghost story, is also set in the 1940s. Her sixth and most recent novel, *The Paying Guests* was published in August 2014 and is set in the 1920s. *Tipping the Velvet*, *Fingersmith* and *The Night Watch* have been adapted for broadcast on BBC television in 2002, 2005 and 2011 respectively, while *Affinity* was filmed in 2008.

Irvine Welsh was born in Leith, Edinburgh, near the Easter Road ground of Hibernian FC, the football team that many of the characters in his Edinburgh-based novels support. When he was a child, his family moved to Muirhouse, a 1960s housing estate on the outskirts of the city. Rumours that Welsh has invented his own biography – for example, while he claims to have been born in 1958, press reports allege the real date is seven years earlier – make it difficult to summarize his early adult life, but he clearly spent time in London and Croydon during the 1970s and 1980s before returning to Edinburgh, where he worked for the district council as a training officer in the housing department and successfully studied for an MBA at Heriot-Watt University. His first novel, *Trainspotting* (1993), is formed of loosely linked stories (some of which had been previously published) of life in the Edinburgh housing schemes of the mid-1980s. Its tales of heroin addiction, sex, violence and boredom, all relayed in local dialect, are fast and often funny but also amounted to an eye-opening snapshot of the state of contemporary Scotland at the time. The book became a cult phenomenon, aided by the popularity of the 1996 film adaptation directed by Danny Boyle, and was sold in non-traditional outlets such as record shops. Welsh has subsequently published a sequel, *Porno* (2002), which also featured characters from *Glue* (2001), and a prequel, *Skagboys* (2012). His other novels are *Marabou Stork Nightmares* (1995), *Filfth* (1998), *Bedroom Secrets of the Masterchefs* (2006), *Crime* (2008) and *The Sex Lives of the Siamese Twins* (2014). He has also written screenplays and published several volumes of short stories including *The Acid House* (1994) and *Ecstasy* (1996). Welsh was a fervent public supporter of the yes campaign during the 2014 Scottish Independence Referendum.

Index

Note: The letter 'n' following locators refer to notes.

Abonji, Melinda Nadj 232
   Tauben fliegen auf (*Doves Ascend*) 232
Ace Books 40
Ackroyd, Peter 82, 202
   Albion: The Origins of the English Imagination (2002) 82
Adebayo, Diran 30, 129, 143
   Some Kind of Black (1996) 143–4
Ahmad, Rukhsana 141
   Hope Chest, The (1996) 141
al-Qaida 13
Alden, Natasha 169, 170
Alibhai-Brown, Yasmin 250
Allen, Richard 61
Allison & Busby 40
Amis, Martin
   postmodernist literary novel 183–4
   prose style 106
   psychological realism 101
   realism principle 228
   Time's Arrow (1991) 184, 197
Anderson, Benedict 69, 70
Anderton, James 40–1, 197
Angel Heart (1997, film) 191
anti-novels 182, 209
Antoine, Patsy 124
Arana, R. Victoria 127, 129, 143
Arrighi, Giovanni 31, 152, 153
   Long Twentieth Century, The (1994) 31, 152–3, 155, 177
Arthur C. Clarke Award 163
Ash, Timothy Garton 163, 164, 176, 220
Attack! Books 61–2, 210
Augstein, Franziska 227
Autobiography of Mark Rutherford, The (1881) 156
avant-garde writing 43, 181, 183, 186, 200–1, 205, 207, 209

Bad Lieutenant (1992, film) 190
Badley, Linda 200
Baileys Woman's Prize for Fiction 38
Baker, Houston A. 124, 129
Bakhtin, Mikhail 52, 77, 175
Balkan conflicts 10–11
Ball, Malcolm 119
Ballard, J.G. 106
   Cocaine Nights 24
   Millennium People 24
   Super-Cannes 24
Bandele, Biyi 141
   Street, The (1999) 141
Banks, Iain 43, 49, 215, 226
   Complicity (1993) 49
   Wasp Factory, The (1984) 43
Bantick, Christopher 53
Barber, Lynn 106
Barker, Pat 20, 22, 30–1, 38, 167
   crime fiction 168
   Double Vision (2003) 167–8
   Eye in the Door, The (1993) 167–9
   Ghost Road, The (1995) 149, 167
   historical fiction 149, 170
   Regeneration (1991) 22
   Regeneration trilogy (1991–5) 20, 31, 155, 167–8
   Union Street and *Blow Your House Down* (1984) 167
Barnes, Julian
   alternative ethnicities 86
   England England (1998) 69, 83–5
   idea of Englishness 83, 85
   on multiculturalism 69
Barry, Kevin 52
   City of Bohane (2011) 52
Bates, Benjamin R. 32n. 1
Baudrillard, Jean 83, 84
   America (1988) 83

Beard, Steve
  Digital Leatherette (1999) 183, 209
  Perfumed Head (1998) 183, 209
Behrends, Jan C. 233
Belfast Peace Agreement 5
Bell, Ian A. 101, 226
Belton, Neil 222, 231
Benjamin, Walter 27, 31, 166, 184
Benson, Dzifa 143
Bentley, Nick 2, 18, 20, 29, 30, 67, 239, 240, 258
Berger, John 149, 229
  G (1972) 149
Berger, Stefan 218, 219, 220, 221
Berhendt, Stephen C. 18
Berlin Wall, fall of 2, 24, 67, 150
Berliner Festwochen of 1998 222
Berners-Lee, T. 3
Bhabha, Homi 70, 136, 139
  Location of Culture, The (1994) 136
Big Breakfast, The (TV show) 2
bildungsroman 89, 191, 232, 260
bin Laden, Osama 11
Bissett, Alan
  Damage Land: Contemporary Scottish Gothic (2001) 44
'black' British Literature
  alternative realism 142
  criticism 124–6, 128
  experimentation 126–7
  political identity 127–8
  postcolonial writing 124
  utopianism 129–30, 135, 140, 143–5
Black Wednesday 6
Blair, Tony 8, 9, 11, 12, 13, 14, 15, 44, 69, 71, 104, 128, 203, 217, 218, 226
Blanchot, Maurice 103, 109
  Writing of the Disaster, The (1980) 103
Bloom, Clive 183
  Literature, Politics and Intellectual Crisis in Britain Today (2000) 183
Böhner, Ines Karin 228
Bond, Ross 30
book publishing in 1990s
  Attack! Books 61–2
  marketing strategies 37–8, 43, 47, 53, 57
  NBA's role 37–8
  practical aspects 44
  prize-giving literary culture 39
  Scottish fiction 43–6
  small presses, impact on 39, 46–7, 52, 57, 61–2
  transgressive forms of literature 39, 41, 43, 45, 52–3
  'Waterstonisation' 38, 46
Booker Prize 28, 39, 43, 52–4, 82, 124, 197
Bosnian War 11
Botting, Fred 2
Bourdieu, Pierre 54, 182
Boyle, Danny 52
Bracewell, Michael 25
Bradbury, Malcom 105, 224
Bradford, Richard 76, 82, 110
Braidotti, Rosi 249
Brennan, Michael 1
Brennan, Timothy 70, 124
'Britain Isn't Working' campaign 25
British Satellite Broadcasting (BSB) 4
Britton, David
  Baptised in the Blood of Millions (2000) 43
  comics 40
  experimentalism 197–8
  impact on small presses 46
  Lord Horror (1990) 37, 39–43, 46, 62, 197–8
  Motherfuckers: The Auschwitz of Oz (1996) 43, 197
  Reverbstorm #1-7 (1994-2000, 2013 comic book series) 197–8
  second and third text 43
  Williams on 42
  Young on 62
Brockmann, Stephen 216, 217, 218
Brooke-Rose, Christine France Evelyn 31, 181, 182, 183, 193, 208, 209
  Between (1968) 182
  Next (1998) 208
  Remake (1996) 193
  Rhetoric of the Unreal (1983) 31, 181
  Stories, Theories, Things (1991) 181
  Textermination (1991) 208
Brooker, Joe 15, 17
Brookner, Anita 224
Brown, Timothy S. 231
Bruguière, Jean-Louis 9
Brussig, Thomas 230
Bryan, Julian 141

Bernard and the Cloth Monkey (1998) 141
Bußmann, Carla 216
buchreport 214
Buckley, William F. 213
Bull, Malcolm 97, 98, 99, 102, 104, 109, 112, 113, 114, 119
   Seeing Things Hidden: Apocalypse Vision and Totality (1999) 97
Burchil, Julie 97
Burroughs, William
   Naked Lunch (1959) 43, 186
Bush, George W. 14
Butlin, Ron 44
Butterworth, Michael 40, 41, 42, 43, 196
Button, Victoria 27
Byatt, A. S. 20, 30, 176
   biographical metafiction 157
   historical fiction 149
   Possession (1990) 20, 30, 111, 131, 149, 156, 176
   on Victorian past 156
Byron 111
   Don Juan 111

Cameron, David 49–50, 128
Campbell, Alistair 12
Campbell, Eddie 172, 203
   From Hell (1999) 172, 202–4
Canetti, Elias
   Auto da Fe 208
Canongate 46, 57
Carr, Rocky
   Brixton Bwoy (1998) 129
Carson, Ciaran 71
Carter, Angela 208, 224
   Magic Toyshop, The 208
Caruth, Cathy 23
Caudwell, Chrisopher 162
   Illusion and Reality (1937) 162
Chadwick, Alan 47
Champion, Sarah
   Disco 2000 (1998) 187
   Disco Biscuits (1997) 187
Chang, Tachun 241, 248, 252, 253–4, 260
   My Kid Sister (1993) 32, 252, 254, 257, 260
Channel 4, 22, 27, 135
Charlotte (Princess, 1817) 18
Chauduri, Amit 225

chemical generation fiction 186–8, 192–3
Chen, Fangming 247
China/Chinese
   immigrant writers 240
   immigrants 244, 248, 253–6
   invasion of Taiwan 244
   KMT government 246–8, 253–4
   literature 241, 247
   Nationalist regime 240, 245–8, 254
   People's Republic of China 247
   society 239
Ching, Leo 245, 246
Chomsky, Noam 8, 12
Chow, Meili 245, 246, 247, 248
Christ's College Grammar School 102
Christian Democratic Union (CDU) 219
Ciocia, Stefania 175
Clark, Melville 96
Clarke, Kenneth 128
Clinton, Bill 9, 11
Clocktower Press 44, 46, 57, 62
club novels 183, 187–8, 193
Coetzee, J.M. 124
Cold War 2, 9, 213, 224
Colebrook, Martyn 29, 37, 44
Collishaw, Matt 25
Colls, Robert 82
   Identity of England, The (2002) 82
Colson, Rob 206
   Seaton Point (1998) 181, 183, 206–8
Conrad, Joseph 187
   Heart of Darkness (1899) 187
Conway, David
   Metal Sushi (1998) 198
'Cool Britannia' 15, 24, 104, 217
Cooper, Martin 206
   Seaton Point (1998) 181, 183, 206–8
Costa Book Awards 38
Costa Short Story Awards 38
Crabtree, James 3
Craig, Cairns 50, 54
Creation Books 61
crime novel/fiction 43, 77, 143, 167, 193, 223
Criminal Justice Act (2003) 7
Crown Prosecution Service (CPS) 6
Cumings, Bruce 246
Cunningham, Valentine 106, 114, 119
Curtis, Ted 206
   Seaton Point (1998) 181, 183, 206–8

D'Aguiar, Fred 138, 140, 141
  Feeding the Ghosts (1997) 140
  Longest Memory, The (1994) 141
Dando, Jill 13
Davison, Gary Marvin 246
Dawes, Kwame 124, 130, 138, 141
de Bernière, Louis
  Captain Corelli's Mandolin (1994) 22
De Groot, Jerome 20–1
Deane, Seamus 69, 71
  Reading In The Dark (1996) 69, 71
Del Ponte, Carla 13
  Madame Prosecutor: Confrontations with Humanity's Worst Criminals and the Culture of Impunity 13
Delany, Samuel R. 196
  Tides of Lust, The (1973) 196
Deleuze, Gilles 81
Dellar, Robert 206
  Seaton Point (1998) 181, 183, 206–8
Dennis, Ferdinand 124, 140
  Last Blues Dance, The (1996) 140
Der Spiegel 214–15, 222, 229
Der Tagesspiegel 215, 217, 222, 227
Derrida, Jacques 183, 199
  Other Heading, The (1992) 183
deVega, Jessica Tinklenberg 105
Devlin, Anne 224
Diana (Princess of Wales) 1, 18
Die Tageszeitung 215, 221–2, 224, 230
Die Zeit 215, 221–2
Dillow, Chris 13, 14
  End of Politics: New Labour and the Folly of Managerialism, The (2007) 13
DIY novels 183, 209
Don't Look Back in Anger (Oasis) 15–18
Donnell, Alison 144
'dotcom' bubble 4
Drabble, Margaret 224
Draesner, Ulrike 228
Drummond, Bill 182, 209
  Bad Wisdom (1996) 209
D'Souza, Frances 42
Duve, Karin 230

Easton Ellis, Bret 189
  American Psycho (1991) 42, 189
Edinburgh Festival 1993, 47

Elliott, Larry 153
Emin, Tracey
  Bed (1999) 28
England
  cultural crisis 86
  Englishness and 82–6
  governmental restrictions 84
  postmodernism 85
English, James F. 28
ethnic diversities
  cultural restrictions 91
  identity crisis 87–8
  immigration, impact on 86–7
  legacies of colonialism 91
  racism 88–90
Evans, Julian 106
Evaristo, Bernadine 129, 141
  Island of Abraham (1994) 141
  Lara (1994) 141
Exchange Rate Mechanism (ERM) 6
Exeter College 102
experimentalism
  anti-novels 209–10
  avant-garde writing 200–1
  chemical generation 187
  club novel 187
  collaborative storytelling 206–7
  conceptual vocabulary 199
  contemporary anti-novels 182–3
  Creation Oneiros books 198
  critical languages 205
  literary postmodernism 183–6
  modern comics 201–4
  New Worlds writers 196
  psychogeography 201, 203, 205
  Savoy's novels 196–8
  social matrices 181

Faber, Michel 176
  Crimson Petal and the White, The (2002) 176
The Face (magazine) 26, 192
'Factory novels' (Raymond) 193
False Memory Syndrome Foundation 19
Fan, Luoping 253
Farrell, J.G.
  Siege of Krishnapur, The (1973) 149, 171
Faulk, Sebastian
  Birdsong (1994) 20, 22

FHM (magazine) 192
Fielding, Helen 225, 230, 239
Finney, Brian 96, 106
Finnigan, Judy 21
First Book Award 22
Flannery, Peter 16
Flottau, Renate 11
Foster, Janet 6
Four Weddings and a Funeral (1990, film) 76–7
Fowles, John 156
  French Lieutenant's Woman, The (1969) 156
Fox, Dan 26
Frankfurter Allgemeine Zeitung 215, 221, 227–8
Franklin, George 19
Fraser, George MacDonald 171
  Flashman series 171
  Flashman and the Tiger (1999) 171
Freeze (show) 25
Freud, Lucian 25
Freud, Sigmund 19
frieze (art magazine) 26
Frye, Northrop 101
  Anatomy of Criticism (1967) 101
Fu, Bennett Yuhsiang 253
Fuchs, Karen 222
Fuentes, Carlos 208
  Terra Nostra (Fuentes) 208
Fukuyama, Francis 30, 31, 84, 98, 99, 105, 149, 150, 151, 153, 163
  End of History and the Last Man, The (1992, Fukuyama) 98–9, 150
  National Interest 99
Fulani, Ifeona 141
  Seasons of Dust (1997) 124, 141
Funck, Gisa 214, 216, 229

Gallagher, Noel 15, 17
Gallix, Andrew 61
Galloway, Janice 44, 78
Gąsiorek, Andrzej 23
Gellner, Ernest 242
General Election May 1997 15
'Genocide in Rwanda' (United Human Rights Council's) 10
Gentle, Mary 31, 149, 163
  Ash: A Secret History (1999) 31, 163

George, Terry 10
German perspectives
  authenticity and resistance ideologies 227–31
  bestseller lists 214–15
  collapse of GDR 214, 216, 218–21, 226, 230
  ethnic writing 214, 222–3, 225, 227
  mood-defining effects 213–14
  national identity 214, 217–19, 223–4, 226
  popularity of British fiction 213–16
  postmodernisms 216
  towards British culture 217–18, 221
Germanà, Monica 43
  The 1980s: A Decade of Contemporary British Fiction (2014) 43
Geyer, Michael 216, 220, 227
Gilroy, Paul 89, 128, 133, 137, 139, 140, 142, 144
  Between Camps (2000) 137
  Black Atlantic: Modernity and Double Consciousness, The (1993) 139
  There Ain't No Black in the Union Jack (1987) 89, 128
Gloer, Will 108
Goodman, Sam 171
Goos, Hauke 226
Goosen, Frank 230
Gorbachev, Mikhail 218
Gordimer, Nadine 222
Gordon, Giles 56
Gorris, Lothar 228, 229
Grahame-Smith, Seth 171
  Pride and Prejudice and Zombies (2009) 171
Grant, Iain 48
Granta 222, 227, 231
Grass, Gunter 221
Gray, Alasdair 43, 68, 78, 79, 82
  Lanark: A Life in Four Books (1981) 43
  Poor Things (1992) 79
Greiner, Ulrich 222, 224
Griffin, Annie
  Book Club, The (2002–3) 22
Griffiths, Niall 52, 68
  Grits (2000) 52, 77
Groß, Thomas 229
Groucho Club 97, 100, 103

Guattari, Felix 81, 182
Guignery, Vanessa 102
Gurnah, Abdulrazak 225
Gustafsson, Lars 208
   La Mot d'um Apiculteur 208

Haas, Birgit 233n. 7
Habyarimana 9
Hager, Martin 222
Hall, Stuart 86, 87, 89, 132
Harms, Ingeborg 225
Harris, Katherine 14
Harris, Wilson 125, 126, 225
Hartley, Jenny 22
   Reading Groups (2001) 22
Harvey, Marcus 26-7
   Myra (1995) 26-7
Hayes, M. Hunter 97, 101, 106
Headley, Victor 141
   Yardie (1992) 141
Heaney, Seamus 71
Heller, Zoe 96, 108
Herald Scotland 47
Herman, Edward 10, 11, 12, 186
   Politics of Genocide, The 11
Heseltine, Michael 128
Hesse, Hermann 186
   Steppenwolf (1927) 186
Hirst, Damien 115
historical fiction
   alternative Victorian values 170-6
   biographical metafiction 153-7
   capitalism 152-3
   global politics 151-2
   hypothetical experiment 158-9
   infestation of ghosts 167-70
   postmodernity 149-50
   science fiction *vs.* 163-7
   on 'short twentieth century' 152
   use of journals and diaries 157, 160
Ho, Elizabeth 203
Hobsbawm, Eric 152, 242
   Age of Extremes: The Short Twentieth Century 1914-1991 (1994) 152
   Nations and Nationalism since 1780 (1991) 242
Hodder Headline 38
Hodgkin, Howard 25
Hodgson, Godfrey 8
   Myth of American Exceptionalism, The 8
Hogg, James 190
   Private Memoirs and Confessions of A Justified Sinner, The (1824) 190
Holman-Hunt, Willaim 196
   Lady of Shallot 196
Home, Stewart 39, 56-7, 62, 182, 201, 209-10
   Come Before Christ and Murder Love (1997) 209
   Slow Death (1996) 209
   Suspect Device: Reader in Hard Edged Fiction (1998) 39
   Whips and Furs My Life as A Bon-Vivant, Gambler and Love Rat by Jesus H. Christ (2000) 210
Hong, Chien-chao 244
Hope, Christopher 224
Hornby, Nick 31, 107, 215, 229-31
   About a Boy (1998) 229
   High Fidelity (1995) 229-30
Hotel Rwanda (2004, film) 10
Howarth, Marianne 226
Hsueh, Hua-yuan 245, 246, 247, 248
Hubble, Nick 1, 30, 31, 149, 162, 165, 167, 169
Huggan, Graham 223
   Postcolonial Exotic, The (2001) 125, 223
Hughes, Thomas
   Tom Brown's School Days (1857) 171
Hulme, Keri 124
Hume, Gary 25
Humphreys, Emyr 76
   Bonds of Attraction (1991) 76
Hunt, Marsha 124
Huntington, Samuel P. 99
Hutcheon, Linda 20, 31, 149, 154, 155
   Politics of Postmodernism, The 20

iD (magazine) 192
Ignatieff, Michael 220, 221, 231
Internet 3, 22, 104, 183, 188, 193, 195, 209, 239
Iraq War 8
Ishiguro, Kazuo 222
Iyer, Pico 222
Izetbegovic, Alija 11

Jackson, H.J. 119
Jackson, Steve
  Warlock of Firetop Mountain, The (1980) 205
Jackson, Rosemary 181
Jacobs, Steffen 229
Jaggi, Maya 135
James, Procter 16
Jameson, Fredric 17, 31, 84, 149, 162, 163
  Postmodernism, or the Cultural Logic of Late Capitalism (1991) 17, 84
Japan/Japanese
  colonialism 239–40, 245
  invasion of Taiwan 246
  nationalism 247
John Llewellyn Rhys Prize 96
Johnsen, William T. 2
Johnson, Amryl 224
Jones, Simon Cellan 16
Jones, Stephen 197
Joyce, James 74, 82
Judt, Tony 219
  Postwar: A History of Europe since 1945 219
Julius, Anthony 27
Jungle Book, The 88
Jury, Louise 26

Kadaré, Ismail 208
  Avril Brise 208
Kafka, Franz 101, 111, 113, 115
  Metamorphosis (1915) 113
Kagame, Paul 9–10
Kamp, David 15
'karaoke pop movement' 18
Keay, Douglas 49
Keen, Suzanne 20
Kelleher, Fatimah 141
Kelly, Aaron 48, 49, 50, 51, 52
Kelman, James 29, 37, 43, 44, 46, 52, 59, 62, 68, 78, 82, 215
  Booker Prize winner 53–4
  on capitalist system 54–5
  A Disaffection (1989) 43
  How Late it Was, How Late (1994) 43, 45, 52, 82
  Lean Tales (1985) 44
  reviewer's comment on 53
  use of vernacular 53, 56
  working class writing 53

Kennedy, A.L. 44, 68, 78, 215
Khan, Naseem 124
Khomeini, Ayatollah 90
Kiberd, Declan 244
Kiefer, Anselm 25
Kincaid, Jamaica 222
King, John 29, 37, 39
  England Away (1999) 69
  on football culture 58–9
  Football Factory, The (1996, King) 57, 59
  on global consumerism 59–60
  science fiction 57
  use of vernacular 58
  working class writing 57
King, Naomi 141
  O.P.P. (1993) 141
Kinson, Sarah 97
Kirk, James T. 183, 187
  cinematic registers 187
  club novel 183
  lyrical associations 187–8
Klaus, Gustav H. 227
Koestler, Arthur 224
Kohl, Helmut 214, 217–20
Korte, Barbara 225, 228
Kosovo Liberation Army (KLA) 11–12
Krauthammer, Charles 18
Kristeva, Julia 261
  Strangers to Ourselves 261
Kuck, Dennis 233n. 5
Kumar, Kristan 83
  Making of English National Identity, The (2003) 83
Kureishi, Hanif 30, 31, 32, 69, 87, 89, 91, 132, 133, 135, 136, 137, 138, 139, 143, 215, 222, 225, 228, 229, 231, 239, 240, 241, 248, 249, 250, 251, 256, 258, 259, 260
  Black Album, The (1995) 89, 135–7, 228
  on black identity 143
  Buddha of Suburbia, The (1990) 32, 69, 87, 89, 132, 228, 241, 248–9, 259–60
  on immigrant experience 249–58
  In a Blue Time 228
  Intimacy (1998) 138
  My Beautiful Launderette (1986, Kureishi) 132
  on racism 135–6

Sleep With Me 228
utopian realism 132, 137
Kurtz, Howard 9
   Spin Cycle: How the White House and the Media Manipulate the News (1998) 9

'lad culture' 192–3
Lancer Books 40
Lancet, The (research paper) 7
Landy, Michael 25
Langford, Paul 82, 86
   Englishness Identified (2000) 82
Le Monde 9
Lee, Robert 124
Legge, Gordon 44
Leith, Sam 48, 51, 96, 106, 116
Lennon, John 17
   Imagine 17
Lessing, Doris
   Shikasta (1979) 165
Levy, Andrea 130, 131
   Every Light in the House Burnin' (1994) 130
   Fruit of the Lemon (1999, Levy) 131
   Never Far From Nowhere (1996) 130–1
Lewis, Justin 4, 7
Li, Ang 239
Liebenstein, Karina 214, 215
Lima, Maria Helena 131
Lin, Yaode 239
Literary Review 47
Livingston, Ian 205
   Warlock of Firetop Mountain 205
Loaded (magazine) 192
London City Airport 4
London Review of Books (2010) 213
London Stock Exchange 5
Longley, Michael 71
'Look Back in Anger' (*Lodger* album) 17
'Look Back in Anger' (Osborne's play) 17
Lucas, Sarah 25
Luckhurst, Roger 13, 19, 21, 23
   Trauma Question, The (2008) 19
Luig, Judith 225
Lukács, Georg
   Historical Novel, The (1981) 154–5

MacClaverty, Bernard 69
   Grace Notes (1997) 69, 71–2
Macherey, Pierre 31, 181

A Theory of Literary Production (1966) 31, 181
MacPherson Report 128
Macpherson, Sir William 6
Maczynska, Magdalena 109, 126
Mad Cow Disease 7
Madden, Deirdre 69, 72
   One by One in the Darkness (1996) 69, 72, 75
Madeley, Richard 21
Major, John 97
Maley, Willy 56
Maliszewski, Paul 115, 116
Mallinson, Keith 206
   Seaton Point (1998) 181, 183, 206–8
Man Booker Prize 38, 149
Manchester City Centre bombing 5
Mandela, Nelson 2
Manly, Stanly
   Raiders of the Low Forehead (1999) 210
Manning, Mark 182, 209, 210
   Bad Wisdom (1996) 209
   Get Your Cock Out (1999) 210
March, Cristie L. 78, 80
Marriott, James 43
Martin, S.I. 129, 130, 133
   Incomparable World (1996) 129–30, 133
Marxism 18
Maxwell, Robert 4
Mazower, Mark 18
McCarthy, Karen 124
McCarthy, Tom 107, 108, 109, 110, 111, 114
McCracken, Scott 53
McElwee, Emma 206
   Seaton Point (1998) 181, 183, 206–8
McEwan, Ian 20, 215
   Atonement (2001) 20
McGee, Alan 15
McGuire, Matt 78
McGuire, Stryker 15
McIlvanney, William 43
   Laidlaw 43
McLean, Duncan 44, 46, 47, 53
McLeod, John 83, 86, 127, 133, 139
   Revision of Englishness, The (2004) 83
McNamee, Eoin 71
   Resurrection Man (1994) 71
McQueen, Steven
   Deadpan (1997) 28

Melville, Pauline 225
'Memory Wars, The' 19–21
Mensing, Kolja 229
Mercer, Kobena 124
Meyer, Michael 219
Mibenge, Chiseche Salome 10
    ex and International Tribunals: The Erasure of Gender from the War Narrative 10
Michaels, Anne
    Fugitive Pieces (1996) 22
Miller, Gavin 81, 82
Milne, Drew 46, 52
Mirror 4
Mitchell, D.M. 198
    Starry Wisdom, The (1994) 198, 200
Mitchell, David 41
Mitchell, George 5
Mitchell, Kaye 78
MMR vaccine 7
Mo, Timothy 225
Mohr, Reinhard 217
Moorcock, Michael 41, 196–7, 201
Moore, Alan 31, 150, 172, 183, 198
    'authorial' exposition 202
    'Courtyard, The' (1994) 198
    From Hell (1999) 172, 202–4
    global ideologies 204
    graphic novel 202
    Haunter of the Dark and Other Grotesque Horrors (2006) 198
    League of Extraordinary Gentlemen, The (1999) 172
    modern comics 201
    on psychogeography of London 203
    V for Vendetta (1990) 172
    Voice of the Fire (1995) 201, 204
    Watchmen (1987) 172
Moore, Brian 69, 71
    Lies of Silence (1990) 69, 71
Moore-Gilbert, Bart 249
Morace, Robert 46, 47, 56, 81
Morgan, Cheryl 41
    Beloved 208
    graphic novels 183
    historical reference 172
    Lovecraft in Heaven 198
    Lovely Biscuits (1998) 198, 201
    short stories 199–201

Moss, Stephen 97
Muldoon, Paul 71
Müller, Anja 231
Müller, C. Amanda 39, 54
Müller, Jan-Werner 230
Müller, Klaus Peter 225, 228
Murdoch, Iris 224
Murray, Janet 107
Myall, Steve 13
Myer, Patrick 13
Myers, Russell 13

Nabokov, Vladimir
    Real Life of Sebastian Knight, The 156
Naipaul, V.S. 222, 251
Nairn, Tom 83
    Break-Up of Britain, The 83
Nathan, Max 3
national identities in 1990s
    Anderson's concept 69–70
    Britain 241–8
    England 82–6
    ethnic diversities 86–91
    Germany 214, 217–19, 223–4, 226
    imagined community 69–70
    literary expression 68, 70
    myths of Englishness 69
    Northern Ireland 71–6
    Taiwan 241–8
    Wales 76–82
Nationality Act of 1981 252
NATO 1–2, 11–13
neocolonialism 8
Net Book Agreement (NBA) 29, 37–8
Neubauer, Jurgen 227
New Formations 21
Newburn, Tim 6
Newland, Courttia 30
    alternative realism 142
    institutional racism 144
    Scholar, The (1997) 141–3
    Society Within (1999) 141, 143
    utopianism 143
New Worlds (magazine) 196
New Writing Scotland 46–7
Newman, Kim 31, 150, 171, 172, 173, 174, 176, 181, 183, 205, 206
    Anno Dracula (1992) 31, 171–3
    Bloody Red Baron, The (1995) 173

Life's Lottery (1999) 181, 205–6
   Role Playing Game (RPG) reader 206
   second-person narrative 205–6
Nian, Dong 239
9/11 attacks 9, 11
1988 Local Government Act 173
Noel's House Party (TV show) 2
Nolan, Simon 229
Nonhoff, Sky 227
Norfolk, Lawrence
   historical fiction 154, 174
   Lemprière's Dictionary (1991) 30, 154–5, 161
   postmodern conceptions of history 30–1
   realism principle 161
Northern Ireland
   economic and class differences 76
   identity construction 72
   sectarian ideologies 72–6
   the Troubles 71–5
Noys, Benjamin 198
Ntaryamira, Cyprien 9

Oasis (British rock band) 15–18
Obscene Publications Act 39, 41, 197
Obscene Publications Squad 40
O'Hagan, Andrew 23, 213
Okri, Ben 124
Oltermann, Philip 216
Ondatjee, Michael 224
   English Patient, The (1992) 20
Ono, Yoko 17
Oprah Book Club 21
Orange Prize for Fiction 38
Orwell, George
   Nineteen Eighty-Four (1949) 165
Our Friends From the North (TV series) 16
Owusu, Kwesi 124
Oyedeji, Koye 144

Parekh, Bhikhu 241
Parker, Emma 111, 116
Parks, Tim 215
Pattern, Dominic 97
Patterson, Glenn 69, 72, 75, 76
   Fat Lad (1992) 69, 72, 75
Paulin, Tom 71
Pavic, Milorad
   Dictionary of the Khazars A Lexical Novel in 100, 000 Words 208
Paxman, Jeremy 83
   English: A Portrait of a People, The (1998) 83
Pease, Donald E. 8
   New American Exceptionalism, The 8
Peterson, David 10, 11, 12
   Politics of Genocide, The 11
Petley, Julian 198
Phillips, Caryl 30, 123, 125, 126, 127
   Cambridge (1991) 133–5
   Crossing the River (1993) 134, 138
   Final Passage, The (1985) 135
   humanist idealogy 133
   Nature of Blood, The (1997) 138
   A New World Order (2001) 139
   on post-ethnicity 138–9
   prose style 134
   utopian realism 132, 134–5
Phillips, Mike 125
   Dancing Face, The (1997) 143
   An Image to Die For (1995) 143
   Last Candidate, The (1990) 143
   Point of Darkness (1994) 143
Physical Impossibility of Death in the Mind of Someone Living The (Hirst) 115
Pilger, John 12, 61
Planet of the Apes (television series) 115
Platt, Charles
   Gas, The (1970) 196
Plog, Ulla 218
Plowman, Andrew 229, 230
poll tax 5
Pope, Alexander 95
   Rape of the Lock, The (1714) 95
   Epilogue of the Satires, The (1738) 96
post-industrial society
   class dynamics 57
   emergence of fiction 37
   landscapes 58, 204
   literary history 29
   male working-class identity 51
   Scottish fiction 44–5
   status of drug use 49
   transnational identities 40
Poutrus, Patrice G. 233n. 5
Prentice, Eve-Ann 11
Priest, Christopher 31, 150, 161, 162

biographical metafiction 157
Prestige, The (1996) 31, 157, 160–2
realism principle 161
use of journals and diaries 160
Procter, James 124
Punter, David 44, 55, 56
Pynchon, Thomas
  cinematic registers 187
  Crying of Lot 49, The (1966) 154, 208
  Deadmeat (1997) 187–8
  lyrical associations 187–8
  subplots 188

Quincey, T. De
  Confessions of An English Opium Eater (1821) 194

Ramdin, Ron 244
Ranasinha, Ruvani 249, 259
Random House 46
Ranger, Terence 243
  Culture, Identity and Politics (1996) 243
Raymond, Derek 191
  He Died With His Eyes Open (1984) 191
  I Was Dora Suarez (1990) 191
Rebel Inc 46–7
Reckwitz, Erhard 225
Reed Books 38
Reinhard, Oliver 233n. 5
Renan, Ernest 242
Rendezvous 100
Rennison, Nick 97, 102, 114
Reyntjens, Filip 10
  Great African War: Congo and Regional Geopolitics, The, 1996-2006 10
Richard and Judy Book Club 21
Richards, David 262
Richards, Yvette 141
  Single Black Female (1994) 141
Robben, Bernhard 224
Roberts, Simon 3
Robertson, George 12
Rogers, David
  Revision of Englishness, The (2004) 83
Rosie, Michael 30
Ross, Leone 141
  All the Blood is Red (1996) 137
  Orange Laughter (1999) 141
Roth, Joseph 208, 224
  Counterlife, The (1986) 208

Rowling, J.K. 2
  Harry Potter (1997) 2
Rowson, Martin 100
Roy, Lucinda 140
  Lady Moses (1998) 140
Royal Academy 26
Rushdie, Salman 31, 90, 96, 124, 125, 135, 208, 215, 224, 230, 239, 251, 252
  Ground Beneath her Feet, The (1999, Rushdie) 230
  Midnight's Children (1981) 124
  Satanic Verses, The (Rushdie) 90, 124, 197, 208
Rwandan Patriotic Front 10

Saatchi & Saatchi 25
Saatchi Gallery 115
Saga Prize 124, 140–1
Salinger, J.D. 229
  Catcher in the Rye, The (1951) 229
Samad, Yunas 91
'Satanic Abuse' case 7
satellite technology 3
Saunders, Max 31, 155, 156, 157
Savoy Dreams (1984) 197
Savoy Publishers 40
Schindler, John R.
  Unholy Terror: Bosnia Al-Qa'ida and the Rise of Global Jihad 11
Schlink, Bernard
  Reader, The (1995) 22
Schnabel, Julian 25
Schröder, Gerhard 217, 218
Schulze, Ingo
  Simple Stories 230
Schulze, Ingo 230
science fiction 43, 57–8, 105, 162–3, 165, 167
Scotland
  literary traditions 78–9
  political ideologies 80
  postmodernism 78, 80, 82
  Victorian culture 79
  working class 78
Scott, Jeremy 106
Scruton, Roger 82
  England: An Elegy (2000) 82
Sealink Club 100
Seaton Point (1998) 181, 183, 206–8
Sebald, W.G. 23
  Austerlitz (2001) 23

Secker and Warburg (publisher) 46–7
Second World War 11–12, 22, 87, 224, 246
Segal, Lynn 18–19
Self, Will
   aesthetic tactics 103–4
   on animalistic aspects of humans 115–16
   apocalyptic concept 97–9, 102, 104–6, 109, 117
   approach to fiction 108–9
   belief systems 99–100
   Cock and Bull (1992) 30, 96, 101, 104, 110–12, 114, 116–17, 119
   cultural assumptions 109–11
   on gender and sexuality 111–14, 116–17
   on *Granta*'s 1993 list 96
   Great Apes (1997) 30, 97, 98, 104, 114–18, 186
   Grey Area (1994) 30, 96
   How the Dead Live (2000) 98, 108–9
   Junk Mail (1995) 96, 101, 103, 107, 111
   on liberty of fictional writer 101–2
   literary prizes 96–7
   media coverage 97
   My Idea of Fun (1993) 30, 96, 99, 106, 185–6
   'The North London Book of the Dead' (1991) 98, 108
   prose style 106
   Quantity Theory of Insanity, The (1991) 30, 96, 104, 107–8, 110
   satirical power 95–119
   sense of endism 98–9, 103–5, 108, 118, 120
   Sweet Smell of Psychosis, The (1996, Self) 30, 98–9, 101
   views on the 1990s 104–6, 119–20
   vision of London 106–7
   'Ward 9' 103, 108
Sellars, Simon 57, 58, 60
Selvon, Sam 124, 126, 129
   Lonely Londoners, The (1956) 124
Sensation (exhibition) 26
Sesay, Kadija George 124
Seward, Keith 43
Shih, Shuching 239
Shone, Tom 96
Simons, Jon 18
Sinason, Valerie 19
   Treating Survivors of Satanic Abuse 19

Sinclair, Iain
   Downriver (1991) 204
   prose style 204
   'psychogeography' 183, 201, 202, 205
   Radon Daughters (1994) 204
   realism principle 23, 205
Sinha, Indra 31, 183
   characterization mode 195
   Cybergypsies, The (1999) 183, 193–6, 284
   form of projection 196
   Internet confessional novel 193–4
   realist epistemology 194
Sissay, Lem 124
Sky Television 4
Smith, Anthony D. 243
Smith, Chris 217
Smith, John 128
Smith, Zadie 20, 69, 87, 91
   White Teeth (2000) 20, 69, 87, 91
Souhami, Anna 6
Srivastava, Atima 140
   Looking for Maya (1999) 140
   Transmission (1992) 140
Stableford, Brian 194, 197
Stallabrass
   High Art Lite (1999) 24
Stark, Lynne 49, 51
Steamboat Bill, Jr (1928, film) 28
Stein, Hannes 228
Stein, Mark 138
Steinert, Hajo 229
Stevenson, Robert Louis
   Strange Case of Dr Jekyll and Mr Hyde (1886) 190
Strategic Studies Institute 2
Strausfeld, Michi 222, 228
Strong, Simon 183, 209
   A259 Multiplex Bomb "Outrage" (1995) 209
Stuckrad-Barre, Benjamin von 230
   Soloalbum (1998) 230
Süddeutsche Zeitung 215, 223, 228
'Sunday Times Purple Prose Award' 106
Sutcliffe, William 229
Swift, Jonathan 95, 96, 113, 115
   Battle of the Books, The (1704) 95–6
   Gulliver's Travels (1726) 115, 186
Syal, Meera 140
   Anita and Me (1996) 140

Taberner, Stuart 218
Taiwan/Taiwanese
   Chinese, comparison with 247
   Chinese ancestry 245
   Chinese immigrants 255–6
   Chinese imperialism 246
   dominant languages 254–5
   Japanese colonization 239–40, 245–7
   KMT government and 246–8, 253–4
   literature 240–1
   nationhood and identity 239, 245
   New Literature Movement 245
   ROC citizens 247
   Western influence 240
   writers 239
Tate Gallery 27
technological revolution 3
Tegmark, Max 159, 160
Tew, Philip 1, 30, 48, 52, 70, 95, 104, 106, 170
TFI Friday (TV show) 2
Thatcher, Margaret 5, 8, 37, 49, 104, 128, 132, 135, 138, 170, 203, 217, 226–7, 288
Thomas, Gina 218
Thorpe, Adam 69
   Ulverton (1992) 69
Thwaite, Mark 57, 59
Tomlinson, John 29
Torrington, Jeff 215
Traynor, Joanna 140, 143
   Sister Josephine (1997) 140, 143
Tremain, Rose
   Restoration (1989) 20
Trocchi, Alexander 48
Turner Prize 27
TV book clubs 21
Two Fingers
   cinematic register 187
   club novel 183
   lyrical associations 187–8
   vernacular modernism 188

Ulrich, Bernd
   Deutsch, aber glücklich 217
United Human Rights Council 10
Urban, Stuart 16
Uthmann, J. von 228, 229
Uwilingiyimana, Agathe 9

Vanity Fair 15–16
Velickovic, Vedrana 141
Vietnam War 11, 17
Virgin Media 4
von Bernruth, Christa 223
von Uthmann, Jorg 228–9

Walberberg seminar 225
Wales
   economic strife 76
   mainstream culture 76–7
   Welsh identity 76–8
Walesa, Lech 2
Wallace, Gavin 45
Walsh, John 106
Walters, Vanessa 141
   Best Things in Life, The (1998) 141
   Rude Girls (1996) 141
Wambu, Onyekachi 124
Warsaw Pact 219
Waters, Sarah 31, 150, 174, 175, 177
   Affinity (1999) 150, 175–6
   Fingersmith (2002) 150, 175
   *Tipping the Velve*t (1998) 31, 150, 155, 174–5
   Wolfskins and Togas: Lesbian and Gay Historical Fictions, 1870 to the Present (1995) 174
Weidinger, Birgit 229
Wells, H.G. 163
   Boon (1915) 156
   Shape of Things to Come, The (1933) 163
   Time Machine, The (1895) 163, 187
Wells, Steven 61, 62, 182, 183, 209
   Tits-Out Teenage Terror Totty (1999) 62, 210
Welsh, Irvine
   acquaintances ideology 49
   on capitalist systems 50–1
   chemical-generation milieu 192–3
   on drug use and consumerism 49–50
   experimentalism 193
   Filth (1998) 188–93
   idea of characterization 189–90
   Marabou Stork Nightmares (1995) 188, 191–3
   'Past Tense: Four Stories from a Novel' 46–7
   publication briefs 47

self-styled persona 47
style culture 192
Trainspotting (1993) 45–9, 51–3, 56–7, 59–60, 62, 77, 80, 191, 193, 228
Trainspotting (1996, movie) 48
typographical play 188–9
use of vernacular 52, 56
visual interruption 189
working-class writing 48, 51
What's the Story (album) 15
Wheatle, Alex 141, 143
  Brixton Rock (1999) 141
Wheeler, Pat 168, 169
White, Lesley 97
White, Tony 39
  Britpulp! (1999) 39
Wild Child 254
Williams, John 68, 134
  Five Pubs, Two Bars, and a Nightclub (1999) 76–7
Williams, Lucy 206
  Seaton Point (1998) 181, 183, 206–8
Williams, Mark P. 31, 181, 198, 210
Williams, Tony 42
Wilson, Robert McLiam 76

Eureka Street (1996) 69, 72, 75–6
Winfrey, Oprah 21
Winterson, Jeannette 239
Wittlinger, Ruth 233n. 4
Wittstock, Uwe 229
Wolf, Chris 208
  Kassandra 208
Wolf Hall (2009, Mantel) 149
  Bring Up the Bodies (2012) 149
The Word (TV show) 2
Wormald, Mark 174, 175
Wynne-Jones, Ros 54

X-Press 124, 141

Yannis, Alexandros 12
yBas (young British artists) 24–7, 115
Young, Elizabeth J. 41, 62

Zenzinger, Peter 226
Zhu, Tienwen 239, 255, 256
  Notes of a Desolate Man 255
Žižek, Slavoj 67
  Tarrying with the Negative: Kant, Hegel and the Critique of Ideology 67

www.ingramcontent.com/pod-product-compliance
Lightning Source LLC
Chambersburg PA
CBHW051804230426
43672CB00012B/2625